MILLER'S
20TH-CENTURY
GLASS

MILLER'S
20TH-CENTURY
GLASS

ANDY McCONNELL

20TH-CENTURY GLASS

by Andy McConnell

First published in Great Britain in 2006 by Miller's,
a division of Mitchell Beazley, imprints of
Octopus Publishing Group Ltd,
2–4 Heron Quays, London, E14 4JP

Miller's is a registered trademark of Octopus Publishing Group Ltd

ISBN-13 978-1-845330-99-6
ISBN-10 1-84533-099-4

A CIP record for this book is available from the British Library.

Set in Frutiger and Versailles
Produced by Toppan Printing Co., (HK) Ltd
Printed and bound in China

Senior Executive Editor	**Anna Sanderson**
Executive Art Editor	**Rhonda Summerbell**
Picture Research	**Andy McConnell**
Special Photography	**Andy McConnell**
Project Editor	**Catherine Emslie**
Copy Editor	**Alison Bolus**
Page Design	**Colin Goody**
Jacket Design	**Colin Goody**
Proofreader	**Naomi Waters**
Indexer	**Sue Farr**
Production	**Jane Rogers**

Front cover, top, from left:
Mould-blown *Nebulosa* vase, designed by Nanny Still for Rihiimäki, Finland, 1967 (p.217); pressed and swung *Chippendale* vase, designed Benjamin Jacobs, US, 1907 (p.112); mould-blown and trailed vase, designed by Jacob Bang for Holmegaard, Denmark, *c.*1935 (p.141).

Front cover, bottom, from left:
Free-formed tourist-quality bull figure, Murano, *c.*1965 (p.85); mould-blown and cased vase by Liskeard Glass, Britain, *c.*1972, (p.179).

Rear cover:
Hand-pressed *Noah's Ark* suncatcher, designed by Michael Bang for Holmegaard, Denmark, 1969 (p.90).

p.1 (half-title page): Free-formed sculptural vase
Designed *c.*1942, by George Thompson for Steuben, US, but reproduced as part of the Steuben Heritage Series, *c.*1983. Engraved *SHS 1983[DP]* 15cm (5⅞in).
£75/$130

p.3 (title page): Bohemian enamelling, *c.*1915
Mould-blown glass decorated with hand-painted transparent enamels in the Werkstätte-style, *c.*1915. The decoration is typical of the high-quality achieved by Bohemian Hausmalers, or home-decorators.14cm (5½in).
£200/$340

p.4 (contents page): Kaj Franck decanter, Finland, 1957
Mould-blown *Kremlin Kellot* (*Kremlin Bells*) decanter (KF500). Designed by Franck for Nuutajärvi. Produced 1957–68, in several forms, combinations, sizes and colours (p.120). 19.5cm (7⅝in).
£100/$170

pp.8–9 ("Introduction to 20th Century Glass" opener), from left:

Chinese *Graal*, 2004
Modern reproduction, probably Chinese, of the *Graal* technique developed at Orrefors, Sweden, *c.*1920 (pp.198–9). 13cm (5in).
£10/$17

Post-war Czech vase, *c.*1965
Hand-pressed vase designed by František Vizner for Rudolfova Hut/Bohemia Glass. c.18cm (7in).
£40/$70

Post-War Whitefriars, Britain
Mould-blown and furnace-worked vase designed by William Wilson for Whitefriars, *c.*1953 [Factory pattern 9386]. 19.5cm (7⅝in).
£90/$155

British *Graal*, 2000
Ruby Rings Graal-technique bowl, designed by Jonathan Harris and made by Tim Harris for Isle of White Studio Glass, Britain (pp.136–7).
£800/$1,360

pp.94–5 ("Identification by Factory" opener), from left:

Val St-Lambert, 1925–30
Mould-blown and cut rust-tinted bowl designed by Charles Graffart or Joseph Simon for Val St-Lambert, Liege, Belgium. 18cm (7in).
£200/$340

Venini, 1960s
Dip-moulded decanter with loose-fitting stopper. Reputedly designed by Paulo Venini for Venini, Murano. Engraved: *Venini Italia*, 26cm (10¼in).
£220/$375

Riihimäki, 1958
Mould-blown *Harlekini* service cream jug by Nanny Still. Produced 1959–71 (p.215).
£85/$145

Alexander Hardie Williamson for Bagley, 1935
Pressed candlestick (3002). Designed by Alexander Hardie Williamson for Bagley, Yorkshire, England. 6.5cm (2½in).
£30/$55

Contents

Foreword

A fundamental difference between the 20th century and preceding eras was that people of all Western countries grew progressively richer and more rapidly than ever before. The spread of wealth down the social ladder, which accelerated from the 1930s resulted in an explosion in the diversity of domestic finery, including glassware.

The years between 1700 and 2000 witnessed a staggering transformation in all Western societies. At the earliest date, the super-rich held a monopoly of political power, owning most of the land and property, including decorative glassware. Coarse forms of glass were available to the poor, mostly in taverns, but the price of even a fine drinking-glass in 1700 was beyond the means of most. Even as late as 1824, when a British aristocrat bought her husband a service of glass, albeit a large one, its price of £2,200 was equivalent to the annual income of an entire village.

By the 1900s, the price of glass had fallen to the point where even shops such as Harrods sold 87-piece matching services for around £2, and within two further generations petrol stations gave away wine goblets to motorists filling up their tanks.

This astonishing transformation was due not only to rising affluence but also to major advances in glass technology and transportation. In 1700, most countries had glassworks scattered across their landscapes, most of which employed just a handful of workers. Two centuries later, the number of factories had reduced dramatically, each with a workforce of hundreds if not thousands.

Today, most glassmaking has been outsourced from developed countries to others with negligible labour costs and less stringent environmental controls. Most of the functional glassware sold across the world today is made in Poland, India, China, and Taiwan, where the cost of manufacture can be less than that of packing and shipping.

The result is that most of the developed world's remaining glassmakers are at risk. The super-rich will doubtless continue to pay premiums for leading brand names, such as Lalique, but many famous factories are in trouble.

A century ago, Europe stood at the dawn of a golden age in glassmaking. Almost two thousand years of experience, recent technological advances, and the rising concept of "design" combined to create the greatest-ever manifestation in the diversity and quality of glass. During the 20th century, more glass was produced and in greater decorative variety than the rest of history combined.

Great glass had certainly been produced before. The techniques used to form and decorate some Roman glass have only recently been unravelled, and the colours created in the Venice of the Doges rank among the glories of the Renaissance. The quality and detail achieved by Bohemian engravers and by English glass-cutters during the 18th and 19th centuries will never be surpassed.

Yet, today, much "historic" glass is either prohibitively expensive or is unfashionable. Some collectors will always be attracted to the naïvety of 18th-century glass and the colours and effects of the finest 19th-century pieces. However, the vision of traditional glass collectors is often blinkered toward just a few categories, such as drinking-glasses, paperweights, or scent bottles and then often only examples made in their own countries.

Of course, some of those attracted to the 20th century remain chauvinistic. For example, few outside the United States collect what is loosely termed Depression-era glass. Yet one of the most inviting aspects of modern glass collecting is that it generally transcends national frontiers. This is largely because the growth of international trade over the course of the last century encouraged its export and import on a previously inconceivable scale. The result is that a great deal of Scandinavian glass, for instance, is present not only in Stockholm, Copenhagen, and Helsinki but also in Berlin, Seattle, and Sydney. The obvious difficulties and cost of acquiring rare pieces naturally encourages the majority to gravitate toward those pieces that are relatively common. So, when it comes to glass, there are few limits, especially for those armed with specialist knowledge.

Twentieth-century glass offers rich decorative possibilities, even for the novice, because it looks so great. However, beyond these obvious attractions, many of those enticed toward it feel a need to rise above the superficial and learn. This book offers a helping hand to those who want to take a further step and trace the work of specific factories and their designers.

In its quest for accuracy, this book is a union of many minds. It would have been impossible to research and write it without the help of dozens of generous individuals, each with their own specialist knowledge. Some helped by effectively directing entire sections, others by allowing their pieces to be photographed, or by selling me objects at generously reduced prices.

The greatest thanks are naturally due to those who made the greatest contributions. It is touching to note that those with the most to give are invariably those who are the most generous in dispensing it. The first thanks go to new-found friends who were so welcoming, hospitable, patient, and understanding when visited abroad, and who continued to respond to persistent requests for further information and clarification over the following months. Without their assistance this volume would not have been possible. They are, in alphabetical order: Gunnel Holmer, curator of the Smålands Glass Museum, Växjö, Sweden; Paivi Jantunen, press attaché at Iittala/Nuutajärvi, Finland; Kaisa Koivista, curator of the Finnish Glass Museum, Riihimaki, Finland; Lis Larsen, guide and archivist at Holmegaard Glasværk, Denmark; Kia Lindahl and Karin Lindahl, formerly the archivist and press attaché at Orrefors Glasbruk, Sweden. Thanks are also due to the companies and institutions who allowed their material to be reproduced here. The names of dozens of other individuals who helped appear in the acknowledgments (p.256), but particular thanks are extended to Graham Cooley, and Roger Dodsworth of Broadfield House Glass Museum, Stourbridge, for their support, understanding, knowledge, and patience.

A few technical points. When known, the measurements of items illustrated are included in the caption. These are always heights unless otherwise stated, and are maximums for irregularly shaped items. "Max." refers to the tallest item shown and "inc." indicates that a decanter measurement includes the stopper. Any numbers in brackets are either the designer's personal number, or the factory production code for the object in question.

Price Guide

Where appropriate, a guide to retailers' prices is included at the foot of the caption to every illustration in this book. These should help give some idea of what readers might expect to pay for pieces that catch their eye.

The problem is that prices are subjective: what is a given piece worth? The most obvious variable is who is selling the piece in question and from where? An Englishman has written this book, so the prices are based on a British perspective, and obviously one expects to pay more for purchases from specialist retailers than at a flea markets, for example. However, price differentials in glass generally extend beyond these simple factors. Size, colour, the presence of a signature, and condition have important bearings on the value of specific designs: larger pieces are invariably rarer than smaller ones, and coloured examples more sought-after than colourless ones. Further, certain objects have been produced for several decades, and early versions are always more expensive than later ones.

Prices are based on the particular items illustrated, on an individual rather than collective basis, with an added star (*) in cases of significant variations due to factors such as those mentioned above. Objects illustrated in advertisements or on catalogue pages have their own prices too. The figures stated were proposed by specialist dealers, most of them exhibiting at the Cambridge Glass Fair, England, on 19th February, 2006 (see page 256).

That explained, the basic laws of commerce remain immutable. These include: an object is worth only what someone is prepared to pay for it, and the example you own usually isn't quite what its prospective purchaser wants! Chips and cracks are seriously detrimental to values, and dealers will always attempt to buy at the lowest price and sell for as much as possible. As one once joked, "I pay too much for everything, and sell it too cheaply!"

Introduction to 20th-century Glass

Identifying & Collecting

The good news for anyone attracted by 20th-century glass is that there is a great deal of it about. While some of it barely merits a second glance, a great deal of it is stylish, handmade, and sits handsomely in modern homes. It is also gaining in value as it attracts increasing numbers of both collectors and casual buyers.

A visit to any flea market, junk shop, or antique fair will confirm that, despite its fragility, 20th-century glass remains abundant: cut, engraved, plain, or coloured; large and small; vases, bowls, and drinking-glasses. In fact, for the approximate cost of one rare 18th-century drinking-glass (picture 1), I have personally accumulated something like 20,000 pieces over the past 30 years, often from large venues with indiscriminate vendors. Indeed, at a recent antiques market, I managed to buy all the glass illustrated in picture 2 for a mere £90 ($160).

So, how many different glass designs were produced during the 20th century? Impossible to say precisely, but it is likely that perhaps as many as 1,000 different glassworks operated across the Western world between 1900 and 1999. Most employed at least one designer, while many used several. For example, Orrefors, the famous Swedish maker (pp.184–99), and Iittala, of Finland (pp.162–77), have each employed about 50. So, for the sake of argument, one might suggest an average of four designers per factory. This means that 4,000 individuals produced glass designs during the 20th century. If each of them produced 100 pieces and patterns – a low estimate, since a single service might comprise as many as 25 vessels – this equates to a total of some 400,000 pieces. With single designers, such as Alexander Hardie Williamson (pp.126–31), having executed over 1,600, the true figure is likely to approach a million.

The bad news is that glass, unlike most other categories of the decorative arts, rarely bears marks that identify its maker. The result is that it can be difficult, if not impossible to attribute given examples even to a country of origin, let alone a specific factory or designer. If only glass were like ceramics, which generally carry basic information printed or impressed on their base, like metalwares, which can be identified through stamped marks, or like paintings and prints, which are applied with artists' signatures or monograms. On the other hand, if the origins and quality of most glass were obvious to everyone, it would not be as easy as it currently is to pick up bargains.

From whichever angle you view it, however, the lack of makers' marks means that it can be difficult to answer the four basic questions that make collecting interesting: who designed it, who made it, when was it made, and for how long was it produced? This information is of little concern to those who occasionally buy pieces of cheap glass and

▲ **1: £30,000/$50,000 18th-century wine glass**
Twist-stemmed English wine glass, one of only four known examples, with a cobalt-blue foot and bowl, c.1760. Sold at Sotheby's, London, in 2002, for almost £30,000 ($50,000). 16cm (6¼in).

desire nothing further. However, for collectors of 20th-century glass, which has become the most sought-after category, knowledge is by far the most crucial asset that can be possessed. More important, even, than a bulging wallet.

Learning about glass

Knowledge is the key to both collecting success and a general appreciation of the subject for several obvious reasons. By far the most important is that it gives those who possess it the ability to differentiate one piece from another: the excellent from the good, the good from the average, and the average from the poor.

A guide to the scale of the historic glass industry is provided by Carolus Hartmann's *Glas-Markenlexikon, 1660–1945,* whose 1,006 pages are crammed with 18,000 unique marks and signatures. It is important to note that the practice of maker-marking increased dramatically during the 20th century, so a follow-up volume covering 1945–2000 would probably rival, if not surpass, the original in size.

Given these facts, how does even the most experienced dealer, let alone a novice, trace a path through the maze of pitfalls, blind alleys, and minefields that constitute 20th-century glass collecting? The answer is: with care. Anybody who claims to know it all is either a fool or a liar. The field is simply too vast and furnished with too little reliable literature for anyone to be an expert in all areas. The answer for those not prepared to devote their entire lives to the subject is to make their choice and specialize.

▲ **2: Recent haul of 20th-century glass**
From left: (a) Hand-pressed vase with fins, designed by Rudolf Jurnikl for Rudolfova Hut, Czechoslovakia, c.1968, 18cm (7in); (b) mould-blown sky-blue Space-Age vase, attributed to Alsterfors, Sweden, c.1965, 23cm (9in); (c) *Sommerso*-technique bowl, Murano, type still produced today, 8cm (3in); (d) Czech optic-moulded ball *Nemo*-series vase with iridescent staining, designed by Max Kannegiesser for Borské Sklo, 1959, 18cm (7in); (e) hand-pressed amethyst ashtray, designed by Rudolf Jernikl for Rosice/Sklo Export, 1962, 17cm (6¾in) diam; (f) optic-moulded ball vase, designed Max Kannegiesser for Borské Sklo, 1959, 23cm (9in); (g) hand-pressed *YORKSHIRE BITTER* ashtray, by Nazeing Glass Works, 1975, 17.5cm (6⅞in) long; (h) mould-blown *Marcel* decanter (FJT15), designed by Frank Thrower for Wedgwood, 1979, 35.5cm (14in); (i) mould-blown and cased vase, reputedly designed by Tamara Aladin (pp.220–3) for Riihimäki, Finland, c.1970, 20cm (7⅞in); (j) hand-pressed *Sunspot* suncatcher (pp.90–1), designed by Geoffrey Baxter for Whitefriars, 1974, 18.5cm (7¼in); and (k) mould-blown bronze-mounted vase, designed by Pentti Sarpaneva for Kumela, Finland, c.1970, 8cm (3in).

Total cost £90/$155 (average £8/$14 each)

A diligent individual could learn virtually all there is to know about the work of René Lalique, for instance, by absorbing the contents of all 1,063 pages of Felix Marcilhac's definitive study, *René Lalique, 1860–1945, Maître-Verrier* (1989), and that of the other 20-plus volumes dedicated to the subject, and, equally importantly, by handling innumerable examples. Then, after studying market trends in Lalique glass, he or she would be adequately prepared to spend the large sums of money required to acquire good examples (picture 3).

However, Lalique is exceptional in having such a huge body of research devoted to him. Excellent books have studied other areas of 20th-century glass – the writers/academics Jan Mergl, Waltraud Neuwirth, Michael Kovacek, Helmut Ricke, Ada Polak, and Lesley Jackson have proved as consistently reliable as it is possible to be. However, their works (picture 4) glow as beacons in a sea infested with poorly written, ill-researched literature that does a disservice to its subject. Though mostly well intended, once published, the mistakes stick.

It is another appalling fact that many, if not most, of the written descriptions applied to glassware by dealers, particularly generalists, are false. When challenged, some dealers can even produce a book containing the source of their fiction! That is not to suggest that all dealers are ignorant, as some, like Kovacek, are the leading authorities on their particular specialities. However, it is a fact that a majority are weak when it comes to glass, largely for the reasons previously outlined.

If prospective purchasers, particularly novices, should be reluctant to believe everything they hear or read, then they should certainly beware

▲ **3: Moulded *Le Jour et La Nuit* clock, *c*.1926**
Designed by René Lalique, after 1926, engraved *R LALIQUE*.
Sold in 2003 for the five-figure sum below. 37cm (14⅝in).
£18,000/$30,600

▼ **4: Selection of the best books on 20th-century glass**
Ada Polak's *Modern Glass*, 1962; Helmut Ricke and Lars Thor's *Swedish Glass Factories, 1915–60*, 1987; Lesley Jackson's *Whitefriars Glass*, 1996; Jan Mergl and Lenka Pánková's *Moser, 1857–1997*, 1997. (*See* bibliography on p.250.)

of the internet, where woeful, criminally inaccurate descriptions entice the unwary into buying glassware of dubious quality and provenance.

For these reasons this book examines the output of certain specific glassworks and designers in some detail rather than opting for a scatter-gun approach to the subject at large. Restrictions of space mean that the selection is subjective rather than definitive. The choice favours factories whose products can be found with relative ease and usually acquired without digging too deep. It also leans toward those that have not previously benefited from in-depth analysis, which partially explains why examples of their production can be found so cheaply. A vast amount of literature has already been devoted to the work of Gallé, Lalique, and the Whitefriars glassworks, for example, so there is little to be gained from retracing such well-trodden ground. Besides, their work has achieved such exalted status and, in the case of Gallé and Lalique, is so clearly signed that large sums are invariably required to acquire it (picture 5).

Most of the pieces illustrated on the following pages can be bought for under £100 ($170). Indeed, I have bought more than half of them over the past two years, in Britain, Scandinavia, and across mainland Europe, for a total of about £6,000 ($10,200). This price equates to an average of around the price of a pint of beer for each piece. The ability to find such bargains is based on knowledge and the willingness to take risks, albeit normally small ones. In many cases they were bought without fore-knowledge of the maker's identity, chosen instead because they were stylish, well made, or simply different. However, now the research is done, many if not yet most of the pieces can be linked to their makers and designers, proving their purchase even more rewarding.

The evolution of 20th-century glass

The character of the glass produced over the course of the 20th century was adapted to and reflected the life and times of its designers, makers, and those who bought and possessed it. In most cases it is possible to

▲ **5: Gallé carved cameo vase, *c.*1900**
Decorated with a lakeside vista. Bearing the cameo signature: *Gallé.* 28cm (11in).
£80,000/$136,000

▼ **6 Evolution of the *roemer* wine glass**
From left: Netherlandish light-green tinted, *c.*1700; Richardsons of Stourbridge pattern drawing, *c.*1850; British, dark green version, *c.*1900; Emile Gallé carved-cameo, *c.*1900; and Werkstätte-style ruby-over colourless cased, Bohemian, *c.*1910.
£40–£2,000/$70–3,400*

distinguish pieces made during the 20th century from earlier ones. Aesthetic taste changed so radically between 1850 and 1950, for example, that even those with the most superficial interest in the decorative arts can differentiate between objects made a century apart (picture 6). However, the dividing line becomes blurred when it comes to those produced in 1890 and 1910. Indeed, a great deal of glass designed as early as 1880 continued to be made as late as 1914. So, do such pieces qualify as 20th-century objects?

The general answer, at least in the case of this book, is no. Certain elements of public taste certainly changed radically between the eras commonly referred to as *Victorian* (1837–1903) and *Edwardian* (1903–14). For instance, the Arts & Crafts Movement evolved into Art Nouveau between *c.*1890 and 1910. Further, many of the designs of Josef Hoffmann and other members of the Wiener Werkstätte (Vienna Workshop), dating as early as 1900, appear more "modern" than most British glass made before 1930 and even later at some Scandinavian works (picture 7). The point is that the term "20th-century" is elastic and can be applied to some pieces made in 1890, but not to others dating as late as 1938.

Identification by mark

On a more specific level, the act of identifying 20th-century glass involves linking individual pieces to their original makers and designers. Again, this is relatively simple in some cases, but not in most. Naturally, the easiest glass to identify bears its maker's name (picture 8).

The practice of signing glassware is an almost exclusively 20th-century phenomenon, though some rare, richly decorated older glass does bear the marks of its makers or decorators. For example, during the 18th century, a small number of goblets and decanters enamelled by the Beibly family of Newcastle and certain cobalt-blue pieces gilded for Isaac Jacobs bear the names *Beilby* and *I Jacobs Bristol* (picture 9). Certain top engravers, such as Friedrich Winter and Jacob Sang, included their monograms or names in their work. Some 19th-century exhibition pieces were also signed (picture 10). However, these are extremely rare exceptions to the general rule.

In theory, it should be simple to determine the maker and nationality of most pieces of 20th-century glass. This is because all manufactured goods, including glass, were required under American law to be maker-marked. The Mckinley/Taft protectionist tariffs progressively imposed on all imports into the USA between 1890 and 1919 required every object to be marked with its manufacturer's name and national origin. With the wealthy American market essential to their financial survival, most European makers of fine glassware conformed in various ways.

Some marked their work indelibly, with acids, through moulded wording, or with an engraver's stylus. This category includes some of

7: 20th-century "Victorian" glass
Mould-blown cruet bottles stylistically dating from the mid-19th century, but illustrated in the 1938 catalogue of the Holmegaard glassworks, Denmark.
£5/$9

8: Argy-Rousseau *pâte-de-verre* vase, *c.*1925
Pâte-de-verre vase by Gabriel Argy-Rousseau, France. Lower body features moulded signature *G. ARGY-ROUSSEAU*. 18.5cm (7¼in).
£6,000/$10,200

9: Rare 18th-century glass signature
The base of a true Bristol-blue decanter, made in Bristol by Isaac Jacobs, *c.*1800, with gilded signature *I Jacobs Bristol 33*.
£750/$1,275

the leading makers, including Venini of Murano/Venice, Moser of Czechoslovakia (picture 12), and Lalique, France. At the other end of the quality scale, the entire range of the pressed-glass *Chippendale* pattern produced by American glassworks was embossed with the words *CHIP-PENDALE KRYS-TOL* (picture 11).

That is the easy part and the reason why pieces by Venini, Moser, Lalique, and Daum, and even *Chippendale*, rank among the most collected of all 20th-century glass. The problem is that they form a minute percentage of all the glassware produced between 1900 and 1999: less than 0.01 per cent of it, in fact. So, what about the overwhelming remainder? Most glassmakers found it cheaper and more expedient to mark their work with a variety of stickers, usually printed with the factory name and location. Some chose metal foil, others paper. Broadly speaking, most Venetian (picture 13) and some Swedish glass-makers (picture 14) opted for foil, at least until the 1950s or '60s, while most others chose paper. Starting in the 1960s, some Finnish and Swedish factories applied marks printed on cellophane (picture 15). The general problem with stickers is that they are easily degraded (picture 16), or removed. Some owners consider that stickers detract from the beauty of glass so scrape them off, and, of the survivors, ink tends to wear, paper disintegrates in water, glues dissolve when damp, and cellophane oxidizes. So, just a tiny fraction of the stickers originally applied to 20th-century glassware have survived the test of time.

Signatures: image and design culture

Aside from the requirements of American import laws, the practice of signing glassware spread immeasurably during the early 20th century for two further reasons. The first was the gradual emergence of "brand marketing", which encouraged consumers to pay more for certain products perceived to be particularly luxurious. This trend encouraged the application to glassware of names such as Tiffany, Gallé, and Lalique, and is closely related to the second reason: the rising social role of "design" and "designers". During earlier periods, designer-decorators had been held on a social par with tradesmen, and their identities, and often the necessity to pay them, were considered irrelevant. However, this perception altered radically as design assumed its modern role at the heart of manufacturing, particularly in the case of decorative objects. It is telling that the name of Christopher Dresser (1834–1904), arguably the first modern designer, was applied to some of the products that flowed from his drawing board.

The situation had certainly changed in Sweden by the 1930s when Edwald Hald was promoted from his drawing board to spend 11 years as Orrefors' managing director (pictures 17 and 18). Around the same time, the neighbouring Kosta Glasbruk works promoted its artistic director, Elis Bergh (1881–1954), by adding his name to the stickers applied to his

MARKS

10

11

12

13

14 ▲ ▼

15 ▶ ▼

16 ▶

10: Exhibition-piece signatures The engraved signatures *W Fritsche* and *W Kny* of the British resident Bohemian engravers William Fritsche and William Kny. The former was applied to a rock-crystal service produced by Thomas Webb & Sons, c.1880. The Kny signature was applied to a set of goblets made for Elbert Henry Gary, president of US Steel, c.1885.

11: *Chippendale* logo From the base of an oval pickle, designed before 1915.

12: *Moser* logo As applied in various forms to the majority of the factory's 20th-century output.

13: *MADE IN MURANO ITALY* Foil sticker as used exclusively by Archimede Seguso, 1960s.

14: *Orrefors Sweden* and *GEHLIN GULLASKRUF SWEDEN* foil stickers, 1950s–60s

15: *pukeberg sweden* and *FOREIGN* stickers *pukeberg sweden* cellophane sticker, 1970s, and anonymous *FOREIGN* sticker as commonly applied to Swedish 1960s glass.

16: Worn foil stickers Top: *GENUINE VENETIAN GLASS, HANDMADE MADE IN MURANO*; Bottom: *MADE IN CZECHOSLOVAKIA*.

▲ **17: Orrefors engraving, Sweden, 1925**
Mould-blown and engraved bowl, *Bacchus Procession*. Designed by Simon Gate, for Orrefors. 22.5cm (8⅞in). Unique exhibtion piece.

▼ ▶ **18: Simon Gate for Sandvik, Sweden, 1924–66**
Astrid drinks service designed by Simon Gate. Produced by Sandvik/Orrefors for 42 years. Decanter 31.5cm (12⅜in) inc.
Decanter £100/$170
Glass £10/$17

designs (picture 19). It is symptomatic of the British glass industry, which crumbled to nothing toward the end of the 20th century, that Clyne Farquharson (1906–72), designer for the bizarrely-named Birmingham glassworks Walsh Walsh, executed his early work in a shed in the company car park. Today, designers can become celebrities, their products retailed adjacent to their portraits emblazoned on giant posters.

The growing desirability of "designer" goods naturally encouraged the proliferation of signatures on glassware in the expectation that they could be sold more expensively. Even the name of poor, disrespected Farquharson was engraved onto the bases of his vases and drinks services during the late 1930s (picture 20), though by that date an office had been graciously provided for his use.

Fine artists generally sign their work literally: by applying their name or monogram, and often the date, in paint to the canvas. This is rarely the case with glass. So, the differing types and forms of "signatures" need to be examined in turn.

The marks applied to 20th-century glass were either indelible or superficial. The first category principally comprises engraved signatures and acid-etched and sand-blasted names and logos; the second, stickers, includes silver or gold foil, paper, and plastic versions.

Engraved and enamelled signatures

True "signatures" often involve painting or scratching the company name, and its nationality and designer, onto or near the base of the item (picture 21). Finishing-room staff traditionally applied engraved marks

◀ **19: Designer-branded glass, Sweden, 1935**
Deeply-cut mould-blown vase and bowl, designed by Elis Bergh for Kosta, Sweden, c.1935. Applied with stickers stating *BERGH-KRISTALL KOSTA*.
Left £600/$1,020; Right £500/$850

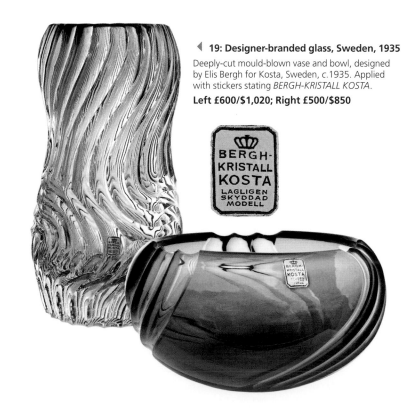

with a diamond stylus, though Dremel-type high-speed electric tools have recently been introduced. Designers and makers rarely apply their own marks, except in the case of small studios.

Typical examples this type include *LALIQUE FRANCE* and *VENINI ITALIA* (picture 22). Such wording is occasionally and variously augmented by further information such as the date, the designer's name, or codes that indicate the type of decoration, the identity of the decorator, or production numbers. For example, many of Per Lütken's designs for the Danish Holmegaard works were stylus-engraved with the word *HOLMEGAARD*, followed by a combination of the date of manufacture framing his *PL* monogram (picture 23). After *c*.1960, the date was superseded by a factory production number, such as *488356*. Still later, around 1965, Holmegaard scrapped the engraving process in favour of paper stickers (p. 139).

If the Holmegaard system appears complex, the rationale behind Orrefors' methodology fills 14 large-format pages of the company history, *Orrefors: A Century of Swedish Glassmaking*, 1998. Basically, the Orrefors' scripted signature is usually followed by a series of letters that indicate the category of manufacture and decoration (a = cut, p = pressed, etc.), followed by a date/number year code (a1 = 1935, f9 = 1988). This is generally followed by a letter that identifies the designer, drawn from a list of the 41 individuals who worked for the company between 1915 and 1990. However, the system changed in 1970, so, for instance, Nils Landberg pieces made between 1927 and 1970 are marked *n*, whereas those made after 1970 are marked *nl*. If this system appears arcane, it occupies just the first two of the 14 pages in question. Those wishing to absorb and digest Orrefors' signature system should be warned that the methodology applied at the neighbouring Kosta glassworks is yet more impenetrable, often neglecting to include even the word "Kosta".

The fundamental point is that signatures are not the be all and end all to identification. For instance, collectors should not be deluded into thinking that the presence of a *LALIQUE* mark on a piece equals hitting the jackpot. Indeed, it does not even necessarily mean that the piece under examination was either designed or made by René Lalique (1860–1945). Some of his work continues to be produced by the modern company that still bears his name and similar marks were and still are applied to objects and vessels designed by his son Marc (1900–77) and granddaughter Marie Claude (1935–).

Signatures can also be misleading in other ways. Some makers "signed" everything they produced, such as Lalique, while others opted, for example, to sign just a decanter from each service and not its glasses. Others signed all their work for certain periods, then ceased or marked their first-quality goods but not their seconds. The methodology of some other makers was so erratic or whimsical that they appear to have applied signatures only when the wind blew from the appropriate direc-

▶ **20: British engraved signature decanter, 1937**
Cylinder decanter decorated with cut *Leaf* pattern, designed by Clyne Farquharson for Walsh Walsh, Birmingham, England. The base is engraved *Clyne Farquharson*. 37.5cm (14¾in) inc.
£300/$510

▲ **21: Enamel-signed decanter, Czech, 1930s**
Enamelled with a colourful coaching scene on a fine opaque-white lattice background, signed *Hand painted in Czechoslovakia*. Similar pieces appear in the 1930s catalogues of Karel Palda, Novy Bor glassmaker and merchant, though most would have been home-decorated, with Palda serving as a middle-man. During the 1920s, 225 people worked in the glassworks of nearby Jablonec, compared with 2,500 outworkers employed on piecework. 22.5cm (8⅞in) inc.
£60/$100

▲ **22: Engraved-signature light shade, Murano, 1958**
Wall light applied with red, blue, turquoise, and opaque-white. Designed by the studio of Paulo Venini, for Venini, in 1958. Engraved *VENINI ITALIA*. 35 x 25cm (13¾ x 9⅞in).
£750/$1,275

23   24

25

26

23: *HOLMEGAARD 19PL59* engraved signature
This mark indicates that the piece was made by the Danish Holmegaard factory in 1959 to a design by Per Lütken.

24: Mdina signature, applied *c*.1972–present

25: *BACCARAT FRANCE* acid-etched logo
This factory used paper labels between 1862 and 1936, then its logo was applied in acid or sand-blasted.

26: British 20th-century acid-etched marks
Top: Royal Brierley/Stevens & Williams. Middle: Stuart Crystal. Bottom: Thomas Webb & Sons and Webb Corbett.

tion. The Mdina glassworks, founded on Malta in 1967 by British glass-maker Michael Harris (1933–94), provides a case in point. The decision as to whether or not to engrave the word *Mdina* onto its products (picture 24) depended on several factors: signatures were not applied if the works were particularly busy, for example, or if its signature writer was absent.

Acid-etched and sand-blasted marks

The two other forms of indelible marking are acid-etching and sand-blasting, which produce apparently similar results. Etching requires the temporary application of a sheet of paper printed with an acid solution of a mirror image of the wording and/or logo. The acid attacks the glass, and, after being neutralized with water, leaves a matt impression. Sand-blasting involves placing the glass on a stencil through which fine sand is fired, under compressed air, to leave a frosted pattern. Acids were used from around 1920 by Baccarat and at most British glassworks (pictures 25 and 26). Blasting, a rare form of marking, was used briefly by Wedgwood after it bought the King's Lynn factory in 1969 (p.234) until the local authority granted permission for the use of acids.

Moulded marks

Moulded signatures appear only on glassware shaped in a mould. They are created by carving the mould with the desired lettering or logos,

◄ 28: Press-moulded mark, *DEUTSCHLAND*

Applied to the vase, left, but not the bowl. Both date from the mid-1930s, but the similarity of colour and decoration are insufficient to enable the bowl to be attributed to the same maker, or even to German manufacture. Vase: 19cm (7½in); bowl: 34cm (13⅜in) diam.

£15/$25

▲ 27: Press-moulded mark, *CZECHOSLOVAKIA*
As applied to the *Loop* patterned vase above. The mark is absent from most examples from this extensive service, which was made in many colours and was widely exported during the 1930s.

£15/$25

which are then transferred, in reverse, to the glass objects formed in them. During the early 20th century, the most common type of glass moulding was pressing, whereby molten glass is forced against the faces of a mould under pressure. While the metals used to make moulds and the means of pressure gradually improved, the basic fundamentals of pressing have remained unchanged for nearly two centuries.

The rarer centrifuge method, used principally in Scandinavia since c.1960, involves spinning a gob of molten glass in an open-topped mould that propels the glass upward and outward into its crevices by centrifugal force (p.193).

The problem with moulded marks is that they were used only rarely, and few of them identify the maker. The most common moulded marks simply state the country of manufacture or attempt to protect a particular design from plagiarism. Accordingly, some pieces simply bear the wording *MADE IN ENGLAND* (or *ITALY*, *CZECHOSLOVAKIA* (picture 27), or *TCHECOSLOVAQUIE*), but no more (picture 28). While certainly better than nothing, these do little to help when attempting to narrow the field to a particular factory.

The most famous maker of moulded-glass, René Lalique, used moulds to create a variety of effects. Examples of his laborious *cire perdu* (lost wax) method are rare and extremely desirable, but even his pressed pieces, mass-produced in tens of thousands, generally command prices far in excess of prices paid for superior pieces by lesser-known factories. Some Lalique pressed glass bears his embossed name, while some other pieces were engraved or etched with one of an evolving series of datable signatures.

Another type of moulded mark, as applied to some British pressed-glass, indicates that the rights to its design were protected. It comprises the embossed letters *Rd* or *Rcgd* followed by a number, which enables the owner of the design, and its date, to be identified (picture 29). Unfortunately for glass spotters, such design registration numbers are fairly rare.

An even rarer form of moulded mark was employed at both the tiny Liskeard glassworks that operated in Devon, England, between 1970 and 1979 (p.178), and by Michael Harris at his Isle of Wight studio in 1973 (p.132). This involved manually branding the base of their work with a seal of hot glass while the piece was still furnace-hot (picture 30).

Stickers

The application of stickers was the most common method used by 20th-century glassmakers to identify their work. As previously explained, stickers were made of various types of lightweight metal foil, paper, and, from the 1960s, cellophane, and were generally printed with a maker's name and sometimes their nationality. Others simply state the country

▲ **29: Design registration number, British, 1926**
Salt cellar decorated in a pattern derivative of *Chippendale* (p.112), the base marked *Rd No 724094*. This number enables its shape and design to be attributed to James Jobling, Sunderland, who registered it at the design registration office, London, 20 September 1926.
£10/$17

◀ **30: *LG* seal**
As applied by the small British Liskeard glassworks, c.1970–9. Branded while still furnace-hot.

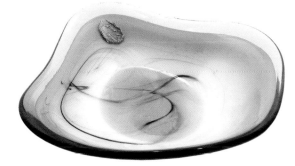

▲ **31: Generic Murano sticker**
Free-formed opaque-blue Murano dish with random trails, applied with a worn foil sticker, 1960s. The sticker reads: *Genuine Venetian glass, handmade in Murano*. A differently coloured sticker with identical wording is illustrated in picture 16. 5.5 x 22cm (2⅛ x 8⅝in) diam.
£30/$55

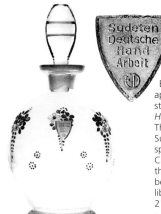

◀ **32: Tell-tale foil sticker, Czech-German**
Enamelled Art Deco decanter applied with a gold foil sticker stating *Sudeten Deutsche Hand Arbeit* (*hand painted*). The Nazis occupied the Sudetenland, the German-speaking border regions of Czechoslovakia, in 1936, so this piece was probably made between that date and the liberation of the area in 1944. 21cm (8¼in) inc.
Price £50/$85

▲ **33: WMF stickers, Germany, 1930s–80s**

The glassworks of WMF, the German metal-maker Württem-burgische Metallwarenfabrik, applied foil and paper stickers to most of its production. These evolved through three stages. The earliest type (top) was used principally before 1939, but also briefly after 1945 because of paper shortages in post-war Germany. Middle: Late 1940s–1972. Bottom (cellophane): c.1970–82.

From left: £80/$135, £75/$130, £30/$55

▲ **34: Whitefriars or not Whitefriars?**

The popularity of Geoffrey Baxter's designs for Whitefriars, Britain, causes problems. One of these is a genuine piece, another is fraudulently applied with a Whitefriars sticker, and the third the subject of an optimistic attribution. Left: blue cased vase, fraudulently applied with a black-and-white Whitefriars paper sticker, which dates from the 1960s and is in fact American. 21cm (8¼in). Centre: genuine mould-blown Whitefriars *Traffic Lights* vase, designed by Baxter in 1966. 12.5cm (4⅞in). Right: cased turquoise decanter, c.1970, applied with colourless nodes, maker unknown, but described by its vendor as "Whitefriars". 22.5cm (8⅞in).

From left: £15/$25, £45/$75, £85/$145

or location of manufacture, such as "Made in Czechoslovakia" or "Murano" (Italy) (picture 31), though even these can sometimes provide a little further information (pictures 32 and 33).

The second problem with stickers, as previously mentioned, is that they not only deteriorate in sunlight, leaving the printing illegible, but are also vulnerable to the fingernail, friction, damp, and washing. However, when still present, they are a delight to the collector and academic because they not only identify that particular piece, but can lead to wider attributions.

The third, though rare, problem with stickers is fraud. This practice involves removing stickers from pieces made by factories that are popular among collectors and applying them to the work of inferior ones. In Britain, this generally involves the designs of Geoffrey Baxter for the Whitefriars factory, which always used stickers. Whitefriars stickers, and some others, have occasionally been known to transfer themselves mysteriously onto superficially similar pieces made by less-desirable glassworks (picture 34 and p.87).

Identification by experience

Very little 20th-century glass is applied with a formal means of linking it to a particular maker or designer. This leaves perhaps 999 pieces out of 1,000 anonymous to the casual observer. This is a problem, even for those who have immersed themselves in the subject for decades, let alone for the uninitiated. The clearest routes to gaining powers of recognition and familiarity with the subject are by digesting reliable literature, by talking to experienced dealers and collectors, and by handling pieces. However, perhaps the single most important factor is retentive memory.

After two decades dealing in glass followed by a further nine years of buying and hoarding it, I still cannot identify the makers of roughly half the pieces I buy. This is partly because I buy a lot of glass, but also because the anonymous pieces are not illustrated in any of my 500+ reference books and catalogues. However, this does not mean I am entirely ignorant as to their origin. All experienced glass dealers and collectors gradually acquire the ability to discern the likely maker or national origin of a given piece through stylistic characteristics (*see* picture 35). It is extremely difficult to explain these in words, because they are composed almost entirely of tints and flavours. To describe the mental processes that might suggest a tentative attribution to Czechoslovakia or Sweden, for instance, is akin to explaining the taste of an apple. One can only acquire intuition though experience.

The greatest problem with books on 20th-century glass, aside from inaccuracies, is that their entire contents needs to be absorbed, yet many remain unread beyond the captions. Many, if not most, books of this type are used only for casual reference, and might as well contain little or no text. In this quick-fire television age, most of us lack the discipline

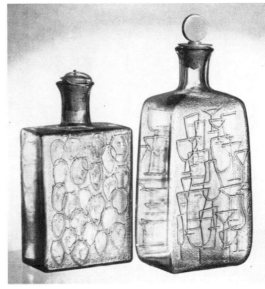

▲ 35: National characteristics, Sweden

Schnapps flasks, formed by various methods but generally fitted with ring-pull cork stoppers, have long been standard production items of Swedish glassworks. This representative group, made c.1956–70, demonstrates both their similarities and differences. From left: Dip-moulded, square-section, attributed to Monica Bratt, Reijmyre, c.1965, 14.5cm (5⅝in); half-post method, square-section, designer uncertain, for Pukeberg, c.1968, 12cm (4¾in); and mould-blown, rectangular section, designed by Lars Hellsten, for Orrefors, c.1965, 15.5cm (6in). Above: two mould-blown variants, designed by Kyell Blomberg, for Gullaskruf, 1956.

Three on left £20/$35, Blomberg variants £60/$100

Problems with 20th-century glass

Newcomers to any field should tread with caution, and not allow wishful thinking to gain the upper hand. There is no denying or avoiding the fact that 20th-century glass collecting can be a tricky area. Beyond the obvious, and the factors previously explained, the remaining danger areas include:

• Endemic design plagiarism between rival glassmakers.

▲ 36: Aino Aalto's *Bölgeblick* and derivatives

Left: The original, 1932; right: *Norman* pattern, Davidson, 1945; above: Jacob Bang's *Broskø* range, Holmegaard, from 1938.
£5–50/$9–85*

◀ 37: Original, 1923, or copy?

This optically moulded piece is similar to an Edward Hald design for Orrefors' sister company, Sandvik, 1923 (p.188). However, the neck of Hald's version has one swelling while this version has two, so this example must be regarded as a copy, probably dating from the 1920s. 17cm (6¾in).

£25/$45

◀ 38: *Veronese* vase, produced since 1920

Designed by Vittorio Zecchin for Venini in 1920, this vase has remained in production ever since. Modelled on a vase featured in Veronese's painting *The Annunciation* (c.1570), copies have been produced by numerous Murano studios in various sizes and colours, for over 80 years.

£50–£5,000/$85–8,500*

▼ 39: Swedish Regency-style cutting, 1934

Simon Gate adopted English Regency-style cutting for his *1000 Windows* series, Orrefors, from 1934, named *Portal* (centre). The decanter (left), signed *Orrefors GA1506*, was designed in 1936. However, the enduring appeal of the optical effects generated by the cutting encouraged Orrefors to modify two of the original vessels, and the vase on the right is from Orrefors' 2003 catalogue.

£100/$170*

- The revival or continuing production of classic designs.
- Condition and restoration.
- The vagaries of the market.
- Retro designs.

Copies and plagiarism

Designers in all fields, and especially those in glass, routinely copy each other's successful designs. On Murano, this was regarded as a compliment to a design's creator. To choose just two examples from thousands: scores of pressed-glass makers produced versions of the American *Chippendale* pattern, from 1907 (pp.112), and Aino Aalto's *Bölgeblick* range, 1932 (picture 36), inspired a legion of look-alikes. (The original *Bölgeblick* designed by Aino Aalto, for Iittala, 1932, shown at the bottom of picture 36, has remained in almost constant production since 1932. Above it are factory drawings of *Broskø*, designed by Jacob E. Bang, for Holmegaard, 1937. Another derivative, WJG Fullerton's Ripple series for Davidson, 1937, is illustrated on p.111). So, if an otherwise anonymous piece simply resembles rather than is identical to one illustrated in a book, it is probably the work of a copyist designer working for another factory (picture 37). If its shape and decoration are identical but the colour is different, it is probably from the same source as that illustrated.

Longevity of greatest hits

Most glass factories operate on the maxim, "If it still sells, keep making it." Accordingly, certain pieces designed almost a century ago, and considerably more from the '30s, remain in production today. For example, the *Veronese* vase, designed by Vittorio Zecchin in 1920, is still produced today at Venini and derivatives of it elsewhere on Murano (picture 38). Orrefors' 2003 catalogue contains recent creations alongside Simon Gate's *1000 Windows* vases (1934) (picture 39), Edward Hald's *Grace* bowls (1932) (p.189) and cognac balloons (1935), and Nils Landberg's *Herkules* jug (1953), *Gabriel* candlestick (1955), and *Illusion* service (1957) (p.191). Iittala/Nuutajärvi has also recently reintroduced certain Kaj Franck designs 16 years after his death (p.120), and the company still makes Alvo Aalto's *Savoy* vase, designed in 1936 (p.163).

The longevity of such designs speaks volumes, underlining the timeless nature of some 20th-century glass. However, the crucial point for a collector is that early *Veronese* or *Savoy* vases typically possess a considerable value that is not enjoyed by later versions. This is why production dates are included in the captions of the illustrations in this book wherever possible.

Murano glass is a nightmare in this respect. The output of its leading factory, Venini, is extensively documented, with several well-illustrated books already dedicated to its production. The cream of Murano glass, produced by the likes of the Seguso family, Salviati, and Barovier & Toso, can also be found in numerous superficial, wide-ranging, coffee-table books. Yet these illustrate *none*, not even one, of the hundreds of pieces I have picked up over the years.

Visiting Murano recently with a sheaf of images of my purchases, I was told with a dismissive wave, "Oh, they are just tourist pieces." What, all of them? Well, apparently yes. The point is that a yawning chasm separates the best, little of which is signed, from the rest, all of which is unsigned. The problem is that "the rest" forms a majority of some 99 per cent, and includes many well-made and distinctive pieces. Compounding matters, Murano-esque glass is now pouring out of glassworks in India and China (picture 41). So, when it comes to general advice, Venetian/Murano glass is probably best left to those armed with the academic knowledge required to avoid its numerous though colourful pitfalls.

Damage and restoration

When space and funds are limited, pieces that are cracked, severely scratched, or bruised, or with severely rubbed gilding should be avoided. Small chips are acceptable to some, including myself, if the price is right, but not to others. Small imperfections can be ignored or professionally restored, but pieces with large chunks missing are best forgotten.

Another problem is "blooming", a cloudy white stain most commonly found in vases and decanters. Caused by prolonged contact with water, blooming requires professional removal through polishing with gentle abrasives or sometimes with acids.

▶ **41: Indian TK Maxx vase**

Modern piece made in India in a vaguely Murano style, containing colour splashes and aventurine copper particles. Available from wholesalers, priced around £6 ($10), and stores such as TK Max for only slightly more. 25cm (9⅞in).

£10/$17

▶ **42: Restoration or vandalism?**

Mould-blown *Kehrä* vases, 1968, designed by Tamara Aladin, for Riihimäki, Finland (pp.220–3). One intact, the other missing its upper half and "restored" (the rim polished to disguise the break). 25cm (9⅞in) when complete.

Complete £65/$110*

▼ **40: "Murano" glass?**

The colourful effects generally associated with Murano have been widely copied. This type of decorative glass, often attributed to "Murano", has been made elsewhere for many years and continues in production in the Far East today.

£5–20/$9–35

▲ 43: Underrated Whitefriars

Most examples of Whitefriars' output designed between Harry Powell's retirement in 1919 and 1954, when Geoffrey Baxter joined the works, remain largely uncollected. Left: mould-blown decanter designed by Barnaby Powell in 1935, 19.5cm (7⅞in) inc. Centre: ribbon-trailed bowl designed by Barnaby Powell c.1932, 14.5cm (5⅝in). Right: Jug and goblet attributed to William Wilson c.1942, max 17.5cm (6⅞in).

Decanter £130/$220*, Bowl £100/$170
Jug & six glasses £75/$130

TOP TEN TIPS WHEN BUYING

- Buy the best of what you like and can afford.

- Concentrate on iconic pieces: generally the best and/or most distinctive pieces by leading designers.

- Buy signed pieces, irrespective of the methodology used to apply the signature.

- Look for pieces that retain their stickers, even if they are worn.

- Specialize in large pieces, as generally fewer were made than small and medium versions.

- Avoid damaged items.

- Buy ahead of the market by identifying decorative pieces made by currently underrated designers or categories.

- Read all you can about your chosen field.

- Cultivate both your memory, and your luck.

- Get out of bed earlier, as early birds invariably catch the biggest and juiciest worms, even glass ones.

Restoration is more problematic because it is often invisible. In the case of sensitive work, it can be difficult to discern whether the foot of a goblet or the lip of a vase has been reduced to lose a chip. Broken stoppers can be reassembled with adhesives, and damaged cutting remodelled. When in doubt, prospective buyers should always ask vendors to indicate areas of restoration in the full knowledge that untruthful answers contravene the law. In the case of dealers being caught out, it is unacceptable for them to claim ignorance.

However, everyone makes mistakes. When visiting Finland recently while conducting research for this book, I bought a textured vase thinking it to be by Tamara Aladin for the Riihimäki glassworks (picture 42, and pp.220–3). As it turned out, I was correct, but its top half was entirely missing and the break polished to disguise the fact! There is only one sure-fire defence against such errors: learn to recognize what you are looking at.

The next big thing

Collectors in all fields are always looking for the next big thing. It is human nature to strive to be ahead of the game, and glass specialists are no exception. Those who "discovered" the Whitefriars designer Geoffrey Baxter a decade ago and bought big are now laughing all the way to the bank. His large and colourful textured *Banjo* (picture 48 on p.69) and *Drunken Bricklayer* vases (picture 98) now regularly fetch over £1,000 ($1,700), and, rumour has it, a particular example in a rare colour has sold for over £5,000 ($8,500). However, Baxter designed hundreds of pieces for Whitefriars between 1954 and 1980, and, while some later examples fetch big money, many earlier ones remain fairly common in Britain, and struggle even to break into double figures. While Baxter is known and some of his work is avidly sought after, the distinctive designs of his predecessors at Whitefriars, such as Barnaby Powell and William Wilson, remain widely unrecognized (picture 43).

Similarly, Timo Sarpaneva and Tapio Wirkkala contributed at least 1,000 designs to Iittala over their careers. Of those that are still produced today, most have negligible value, but a few command thousands. Such are the vagaries of the market, and serious collectors must learn that blue versions of a given vase might be much rarer than red or green ones, and thus "worth" three times more. However, it might all change tomorrow if the bottom falls out of the market for the work for a particular factory or designer, as it did for Emile Gallé pieces when the economy of Japan, the biggest market for Gallé, suffered a downturn in the mid-1990s.

Modern reproductions

The rising popularity of stylish, post-war glass has recently inspired a swathe of modern reproductions, copies, and derivatives. Sold through modern design stores, some are virtually indistinguishable from originals, while others simply approximate them. A recent visit to Ikea netted a haul of new pieces, all made in Poland and China, some clearly derived from classic designs by Nils Landberg and Tapio Wirkkala, while others were more vaguely descended from the Scandinavian repertoire (pictures 44 and 107, p.49).

The reason for the success of these pieces is two-fold. First, they are very cheap: made in countries largely without environmental controls and with lower labour and energy costs. Second, they are convenient, with their acquisition and appreciation demanding nothing from their purchasers other than payment and occasional dusting.

The rise of new glassmaking centres not only adds to the challenges facing collectors of period pieces, but also causes the owners of historic glassworks to quake in their boots, with thousands of jobs threatened by low-cost competition. Recently, when a freelance Swedish designer was commissioned to produce a new range for Ikea, she suggested that Orrefors should quote to make it. However, the bottom line was that the cost of making the pieces at the traditional European factory was ten times greater than making them at a Chinese glassworks. It is ironic that Ikea, based in the traditional Swedish glassmaking region of Småland, and a short drive from Orrefors, Kosta, Boda, and several other glassmakers, threatens to undermine their very survival.

In general

Some collectors make money from their hobby, but few are motivated exclusively by the prospect of financial gain. An increasing number sell surplus items over the internet or at specialist fairs, though they often do so simply to finance new acquisitions. Nobody can predict the future, but history has shown that the best pieces are the safest long-term bet. However, collecting should above all be stimulating and fun, and investing money in decorative objects is a great deal more enjoyable than leaving it in a savings account.

▲ **44: Spot the difference**
Four apparently similar free-formed dishes, two designed and produced in the 1950s, one made by a modern studio, and another available today from Ikea. From top: Designed by Ernest Gordon, for Åfors, Sweden, late 1950s, base engraved *GM376 E Gordon*, 24.5cm (9⅝in); Ikea, designer unknown, paper label with *Made in China*; triform *Fionia* vase designed by Per Lütken, for Holmegaard, Denmark, c.1955, base engraved *HOLMEGAARD 19PL57*, 18cm (7in); modern studio glass dish, both designer and maker unknown, base engraved *MICKE of-99*, 25cm (9⅞in).
From top £65/$110, £5/$9, £75/$130, £45/$75

WHERE TO BUY

After reading this book and absorbing its contents, you will probably want to know where to apply your new-found knowledge. Twentieth-century glass can be located and bought from three types of venue:

GROUND FLOOR: General flea markets, open-air "antiques" fairs, yard and boot sales, charity and junk shops. These offer the greatest potential for bargains but are time-demanding.

MIDDLE FLOOR: Antiques centres and eBay. Prices are variable according to luck, your knowledge, and that of the vendor and the current competition.

TOP FLOOR: Specialist dealers and websites. They offer expert knowledge but few bargains. However, purchases can be returned if they turn out not to be as described. To be used only by the sufficiently rich, or those desperate to fill holes in their collections. Always ask for areas of restoration to be identified.

A Short History

Decorative domestic glassware evolved through a series of five basic stylistic eras during the 20th century, each allied to a combination of changing aesthetics and technological advances. Yet, aside from style, the predominant trend was that the volume of glass produced between 1900 and 1999 grew immeasurably as its price fell relative to incomes. Of course, it was entirely possible to pay a small fortune in 2000 for a single brand-new wineglass by a leading maker, but, generally, prices continued the historic trend by dropping markedly over the course of the century.

Working by sociological and financial, as well as aesthetic, trends, the 20th century might reasonably be divided into the following periods:

1900–1919: Straddling the centuries This period ushered out the past and heralded the new, yet it all took time. The social order remained broadly unchanged until after the First World War, when the ruling classes were found to share the same faults and frailties as those who had previously been prepared to be their subordinates.

1920–49: The rise of the masses The working classes became increasingly organized and prepared to flex their new-found political and economic muscles through the ballot box and their wallets. Hard, filthy work in return for meagre crusts was no longer acceptable, and was duly replaced by a fair day's work for a fair day's pay, plus a pension, sick leave, and annual holidays. Then came another war.

1950–67: Commercial modernism After the bitterness of war, rationing, and reconstruction, a consensus was agreed: it was time for a brave new world whose inhabitants would be happier, healthier, wealthier, and wiser. These objectives would be achieved through technology, compassion, and good design, as long as everyone worked together toward the shared ideal.

1968–84: Get rich quick The pace of life accelerated faster than ever. Choice, opportunity, and personal wealth soared to new peaks, with even manual workers owning their own homes and cars and enjoying foreign holidays. After the darkness of the past, it was true: we had never had it so good.

1985–2000: Dumbing down This was the era of globalization: why pay Westerners in gold when workers in other parts of the world would work for peanuts? Banks and supermarkets counted their profits in billions, while celebrity, brands, and bargains became the new gods.

1900–19: Straddling the centuries

Most of the glassware produced before 1920 is of little or no interest to collectors of "modern" glass. Countless, unimaginative pressed pieces, many decorated with pseudo-cutting and some designed as early as the 1860s, continued to pour from factories across Europe and the United

▲ **45: Renaissance Venice Revisited**
Renaissance-style tazza (c.1550), by Fratelli Toso, c.1891. 6.5cm (6½in).
£500/$850

States. A great deal of fine glassware was also made over the period, but, despite its outstanding craftsmanship, most of it is currently unfashionable and of little relevance to 20th-century design.

Arts & Crafts and Art Nouveau glass is a grey area. The Arts & Crafts Movement evolved during the 1880s, and although some of it was regarded as avant-garde, much, if not most of it, drew its inspiration from the past, most notably from Renaissance Venice (picture 45). Such revivalist glass was produced into the early 20th century in all major glassmaking centres, from Pittsburgh to Venice itself (pp.84, 139, 185).

Europe

European taste fragmented toward the end of the 19th century. In central Europe, for example, a taste for tradition cohabited alongside the forward-looking designs of the Successionist Movement. The retrovists opted for historical revivals, known in German as *Historismus*. *Historismus* glassware is typified by large *Humpen* beer glasses and ewers with metal mounts, often decorated in gold and bright enamels, with rococo scenes or Gothic shields and armorials (picture 46 and p.92). Most of the leading makers produced such work, including the Viennese designer/retailer J&L Lobmeyr, some of whose reproductions were in turn copied in the United States into the early 20th century.

The roots of modern design are generally traced back to Christopher Dresser (1834–1904), who is widely credited as having been the world's first professional designer, although little glassware has yet been linked definitively to his drawing board (picture 47). However, Harry Powell (1835–1922) is seen as possibly the world's first full-time glass designer. Even so, a great deal of Powell's work, all for his family's Whitefriars glasshouse in London, looked to the past, combining a raft of historical references gathered during his tours of Europe's leading museums.

Powell belonged to a small but distinguished clique of glassmakers/designers whose careers spanned both the 19th and 20th centuries and the Arts & Crafts and Art Nouveau eras. While he designed a large body of distinguished Art Nouveau glass (picture 48), the greatest designer of the genre was Emile Gallé (1846–1904). Gallé, firmly based on his extensive education and bold sense of curiosity, elevated glassmaking to a new level of ingenuity and excellence, and enjoyed critical and commercial acclaim before losing his battle against leukaemia at the age of 58. Yet, despite the revolutionary nature of some of his techniques, his floral designs are arguably better categorized as defining the end of the 19th century rather than as heralding the birth of the 20th (picture 49).

The United States

Gallé's American counterpart, Louis C. Tiffany (1848–1933), was no glassmaker, but he knew what he wanted and enjoyed the wherewithal to ensure that he got it. Tiffany's rainbow visions, often inspired by ecclesi-

▲ 46: *Historismus*-style ewer

Aquamarine glass with base-metal mount. The cover is dated 1892. German or Austrian, maker unknown. 41cm (16⅛in).
£500/$850

▲ 47: Dresser *Crow's Foot* claret jug, 1878

One of Christopher Dresser's most Modernist designs, made by Hukin & Heath. 33cm (13in).
£3,000/$5,100

◀ **48: English Art Nouveau**
Wine glass with applied green trails, designed by Harry Powell, for Whitefriars, 1899. 20.5cm (8in).
£250/$425

▶ **49: Gallé acid-cameo vase**
Floral vase, designed by Émile Gallé c.1905. 36cm (14⅛in).
£8,000/$13,600

▼ **50: Iridescent Tiffany and Carnival glass, US, c.1910**
Iridescent wave-rimmed Tiffany vase, designed by Louis C. Tiffany, 1910 (factory number 5242), signed *LC Tiffany*. 11.5cm (4⅛in). Also an apparently similar Marigold-tinted Dugan/ Diamond Carnival glass bowl, c.1920. 24cm (9½in).
Tiffany £700/$1,190*, Carnival £25/$45

astical stained glass, were translated by his carefully recruited staff from scribbled scraps of paper into a magnificent range of lighting and iridescent *Favrile* table-glass, so sought-after today by wealthy collectors (picture 50 and p.80). Frederick Carder's Steuben workshops at Corning also produced exotically tinted glass but, like Tiffany, this suffered with the advent of superficially similar, though extremely cheap, pressed Carnival glass that poured in from numerous West Virginia glassworks from around 1904 (picture 50).

Bohemia

Across the Atlantic in Bohemia, the sleepy Loetz glassworks was inherited and gradually transformed from 1879 by Max Ritter Von Spaun (1825–1909). Inspired by Tiffany's *Favrile*, he patented a form of glass with a metallic shimmer in 1895, and employed many of the Hapsburg Empire's leading designers to develop a repertoire of over 8,000 shapes within a decade (picture 51). Loetz's output was further redefined from 1906 by the introduction of more adventurous shapes and decorative schemes devised by the various members of the Weiner Werkstätte (Vienna Workshop).

The Werkstätte, led by the architect/draughtsman Joseph Hoffmann (1870–1956), was a revolutionary design concept. Following Dresser's example and marking the dawn of a new age in design, most of its members worked in several media, including Hoffmann himself (picture 52 and p.54) and Otto Prutscher (1880–1949) (picture 53). Werkstätte glass, *c.*1900–30, was often the result of collaborations between its members. It drew on Bohemia's rich and historic decorative palette to create original and distinctly 20th-century forms that tower above most of the derivative work being produced elsewhere at the time.

Most of the glassware produced between 1900 and 1920 was dull and unchallenging, although a few dazzling beacons lit a path to the future. However, avant-garde pieces were produced in relatively small quanti-

◀ 53: Otto Prutscher wine glass, 1907
Cased and cut "ladder" stem hock glass. Designed by Otto Prutscher, for Meyr's Neff, Bohemia. 20cm (8in).
£4,000/$6,800

▶ 51: Iridescent Loetz, Bohemia, *c.*1905
Spherical iridescent decanter (346/347), produced by Loetz, for its London retailer, Max Emmanuel & Co., 1898–1905. 20.5cm (8in).
£400/$680

▼ 52: Josef Hoffmann for Lobmeyr, 1914
Bronzit series bowl, designed by Joseph Hoffmann, for Lobmeyr, 1914. Hand-painted black enamels on acid-matt surface. 22cm (8⅝in).
£4,000/$6,800

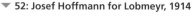

▲ 54: Bohemian enamelling, *c.*1915
Seccessionist/Werkstätte-style. Designer unknown. 14cm (5½in).
£200/$340

ties, were expensive when originally retailed, are now rare and highly sought after, and often require academic knowledge to attribute them to their makers and designers.

1920–49: The rise of the masses

The period following the First World War was marked by rapid economic growth across the board. This was fuelled by many factors, including an increasing awareness of design and style encouraged by greater diversity of wealth and taste. Lower prices, facilitated by fiercer competition and improving technology, acted as catalysts to the growth of consumerism. It was the age that gave birth to Art Deco and Scandinavian design. Another major factor was that the working classes, previously lacking the means to purchase decorative objects, became major buyers of glassware, which led to an explosion in the production of colourful pressed glass.

The age of consumerism, or shopping, dates from the latter part of the 18th century. Josiah Wedgwood had grasped its principles by 1781, when he observed that the decoration of his porcelain "must every few

▶ **55: Lalique *Ondines* dish, *c.*1921**
With green staining and a moulded mark, designed by René Lalique. 27.5cm (10⅞in).
£950/$1,615

days be altered, reversed and transformed as to render a whole new scene". Using this now familiar tactic, customers could be encouraged to acquire his new objects not because their old ones were broken but because they had become old-fashioned.

France

The mood of the world was radically transformed by the carnage of the trenches and social upheaval after 1918. Accurately reflecting this seed change, the romantic idealism of Art Nouveau was immediately superseded by geometric Art Deco, as seen in the work of René Lalique (picture 55). Abandoning a career in jewellery design, Lalique bought a glassworks in 1918 and within a decade had instigated a massive transformation in the way in which pressed glass was perceived. He designed and produced glass tableware, architecture, fountains, trans-Atlantic liners, cars, and cathedrals as well as jewels and lighting. He won prizes, was internationally fêted, and made a fortune; he also turned the name *Lalique* into an international brand that has endured for almost 100 years and generated vast profits.

Lalique's designs from the 1920s transformed the public perception of pressed glass from a second-class substitute for cut glass into an art form, retailed by the world's most exclusive emporia. Yet, despite having developed some new production methods, Lalique generally relied on familiar, even ancient technology. The secret of his success lay in the way he combined his extraordinary design sense and feel for glass moulding with an innate understanding of his market.

Lalique's success inspired a legion of copyists and imitators, and extended the boundaries of glass design by making pressed glass posh. The French-naturalized Sicilian Marius Ernest Sabino (1878–1961) (picture 56 and p.70), led Lalique's followers, but it might be claimed that only the German-Bohemian partnership of Heinrich Hoffmann and Henry Schlevogt (1904–84) significantly advanced his work (picture 57 and p.58). Lalique's direct disciples were followed by a swathe of colourful, mostly cheap and cheerful pressed glass from the world's glassworks, a great deal of which was stylish and cleverly modelled, and which remains plentiful and affordable.

Elsewhere in France, Gallé's legacy of acid-cameo was maintained through Daum (picture 58) and in Schneider's striking Art Deco vases and lamps (p.70), while the long-established Baccarat produced the more subtle designs of Jacques Adnet and Georges Chevalier (picture 59 and p.72). Despite Lalique's enduring fame, it is arguable that Maurice Marinot (1882–1960) was equally influential in the long-term as the first designer/artist to use glass as a means of self-expression. Unlike his contemporaries and forebears, Marinot rejected the concept of function and produced pieces best described as "art objects" (picture 60).

▲ **56: Sabino opalescent fish, c.1930**
Designed by Marius Ernest Sabino, Paris, c.1930. Engraved signature. 7cm (2¾in).
£75/$130*

▲ **57: Hoffmann/Schlevogt pressed tortoise, c.1925**
In marbled *Malachite* glass. Designed by Henrich Schlevogt, partners with Hoffman, c.1925. From their 1939 catalogue. (See explanation on p.57).
£150/$255

▲ **58: Daum Modernist vase, c.1925**
Acid-etched vase, designed by Paul Daum, c.1925, revealing the influence of Maurice Marinot. 14.5cm (5⅝in).
£650/$1,105

Czechoslovakia

While a significant proportion of the work of French glassmakers can be identified through their signatures, the opposite was the case in the ancient kingdom of Bohemia, absorbed into the Republic of Czechoslovakia at its foundation in 1918. Aside from the distinguished production of Moser (picture 61 and pp.54–5) and some occasional pieces etched or moulded with the words *TCHECO-SLOVAQIE* (picture 62) or *CZECHOSLOVAKIA*, Czech glass rarely bears marks that identify even its national source, let alone its maker or designer.

The historic Czech glass industry was managed and staffed almost exclusively by German-speakers, almost all of whom were dispossessed and forcibly removed from Czechoslovakia in 1945, and most of their records lost or destroyed. The resulting absence of information is both irritating for collectors and problematic for historians and academics: how can pre-war Czech glass be adequately appraised when so much of it cannot be reliably identified? However, the scenario was very different during the 1950s, '60s, and '70s, because the cash-poor Communist regime was proficient at advertising its glassware abroad through the *Czech Glass Review*.

The grey area of pre-war central Europe would be irrelevant if Czechoslovakia had not been such an important and prolific glass-

▲ **59: Baccarat Modernism, 1925–30**
Mould-blown and cut candlestick, probably designed by Georges Chevalier, c.1925–30. 10cm (3⅞in).
£100/$170

▲ **60: Marinot art object, 1920s**
Free-formed object containing metallic inclusions. Designed by Maurice Marinot. Engraved *MARINOT*. 15.5cm (6in).
£5,000/$8,500

▲ **61: Moser Art Nouveau, c.1902**
Amethyst-to-colourless, with *Eckentiefgravur* floral decoration. Designer unknown. Etched: *Moser Karlsbad*. 15cm (5⅞in).
£225/$380

making nation, having produced a greater variety of shapes and styles and employed more decorating techniques than any other country (picture 63). The fact that its designers and makers were also great plagiarists adds to the problem. While Bohemian/Czech glassmakers developed innumerable distinctive styles and techniques of their own, their great experience also enabled them to produce convincing copies of almost anything made elsewhere. Furthermore, their output was enormous, with hundreds of factories and workshops, large and small, dotting the Czech landscape. The forming and decorating of glassware occupied the working lives of some 25,000 of its 14 million population during the 1920s and '30s, proportionately more than any other country.

The United States

America's most prestigious 20th-century glassworks was Steuben, established in Corning, New York State, in 1903. Though Steuben originally focused on the colours and effects developed by Frederick Carder (1863–1963), the appointment of sculptor Sidney Waugh as its artistic director in 1934 marked a switch toward bold, Swedish-style, colourless, monolithic forms. With Steuben crystal aimed at America's elite, its masses were served by scores of lesser glassworks, most centred on the Virginia coalfields, which produced a huge array of utility pressed glassware (picture 64). Certain patterns, including *Chippendale* and *Cubist*, established notable export markets, but most was sold within

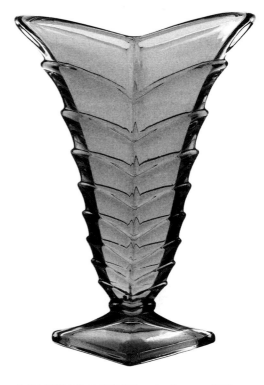

▲ **62: *TCHECO-SLOVAQIE* pressed vase, c.1930**
One of many vases of uncertain origin, all with the base embossed *TCHECO-SLOVAQIE*. Reputedly by Walther, Radeberg, Germany, c.1930. 24.5cm (9⅝in).
£40/$70

▼ **63: Anonymous pre-war Czech glass**
From left: Iridescent and intaglio-cut lampshade, 1920s; green pressed powder pot, 1930s; and lightweight decanter and tumbler with floral enamelling, 1930s. Decanter 20cm (7⅞in).
£5-35/$9–60

▲ **64: American Depression-era glass**
Jeannette Glass Co. *Poinsettia* pattern pitcher, 1931, 26cm (10¼in); *Romba Rubic* Modernist ashtray, 5.5 x 11cm (2⅛ x 4¼in); and Hazel Atlas Royal Lace plate, 1934, 25.5cm (10in).
Pitcher and plate £5–50/$9–85, Rubic ashtray £50/$85

the United States, where it is avidly collected today. It is generically known as Depression-era glass, though some of its patterns were produced into the 1960s and beyond.

Britain

British glassmakers took a considerable time to adjust to the 20th-century decorative trends. In more ways than one, they had ruled the world from around 1770, with their extraordinary style of cutting becoming universally known as the *façon d'Angleterre*. Their dominance had been challenged by the high-quality coloured glassware developed in Bohemia and France from the 1820s and '30s, but having successfully copied these, the British maintained a lead through a combination of early industrialization, technical excellence, and their broad base of colonial markets.

The British dominance in world glassmaking began to crumble toward the end of the 19th century. This was due to a variety of factors, including inept management and intransigent labour unions at home, and to general improvements abroad in the designs, production methods, and marketing strategies of its competitors, as well as their lower wage costs. It was not until the late 1920s that the output of British glassworks showed any significant signs of adapting to the 20th century, but by then the country was importing five times more glass than it exported.

It took a combination of heavy tariffs on imported glass and a series of government-sponsored exhibitions during the early 1930s showcasing glassware designed by some of the country's leading artists to kick-start a revival (picture 65). Suitably encouraged, most British glassworks

▲ **65: Pre-war Stuart Crystal, Britain**

The vase, rear, was designed by the painter Paul Nash for the British Art in Relation to the Home Exhibition, 1933. 20cm (7⅞in). Bowl designed by AR Pierce, c.1935, 20cm (7⅞in) diam.
Vase £1,750/$3,000; Bowl £300/$510

▲ **66: *Cloud* glass bowl, Britain, 1931**

Pressed *Cloud* bowl, designer unknown, for George Davidson & Co. This shape was introduced in 1931. Black plinths were optional extras for most British pressed-glass ranges. 30.5cm (12in) diam.
£45/$75

▲ **67: Early Orrefors, Sweden**

Decanter blueprint by Edward Hald, 1923 and mould-blown and cut *Triton* vase, by Simon Gate, 1916. Vase 29cm (11½in).
Triton vase £1,250–2,500/$2,125–4,250*

recruited college-trained designers, some for the first time, with the result that certain rejuvenated elements of the British industry began to produce some stylish fine and pressed Art Deco and Modernist glass (picture 66).

Scandinavia

The most radical transformation in pre-war glassmaking occurred in Scandinavia, whose previous output had been undistinguished. Sweden led the way from around 1920, with an outpouring of top-quality, even iconic designer glass from several glassworks, but one in particular: Orrefors, which developed from a small, backwater concern into arguably the world's greatest glassworks. Most 20th-century works were lucky to recruit and retain one great designer, but Orrefors' initial partnership of Simon Gate and Edwald Hald (picture 67) was augmented within a decade by Nils Landberg, Sven Palmqvist, and Vicke Lindstrand, who worked for the company for a combined total of 100 years.

Norway and Denmark's emergence as significant glassmaking nations was more gradual than Sweden's. However, the distinguished work of Jacob E. Bang from the 1920s established the importance of the Holmegaard works (picture 68). Aside from certain notable designs, Finland did not emerge as a major international glassmaker until after the Second World War.

Italy

The development of the Venetian glass industry during the second quarter of the 20th century almost rivalled that of Scandinavia. Dr Antonio Salviati's late-19th-century reproductions are widely credited with having averted the extinction of the Murano industry, but Paulo Venini (1895–1959) was largely responsible for its rejuvenation. Venini founded the luxury glassworks that still bears his name in 1921, and established it among the world's most influential and adventurous through the work of a roll call of world-class designers, including Carlo Scarpa, Napoleone Martinuzzi (picture 69), and later, Venini himself.

Several other designer/makers contributed to Murano's 20th-century success, including some of the descendants of some of the island's oldest glassmaking families: the Baroviers, Tosos, and Segusos. Retaining handicraft at its centre, Murano glass has always tended toward size, colour, and effect, but attempts at specific attributions are fraught with complications. Murano design classics now command big prices, but close copies, modern reproductions, and fakes can leave novices vulnerable to expensive mistakes.

The effects of war

Many of the world's leading fine glassmakers naturally experienced a hiatus from 1939 to 1945, when production switched from domestic finery to military applications, with vases and goblets being replaced by

▲ **68: Jacob E. Bang, Denmark, 1934**
Mould-blown and trailed Modernist decanter, designed by Jacob Bang, for Holmegaard (pp.140–5). 19.5cm (7⅜in).
£250/$425

▲ **69: Martinuzzi for Venini, Murano, 1933**
Rib-moulded opaque red vase with applied handles, designed by Napoleone Martinuzzi, for Venini, in 1933. 33cm (13in).
£4,000/$6,800*

◀ **70: Nanny Still *Harlekini*, Finland, 1958**

Mould-blown and colour-cased decanter from Still's *Harlekini* range (pp.95 and 215), for Riihimäki. 28cm (11in).

£225/$380*

▼ **71: Wirkkala original, 1946, and anonymous derivative**

Left: Free-formed and engraved *Kantarelli* art object. Designed by Tapio Wirkkala, for Iittala, in 1946. Winner of the Milan Triennale, 1951. 21cm (8¼in) (p.167). Right: Copy by unknown Scandinavian maker. 10.5cm (4in).

Left £2,000–£30,000/ $3,400–51,000* **Right £30/$55**

▼ **72: Typical 1950-early-60s glass colours**

Random selection of mostly 1950s and 1960s jugs, demonstrating some of the typical colours of the period, and several sharing conformity of design. The ones in the flattest colours are the earliest, and those in the most vivid the latest. Max. 34.5cm (13⅝in).

£15–£75/$25–130*

radar screens and periscope lenses. Yet, in certain countries, notably across Scandinavia and in Italy, the everyday lives of many escaped relatively unscathed. It would be from these sources that some of the most dynamic glass would emerge after the restoration of peace in 1945.

1950–67: Commercial modernism

It is unsurprising that the nations that suffered the worst ravages of the Second World War took the longest time to recover. The industrial areas of Britain and Germany, for example, had been pounded, if not flattened, by each other's bombs, and their populations continued to suffer the privations of wartime rationing well into the 1950s.

Nevertheless, the general feeling for the majority during the post-war period was one of optimism and, in the medium- to long-term, one of growing affluence and prosperity. Incomes continued to rise in relation to living costs across most of the Western world as bigger and better goods were produced more cheaply and more colourfully than ever before.

Changes in glassmaking

Post-war glassware tended to reflect the societies that produced it, even more so than ever before. With much of the world emerging from the ashes, it tended toward bold, Modernist shapes (picture 70). Perhaps the greatest change was that, for the first time, most glassware did not evolve empirically, around the practical needs of the product, but was designed by professionals, many of them young graduates of colleges of art and architecture. With few of them scarred by military service, the mood of this new breed of designer was optimistic and dynamic, with many feeling charged with a sense of duty to improve the world through design.

While the fundamentals of glassmaking remained largely unchanged, the price of products fell faster than ever. This was due partly to the effects of technology and competition, but perhaps more importantly to the desire of those who conceived it to provide good design at low prices.

Certain defining characteristics, such as form, colour, and decoration, enable most pieces of 18th- and 19th-century glassware to be securely attributed to its country of origin. The rigidity of such national idiosyncrasies softened from the mid-19th century as the world gradually "shrank" through the catalysts of international fairs and improved trade and transport links, and the individualization of individual taste. From the mid-20th century, however, specific design trends emanating from one factory could be, and indeed were copied within days by its neighbours, and within weeks by others great distances away (pictures 71 and 72).

Trade fairs and the *Studio Yearbooks*, each containing photographs of hundreds of new glass designs from around the world, continued to play their role in the homogenization of international taste. However, perhaps the greatest change in the post-war period was the spread of car ownership, which enabled individual designers to travel abroad to visit rival factories, talk to their counterparts … and copy their ideas.

Pre-war designs continued in production at most glassworks into the 1960s at least, and many works faced lean times as the world economy took time to rebuild. Post-war glass design drew from a limited palette, with colourless pieces forming the majority, and most coloured designs produced in largely flat or soft tints, smoke, or even black (picture 73).

Italy

The exceptions to the generally muted colours of post-war glass were, of course, pieces produced in the ever-flamboyant Venice, whose fiery hues have always been the defining characteristic of Murano glass. The trend continued unabated after 1945, when Venice enjoyed a second golden age to rival that of four centuries before. Imaginations and techniques were pushed to the boundaries and beyond by the likes of Paulo Venini (picture 74), Fulvio Bianconi, Ercole Barovier, Dino Martens, Flavio Poli, Carlo Scarpa, and Archimede Seguso. This trend toward daring, technically demanding, and expensive art objects established by the leading

▲ **73: Post-war organic shapes**
Muted, dark tints recalling wartime camouflage and organic shapes were typical of much post-war European glass production, *c*.1950–early '60s. All solid colours in soda glass. From left: Smoke-grey vase, 14cm (5½in); smoked amethyst skittle-shaped vase, 25cm (9⅞in); tall blue vase, probably Magnor, Norway, 27cm (10⅝in); slash-rimmed smoked amethyst carafe/vase, 40cm (15¾in); blue bulbous vase, probably Magnor, 21cm (8¼in); and tall, smoke-brown, funnel-mouth vase, possibly Gullaskruf, Sweden, 34.5cm (13⅝in).
£30–45/$55–75*

▲ **74: Paolo Venini *Inciso*, c.1956**
Designed by Paolo Venini. Acid signature: *Venini Murano*. To achieve *Inciso*, the surface was laboriously cut with a series of parallel grooves, which were then almost entirely polished away to leave a matt surface. These pieces remain in the modern Venini repertoire but bear different signatures. Max. 37cm (14⅝in).
Rear, from left £1,200/$2,050; £1,000/$1,700
Front £900/$1,530

studies spilt into dozens of nearby anonymous workshops, where they were mimicked and modified for the mainstream "tourist market".

These trends were, of course, gradual, and fancy glass was hardly top of British and German household shopping lists in the late 1940s and early '50s, when rationing was still in force. Yet, even though Venice and much of Scandinavia had endured Fascism or Nazi occupation, life returned to normal relatively quickly, and glassworks not only retained their best designers, but began recruiting the names of the future (pictures 76 and 77).

Czechoslovakia

While most of Europe enjoyed the calm after the storm, the aftermath of war heralded new and grave concerns for others. For Czechoslovakia, an independent nation since just 1918, the future appeared bleak. In 1938, Franco-British appeasement had allowed Hitler to annex Czechoslovakia's German-speaking Sudetenland region, and the remainder of its population suffered a particularly brutal Nazi occupation. Yet, within just weeks of its liberation in April 1945, Communist-inspired uprisings began to destabilize the fledgling Prague regime, and three years later, Czechoslovakia fell behind the Iron Curtain, its industries were nationalized and its people banned from looking west.

The collectivization of the Czech glass industry in 1948 saw previously independent factories regrouped through a bewildering series of realignments and reorganizations over the following decades. Initially viewed as nothing more than a source of hard currency through exports, Czech glass began to win international awards for their work, notably at the Brussels Expo in 1958. The commercial designs of over 20 individuals,

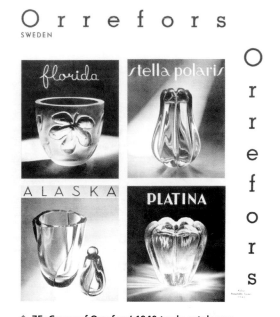

▲ 75: Cover of Orrefors' 1940 trade catalogue
Illustrating new designs by Sven Palmqvist and Vicke Lindstrand.
£80–125/$135–210*

◄ 76: Wartime Danish vase, 1944
Holmegaard mould-blown vase. The shape was designed by Jacob Bang, the cutting by Per Lükten. Base engraved *19PL44*. (p.146). 21cm (8¼in).
£350–500/$595–850*

▶ 77: Czech diplomatic presentation vase
Unique piece, presented in 1947 as a diplomatic gift by Jan Masaryk (1886–1948), Czech war hero and post-war Foreign Minister, to Harold Laski, chairman of the British Labour Party. The base is engraved with these details. Mould-blown, cut, engraved, and frosted. Designer and maker unknown. 32cm (12⅝in).
£300/$510*

Left: Vase designed by Adolf
Matura, for Rosice, c.1962.
8.5cm (3¼in). Middle: Vase
designed by František Vizner
c.1968. 28cm (11in). Right:
Vase designed by Rudolf Jernikl
c.1964, for Rudolfova Hut/
Bohemia Crystal. 12cm (4¾in).
**From left £20/$35,
£35/$60, £25/$45***

▶ **79: Finnish exhibition
piece, Paris 1937**

Designed by Gunnel Nyman, for
Karhula, in 1936. Exhibited in
Paris, 1937.
£2,000/$3,400*

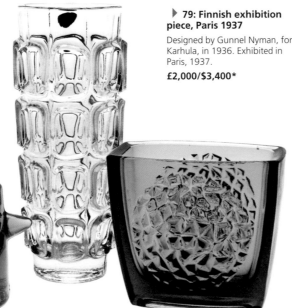

including Adolf Matura, Rudolf Jurnikl, and Frantisek Vizner, were characterized by bold, geometric pressed vases, ashtrays, and utilty wares (picture 78). The success of the Corning Museum of Glass' 2002 exhibition *Czech Glass, 1945–1980*, is symptomatic of the rising interest in both Czech art and household pieces of the period.

Scandinavia

Whereas Czechoslovakia was simply absorbed into the Soviet bloc, Finland, independent since 1919, faced a different but equally stark reality. Finding itself in a geographical vice between Germany and Russia in 1940, and mindful of previous Russian domination, the Finns had chosen the Nazis as the lesser of two evils. However, when the tables turned in 1944, Finland surrendered to the advancing Russians and, following the Treaty of Paris, 1947, faced a bill for war reparations to Russia of $300 million. Driven by a sense of shame for the past, hope for the future, and a fear of late-payment penalties, the Finnish economy went into overdrive.

Glass had been produced in Finland since at least the 18th century, but its styles had remained entirely derivative until the early 1930s, when focus shifted. Aino and Alvar Aalto's ground-breaking work for Iittala was soon followed by a new wave of designers, including Göran Hongell, Arttu Brummer, and Gunnel Nyman (picture 79). However, the big international breakthrough for Finnish glass came in 1951, when Tapio Wirkkala's *Kantarelli* vases (picture 80) won the Grand Prix at the Milan Triennale, 1951. Drawing from a population of only four million, Finland produced several of the world's leading post-war glass designers, including Wirkkala himself (pp.166–71), Timo Sarpaneva (pp.172–7), Kaj Franck (picture 81 and pp.116–25), Nanny Still (pp.214–19), and Helena Tynell (pp.208–13).

▲ **80: Finnish fungus, 1949**

Publicity photograph of Tapio Wirkkala's *Tatti* (*Boletus*) mushroom vases for Iittala in the *Finnish Trade Review*, 1949, two years before they won the Grand Prix at the Milan Triennale.
Small £150/$255, Large £1,000/$1,700*

◀ **81: Franck *Kartio*
carafe, 1959**

Mould-blown carafe,
designed by Kaj Franck,
for Nuutajärvi, in 1959.
The pouring lips of
original versions were
drawn manually while
those of recent
reproductions are
formed with a tool and
are more angular.
19.5cm (7⅝in).

£35/$60

▲ **82: Free-formed Danish vase/sculpture, 1956**
Designed by Per Lütken, for Holmegaard. Engraved: *19PL59*.
12cm (4¾in).
£75/$130*

▲ **83: Stromberg modernist vase, Sweden, *c*.1945–50**
Designed by Gerda Strömberg, for Strömbergshyttan. Unsigned.
7.5cm (2⅞in).
£30/$55*

▶ **84: Steuben ashtray, US, *c*.1947**
With applied trails. Probably designed
by George Thompson, for Steuben.
14cm (5½in) diam.
£35/$60

The story was repeated across Scandinavia, through the work of Per Lükten (picture 82 and pp.146–7), Jacob Bang (pp.141–9), and his son Michael (pp.158–9) at Holmegaard, Willy Johansson for Hadeland in Norway, and at new Swedish factories, as well as previously unremarkable ones that were invigorated by Orrefors' success. Though limited in scope, Strömberg's austere, thick-walled vases with polished rims, left plain, engraved, or cut with deep slashes, remain among the most distinctive glassware of their kind (picture 83 and p.77). Starting in the 1930s, this elegant new style developed an international resonance and became popularly known as Swedish Modern.

The United States

In America, another nation physically untouched by war, the story remained the same, with Steuben's crystal maintaining its umbilical connection with its plain, sculptural Swedish role model (picture 84). Lesser factories generally merged with one another to form glassmaking giants, as their products switched from the light colour tints used widely during the 1920s and '30s toward boldly printed, sprayed, and mould-textured table- and oven-glass (picture 85). The rare exceptions include Blenko, renowned for its bold, mould-blown table-glass, much of it in strong colours and exaggerated forms.

France

Steuben's colourless sculptural crystal was mirrored in France by an unlikely source, Daum, whose reputation remains inextricably linked with striking, acid-etched Art Nouveau cameo and acid-etched Art Deco vases (picture 58). Guided into the post-war era by Henri and Michel Daum, son of the founder, Antonin, colourless production was largely abandoned after the war in favour of free-formed and furnace-worked objects. The range, entirely designed by Michel himself, included lamps, ashtrays, and animals, and some vessel glass, all bearing the engraved signature *DAUM FRANCE* (picture 86). Like other niche glassmakers, Daum today specializes in limited edition collectors' pieces.

Britain

As we have said, British glassmaking took three decades to adapt to the 20th century, then enjoyed just a few years of creativity before production was switched to military applications. During the war years, Stuart Crystal made radio valves and scientific glass, for instance, while Davidson produced tumblers and aircraft runway lamps. Even after 1945, the production of decorative glass was entirely banned, except for export, until 1952, when a 100 per cent tax was placed on its retail price. It was not until the tax fell to 30 per cent in 1955 that the prospects of british glassmakers began to improve. By then, and anticipating a bright future, a significant group of Royal College of Art graduates was already working at Britain's leading glassworks, including Irene Stevens, who joined Webb Corbett in 1946, and John Luxton, who worked for Stuart Crystal from 1948 (picture 87).

The problem facing Britain's young glass designers was that they worked for conservative employers who proved unwilling to invest in the moulds required to produce new shapes and effects. Instead, they

▲ **86: Michel Daum geese sculptures, France, 1961**
From a series of free-formed crystal animal sculptures, designed by Michel Daum for Cristallerie Daum in 1961.
£50–250/$85–425*

▲ **85: Fostoria *Coin Glass* pressed pattern, US, 1959**
This pattern, which illegally reproduced American coins dated 1892, was banned in 1992 and the moulds seized and smashed by government agents. From Fostoria catalogue, 1975–6.
£25/$45*

▲ **87: Cream of British post-war cutting, 1951–5**
Left: Designed by Irene Stevens, for Webb Corbett, *c*.1951. 25.5cm (10in). Right: Designed by John Luxton, for Stuart Crystal, *c*.1955. 23cm (9in).
Left £180/$305, Right £120/$205

Variously tinted tube vases designed by Tamara Aladin, Nanny Still, Aimo Okkolin, and Helena Tynell, for Riihimäki, c.1965–70. Max. 28cm (11in).
£25–60/$45–100

▲ 89: Swedish primitive, 1950s
Cast and press-moulded candlesticks, designed by Erik Höglund, for Boda, c.1955. Publicity photograph. Max. c.22cm (8⅝in).
£60–100/$100–170*

preferred to stick with designs with proven track records and to play safe with colourless crystal cut in the time-honoured fashion.

Yet while British glassmaking was on the wane, the sun was rising on a host of new centres of excellence. By the mid-1960s, the stage was set for a bewildering outburst of outrageously varied glassware, shaped, sculpted, and coloured by the mood of its times. The Western world had emerged from the shadow of war and economic uncertainty with money in its pocket, a swing in its step, and a smile on its face.

1968–84: Get rich quick

By the end of the Swinging Sixties, consumers were spoilt for choice. Glassware was being formed in every conceivable size, shape, and texture, available across the quality range. Vases in vivid colours, including purples, yellows, reds, and tangerines (picture 88), were stocked on department store shelves next to entirely plain, functional vessels. The range of decorative variations included casting, cutting, texture-moulding, sand-blasting, applied effects, and gold leaf, with styles ranging from screamingly bold to whisperingly subtle.

From craft to art

Following the precedent established by Maurine Marinot in Paris in the 1920s, adopted on Murano during the 1930s, and consolidated by Wirkkala (p.166–71) and Sarpaneva (p.172–7) in Finland in the early 1950s, decorative glass continued its gradual shift in status from craft to art.

Design became a buzz-word, as the emphasis switched from function to appearance: vases evolved from vessels for displaying floral bouquets into objects in their own right. Glass was increasingly designed by sculptors, artists, architects, and others working across several media. With young couples now able to afford their own homes, stores sprang up specializing in birch furniture, wooden kitchen utensils, stainless steel cutlery, and, of course, Scandinavian-style glass. The British designers Ronnie Stennett-Willson (pp.224–33) and Frank Thrower (pp.242–7) both opened shops selling butcher's blocks and aprons, their own glass, and other chic household accessories.

The most fashionable new style was, and remains, Scandinavian Modern (better known today as the Ikea Look). As *House & Garden* noted in 1964, "it is chic to shudder at British cut-glass and set your table with uncut Scandinavian instead". Fortunately for most British glass-works, for which cut-crystal remained their life-blood, large sections of their domestic and American markets remained sufficiently conservative and wealthy to sustain them.

The glass produced during the late 1960s and early '70s reflected society at large by breaking with its local traditions. After the vivid outbursts of the 1950s, Murano became more muted, while Scandinavian glass grew louder. To some eyes the results were gaudy and kitsch, while to others they were electrically attractive. Alternately monumental and amorphous, daring and subtle, glass became fun. It may seem contradictory to those who accept the stereotype that Scandinavians are dull, but some of the glassware produced in post-war Sweden, Finland, and Denmark not only led the rest of the world but had a laugh on the way.

Scandinavia

The humorous trend had been established in Sweden in the 1950s at Boda. The catalyst was Erik Höglund (1937–88), who had joined the works in 1953 as a young sculpture graduate. Backed by its proprietor Eric Åfors, Höglund broke entirely from the cool sophistication of the Orrefors design A-team of Hald, Gate, Lindstrand, and Landberg. Working often in coarse, uneven, and striated glass, he applied his crudely formed pieces with running, laughing, naked figures or sealed them with box-headed faces apparently derived from comic books or cave-paintings (picture 89).

Höglund's off-beat approach was both ridiculed and acclaimed, but it certainly proved influential. His most notable disciples included Viktor Berndt, chief designer at Flygsfors 1955–74, and Lars Hellsten (1933–) (picture

▲ **90:** *Red Square* **sculpture, 1965**
Free-formed and furnace-worked glass sculpture. Designed by Lars Hellsten, for Skruf, in 1968. 50cm (19¾in). Made in various sizes into the early 1970s.
£1,000/$1,700*

▼ **91: Moulded glass camera, Swedish, 1975**
Designed by Christof Sjögson, for Lindshammar, Sweden, c.1975. 16cm (6¼in).
£75/$130

90). Hellsten, the *enfant terrible* of the new wave of Swedish glass, cut his teeth with Skruf Glasbruk before joining Orrefors in 1972, where he remained until the works was sold to the New Wave Group in 2004.

In Denmark, Michael Bang maintained the Bang dynasty by joining Per Lütken at Holmegaard in 1968, just two years after his father Jacob's retirement (pp.138–61). Reflecting the times, Lütken abandoned his previous propensity for monolithic forms in muted tints in favour of freer, more organic shapes and greater colour. Lütken and Bang's similarly vivid colour-cased *Carnaby* and *Palette* decorative, utility, and lighting ranges, designed between 1967 and 1970, were probably the most distinctive utility glass of the period (picture 92).

The centre of the greatest transformation in post-war glassmaking was Finland. Defended in its home market by a protectionist ban on imported glassware until 1973, the reputation of Finnish glass was boosted by the kudos of Wirkkala's international success. Iittala continued as the darling of the design establishment, its ice-blasted textured ranges, inspired by the region's climate, proving particularly influential (picture 93). However, Iittala's supremacy was soon threatened by pretenders. The country's largest glassworks, Riihimäki, launched its relatively low-priced products onto the world market from the early 1960s, followed by from the smaller Humppila, Kumela, and Muurla.

Riihimäki's daring new designers, all recruited during the late 1940s and early '50s, made major contributions. Helen Tynell and Nanny Still

▲ **92: Danish kitchen glass, 1969–70**

Michael Bang's opaque colour-cased *Palette* range of utility kitchen glassware designed for Holmegaard. From Holmegaard's 1970 catalogue. Jug 21cm (8¼in).

£25–75/$45-130*

▲ ▶ **94: Riihimäki, Finland, 1960s**

Typically idiosyncratic late-1960s vases by Nanny Still and Helena Tynell, for Riihimäki, Finland. Above: Mould-blown *Kometti* vase, designed by Still, 1967. 20cm (7⅞in). Right: Mould-blown *Aitan Lukku* vase, designed by Tynell, 1968. 20.5cm (8in).

Left £135/$230*, Right £90/$155*

▲ **93: Finnish ice-blasted glass, 1960s**

The chill of Tapio Wirkkala and Timo Sarpavena's ice-blasted texture moulding for Iittala extended far south of the tundra regions. Left: *Ultima Thule* jug designed by Wirkkala c.1969. 20cm (7⅞in). Right: *Festivo* goblet designed by Sarpaneva in 1967. 19.5cm (7⅝in).

Jug £35/$60, Goblet £12/$20

made the loudest splash with their iconic and inimitable vases (picture 94), while Tamara Aladin's brightly cased vases sold in tens of thousands (pp.206–23). Yet they were not all that Finland had to offer. Humppila chose an even more populist route during the early 1970s, with outrageous, thick-walled, and dark-toned pieces that caused the design establishment's hair to stand on end (picture 95).

Britain

The leading British glassworks might have been wearing blinkers at this time, so completely did they ignore the colours and textures exploding across Scandinavia. The Stourbridge Big Four, Thomas Webb, Webb Corbett, Brierley, and Stuart, continued along their familiar path, apparently oblivious to the fact that it was a road to nowhere. With the American market continuing to soak up faux Regency cutting, their designers found themselves shackled by managers unwilling to take risks, though certain fine examples of Modernist cutting shine out from the humdrum (picture 96).

Slightly more adventurous work was produced by a small clutch of new British glassworks. Caithness was established in Scotland in 1961, followed by Dartington and King's Lynn in 1967 (picture 97). All followed the Scandinavian model, evidenced in clean-lined, mould-blown vessels and vases, often in pastel tints. This was hardly surprising in the cases of Dartington and Lynn, as the founders of both had previ-

▲ **95: Wacky Finnish cast glass, 1974**
Centrifuge-cast *Kivi Set* chalice. Designed by Pertti Santalhti, for Humppila, in 1974. 17cm (6¾in).
£40/$70

▼ **96: Stuart Modernist cutting, 1960s**
Conical vase, designed by John Luxton, for Stuart Crystal, mid-1960s. 20.5cm (8in).
£150/$255

▶ **97 Anglo-Swedish glass**
Left: Dartington decanter (FT44) designed by Frank Thrower, 1966 (pp.242–7). 27.5cm (10⅞in) inc. Centre: Caithness bowl, designer uncertain c.1968. 10cm (3⅞in). Right: *Top Hat* vase designed by Ronald Stennett-Willson, for King's Lynn, in 1967 (pp.230–3). 10cm (3⅞in).
From left £30/$55, £15/$25, £55/$95

ously been salesmen for Nordic factories, and in fact, the entire Lynn and Dartington factories, including their furnaces and workers, were imported from Sweden.

The fire in British glass of this period was provided by Geoffrey Baxter for Whitefrairs, and Michael Harris, whose designs for Mdina on Malta radiated Mediterranean heat. Baxter's earlier work had been largely derivative, but became increasingly dynamic from the mid-1960s, expressed in several series of colourful, textured, and oddly shaped vases (picture 98). Harris' work looked toward Murano, with its vivid colours, random trails, and exaggerated forms (picture 99).

Italy

Murano, in contrast, took breath after the dynamism of the 1940s and '50s, with Paulo Venini's death in 1959 drawing a line in the sand. The brilliance of Venini's management, marketing, and design skills, combined with an unparalleled gift for spotting and tutoring talent, had probably been the greatest single factor in re-establishing the island as a centre of modern glassmaking. So, it was perhaps inevitable that his death symbolized the end of an era, leaving exuberance to others for once.

Tapio Wirkkala (picture 100) worked on the island from 1966, and three young Americans also spent time there honing their skills and composing their visions: James Carpenter, Dick Marquis, and Dale Chihuly. Yet, while big names continued to make the headlines, and their work fills today's lavishly illustrated books on the subject, the over-

▲ **98: Baxter's *Drunken Bricklayer*, Britain, 1966**
Designed by Geoffrey Baxter, for Whitefriars. 33cm (13in).
22cm £270/$460, 33cm £800/$1,360

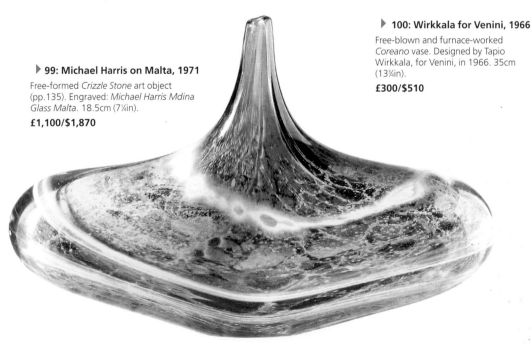

▶ **99: Michael Harris on Malta, 1971**
Free-formed *Crizzle Stone* art object (pp.135). Engraved: *Michael Harris Mdina Glass Malta*. 18.5cm (7¼in).
£1,100/$1,870

▶ **100: Wirkkala for Venini, 1966**
Free-blown and furnace-worked *Coreano* vase. Designed by Tapio Wirkkala, for Venini, in 1966. 35cm (13¾in).
£300/$510

whelming majority of Murano's production flowed not from the front-doors of its luxury establishments but from scores of smaller, largely anonymous studios (picture 101).

The United States

The USA, best-known for its unadventurous pressed glass, began to revitalize itself from 1962. In that year Harvey Littleton (1922–) (picture 102) and Dominick Labino (1910–87) staged a pioneering glass workshop at the Toledo Museum of Art, an institution richly endowed by the industrial giant Libbey Corporation. Their idea, that individuals could establish their own furnace/workshops to elevate glass into an art form, spread like wildfire.

The increasingly vivid creations of Dale Chihuly (1941–) (picture 103) caught the public imagination and helped to place the American studio-glass movement firmly on the aesthetic and commercial map.

The movement comprised a series of small studios that avoided the commercial pressures of formal, bureaucratic structures in order to liberate the creative spirit of the artist/designer/maker. Founding member Fritz Dreisbach (1941–), for instance, has notched up hundreds of thousands of kilometres driving his mobile furnace across the States in his evangelical

▲ **101: Anonymous Murano *Sommerso***

Textured and polished *Sommerso* (cased) bowl. Pieces of this type were produced on Murano in the 1970s, but their makers remain unrecorded. 6.5cm (2½in).
£35/$60

▼ **102: Littleton sculptures, US, 1983**

Free-formed *Red Pairs Descending Forms*, designed by Harvey Littleton in 1983. Signed: *Harvey K. Littleton 1983*. Sold in 2003 for $33,000. Max. 33cm (13in).
$33,000 (£20,500)

▲ **103: Free-form Chihuly, US, 1977**

Free-formed *Tabac Basket with Oxblood Spots*. Designed by Dale Chihuly in 1977. 35.5cm (14in) diam.
£5,000/$8,500*

△ 104: Royal Brierley's last gasp
Mould-blown decanter and iridescent bowl from Royal Brierley's *Studio Glass* range, *c.*1978 and 1986. *Rio* decanter designed by Gwyneth Newland in 1986. These were among Brierley's last notable design commissions before its closure in 1996. 21cm (8¼in) and 7.5cm (2¾in).
Decanter £50/$85, Bowl £45/$75

△ 105: Eurovision Song Contest trophy
Designed by Jan Johansson, for Orrefors, in 2004, and available as a limited-edition sculpture. As Johansson explained, "The bubbles symbolize the stars, the glamour and the elegance while the hole at the top right corner is the source of the music".
£400/$680

quest to take the art of glassmaking to the masses, earning the soubriquet of the "Johnny Appleseed" of the American studio glass movement. The subsequent outpouring of art and craft quickly captured the American imagination (and wallet) and pointed a clear finger to the future.

1985–2000: Dumbing down

Despite the relatively easy ride for glassmakers during the post-war era, by the 1970s there was a chill in the air and the climate was about to change. The oil crises of the early 1970s caused casualties, especially in sectors with high energy costs, including glassmaking.

However, most recovered and continued to flourish as consumers got ever richer. Wages rose but technology and infrastructures improved, and some prices fell. In 1930, a three-minute transatlantic phone call cost $298, yet in 1998 the same conversation was billed at 30 cents or less, and the cost of international shipping dropped by 80 per cent in the 40 years to 1996. With transport and communications improving and getting cheaper, it became easier to conduct business at long-range and so competition intensified.

In the modern commercial world, it was no longer sufficient just to make a profit; banks and shareholders demanded more, much more. The easiest route to achieve growth was through corporate acquisitions. It is an astonishing fact that between 1967 and 1996 all of Britain's major glassworks were taken over by non-glassmakers: Webb Corbett was bought by Doulton, and King's Lynn by Wedgwood in 1969; Coloroll took over Thomas Webb in 1987; Wedgwood bought Dartington in 1982; Waterford/Wedgwood bought Stuart Crystal in 1995; and Epsom Activities acquired Royal Brierley/Stevens & Williams in 1996 (picture 104). Indeed, Dartington changed hands six times between 1967 and 2000, and Caithness three times within a decade. The net result of this megalomania is that just Dartington, founded in 1966, survives today, with all the others now closed.

The destruction of Britain's historic fine-glass industry was a depressing phenomenon. Naturally, its roots lay beyond mere corporate rapaciousness: feeble management, lack of investment, poor design, awkward labour unions, inflation, and cheap imports also played their part.

While orders that would previously have been placed with British glassworks were switched to its foreign competitors, these too remained vulnerable to the realities of modern commerce. In Finland, Iittala, itself owned until 2004 by a washing-machine manufacturer, controls Nuutajärvi and Humppila. The diversity of the Swedish glass industry has also been narrowed, though at least many of its components currently survive. Today, Orrefors owns Kosta, Boda, Åfors, Johansfors, and SEA (picture 105). However, the Orrefors story is not so simple, as it, in turn, was owned by Royal Copenhagen, along with Holmegaard (Denmark) and Venini (Murano). So who owned Royal Copenhagen?

Carlsberg, owned itself by the Tuborg brewery! However, the brewers tired of mounting losses, and in 2005 sold it to the New Wave Group, who promptly jettisoned 67 jobs.

The challenge from cheap glass

The insecurities of fine glassmaking rest on one simple fact: prospective customers find it difficult to justify spending ten or even 50 times more on a handmade wine glass than on a mass-produced one. Today, very few consumers are concerned by the source of goods or how they are made. Given the choice between a set of Ikea goblets made in the Far East for cents or a single handmade example by Baccarat, Riedel, or Lalique from Harrods for £85 ($145) (picture 106), there is no contest for all but the wealthy and the ultra-design/quality conscious.

It is an ironic fact that, as the general population has grown ever more affluent, the more bargain-hungry it has become. Ikea recently launched a new British store with promotional reductions on beds and sofas sold before 3am on its opening day. Anxious not to miss any good deals, a crowd of 7,000, all of whom presumably already owned beds and sofas, stormed the building, leaving 70 people requiring hospital treatment.

Faced with such acute price-sensitivity, fine glassmaking has found itself increasingly in trouble. In 1980, Whitefriars, founded in 1720, was finally closed. The economics were simple: the site it had occupied for 60 years was worth more than the business. Taking the view that the company had become more trouble than it was worth, its owners shut its doors, sold the site into development, and made the workers redundant; so Britain lost its oldest glassworks.

▲ **106: : Modern Lalique**

Marc Lalique's *Angel* flute (*flûte ange*), designed in 1948 and modelled on a medieval stone sculpture at Reims Cathedral. Available at leading stores, at around the price below.

£100 ($170)

▼ **107: Derivative modern Polish and Chinese glass**

Modelled on original 1950s designs by Edward Hald (glass), Nils Landberg (decanter), Kaj Franck (short decanter), Tapio Wirrkala (red and blue vases), and Erik Höglund (green vase), most are made by Krosno or for LSA International. The Krosno glassworks was founded in the Polish town of the same name in 1921 and has been an independent company since the fall of the Communist regime in 1991, while LSA is a London-based company that commissions designs from Polish glassworks. Tall Landberg-style decanter: 38cm (15in) inc.

£5–10/$9–17

▲ **108: Kaj Franck revisited, 2005**

Kaj Franck's *Kartio* (*Cone*) functional glassware, originally designed in 1958 but remodelled by Oiva Tiokka and commercially relaunched by Iittala in 2005.

£20/$35

▲ **109: British and Canadian studio glass**

Left: Glass by British Royal College of Art graduate, Laura Birdsall, engraved *Laura Birdsall*, c.2000. 12.5cm (4⅞in). Right: Glass made by Canadians Ron Lukien and decorated by Gail Hall, engraved *R Lukien G Hall 1995*. 14.5cm (5⅝in).

Left £30/$55, Right £40/$70

The root of the problem for traditional glassworkers is that they lack one of the basic prerequisites to most types of modern manufacturing: economy of scale. Their products are generally formed, decorated, and finished by hand and some companies are often prepared to accept small commissions. As late as the 1980s, Brierley advertised the fact that it was prepared to recreate anything from its vast range of historic patterns, numbering 80,000 and many dating from the 19th century. However charming the idea, the resulting orders were entirely uneconomic because every one lost money.

The battle of the brands between today's glassmakers pits cheap, mass-produced, and handmade pieces from low-cost economies against expensive, high-quality objects from traditional sources. Faced with a deluge of very cheap, superficially attractive pieces, mostly mould-blown in Poland or China and based on Scandinavian design classics (picture 107), the established names have been forced to play safe and head upmarket. This has led to a greater emphasis on branding and revivals of the greatest hits of famous designers, including Wirkkala, Gate, Bianconi, and Franck (picture 108). The Venini brand name now appears on perfume and jewellery, while the factory itself produces Versace glass, and Holmegaard, Denmark, has reproduced its classic *Gulvæse* for Ralph Lauren (p.161).

Studio glass

The realities of modern manufacturing have also encouraged the growth of studio glass, both the type made within large glassworks and by individuals at their own premises (picture 109). The advantages of studio pieces for traditional glassworks are that they can be sold for higher prices than standard pieces while keeping their craftspeople and designers profitably occupied when demand is slack for their standard ranges.

The American Studio Glass movement, tapped into the same consciousness as the Arts & Crafts movement almost a century before. It became successful and profitable largely because its products were either exclusive or obviously handmade, especially when compared to the products of other glassworks discussed on these pages. Yet it is an ironic fact that virtually the entire output of factories such as Orrefors, Riihimäki, Holmegaard, and Stuart Crystal was handmade too, though in this age of mass production it generally lacks the uneven characteristics that most people recognize as derived from craft.

It requires training, aptitude, and skill to blow and decorate glass successfully. The apparently simple act of cutting a single groove in a piece of glass is, in fact, very demanding. Although Swarovski and Baccarat now use lasers to achieve similar effects, this is a recent innovation. All the cut-glass illustrated in this book required at least three manual processes during which every element of the pattern had to be roughed, cut, and polished against rotating wheels. Acids replaced some of the polishing processes from around 1930, but the basic stages of cutting, as well as of blowing fine glass, have remained largely unchanged since the days of ancient Rome nearly 2,000 years ago. Yet the understanding of these basic facts is almost entirely lost on the greater population, most of whom are entirely disinterested in such details.

The studio movement took its lead from Murano, where several of its leaders worked during their formative years. Borrowing from the island's traditions, ancient and modern, most studio glass rejects the concept of function and depends almost exclusively on its form and colour. It would be impossible to drink from most studio glassware, for instance. The vast majority exists purely to be admired (picture 110).

Today, most consumers are incapable of discerning between the design classics and limited-edition studio work of famous glassworks, and cheaply-made Polish or Chinese clones of them (picture 111). And even if they could, would they care? Some would, but their numbers dramatically decrease when the former are ten times the price of the latter. To conclude, one wonders what academics, writers, and collectors in 2105 will have to say about 21st-century glassware. Their attentions will doubtless focus more on the work of studio designer/makers than factories producing 6 million pieces per day.

▼ **111: Design classics and an Ikea clone**

Left: Two versions of the *Sandringham*, designed by Ronald Stennett-Willson, for King's Lynn, in 1967. Tallest 24cm (9½in). Centre: Clone/ derivative copy, made by Krosno, Poland, retailed by Ikea. 20cm (7⅞in). Right: *Gabriel*, designed by Nils Landberg, for Orrefors, in 1956, still produced today. 27cm (10⅝in).

From left £100/$170, £75/$130, £2/$3, £125/$210

◀ **110: Dante Marioni, US, *Blue Trio*, 1994**

Like many of his contemporaries, Marioni studied at Dale Chihuly's Pilchuck Glass School, Seattle, Washington, 1984–5. After he won a $15,000 Tiffany fellowship in 1987, examples of his work were later included in the Young Americans exhibition at the American Craft Museum, and acquired by Hilary Clinton for the White House Collection. Max. 100cm (39½in).

For whole *Trio* $22,000/£13,000 (retail)

Collecting by Country

▶ **1:** *Schwartzlot* **enamels, 1720**

Spirit decanter enamelled in *Schwartzlot* (black lead) and red oxide pigments by Ignaz Preissler, Bohemia c.1720–30. The scene shows the grape harvest near Caub on the Rhine, from an engraving by Raphael Sadeler, 17.5cm (6⅞in).

£10,000
$17,000

Czechoslovakia and Germany

Glass has been made and decorated in Bohemia, within the borders of the modern Czech Republic, since at least the 14th century. Abundant with all the ingredients essential to glassmaking, Bohemia lay at the centre of Europe, so its exports provided employment for thousands. Its resources of sand, fire clay, furnace fuel, and cheap skilled labour were complemented by the patronage of the Church, the aristocracy, and the Viennese gentry, which increasingly viewed fine glassware as a suitable means through which to express their wealth and status (picture 1).

After enduring a depression between c.1775 and 1835, the Bohemian industry revived during the 19th century, initially through its pioneering colours and decorating techniques (picture 2). The foundation of glass-making schools, at Kamenický Šenov in 1838 (expanded in 1856) and Nový Bor in 1870, augmented local skills and provided the nucleus of an

---

CZECH GLASS – KEY DATES

1905 Inwald takes over the Rudolfova Hut, a metal factory at Teplice, and converts it into a pressed-glass works, making the sixth factory in the Inwald group.

1907 Hermanova Hut founded by Stözl brothers.

1922 Inwald designer Rudolf Schrötter creates new pressed-glass range, named *Lord* across most of Europe, but *Jacobean* in Britain.

1928 300 glassworks operating in Nový Bor.

c.1930 Inwald takes over Josef Rindskopf & Söhne, pressed-glassmaker in Teplice, which had previously absorbed the Dux and Tischau factories.

1930s Employment at Hermanova Hut reaches 740.

1935 Inwald's *Barolac* registered as a trademark in Britain by its importer, John Jenkins & Son, London.

1935 Czech glass wins 14 prizes at World Expo, Brussels.

1937 Czech glass wins Grand Prix at World Expo, Paris.

1938 The Sudetenland, which includes most Czech glassmaking towns, annexed by Nazi Germany.

1939 Remainder of Czechoslovakia invaded by Germany, its artists and intellectuals dispatched to concentration camps.

1945 End of the Second World War, Czechoslovakia liberated. Gradual rebuilding of industries starts.

1948 Communist takeover followed by nationalization of industries

and commercial property. Czech artistic tradition dismissed as decadent, replaced by Socialist Realism. Fine artists directed toward propaganda; architects and designers restricted exclusively to decoration. Inwald amalgamated with Pallme König & Slanina glassworks into new company employing 3,000 in making a broad range of products, from headlamps to art glass. A second holding company, Borocrystal, founded at Nový Bor, incorporates several factories and 55 decorating shops, many others closed down.

1948–53 Fine artists migrate toward decorative arts as a covert means of self-expression. New school of glass enamelling established at Prague Academy of Applied Arts, directed by Josef Kaplicky.

1950 Inwald's Podebrady factory becomes Poděbradská Sklárny National Corporation, later renamed Bohemia Glassworks.

1953 Borské Sklo merges three holding companies founded in 1948: Borské Sklárny, Borocrystal, and Umělecké Sklo. Company also includes Egermann-Exbor, founded in Nový Bor by Freidrich Egermann (1777–1864) in 1832.

1954 Individual glass designers allowed studio space to develop ideas within large, state-owned glassworks.

1954 Jiří Řepásek (1927–) and Vladimir Zahor (1925–) join Poděbradská design staff. Adolf Matura (1921–79) used freelance.

mid-1950s Inwald and Hermanova Hut transferred to new company, Sklo Union ("Sklo" meaning "Glass").

mid-1950s Production at Rudolfova Hut becomes fully automatic.

1957 Czech glass exhibited internationally for the first time since

industry that employed around 25,000 people by 1900. Enterprises ranged from a few works employing hundreds, to countless *Hausmaler (home decorators)*, working in their own homes. This trend continued into the 20th century: during the late 1920s, for example, the glassworks of Jablonec employed a total of 250, with a further 2,250 *Hausmaler*.

It is difficult to separate the glassmaking identities of Bohemia and Germany because their industries were largely owned and staffed by Germans, and craftspeople constantly migrated between the two. Most important glassworks were located in a long, narrow geographical strip straddling the modern border that divides the Czech Republic from Poland and Germany. The area was absorbed into what became Czechoslovakia in 1919, when Bohemia ceased to exist as a nation, and was known to ethnic Germans as the Sudetenland, where most of the population spoke German rather than Czech.

Early 20th-century glassmakers

Typically, the patriarchs of Bohemia's leading glassmaking dynasties at the turn of 20th century were all German: Josef Lobmeyr, Ludwig Moser,

◀ 2: Historic Bohemia, 1835

An historic masterpiece in Bohemian glassmaking: The *Culm Goblet*, probably made by the Harrachov glassworks and decorated by Friedrich Eggermann at Nový Bor, c.1835. 41.5cm (16⅜in). Sold in 2002 for the huge sum below.

£140,000 ($235,000)

1948 at the Milan Triennale. Positive reaction encourages continuing liberalization.

1957–60 Václav Hanuš (1924–) resident designer at Rudolfova.

1958 Czech glass wins Grand Prix at World Expo, Brussels.

1958 František Pečený (1920–) appointed resident designer at Hermanova.

1958 Further reorganization of Czech industry: Inwald name disappears but production continues at Rudolfova Hut.

1959 Czech studio-glass artists acclaimed at *Glass 1959*, Corning Museum of Glass, but attacked as decadent at Moscow exhibition.

Late 1950s Miloš Filip (1926–) designs pressed glassware for Rudolfova.

1960 Rudolf Jernikl (1928–) replaces Hanus as Rudolfova resident designer.

1962–7 František Vízner (1936–) on Rudolfova/Sklo Union design staff.

1964 *Czech Glass* exhibition at the Museum of Contemporary Crafts, New York, but excludes most artistic pieces.

1965 Bohemia Glassworks formed by merger of five glassworks, based at Poděbradská, a spa town near Prague.

1967 Large Czech representation at Montreal Expo. Postitive reaction encourages Western studio-glass artists to visit Czechoslovakia, including James Carpenter, Dale Chihuly, Erwin Eisch, Marvin Lipovsky, and Harvey Littleton.

1968 Liberalization collapses after Czechoslovakia invaded by 750,000 Warsaw Pact troops.

1970s Gradual thaw in controls over Czech studio glassmaking.

1971 Hermanova production switched to fully automated.

1974 Bohemia Glassworks absorbed into Crystalex, based at Nový Bor.

1979 Large Czech representation at Corning exhibition: *New Glass: A Worldwide Survey*. Includes representative pieces by Antonín Drobník, Jirí Harcuba, Pavel Hlava, Vladimír Jelínek, Stanislav Libensky and Jaroslavá Brychtová, Ladislav Oliva, and František Vízner.

1982 Stanislav Libensky and Jaroslava Brychtová invited by Dale Chihuly to teach at Pilchuck Glass School, Washington State, USA.

1989 The Velvet Revolution ends Communist rule in Czechoslovakia. Writer Václav Havel becomes president. Czech glass industries privatized.

1992 Rudolfova taken over by American Owens-Illinois, production switched to container glass.

1993 Czechoslovakia divides into Czech and Slovak republics. Lobmeyr reopens its factory in Kamenický Šenov, confiscated by the Communist government in 1951. Czech artists gain total artistic and commercial freedom.

2005 Czech glassmaking struggles against tighter EU environmental controls and competition from cheap Far Eastern imports in its traditional markets.

▲ 3: Hoffmann for Lobmeyr, 1912

Mould-blown, frosted, and black-enamelled *Bronzit* series decanter. Designed by Joseph Hoffmann, for Lobmeyr, in 1912. 27.5cm (10⅞in) inc.

£5,000/$8,500*

◀ 4: Hoffmann/ Loetz acid-cameo

Mauve-over-colourless acid cameo vase. Designed by Josef Hoffmann for Loetz, 1912. 18cm (7in).

£1,000–2,000/ $1,700–3,400*

▶ 5: Eschler for Moser, 1930s

Mould-blown spherical *Culbutto* decanter. Designed by Rudolf Eschler for Moser, 1935 (16520). 18.5cm (7¼in). Background: Rudolf Eschler designs for Moser, 1932–3.

***Culbutto* £300/$510**

and Joseph Riedel. The Lobmeyr family were Viennese retailers who had commissioned Bohemians to produce their designs since 1821; the Moser glassworks had been founded in Karlovy Vary in 1857, while Riedel, a seventh-generation glassmaker, was head of a family firm established near Jablonec in the early 18th century. Lobmeyr and Moser occupied the top of the range, designing or producing colourless and decorated ranges of the finest quality. The Riedels were more broadly based: makers of plain and coloured vessel glass, beads, jewellery, and, most influentially, a range of 600 glass colours.

Lobmeyr maintained a relatively small base at its shop in Vienna, from where the company commissioned designs from outsiders, including members of the Wiener Werkstätte, whose mentor, Joseph Hoffmann, produced numerous designs for Lobmeyr from c.1900. These included the gilded or black-enamelled *Bronzit* ranges, from 1910, which remained influential for decades (picture 3). Hoffmann also executed series of stylish glass designs for Johann Oertel, Moser, and Loetz (picture 4) in Bohemia.

Moser's notable early 20th-century ranges included vases deeply engraved with Art Nouveau lilies (p.32) and the *Fipop* series, from c.1914. *Fipop* was an ingenious and stylish method of banding glassware with acid-etched and gilded Neo-classical friezes. These inspired a rash of derivatives, some of which matched Moser's quality, while others were cheaply pressed, produced by companies including Inwald, Brockwitz, and Walther & Söhne, whose catalogues illustrated them into the mid-1930s (picture 6). Several American glassworks produced copies of *Fipop*, between 1927 and 1933, including US Glass and Paden City Glass, variously naming it *Woodland* and *Deerwood*, featuring typical Bohemian scenes of stags, foals, and rabbits in woodland (p.81).

Moser expanded rapidly after 1916 under the direction of Ludwig's son, Leo, through capital improvements and takeovers. He also commissioned designs from Gabriel Argy-Rousseau (pp.14 and 70), draughtsman Rudolf Eschler (picture 5), Swedish sculptor/glass designer Tyra Lundgren (p.76), and graphic artist Heinrich Hussmann (picture 7). The resulting

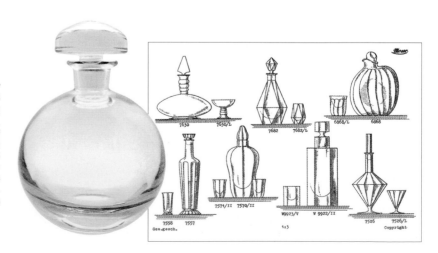

outburst of diverse and dynamic designs, combined with top-quality craftsmanship, earned Moser a Grand Prix at Paris, 1925.

However, the Moser family paid a high price for its ambitions. The Depression exacted its toll and, in 1932, with company employment down to 240, Leo Moser resigned. The rising tide of anti-Semitism forced the family to flee the country, and the glory days were over. The company retained relative independence during the Soviet era and continues, like Lobmeyr, to the present day. Both companies still produce some of their classic designs, including Moser's *Fipop* and Lobmeyr's *Ambassador* service, c.1929 (picture 8).

Riedel also survives, though now in Austria. The company entered the 20th century under the guidance of Josef Riedel, a technologist who had studied under Nobel prize-winning chemist Richard Zsigmondi. Riedel applied his passion for science to the creation of a spectrum of 600 glass colours. Riedel used these to make pressed and cut decorative drinking services, scent bottles, and beads (picture 9), and also sold them to other glassmakers to tint their own products. By 1924, the company employed 3,200 people, almost twice as many as in 1900.

Facing a slump after 1918, Josef's sons, Walter and Arno, were responsible for the invention of fibreglass, the red/amber/green traffic-light system, and several other forms of technical and scientific glass. The Riedel plants were captured in 1938 when the Nazis occupied the Sudetenland and production switched to military applications.

In 1945, Riedel's properties were confiscated and Walter, regarded as an "important warfare scientist", endured ten years of forced labour in Russia. Meanwhile, his son, Claus Josef escaped to Austria, where he bought a redundant glassworks for 1 schilling and acquired debts of 18

▲ **6: Moser *Fipop* and copies**
Left: Pressed version, probably Walther & Söhne, Germany, c.1930. Middle: Signed Moser example in violet cut glass, c.1925. 14cm (5½in). Right: Superior mould-blown and cut version, unsigned, c.1920–25. 14.5cm (5⅝in).
From left £30/$55, £130/$220, £250/$425

▲ **7: Free-form Hussmann/Moser sculpture**
Free-formed and deeply cut light sensitive sculpture in *Alexandrite* glass. Designed by Heinrich Hussmann, for Moser, c.1929. 19.5cm (7⅝in).
£350/$595

◄ **8: Lobmeyr *Ambassador* service, 1925**
Mould-blown service. Designed by Oswald Haerdtl, for Lobmeyr, 1925, still produced today. Decanter 38.5cm (15⅛in).
Decanter £400/$680*, Glasses from £10/$17*

million. Duly rejoined by Walter, the Riedels gradually re-established the family firm, which today employs 250 people producing handmade and auto-blown wine-ware (picture 10).

Czech and German pressed glass

The central European pressed-glass industry grew rapidly during the inter-war period. From 1920 to 1923, Czechoslovakia annually exported 5,000 barrels of decorative pressed glass, compared with 66,000 of finer vessel glass. However, 15 years later, exports of pressed glass had more than doubled to over 12,000 barrels, while fine-work shipments had almost halved to 39,000. Further, while most wine glasses have since been lost to accidents, more robust vases and bowls remain relatively abundant.

Czech pressed production was based around Jablonec, the centre of Riedel's operations. Riedel supplied colours and manufacturing facilities

▶ **9: Pressed Art Deco**
Asymmetrical Art Deco pressed-glass candlestick. Designer unknown, but reputedly made by Riedel, c.1930. 28.5cm (11¼in).
£45/$75

▲ **10: Riedel *Columbo* glasses, 1967**
Mould-blown suite of *Columbo* glasses. Designed by Joe Columbo, for Riedel, in 1967. Various sizes.
£25–40/$45–70

▶ **11: Czech cocktail suites, 1930s**
Decanter sets from the 50th anniversary Karel Palda catalogue of its current lines, published in 1938.
Complete sets £250–500/$425–850*

to numerous Czech and German glassmakers, including its neighbours, Heinrich Hoffmann and Henry Schlevogt. A mould-maker, Hoffmann also owned a bead shop in Paris, where he met René Lalique, a genius at glass moulding, in the 1920s. Hoffmann duly reproduced some of his acquaintance's best designs (pictures 12 and 14) alongside a series of angular table-pieces in Reidel's mauve *Alexandrite* glass (picture 13) and a range of stylish ashtrays and scent bottles impressed with frosted Neo-classical and Art Deco intaglio friezes (picture 15).

In 1927, Hoffman formed a partnership with his son-in-law, Henry Schlevogt, a second-generation glassmaker. Their relationship became so intertwined that it can be difficult to separate their professional entities, and Hoffmann's open-winged butterfly logo was moulded into some of their products. There is no doubt as to the most distinctive range credited to Schlevogt: the marbled *Ingrid*, copied from Lalique (picture 16). Unveiled at Liepzig in 1934, it is still produced by Desna at Jablonec using Hoffmann/Schlevogt's original moulds.

The greatest attributes of historic Bohemian glassmaking – its diversity and versatility – were maintained during the 20th century. However, while Bohemians and Czechs have been great creators, they have also proved incorrigible plagiarists, prepared to copy virtually any design or style with profit potential. It is for this reason that otherwise anonymous glassware of any age and category is often awarded vague attributions to "Bohemia/Czechoslovakia".

Attempting to pinpoint the precise source of Czech glass is often impossible. Aside from the problems arising from design theft, the area was shaken to the core between 1938 and 1948. The historic, economic, and political supremacy of Bohemia's ethnic Germans had been overturned in 1919 by the foundation of Czechoslovakia. Disgruntled at the loss of their power and prestige, many agitated for Nazi intervention and welcomed its occupying armies in 1938. However, when the dust settled in 1945, the Czechs exacted their revenge through ethnic cleansing, expelling nearly three million Germans on foot and at gunpoint. Then the Russians moved in, and stayed for 30 years.

The consequent loss to the Czech economy of many of its proprietors, managers, and craftspeople was crippling, at least in the short term. It also resulted in the destruction of their records. Some pre-war glass manufacturers' catalogues survived, but even these can be problematic. While some designs can be attributed definitively (picture 17), others appear in the catalogues of two or more makers, while a small number, marked *MADE IN BELGIUM* and *TCHECO-SLOVAQIE* (p.33), have been linked to August Walther & Söhne, of Radeberg, Germany.

Pre-war Czech and German fine glass

The makers of some 1920s and '30s central European glassware are known, but probably only a minority. The Passau Glass Museum, situated

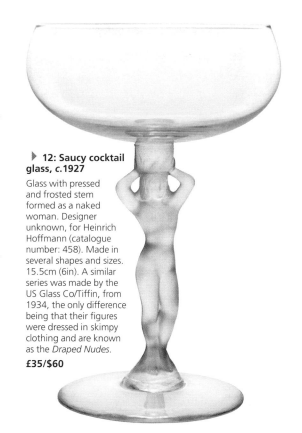

▶ **12: Saucy cocktail glass, c.1927**
Glass with pressed and frosted stem formed as a naked woman. Designer unknown, for Heinrich Hoffmann (catalogue number: 458). Made in several shapes and sizes. 15.5cm (6in). A similar series was made by the US Glass Co/Tiffin, from 1934, the only difference being that their figures were dressed in skimpy clothing and are known as the *Draped Nudes*.
£35/$60

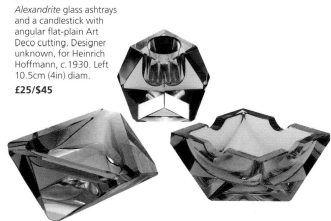

▼ **13: Angular table-pieces, 1930**
Alexandrite glass ashtrays and a candlestick with angular flat-plain Art Deco cutting. Designer unknown, for Heinrich Hoffmann, c.1930. Left 10.5cm (4in) diam.
£25/$45

▼ **14: Cheeky pup, c.1927**
Pressed amber dog with a plastic collar fixed to a pressed and polished black/amethyst base. 8cm (3in) wide.
£40/$70

on the German/Czech/Austrian border, specializes in Bohemian/Czech glass of all ages, and recounts its evolution through a 30,000-piece collection. Yet, while its curators propose secure attributions to many of its 18th- and 19th-century objects, the source of a large proportion of those pieces made within living memory still eludes them. In addition to the factors previously indicated, the story is further clouded by the role of *Hausmalers*, who numbered 2,250 around Jablonec alone in the 1920s. These individuals or family enterprises decorated blanks made by various manufacturers, then sold them on, often piecemeal. An inevitable result of this outsourcing is that these pieces never appeared in catalogues.

One of the most colourful sources is the catalogue produced in 1938 to celebrate the 50th anniversary of the Karel Palda works at Nový Bor (picture 11). Founded in 1888, Palda grew to become one of Bohemia's largest producers of table- and lighting glass. The factory's more stylish output will be familiar to modern collectors, such as its distinctive Art Deco trinket sets flashed in sharp, geometric enamels. It also produced perfume atomizers, vases, and lampshades in marbled and plain coloured glass, often stencilled with patterns, as well as land and seascapes, domestic pets, and so on. Other Palda ranges were painted and transfer-printed with traditional scenes portraying hunting, coaching, and farm animals.

The glassmakers' catalogues that do survive from the 1930s reveal a staggering array of styles and decorative techniques, many of which are now considered to be in atrocious taste. However, perhaps their most surprising feature is the continuing dominance of Victorian-style glass of all descriptions. Seemingly endless pages of colourless pressed milk jugs, American-style *Lacy* pattern plates, and *faux* cut vases demonstrate the conservative nature of a large section of the pre-war market for decorative glass.

Post-war Czech glass

It is difficult from today's comfortable perspective to appreciate fully the extent of the traumas and disasters that befell the still-embryonic Czechoslovakian Republic from 1938. Then just 20 years old, it was abandoned by Britain and France in their vain attempt to appease Hilter, then suffered Nazi occupation until 1945. Three years of murderous political turmoil then passed before it fell behind the Iron Curtain, where it remained until its eventual liberation in 1989.

The Nazi occupation was not entirely catastrophic for Czechoslovakia's glass industry, however, because it had long been dominated by ethnic Germans, and most were unthreatened by the presence of invaders who shared their culture and language. Whilst the production of certain works was switched to military applications, decorative glassware continued to be made for the expanding German empire. However, when the tables

▲ 15: Neo-classical pin trays and ashtrays

Mouled and polished, with intaglio friezes. Designed by Frantisek Pazourek, for Heinrich Hoffmann, from c.1925. Central dish: 10cm (3⅞in) diam.

£15–25/$25–45

▲ 16: Lalique and Schlevogt

Left: Acid-frosted *Bacchantes* vase by René Lalique, after 1927. Etched mark: *R Lalique, France*. 24cm (9½in). Right: Copy of Lalique – *Ingrid* vase from Schlevogt's 1939 catalogue. Both still produced.

Lalique £4,500/$7,650; Schlevogt £250/$425*

turned in 1945, virtually all German speakers were expelled, despite having lived in the region for centuries. The resulting losses to the Czech glass industry left its factories largely intact but suffering acute shortages of design and production skills.

This situation would have provoked limited concern in some nations, but glassmaking ranked among Czechoslovakia's most important economic activities. However, the tentative processes of reconstruction were almost immediately disrupted by the advent of Communism from 1948, after which every aspect of commercial, industrial, artistic, and social life was placed under the closest scrutiny.

The nationalization of the Czech glass industry in 1948 involved the grouping of previously separate factories into a series of larger conglomerates, with only Moser retaining relative independence by virtue of its international reputation. Local glassmaking schools went into overdrive to train the hundreds of skilled and semi-skilled workers required to produce industrial and domestic glassware both for the Soviet bloc and for export to the West as part of a growing appetite for hard currency.

Virtually every factory was renamed, with original German names superseded by Czech ones. These were then merged into larger organizations. The Inwald empire, for instance, was dismembered, its

▲ **17: Identifiable Czech 1930s pressed glass**

Left: Lime-green dessert bowl, designed by Rudolf Schrotter (p.114), for Inwald/Rudolfova Hut, c.1935. 7cm (2¾in). Middle: Yellow glass fish dish, Hermanova Hut (19438), produced c.1935–60s. 14.5cm (5⅝in) diam. Right: Amber lidded pot, produced at Hermanova Hut, c.1935. 10cm (3⅞in).

£5–15/$9–25

▼ **18: Czech glass from 1950s and '60s catalogues**

Czech glassmakers continued to make a huge range of lighting, functional, and decorative glass after the Communist takeover. These images provide some idea of their range, much of which was retro-based.

£30–65/$55–110

▲ 19: Matura pressed designs

Glass by Adolf Matura. From left: Blue pressed vase, for Rosice, 1961, 8.5cm (3¼in); elements of a pressed service for Rosice, 1962; sky-blue pressed ashtray for Rosice, 1971, 15.5cm (6in) diam.; and mould-blown and cut vase for Karlovarske Sklo (Moser), 1966, 17cm (6¾in).

£20–100/$35–170

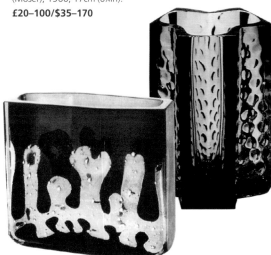

▲ 20: Studio glass, 1960s

Left: Cut and polished ruby vase with fused silver decoration. Designed by Pavel Hlava, for Exbor, Nový Bor, in 1967. Right: Deeply cut amber vase. Designed by Karel Wünsch, for Nový Bor Glassmaking School, in 1965.

Left £450/$765*
Right £1,000/$1,700*

▶ 21: Hospodka or not Hospodka?

Josef Hospodka's designs for Chřibská rank among the most copied of all post-war Czech glass. Their distinctive colours and shapes commonly lead to vague but mistaken attributions to "Murano", but similar pieces were made in many locations. Individual examples are impossible to attribute without signatures or stickers. 26cm (10¼in).

£20–75/$35–130*

components renamed, then progressively transferred and reshuffled over the following decades into the Sklo Union group, Poděbradské Sklárny, Bohemia Glassworks, Crystalex, and others (pictures 21 and 24).

These complex bureaucratic machinations remain of limited interest to all but hardcore academics. Nevertheless, the fundamental point remains that despite the obvious difficulties and against all odds, Czech glassmaking flowered during the 1950s, '60s, and '70s, and, ironically, this was as a direct result of the Soviet regime. With fine art virtually banned as decadent and potentially subversive, liberal art-school tutors directed their students toward glassmaking as a covert means of self-expression.

Czechoslovakia in general, and Prague in particular, had traditionally ranked among Europe's leading artistic centres. It had played an important role in the development of many of the 20th century's principal decorative movements, including Bauhaus, Modernism, and Cubism, and its art colleges were hotbeds of radicalism. Despite the best endeavours of the authorities, this tradition continued and even thrived after 1948.

With the glass industry in need of direction, several of the country's leading artists migrated north from Prague to the glassmaking towns of Nový Bor, Kamenický Šenov, and Železný Brod, where they became established as designers and art-college teachers. Josef Hospodka (1923–89) (picture 21) directed glass education at Nový Bor, while two liberal professors at the Prague Academy of Applied Arts directed budding talent toward glass. Josef Kaplicky and Karel Štípl, who kept abreast of trends in Western art, drenched their students in contemporary drawing, painting, ceramics, and sculpture, and urged them to

apply their experience to the form and decoration of functional and, increasingly, artistic glass.

Kaplicky and Štípl's graduates form a roll call of the major players in post-war Czech glassmaking: Jaroslavá Brychtová, Pavel Hlava (picture 20), Vladimír Jelínek, Marta Kerhartová-Perinová, Vladimír Kopecky, Stanislav Libensky, Oldrich Lipá, Vera Lisková, Adolf Matura (picture 19), Jan Novotny, Ladislav Oliva, René Roubícek, Miluse Roubícková, Marie Stáhlíková (picture 22), Dana Vachtová, Karel Vanura, Karel Wünsch (picture 20), Vladimír Zahour, and Jirina Zertová.

The methodology of Czech glass designers was as varied as the personalities of its exponents. However, most were allowed after-hours access to the furnaces, and the provision of private studio spaces was first tolerated, then encouraged. The result was a flowering of individualism and, in effect, the foundation of the first studio-glass movement. Positive critical reaction to Czech exhibits at Milan in 1957 was followed by the Gold Medal at the Brussels Expo, '58 (picture 23).

The further international acclaim accorded Czech glassmakers at Corning, 1964, and the Montreal Expo, 1967, loosened the chains and enabled important visits from several emerging American studio artists.

However, the path was not always smooth for the Czechs. The teacher/engraver Jirí Harcuba, for instance, was jailed for making a medallion in memory of Jan Palach, who had burnt himself alive in Prague's Wenceslas Square in 1968 as a desperate protest against the Russian invasion.

Czech glassmaking, both studio and industrial, had gradually re-established a firm footing by the time of liberation in 1989. However,

▲ **22: Hospodka style**

Free-formed objects in the style of Josef Hospodka, designed by Milena Velísková (1926–) and Maria Stáhlíková (1922–), for Škrdlovice, 1969.

From left £30/$55, £60/$100, £30/$55

◄ **23: Brussels Expo 1958 sticker**

Applied to certain Czech glassware after the award of the Grand Prix for glass to Czechoslovakia at the Brussels Expo, 1958.

▼ **24: Rudolf Jurnikl pressed glass**

From left: Grey-green vase, designed for Rosice/Moravia National Glass Corporation, 1962, 24cm (9½in); finned pressed bowl and contemporary publicity photograph, designed for Rudolfova Hut, c.1970, tallest bowl: 7.5cm (2⅞in); blue ashtray (185), designed for Rosice, 1962, 6cm (2⅜in) high; and a series of pressed vases, designed for Rudolfova Hut, 1964, tallest (left) 22.5cm (8⅞in).

From left £15–40/$25–70*

▲ 25 British silver-mounted Art Nouveau decanters

The cheapest (top, second from right) cost 13/- (65p/$1), and the most expensive (bottom, second from right), 27/- (£1.30/$2). Each was based on the same blank, the only differences being their stoppers and the engraving on the lower one, which doubled its price. Illustrated in the Army & Navy Stores' 1907 catalogue.

£200–250/$340–425

▲ 26: Art Nouveau British decanter

Amethyst-over-colourless cased. Produced by Webb or Stevens & Williams, c.1900–1910. 23cm (9in) inc.

£1,000/$1,700*

while its individual artists now enjoy widespread respect and prosperity, its recently privatized factories find themselves struggling against competition from Far Eastern imports.

Britain

The history of the 20th-century British glass industry is a lamentable saga of decline and fall. In 1900, it was the envy of the world, with a roster of famous glassworks employing thousands in the production of a vast range of functional and decorative pieces for a market that encircled the globe. By 2000, there was virtually nothing left; instead, supermarkets, apartments, and sports halls stood on old glasshouse sites, and most of Britain's glassware was imported from Eastern Europe and the Far East.

This extraordinary collapse was not spread evenly over the course of the century. Rather, it took place recently and within a single decade: Thomas Webb closed in 1990; Webb Corbett in 1995, Royal Brierley/ Stevens & Williams in 1998, and Stuart Crystal in 2001. Today, Dartington, established in 1967, remains Britain's sole surviving fine-glassworks.

1900–14

The situation was very different in 1900. While foreign competition was beginning to make inroads into Britain's markets, ships laden with table-glass of all qualities sailed from British ports every week. The glass industry was settled in two principal areas: around the port cities of Sunderland and Newcastle, where pressed-glassmakers Sowerby, Greener/Jobling, and Davidson produced cheap functional and decorative pieces, and land-locked Stourbridge, west of Birmingham, which had become the virtual monopoly producer of finer British wares.

Most British glass design was based on two long-established characteristics: lead crystal and the English style of cutting it. It was associated domestically with the Regency period, c.1800–25, and known internationally as the *façon d'Angleterre*. For many, deep, geometrically cut, colourless crystal remained unassailed as the epitome of good taste. The composition of crystal, or what its makers called *flint*, had been perfected in 1676 by George Ravenscroft, whose formula was based on crushed flint pebbles. Though fine sand soon replaced flints as their source of silica, the term persists to the present day.

The popularity of cutting remained fundamentally unaltered at the dawn of the 20th century. Other styles certainly attracted the attentions of the artistically minded, such as the Arts & Crafts designs of Harry Powell for Whitefriars. However, while these remain sought-after today, they formed a tiny fraction of the massive output of British glassmaking. The fact was that the British have always been conservative in outlook and taste, and the combinations of mitres, grooves, and lenses that define Regency cutting remained the staple product of its historic glassworks until their demise toward the end of the 20th century.

Mindful of this background, it is hardly surprising that Art Nouveau caused problems for delicate, if not hypocritical, British sensibilities. Its free-flowing organic lines and obvious sexual undertones provoked outraged headlines and consternation in the drawing rooms of pompous Empire-builders. Besides, it was so obviously foreign, in more ways than one. So, while Europe's leading glassmakers and stylists became increasingly audacious, their otherwise rudderless British counterparts generally resorted to reproductions of their former glories.

Some British glassware dating from 1900–14 bears hints and flavours of Art Nouveau (picture 25). Harry Powell designed certain outstanding pieces, but the major Stourbridge glassworks generally tagged along half-heartedly, producing only a limited number of ranges. Nevertheless, some of these pieces invariably demonstrate a high degree of skill, if not innovation (pictures 26 and 27).

So, while some Art Nouveau glassware was produced in Britain before 1914, the majority of local production broadly continued to followed safe, traditional paths. The surviving illustrated catalogues of both pressed- and fine-glassmakers of the period demonstrate only slight deviations from well-established paths, with cutting – real or pressed approximations of it – remaining the prevalent decorative style.

The 1920s

The fading international appetite for Art Nouveau after 1918 should have been good news for British glassmakers, who had never fully engaged with it. The problem was that its successor was Art Deco, which they didn't like either. After all, it, too, was French-inspired and, they argued, doubtless a passing fad. Naturally, what they really longed for was a revival in the popularity of Regency cutting. So, in the absence of serious competition, they continued to produce it themselves.

This may appear to have been tantamount to commercial suicide. However, the 1920s were a far cry from today, when personal taste moves in international rather than parochial waves, and a market still existed for these conservative products. As wealth continued to trickle down the social ladder, workers raised with only pressed glass at home (not just in Britain, but also across its Empire and in the United States) discovered that they could afford the luxury of luxuries, real cut glass.

A high proportion of British glass of the 1920s took its lead from the Regency model, then a century old. The resulting pastiches were based on period shapes cut with traditional motifs, sometimes complemented by localized intaglio cutting or engraving (picture 28). While unfashionable today, such pieces were laborious to decorate and were not cheap when originally retailed.

The Edwardian appetite for reproductions reflected an international trend. A rising appreciation of antiques, started by a small group of late 19th-century American billionaires, gradually spread to the middle

▲ **27: British Art Nouveau engraving**
Green baluster-shaped decanter, finely engraved with a flying dragon. Maker uncertain, possibly Webb, 1910. 33cm (13in) inc.
£200–400/$340–680*

▲ **28: Typical 1920s English glassware**
Made by Stuart Crystal (pp.234–41), the cutting designs echo those produced during the Georgian Regency, over a century earlier.
£20–50/$35–85*

classes. However, as dealers across the quality range soon discovered, stock was hard to find. The original purchasers of period finery generally remained wealthy and had no reason to sell. So, faced with the resulting shortage, manufacturers responded with reproductions (picture 31). The contemporary pattern books of the leading British glassmakers and retailers on both sides of the Atlantic illustrate substantial ranges of reproductions of Georgian glassware (pictures 29 and 30).

The moribund nature of 1920s British glassware had predictable consequences. Facing increasingly dynamic foreign competition but unable, or unwilling, to offer anything fresh, its sales nose-dived when American Prohibition was followed by the Wall Street Crash. A traditionally healthy British trade surplus in glass gradually reversed to a point, around 1930, where imports were five times greater than exports.

The 1930s

Fearing a total collapse of its entire glass industry, the British government slapped a 50 per cent protectionist tariff on imports in 1931 and established an inquiry into the industry's failings. The findings, published in 1932, lamented the absence of design talent in British ceramics and glass. It proposed a series of showcase exhibitions for which Stuart Crystal (pp.234–41) produced a series of designs submitted by some of Britain's leading fine artists (pictures 32 and 33).

Suitably encouraged, trained designers were soon engaged by most British glassworks, a trend rapidly reflected in their products. Even pressed-glassmakers Bagley and Davidson (pp.96–101 and 108–15) hired outside help during the 1930s for the first and only time in their histories, though Sowerby, the leading Victorian pressed-glassmaker, resisted such frivolity (picture 34).

Britain's best-known designer of the period was New Zealand-born architect Keith Murray. Finding building work scarce during the Depression, he worked for Royal Brierley between 1932 and 1939. His interest in modern glass had been kindled by the French, Swedish, and Czech displays at the Paris Exposition in 1925. It was further boosted by the Orrefors display at the London Exhibition of Swedish Industrial Art in 1931, on which many of his own designs were based (picture 35).

Murray's designs are characterized by bold engraving and deep cutting on clear and bi-coloured glass, with pieces sometimes fitted with contrasting black feet and/or stoppers in the manner of Simon Gate (pp.187). Brierley claimed that Murray's work was "designed for blowing in moulds, and therefore for mass production methods". However, its reluctance to make the required investments without a proven market resulted in few of Murray's designs entering commercial production.

Britain's leading 20th century cut-glass maker was Stuart Crystal, whose output is examined on pages 231-41. Clyne Farquharson, who worked for Walsh Walsh, Birmingham, during the 1930s, remains another respected designer of inter-war colourless crystal. This is partially because of his stylish patterns, but also because his work often bears his engraved signature. However, demand for his work is largely limited to Britain; it is hard to believe that it is widely collected in Sweden, for instance. Walsh Walsh's 1920s output was typically nondescript. However, heavily promoted by the company, Farquharson's crisp, fine outlined *Leaf* (picture 36), *Albany*, *Kendal*, and *Barry* services enjoyed limited commercial success.

A lack of documentary evidence currently obscures the inter-war output of the three remaining major Stourbridge works: Richardson, Thomas Webb & Sons, and Webb Corbett, founded in 1897. The distinguished Richardson glassworks, established in 1829, was ended almost exactly a century later by Thomas Webb's takeover around 1930. This means that rare objects acid-badged with Richardson's name probably date from the 1920s (picture 37).

Thomas Webb and Webb Corbett's output can be identified by their etched logos. Yet, while the names of their designers are known, it remains difficult to date and attribute their work (picture 38). Thomas Webb produced cut glass at this time, but its most colourful ranges were formed in optic-moulds to create a variety of patterned effects (picture 39). The earliest of these was the *Cascade* series, introduced in 1900, followed by *Fir Cone* and *Old English* (1903), *Lattice*, *Pineapple*, and *Mirror* (1905), *Ondé* (*Waved*) (1908), *Ribonette* (1910), and *Pea* (1933).

Whitefriars, Britain's only London-based glassmaker, took time to recover from the retirement in 1919 of its leading designer, Harry

▲ **31: British 18th-century-reproduction glassware**
All 1920s, from left: Facet-stemmed wine glass, stylistic date 1770, 15cm (5⅞in); gadrooned syllabub glass, the base etched *T GOODE* (the top Mayfair retailer), stylistic date 1730, 11.5cm (4½in); pedestal-stem wine glass, stylistic date c.1720, 15cm (5⅞in); and trumpet-bowl wine glass, stylistic date c.1750, 13.5cm (5¼in).
£25–50/$45–85*

▲ **32: 1930s exhibition piece**
Vase designed by fine artist Dame Laura Knight, made by Stuart Crystal, c.1933, and displayed at a series of showcase London exhibitions during the 1930s.
£1,500/$2,550

▲ **35: 1930s British-Swedish style**
Deeply-cut vase, etched *Keith Murray/S&W*, and a Royal Brierley advertisement, 1935, for the designs of Keith Murray, Harry Whitworth, and R.S. Williams-Thomas. Murray was influenced by Swedish glass he saw at the 1925 Paris Exposition and the London Exhibition of Swedish Industrial Art, 1931. Despite the signature, this vase was the result of remodelling during the 1950s by Williams-Thomas for Tiffany, New York. 26cm (10¼in).
1930s example £1,200/$2,050; 1950s version £300/$510

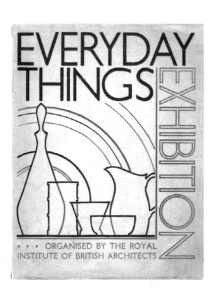

▲ **33: Everyday Things Exhibition, 1936**
Catalogue cover for the exhibition staged at the Royal Institute of British Architects, 1936, to promote new designs in British ceramics and glass.

▲ **34: Sowerby centrepiece, 1933**
Although this pressed-glass maker was one of the few British glassworks not to engage professional design services, these vases proved to be best-sellers. 16cm (6¼in). From Sowerby's 1933 catalogue.
£20/$35

▲ 36: Clyne Farquharson for Walsh

Leaf is Farquharson's best-known pattern for Walsh Walsh, Birmingham, *c*.1935, though this biscuit barrel was designed in 1939. The stems are engraved, the leaves simply cut in two planes. Base engraved *Clyne F, NRD 39*. 16.5cm (6½in).

£150/$255

▲ 37: British Swedish-style engraving

Vase with bubble inclusions, produced *c*.1925–30. Engraved with a salmon caught on a fishing hook. Base acid-badged *RICHARDSON MADE IN ENGLAND*. 18cm (7in).

£140/$240

◀ 38: Stylish Art Deco vase

Green-over-colourless cut vase, *c*.1930–5. Base acid-etched *WEBB CORBETT MADE IN ENGLAND*. 20cm (7⅞in).

£300/$510

▲ 39: Thomas Webb optic-moulding

Optic-moulding formed a major part of Thomas Webb's inter-war and early post-war production. Most acid-badged *Webb Made in England*. These are often confused with similar effects produced by Whitefriars. Max. 30cm (11⅞in).

£20–80/$35–135*

Powell, and its relocation to suburban Wealdstone in 1923. Many of Powell's designs were produced until the outbreak of war in 1939 and were supplemented only gradually by fresh ones. Powell family members Marriott and Barnaby both made stylish contributions during the 1930s before outsiders, including William Wilson and James Hogan, gradually assumed the reins.

Post-war

British glassmakers endured a tough time after 1945. As military contracts died away, they faced an outright ban on selling their work, utility glass excepted, to the home market until 1952 in order to encourage currency-earning exports (picture 40). It was not until 1955, when a 100 per cent luxury tax imposed on their work since 1952 was reduced to 30 per cent, that the outlook began to brighten.

Mindful of this uphill struggle, it is a testament to the optimism of British glassmaking that most of its leading post-war designers were recruited during this period. Alexander Hardie Williamson (pp.126–31) began designing for United Glass in 1944; Irene Stevens joined Webb Corbett in 1946; David Hammond, Thomas Webb in 1947; John Luxton, Stuart Crystal (p.234) in 1949; and Geoffrey Baxter, Whitefriars in 1954. As members of a dynamic new breed of Royal College of Art graduates, each felt duty-bound to lift society from the wreckage of war, a passion shared by their colleagues in architecture and across the decorative arts.

The Festival of Britain, 1951 (picture 41), played an important role in galvanizing the varied visions of this new generation of designers toward what became known as the Contemporary style. The festival, based at RD Russell and Robert Goodden's (p.102) Festival Hall, shared a dual purpose: to celebrate the centenary of the Great Exhibition, 1851, and to act as a jamboree of art and industry to cheer the population after 12 years of austerity. In the words of its director, Gerald Barry, its series of nationwide events was intended to be a "tonic for the nation".

Examples of early post-war British fine glass are rare for several reasons: little was produced, it was expensive, and most was exported. However, surviving pieces exhibit varying degrees of Modernism (pictures 42 and 43). Marking the start of an evolutionary trend, edges and cuts grew more curvilinear rather than geometric, shapes became more organic, and colours cooled into leaf green, sky blue, and smoke pastels.

The other reason for the rarity of daring early-1950s British glassware is that the public, short of disposable income, remained unconvinced of its merits. It was one thing for academics to encourage designers to be daring, but it proved quite another to persuade consumers to buy the results (picture 44). While design history books often herald the early 1950s as a period of dramatic change, in reality the process proved very slow as manufacturers and their customers played safe (picture 45).

The ban on domestic sales of decorative glass, the relative poverty of the period, and the conservative nature of consumers combined to ensure that early-1950s glassware was most commonly of the cheap, pressed variety. Companies such as United Glass, Sherdley, Bagley, and Chance Brothers understood their market and responded with a variety of innocuous, often homespun products that outsold finer pieces, probably thousands of times over (picture 46).

Chance's *Handkerchief* vases, launched in 1958, typify this trend. Derived from Fulvio Bianconi's expensive and technically demanding 1940s originals for Venini, Chance's versions were easy to make, eye-

▲ 40: Cheap *CELERY* vase, c.1950

The addition of the word "celery" enabled this Thomas Webb vase to be categorized as utility glass, so avoiding the ban on sales of fancy glass in Britain between 1942 and 1952. 15.5cm (6in).
£25/$45

▲ 41: French Festival of Britain tumbler

The logo of the festival, held in 1951, applied to a tumbler probably made in France by JG Durand (p.73). 6cm (2⅜in).
£5/$9

◄ 43: Post-war Stuart Crystal

Designed by John Luxton, from Stuart's 1954 catalogue. While all were recent designs, only two (centre and bottom right) could be described as Modernist, the others being more retro. 25cm (10in).
£125–150/$210–255*

29599

29636

29538

29537

29578

**◄ 42: Irene Stevens'
Modernist vase, 1946**

A spectacular example of British Modernist glass, designed by Stevens for Webb Corbett. However, its original top rim was horizontal and the wavy version seen here is the result of extreme so-called "restoration". At 25.5cm (10in) max, it is probably short of its original height.

**Original condition £1,200/$2,050
Sold as seen £600/$1,020**

" *Of course, it's very, very beautiful, but I don't like it.*"

▲ 44: British taste satirized in 1947
This cartoon crystallized the problem faced by contemporary designers of all nations: consumers felt safer with old-fashioned objects than with modern ones.

▲ 45: Conservative British taste
A 1960s biscuit tin is printed with a contemporary vision of middle-class sophistication. A Georgian silver salver is laden with cocktail biscuits and a reproduction Georgian decanter (with matching glasses) is filled with sherry. The biscuits apart, the scene could be from a Regency drawing room, 1825.

▼ 46: Best-selling post-war British glass
From left: *Waverley* sugar bowl with chrome fittings, Chance, c.1950; frosted and painted *Somerset* vase, Bagley, c.1953; *Spiderweb* bowl, Chance Brothers, c.1950; *Ripple* jug, designed by Alexander Hardie Williamson, for Sherdley, in 1938 (as distinct from W.J.G. Fullerton's *Ripple* for Davidson, p.111); and *Spinette* vase and plinth, Bagley, c.1953. Max. 21cm (8¼in) diam.
£5–20/$9–35

catching, cheap, and sold like hot cakes (pp.107). Of course, finer pieces were available, but the British market for them remained small until the 1960s, when customers became more sophisticated and enjoyed greater disposable incomes.

1955–2000

With the luxury tax reduced to 30 per cent in 1955, the British glass industry issued a collective sigh of relief and stepped up a gear. Probably the most ingenious innovation of the period was Chance's *Fiesta* range. With Chance owned since 1945 by glazing-glass specialist Pilkington, it was appropriate that *Fiesta*, its best-selling post-war range, was formed in sheet glass. Early versions printed with lace doily patterns were followed by the most popular of all, *Swirl* (1955), then Margaret Casson's *Night Sky* (1957), and Michael Harris' *Calypto* (1959).

Fiesta's success, selling in millions over its 50-year production span, encouraged a swathe of transfer-printed glass, ranging from patterned *Pyrex* (p.204) dishes to advertising ashtrays (p.180). These were achieved by soaking the transfer off its backing paper, floating it onto the glass, then firing the image onto the vessel in a furnace (picture 47).

The manufacturers of cheap glass knew their job and stuck to it, but the fine-glassworks, principally the Stourbridge Big Four – Webb, Webb Corbett, Stuart, and Brierley – were torn between experimenting with the daring Contemporary look and following their natural inclination toward the traditional. They also knew that the buyers for Britain's major department stores were equally dubious as to the commercial potential of Designer Glass. The result was more of the same: heavy, deeply cut crystal, and even Whitefriars joined in with series of cut vases and drinking suites, designed by Geoffrey Baxter between 1955 and 1980 (picture 48).

Certain exceptions to the generally low standard of Stourbridge glass design were produced by Webb Corbett, which backed Irene Stevens' bold drive toward Modernism; Stuart, which occasionally allowed John

Luxton some latitude, and Whitefrairs, whose output under Baxter became increasingly colourful and expressive.

Webb Corbett continued to support dynamic cutting after the end of their association with Stevens in 1963 by engaging the freelance services of the Royal College of Art professor David Queensberry, best known for his geometric designs for Midwinter pottery (picture 49).

With the wartime ban on glass imports lifted in 1955, British agents were soon acting for a host of Scandinavian glassmakers, including Orrefors (pp.184–99), Holmegaard (pp.138–61), Kastrup (pp.140–4), and Nuutajärvi (pp.116–25). Although Stourbridge reamined blinkered to this mounting threat, other British glassworks rose to meet the challenge. The Scandinavian Modern template was soon adopted at Whitefriars and by newcomers King's Lynn (pp.232–5) and Dartington (pp.242–7), both founded in 1967. Whitefriars' Geoffrey Baxter, Lynn's Ronnie Stennett-Willson, and Dartington's Frank Thrower had all visited Nordic countries, and R.S.W. and Thrower had been colleagues at J. Wuidart & Co., London agents for Orrefors and Kosta.

Baxter, Stennett-Willson, and Thrower routinely plagiarized Nordic themes, including those developed by Jacob Bang (pp.140–5), Per Lütken (pp.146–57), and Orrefors' Nils Landberg (pp.190–1), and it was not until the late 1960s that each developed an individual style. Stennett-Willson's finest designs were probably his candlesticks for King's Lynn, 1967, while the merits of some of Baxter's texture-moulded vases from 1966 are reflected in the extraordinary prices they fetch today (picture 48). Thrower remained the most consistent of the trio, producing mostly plain, colourless, functional services, vases, and kitchen glass throughout his career.

At the end of the 20th century, Dartington remained Britain's sole surviving fine-glassmaker. Perhaps surprisingly, the industry collapsed not so much because it had failed to develop a modern identity but because of global economics. The margins available today to both standard- and fine-glassmakers in developed nations are simply too narrow to be sustainable. Most British glassworks were situated in urban conurbations

▲ 47: Post-war glass transfers

1967 advertisement for Johnson Matthey transfers, as applied to a huge number of items of cheap British post-war decorative and functional glassware.

◀ ▼ 48: Baxter for Whitefriars

Geoffrey Baxter's enduring reputation is based on his eccentric textured vases. However, he also designed cut drinks services and vases throughout his career (1954–80). This crystal vase (C480), left, appeared in Whitetfriars' 1970 catalogue. 14cm (5½in). The indigo-tinted *Banjo* vase (9681), below, 1968, is in front of Whitefriars' last catalogue, 1978. 33cm (13in).

**Vase
£55–80/$95–135*
Banjo
£750–1,200/$1,275***

◀ ▼ 49: Queensberry for Webb Corbett

Geometrically cut vase and bowl, designed by David Queensberry, for Webb Corbett, 1966–7. Left: *Mitre* vase. Below: *Harlequin* bowl.

**Left £150/$255
Right £125/$210`**

△ 50: Argy-Rousseau *pâte-de-verre*, 1920

Danseuses, the mottled amber ground with three panels framing dancers. Moulded mark: *G. ARGY-ROUSSEAU*. 1920. 10cm (3⅞in).

£3,500/$5.950*

△ 51: Schneider acid-cameo, 1930

Cerises (*Cherries*) vase. Engraved *Le Verre Français*. 20cm (7⅞in).

£1,000/$1,700

▽ 52: Publicity ashtrays, 1930s–60s

From top: *HOTEL RITZ PARIS*, *c*.1930, 12.5cm (4⅞in) long; *Dom Perignon 1638–1715 CHAMPAGNE MOËT & CHANDON*, *c*.1950, 10cm (3⅞in) long; and *STELLA ARTOIS*, *c*.1960s, 20cm (7⅞in) diam.

£10–20/$17–35

▽ 53: Lalique and Sabino statuettes, 1927 and 1930

Contrasting statuettes by, left, René Lalique, *c*.1927, and right, Ernest Sabino, *c*.1930. Lalique: *Taïs*, 23cm (9in); Sabino: 22cm (8⅝in).

Lalique £5,000/$8,500; Sabino £3,000/$5,100*

where development land commands premium prices, and, as with most other traditional industries, it simply proved expedient to shed their workers, sell their plots, and let consumers buy from abroad.

France and Belgium

The French contribution to glassmaking history before 1830, the year that the state of Belgium was created, remains a grey area. Such was the derivative nature of its forms and decoration that it requires specialist knowledge to differentiate between French-made pieces and their foreign-made role models. Early vessel glass illustrated in French glass literature generally appears to be more Venetian, *Venise*, Dutch, Spanish, Bohemian, *Bohème*, or German and English than characteristically "French".

Aside from certain exceptions, the first French post-medieval glass-ware of international consequence post-dates the Napoleonic Wars, and all of it was introduced within a decade of Bonaparte's final defeat. The group comprises the sulphide inclusions perfected and patented by Barthélemy Desprez in 1818, Baccarat's *moulé en plein* method of pres-sure-moulding, invented *c*.1820, and the development of a spectrum of opaline colours from 1823.

France's geographic location at the crossroads of Europe could have proved a boon to its glassmakers. However, war and religious intolerance proved costly, because their industry was regularly depleted of craftsmen. For instance, the Peace of Alès, 1685, which effectively outlawed Protestantism, caused the exit of 400,000 Huguenots, among whom were most of France's glassmakers. During the 19th century, political and social anarchy around 1850 closed several leading works, including Choisy-le-Roi, and encouraged the emigration of many of its best glassmakers,

incluing the influential Georges Bontemps to Chance Brothers (pp.102–7) in 1848. Similarly, Jules Barbe, one of France's finest enamellers, moved to England in 1872 after losing his family to the Franco-Prussian War.

Art Nouveau

The scenario changed entirely with the advent of Art Nouveau from around 1890, when French glassmaking began its most spectacular flowering, almost literally, with similar trends echoing in Belgium. Art Nouveau drew on myriad influences, including the *Beaux-Arts* style that had been dominant in France from the 1870s, but further flavoured with flighty eroticism, sinuous botany, and symbolism.

Art Nouveau glass is epitomized by the work of its greatest creative genius, Emile Gallé, one of several French glass artists who emerged during the 1870s. Based in his hometown of Nancy, Gallé's early commercial "transparent period" was marked by clear, lightly tinted vessels decorated with colourful enamels. The turning point came at the Paris Exposition in 1878, where he won four gold medals and witnessed the multilayered cameo glass exhibited by Webb and Stevens & Williams, iridescent art glass by Pantin, Paris, and Argy-Rousseau's daring *pâte-de-verre* (picture 50 and p.14). Duly inspired, Gallé dedicated the rest of his life to expanding the boundaries of glassmaking, notably through the use of acids on multilayered blanks (pp.13 and 28).

The New Wave

The new momentum in French glass was maintained by others, most working with acids to create three-dimensional effects (picture 51), including Antonin Daum, Nancy, and Maurice Marinot, who together formed the next New Wave of French glassmakers (pp.31–2).

Marinot and Majorelle were already successful painters before turning to glassmaking. Yet, while Majorelle, Daum, Schneider and others continued Gallé's path, Marinot's distaste for Art Nouveau manifested itself in severe Modernistic forms, characterized by deep cutting and acid-etching, that anticipated the future. However, where Marinot used glass as a means of self-expression and produced just 2,000 crafted pieces, others turned to the production of eye-catching designs by semi-industrial means. This trend is epitomized by the work of René Lalique, the world's most famous and fashionable glassmaker. With experienced staff scarce after the First World War, Lalique combined his extraordinary design sense with a genius for moulding techniques to create mass-produced pieces sold as *objets d'art* by glamorous retailers.

Lalique inspired a legion of copyists, both in France and abroad, the best-known of whom was Marius Ernest Sabino (picture 53). The trend toward moulding was particularly prominent in France and Belgium, where 1.5 million men had been lost in the 1914–18 war. While the work of Lalique, Gallé, and other leading French glass designers/makers of

▲ **54: French effects, *c.*1930**
Inter-war French glassmakers produced a variety of moulded and mottled effects. These 1930s mould-blown lamp bases, originally fitted with brass mounts, are unsigned, but unmistakeably French.17 and 15cm (6¾ and 5⅞in).
Left £75/$130, Right £50/$85

▲ **55: Val St-Lambert, Belgium**
From top: Cut and acid-decorated Art Deco vase, probably designed by Charles Graffart or Joseph Simon, *c.*1930, 30cm (11⅞in); *VAL St LAMBERT BELGIQUE DESPOSÉ* sticker, 1930s; cased ruby-over-colourless and brilliant cut basket, probably Val Saint-Lambert, *c.*1950s, no mark, 20cm (7⅞in); and amethyst Modernist fruit bowl, *c.*1935, part of VSL's *Luxval* range of 1930s pressed glass, impressed mark: *Val Saint Lambert BELGIQUE*, 30cm (11⅞in) diam.
From top £600/$1,020; £75/$130; £30/$55

▼ **56: Georges Chevalier for Baccarat, France, 1930s**

Mould-blown *Davos* decanter, 1930, and *Bain d'Oeil* (*Eye Bath*) goblet, 1937, both by Chevalier for Baccarat. Founded in 1763, and with nearly 800 employees in 2006, Baccarat remains France's most prestigious glassmaker. With demand for fine table-glass falling, it has diversified into jewelry (now 26 per cent of its output), and lighting (32 per cent). However, its mid-20th-century output was distinguished by the decanters and glasses of Georges Chevallier, its chief designer 1916–76.

Decanter £150/$255
Goblet £30/$55

the inter-war years has been the subject of comprehensive literature, the work of most French and Belgian 20th-century glassmakers remains almost entirely undocumented. Some lesser names applied signatures, but the identities of the majority currently remains lost and the extent of their repertoire unknown (pictures 52, 54, and 57).

Art, craft, and mass production

As elsewhere, table-glass of all qualities, not vases and *objets*, formed the majority of French and Belgian glass output. The unrivalled leader in this field was Baccarat, founded in 1765 in what is now Belgium. Based in modern France since 1816, Baccarat has produced high-quality table- and lighting glass for the rich ever since. The company commissioned ranges from many sources, but its leading designer was the remarkable Georges Chevalier, who designed so many decanters and glasses between 1916 and 1976 that they have proved unquantifiable. His bold, geometric forms, mostly in cut-crystal, became the company's hallmark (picture 56).

The scenario was echoed in Belgium, which housed dozens of small glassworks (picture 60) but only one giant: the Verreries de Val Saint-Lambert, founded near Liège in 1828 (picture 55). VSL's payroll grew from 1,200 in 1856 to 6,000 in 1900 before shrinking to 4,000 in 1926. VSL's four glassworks produced all the familiar forms: from pressed utility and fancy work through cut, engraved, and etched services, and *pâte-de-verre*, to daring Modernist pieces. It employed many leading designers, including Henri van de Velde, Nanny Still (p.214), and Harvey

◄ **58: 1960s Post-war Daum**

Left: Mould-blown table-lamp base. 20cm (7⅞in). Right: Free-formed duck. Engraved *DAUM FRANCE*. 11.5cm (4½in) long. Both designed by Michel Daum.

Lamp £80/$135, Bird £150/$255

▲ **57: Idiosyncratic 1950s–60s Franco-Belgian forms**

Top: Mould-blown smoked glass fruit bowl with intaglio engraved roses. Unmarked. 35.5cm (14in) diam. Bottom: Free-formed crystal basket sculpture. Unmarked. 35.5cm (14in) diam. Similar pieces were produced by numerous French works, including Baccarat and Daum.

Bowl £60/$100, Sculpture £60/$100

Littleton, but its most distinctive ranges were the striking Art Deco pieces designed by the in-house team of Charles Graffart, who joined the works aged 12 in 1906, and Joseph Simon, who succeeded Graffart as its chief designer from 1942 to 1958 (picture 55).

Prohibition in the USA, 1920–33, and the Depression following the Wall Street Crash of 1929, wrought havoc on French and Belgian fine and art glassmaking, and the region's role as a major player diminished rapidly. With markets and jobs evaporating, the emphasis switched toward cheaper lines, including VSL's stylish pressed *Luxval* (picture 55). Lalique, Baccarat, VSL, and Daum survived, but many did not.

Post-war, Marc and Marie-Claude Lalique and Michel Daum designed some interesting pieces for their family enterprises. Vannes-le-Châtel, which now makes Daum's ranges, produced a stylish series of crystal vases and animals during the 1960s and '70s (pictures 58 and 59). However, the greatest success story in French glassmaking has not been in this field.

The name Jacques Durand will not register with many, but his company, founded near Calais in 1825, is Europe's largest producer of table-glass. The company, 100 per cent family-owned since 1897, operates 24 hours a day, 365 days a year. The site produces 6 million items of glassware that consume 1,400 tonnes of melted glass every day (picture 61). Succeeding generations of Durands skilfully identified and adopted new technology, including the installation of France's first tank furnace, followed by automatic blowing machines. Durand's products are now marketed under the brand names of *Luminarc*, *Cristal d'Arques*,

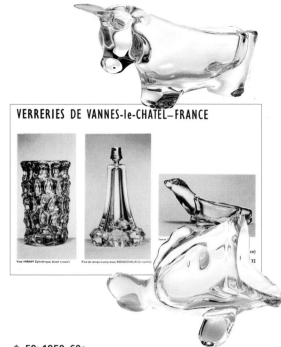

▲ **59: 1950–60s**
Verreries de Vannes-le-Châtel
Founded under aristocratic patronage in 1765, the Verreries de Vannes-le-Châtel in Lorraine employed around 600 glassmakers in 1960. Its production included lead-based artistic pieces formed in moulds bought from defunct makers, including Cristal de Sèvres and Paris wholesaler Etling, and it has produced all Daum's ranges since 1980. Its 1950s and '60s output included a large range of mould-blown, furnace-worked, and polished animal figures designed by Auguste Houillon. The works now houses Europe's largest glassmaking school. From top: Bull, 18.5cm (7¼in) long; trade advertisement, 1967; Vannes gold foil sticker; and fish, 14.5cm (5⅝in) long.
Animals £25/$45

◀ **60: The post-war period**
The 1950s–70s were marked by the closure of dozens, if not hundreds, of small French and Belgian glassworks. The casualties included Michotte, near Charleroi, Belgium (1899–1972), and Belotte, Valenciennes. Top: Mould-blown lemonade set applied with sticker: *Michotte Belgium*. 18cm and 26.5cm (7 and 10½in). Below: Pressed promotional plate/ashtray, printed with *VERRERIES DE LA GARE. &. A. BELOTTE REUNIES-VALENCIENNES*.14.5cm (5⅝in) diam.
Lemonade set £45/$75, Plate £5/$9

▲ **61: J.G. Durand, 1930s–present**
Producing all manner of glassware, from storage jars and bottles to coffee cups and wine glasses, J.G. Durand (founded 1828) is the world's largest glassworks. By adopting new technology and aggressive marketing, the family-owned company expanded rapidly and today employs 16,000 in the production, distribution, and sale of its daily production: 6 million items weighing 1,400 tonnes. From left: *Windsor Rubis* vase, 1970, several sizes; *Etoile Rosalin* decanter service, 1930s–70s, from an extensive range of table-glass; Luminarc *Lido* tumbler, 1970s, 12cm (4¾in); Luminarc *Ligne Verte* (*Green Line*) tumbler, 1980s, 10cm (3⅞in).
£5–20/$9–35

Studio Nova, *Mikasa*, and the luxury, handmade *Salviati*, originally established on Murano in 1859. These days, most glassworks can only survive if they are very large or very small, and J.G. Durand has certainly proved the viability of super-sizing.

Scandinavia

The transformation in Scandinavian glassmaking's status between *c.*1920 and the 1950s, from irrelevant to world-leading, was an astonishing achievement. It is no an exaggeration to state that over the preceding four centuries the combined glass industries of the four Nordic countries, Sweden, Denmark, Norway, and Finland, had produced virtually nothing of international consequence. Yet during the middle of the 20th century, their designers produced ranges of furniture, ceramics, metal, and glassware that redefined the appearance of the world's interiors.

The rise of Scandinavian glass

Historically, Scandinavian glassmaking had been characterized by numerous small works, most in noble ownership, producing derivative wares under German and Bohemian direction. Its sole notable contribution had been a limited range of goblets and decanters produced at the Royal Norwegian glassworks at Nøstetangen during the 18th century (picture 62). Despite this lack of originality, Scandinavia possessed most of the ingredients essential to glassmaking, and, by 1900, the largest works in the region, Kosta Glasbruk, founded in 1742, employed 500 in Sweden's Småland.

The problem for Nordic glassworks, as the Swedish connoisseur Ludvig Looström noted in 1898, was that "they lack imagination and are in need of a new design sensibility". An ensuing philosophical debate within the Swedish artistic establishment pitted crafts-oriented traditionalists against progressive modernists. Not that this theorizing had any discernable impact on Scandinavian glass design, because consumers continued to vote with their wallets: the rich opting for complex, brilliant cutting, *Bohème* gilding and enamelling (picture 63), and imitations of Gallé acid-cameo, while the poor remained content with pressed approximations of cut-glass.

The tide began to turn when Johan Ekman acquired the previously undistinguished Orrefors glassworks in 1913. Siding with the modernizers, he hired artist/designers Simon Gate and Edward Hald, who brought a radical new approach to glass: uniting philosophy and form to lay the foundations of a new style that would later become known to the world as Scandinavian Modern.

Retro *Venise* table-glass ranges by Gate and Hald for Orrefors and Edvin Ollers for Kosta (picture 64) were unveiled at the Home Exhibition at Stockholm in 1917 under the Dresser-esque motto: "vackrare vardagsvara" ("beautiful things for everyday use"). Yet despite critical acclaim, the results met with disinterest from the general public.

◀ **62: Norwegian *Venise* goblet, 1750**
Lidded ceremonial goblet. Probably made c.1750 at the Royal Norwegian glassworks at Nøstetangen (1741–77). 45.5cm (18in) inc.
£65,000/$110,500

▲ **63: Swedish *Bohème* drinking-glasses**
Gilded and enamelled at Boda Glasbruk, c.1900. Centre: *Roemer* white wine glass, 17.5cm (6⅞in).
£100/$170*

Gate and Hald's daring new approach to the unfashionable art of engraving (picture 65) won increasing praise at Scandinavian exhibitions during the early 1920s. As a Swedish critic remarked in 1924, "Who could resist the charm of these airy pieces, seemingly conjured up with playful ease? What has happened in Sweden must be almost unparalleled, creating a production of this scope and quality in just a few short years." Further afield, similar pieces were lauded at shows in Paris (1925), New York, Detroit, and Chicago (1927), and London (1931). Designers in New York, Paris, and London were soon creating their own "Swedish" glass.

However, Nordic glassmaking did not revolve around Orrefors alone. Important contributions to its rapid emergence were made by, among others, Elis Bergh, Sven Erik Skawonius, and Tyra Lundgren (picture 69) at Kosta, and Gerda Strömberg. Strömberg joined her husband, Edvard, formerly Orrefors' managing director, when he bought the Eda works in 1933, which she supplied with distinctive designs, often in steel blue, into the 1960s (picture 71). Her bold, Modernist forms were widely copied, notably by Per Lütken at Holmegaard (p.149) and Geoffrey Baxter at Whitefriars.

The output of the numerous but disparate Scandinavian works drew on numerous influences, including contemporary painting, architecture and sculpture, and medieval and Art Deco, geometric, figurative, and abstract shapes and motifs. These were combined to create a distinctive, contemporary, and modern look that proved hugely influential and was widely copied. The leading trends included:

- Before 1920: Continuing dominance of foreign influences.
- 1920s: *Venise* retro forms (picture 64), grey and brown smoked

▲ **64: *Venise* decanter, 1918**
Designed by Edvin Ollers for Kosta in 1918. Most Scandinavian glassworks produced foreign-inspired designs until the 1920s. 30cm (11⅞in). Background: a contemporary magazine advertisement for Ollers' work.
Decanter £150/$255

66: Swedish enamelling

Enamels continued to be applied to Scandinavian glass into the 1950s, well after the widespread adoption of Modernist design principals during the 1920s. From left: Swedish decanter in the form of a peasant woman, c.1935–50, 24cm (9½in) inc.; Swedish schnapps barrel, c.1930, 15cm (5⅞in) inc.; and cobalt-blue tumbler designed by Hugo Gehlin for Gullaskruf Glasbruk, Sweden, given to delegates attending a glassmakers conference in 1950. 6cm (2⅜in).
Decanter £125/$210, Barrel £75/$130, Beaker £150/$255

▲ **65: A revolution in Scandinavian glass engraving**
Top: Edward Hald's extraordinary *Sönderslagna Bryggan* (*Broken Jetty*) dish, inspired by his teacher Matisse. Designed in 1920. 27.5cm (10⅞in) diam. Left: Traditional Bohemian-style wedding scene applied to a tankard. Designed c.1920s. Signed: *KOSTA*. 12cm (4¾in). Right: Modernist vase with an engraved nude. Signed: *KJELLANDER*. 25cm (9⅞in). Lars Kjellander (1868–1931), Kosta's leading engraver, worked on his own account after his retirement in 1925.
£600/$1,020*

▲ 67: Swedish artist turned glass designer
Sven Erixson (1899–1970) was among many fine artists recruited by 20th-century Scandinavian glassworks. Best known for his hot Mediterranean paintings, in 1930 he was based in Paris, from where he sent glass designs to Kosta. Overlaid with his calling-card.

▲ 68: Swedish pressed utility glass
Vases and art objects represent a fraction of Scandinavian glass. The vast majority of the output of Nordic glassworks in the 1930s was of utilitarian objects, priced at pennies. This Swedish pressed jug is typical, in being similar to equivalent designs produced in Germany and Czechoslovakia at the same time. 12.5cm (4⅞in).
£10/$17

tones, Neo-classicism and Baroque, fine engraving (picture 65), cross-overs from fine art.

- 1930s: Black feet and stoppers (p.187), bold Modernist shapes and decoration (picture 66), bolder and deeper engraving and cutting.

Notwithstanding the international success of Scandinavian "designer glass" among critics and connoisseurs, its creators faced an immutable contradiction: while they espoused egalitarian principles, the rich provided their market. As the Swedish critic Derek Ostergard observed, "Even simple stemware promoted as 'inexpensive' was not for those of limited means. Few lower income families had the means or the need to purchase a variety of wineglasses, champagne flutes, aperitif glasses… they were created for those whose lifestyles required them."

Post-war growth

While Swedish glass designers held the ascendancy pre-war, they had not been alone. Jacob Bang's artistic pieces (p.140) for Holmegaard, Denmark, gave Marinot's themes a new momentum, and Finnish glassworks were on the rise. The excitement generated by Alvar Aalto's *Savoy* (p.163) vases was maintained, albeit more quietly, by Gunnel Nyman and others (pp.164–5). However, the pace of Finnish design accelerated rapidly after 1945.

Finland's painful decision to fight the Soviets rather than the Nazis from 1940 left it, five years later, with a $300 million bill for war reparations. So its population, desperate to maintain their independence, united in the national interest: to clear the national debt through exports. Traditional categories, such as timber and electrical and mechanical engineering, played vital roles, but few would have predicted the contribution made by furniture, cutlery, and glassware. Defended in their home

◀ 69: Tyra Lundgren
Lundgren (1897–c.1980), painter/designer/journalist, was a trail-blazer in pre-war Scandinavian decorative arts. She designed ceramics for Röstrand/Arabia and glass for Moser (pp.54–5), Riihimäki (pp.206–23), and Kosta. However, her greatest achievements in glass stemmed from her association with Paulo Venini, for whom she designed 100 pieces, 1937–48, becoming Murano's first-ever female glass designer. Left: Three Lundgren designs for Kosta, 1935. Right: *Foglie* art object. Designed for Venini in 1938. 35cm (13¾in).
Vase £450/$765*
Sculpture £700–1,350/ $1,190–2,300*

market by prohibitive import tariffs, Finnish makers of decorative goods exported aggressively, often at close to cost-price, to raise hard currency.

By fortuitous coincidence, Iittala, Finland's leading glassworks, hired two new designers in 1946, Tapio Wirkkala and Kaj Franck, and another, Timo Sarpavena, in 1950 (pp.162–77). During the same period, neighbouring Riihimäki recruited two further names of the future: Helena Tynell and Nanny Still (pp.208–19). So the die was cast: Finland suddenly enjoyed an abundance of glass design talent.

Indeed, the story was repeated across Scandinavia during the immediate post-war era. Among others, Vicke Lindstrand returned to glass at Kosta, and Landberg, Palmqvist, and Öhrström flowered at Orrefors, Sweden, while Bang and Lütken worked for Kastrup and Holmegaard, Denmark (pp.138–57). So, it is an astonishing fact that the Nordic countries, with only 20 million inhabitants, produced more post-war glass designers of international consequence than the rest of Europe and North America combined, with a population 15 times greater.

Inevitably, rivalries abounded within such a large, disparate group of strong-minded, egocentric individuals. Sparks flew and ideas were transplanted when they met each other and witnessed the results of their work, both at their employers' premises and at the regular prize-orientated exhibitions of the period. The result was an outpouring of designs of all types. Nevertheless, certain trends remain discernable in post-war Scandinavian glass. These include:

• 1950s: Organic shapes, fine-line engraving, and "camouflage" tones.

▲ 70: Scandinavian stickers

The scale of the 20th-century Scandinavian glass industry, involving hundreds of different works, is mind-boggling. Most did not sign their output, preferring cheaper stickers, the designs of which were often adapted or entirely changed. These are just a tiny selection of them, including some simply stating *FOREIGN*.

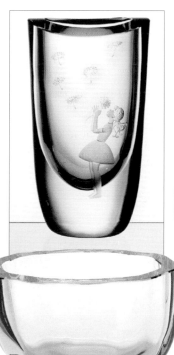

◀ ▼ 71: Strömberg blue

The international influence of Gerda Strömberg's Modernist designs proved disproportionate to the relative small scale of her family's *Strömbergshyttan* (Strömberg glassworks). Generally produced in aqua blue and occasionally cut or engraved, some pieces continued in production even after Strömberg's closure in 1979, a year after its take-over by Orrefors. Clockwise from top left: Engraved vase, c.1960; *Strömbergshyttan* engraved signature; and Gerda Strömberg vase, c.1939. 6cm (2⅜in).

Top £80/$135, Bottom £40/$70

▶ 72: *Coquilles* and copies

Paul Kedelv's *Cocquille* (Shell) sculptures, designed for Flysfors, Sweden, 1949–56, were widely copied. Original versions are usually signed, unlike these examples, which could have been made in Sweden, Czechoslovakia or the Unites States. 23.5 and 31cm (9¼ and 12¼in).

£25/$45*

▲ **73: Höglund the Sculptor**

Erik Höglund (1932–98) was probably Scandinavia's most idiosyncratic glass designer. Sculpturally trained, his designs for Boda (1953–73), remain the antithesis of the cool sophistication generally associated with Swedish glass. From left: People decanter, 26cm (10¼in); green tumbler with sticker *BODA Sweden Erik Hoglund*, 16cm (6¼in); amber tankard, 12cm (4¾in); and blue/grey vase, 19cm (7½in). Background: Boda publicity photograph, 1955.
From left: £125/$210, £15/$25, £25/$45, £45/$75

▼ **74: Scandinavian colours and effects**

From left: sky-blue vase, *c.*1965, from a series by Alsterfors, Sweden, 23cm (9in); grey lamp base, *c.*1955, stickered *Konstglas Vetlanda*, 30cm (11⅞in); *Harlequin* tumblers, Reijmyre, Sweden, probably designed by Monika Bratt *c.*1950, 15cm (5⅞in); textured aquamarine vase, 1968, Magnor, Norway, 13.5cm (5¼in); ruby liqueur glass, designed by Monika Bratt, for Reijmyre, Sweden, *c.*1965, 5cm (2in); green textured vase, *c.*1967, Alsterbro, Sweden, 25cm (9⅞in); goblets with bubble inclusion ball feet, designed by Bo Bergström for Aseda, Sweden, 1960s, 13cm (5in); red tube vase, *c.*1972, probably Alsterfors, Sweden, applied with sticker for British glass importer *S Jones*, 15cm (5⅞in); sky-blue vase, 1970, signed *PO Ström 70*, Alsterfors, 25cm (9⅞in); cast *Snowball* night-light holder, designed by Ann Wärff for Kosta in 1973, 7.5cm (2⅞in); and cast *Maljakko* chalice from the *Kivi-Set* series, designed by Pertti Santlahti for Humppila, Finland, in 1970, 25cm (9⅞in).
£5–50/$9–85*

- 1960s: More exuberant, off-beat shapes, brighter colours, increasing use of textured decoration and a Swedish trend towards primitive forms and decoration and casting.
- 1970s: Even brighter colours, more exaggerated texturing, more casting (picture 77).

The 1950s and '60s witnessed rapid growth in Nordic glassmaking, with the establishment of new works to meet international demand: 21 new enterprises were founded in Sweden alone from 1945 to 1970 (picture 70). These were supplied with fresh design impetus by further waves of fresh talent. For example, between 1963 and 1965, Bertil Vallien joined Åfors, Ann and Goran Wärff went to Kosta (picture 76), Lars Hellsten joined Skruf, Christer Sjögren arrived at Lindshammer, and Monica Backström was united with Erik Höglund at Boda.

The resulting momentum in Scandinavian design inspired Frederik Lunning, a New York-based Dane, to establish a prize in their honour. The following recipients of the Lunning Prize (1951–70) form the glass-making *crème de la crème* of Scandinavian post-war design: 1951: Tapio Wirkkala, Iittala, Finland; 1954: Ingeborg Lundin, Orrefors, Sweden; 1955: Kaj Franck, Nuutajärvi, Finland; 1956: Timo Sarpaneva, Iittala, Finland; 1957: Erik Höglund, Boda, Sweden; 1966: Gunnar Cyrén, Orrefors, Sweden; 1968: Ann and Göran Wärff, Pukeberg, and Orrefors and Kosta respectively, Sweden; 1970: Oiva Toikka, Nuutajärvi, Finland.

Höglund, chief designer at Boda for 20 years from 1953, possessed an exceptional talent. Trained as a sculptor, his unique perspective catapulted glass into previously uncharted territory. Breaking from the style of cool Modernism, he injected the medium with humour and insisted that his

designs be produced in impure bubbly, streaky, and striated glass (picture 73). His wonky mould-blown shapes were decorated with scenes of comic/erotic slapstick, or applied with large blobs sealed with primitive symbols or naked women. Following his lead, Viktor Berndt recreated scenes from cave paintings for Flygsfors, and the success of Lars Hellsten's robust figurative and expressive designs for Skruf encouraged Orrefors to recruit him in 1972.

Norway's previously leading role subsided during the 19th century. However, the generally sober of designs of Willy Johansson for Hadeland (1947–88), and the colour-splashed and oxide-stained work of Benny Motzfeldt, for Randsfjord and the Plus Studio, are beginning to draw international attention.

The oil crisis of the late 1960s and the ensuing economic downturn took its toll on glassmaking. In 1970, Sweden employed 4,000 glass-makers, including 700 at Åfors and 450 at Orrefors. By 1979, the total had halved to 2,050. During the interim, Orrefors had increased its domi-nance while its lesser competitors had crumbled. Under new ownership itself from 1971, Orrefors bought Alsterfors in 1972, Flygsfors in 1975, Strömberg in 1976, and Gullaskruf in 1977, all of which were closed by 1980. The trend toward centralization continued with Orrefors' takeover of Kosta/Boda/Åfors in 1990. Then Orrefors was sold to Royal Copenhagen (already the owner of Venini and Holmegaard) in 1996, and again in 2005 to the New Wave giftware conglomerate.

The story was repeated elsewhere, with Finland's Riihimäki closing in 1990 and Nuutajärvi now a shadow of its former self. Iittala was only recently liberated from the shadow of a multinational combine. Elsewhere, Holmegaard gradually swallowed its rivals to become Denmark's only

△ 75: Post-war Kosta

Art school-trained Mona Morales-Schildt quit her job as a department store manager in 1957 to emerge as Kosta's leading 1960s designer. Her work is distinguished by strong colour combinations, often complemented by radical cutting. *Hourglass* vases, 1965, 32cm (12⅝in), and *Venata* vase (centre), 1961.

Hoursglass vases £150/$255, Centre £250/$425

◄ 76: Scandinavian art glass

Top: Monolithic sculpture, designed by Göran Wärff for Kosta in 1966, signed *Kosta 95691 Wärff*, produced at least until 1971.29.5cm (11⅝in). Below: *Aurinkopallo* (*Sun Ball*), designed by Timo Sarpaneva for Iittala in 1960, produced until 1970. 10–25cm (3⅞–9⅞in) diam.

Ball £245/$415
Obelisk £450/$315

◄ 77: Pukeberg casting and pressing

Pukeberg, of Nybro, Sweden, is best known for its 1970s cast and hand-pressed glass, designed by Uno Westerberg (rear), Göran Wärff (front) and Eva Englund (right). However, many *solifleur* block vases by Walther of Germany, similar to that on the left, are erroneously attributed to Pukeberg. Candlestick (*c.*1970): 19cm (7½in). Flower block (*c.*1970): 10cm (3⅞in). Blue ashtray (1962): 12.5cm (4⅞in) wide. Eggcup/salt (1965): 7.5cm (2⅞in) wide.

£20–45$/35–75

▲ **78: Tiffany, Loetz, and Quezal**

From left: Top: Iridescent bowl by Quezal, New York, 1902–24, 35.5cm (14in) diam; Loetz iridescent vase applied with fake LCT signature, c.1895, 25cm (9⅞in). Bottom: Tiffany table-lamp, 1900–1910, sold in 2002 for the sum below, 67cm (26½in); Tiffany Favrile goblet, c.1905–10, 24.5cm (9⅝in).

Bowl £650/$1,105; Vase £200/$340*; Lamp £200,000/ $340,000; Goblet £900/$1,530

▲ **79: Carnival glass**

Iridescent Carnival glass was Tiffany glass for the working classes. Originally sold for a few cents, certain rare examples now change hands for mega-money. Top: *Pony* pattern bowls, one in marigold, the other in deep amethyst. Both by Dugan/Diamond (1913–31). 25cm (9⅞in) diam. Bottom: Footed bowl in the Imperial Glass Co.'s *Rose Lustre* pattern. 16cm (6¼in) diam.

£25/$45

sizeable glassmaker, though Hadeland and Magnor both survive at least partially by virtue of Norway's oil wealth. With the cost of producing handmade glass in Europe rising ever more steeply, the few remaining survivors will need steely determination and cost-control, combined with excellent design, to survive another generation.

United States

The story of American 20th-century glassmaking mirrors that of other nations, but, characteristcally, in a more exaggerated form. Its basic recipe is familiar: a thin upper crust of luxury producers above a thick slice of cheap, low-grade utility makers, and sandwiched between the two, a narrow filling of fine decorative glass.

The most important differences between American and European 20th-century glassmaking are, first, the scale of their respective markets and, second, America's greater use of industrial/automatic production methods. The United States, with a population of around 80 million in 1900 rising to 300 million in 2000, formed the world's largest consumer market, and both produced and imported more goods than any other nation. To provide an idea of the scale of American table-glass making, its industry employed 50,000 in 1969, when the equivalent figure in Sweden was 4,000.

The top American makers, led by Louis C. Tiffany and Steuben Glass Works, of Corning, New York State, were entirely craft-based. They were followed by a limited number, including Fenton and Imperial Glass, which employed traditional skills alongside automatic processes. Beneath them lay the remainder, which used technology to mass-produce cheap and cheerful utility ware.

American craft glass

Louis Tiffany, heir to the jewellery fortune, founded his first glassworks in Brooklyn in 1885, and designed objects, stained-glass, and lamps. Some of his effects, particularly the iridescent *Favrile*, were derivative, borrowed from Britain's Webb and France's Pantin, with whose products they can be confused (picture 78). Nevertheless, Tiffany's best work ranks among the greatest in Art Nouveau glass, and the presence of his distinctive *LCT* signature remains a serious value-booster.

Tiffany was not alone during the heyday of American iridescent glass, c.1900–25. His studios continued long after his retirement in 1919, and similar effects were devised by Quezal of Brooklyn (picture 78), from 1901, and Steuben at Corning, New York State, from 1903. However, their market was dented by the advent of superficially similar Carnival glass, pressed in the coal-rich Pennsylvania/West Virginia/Ohio tri-state area of the Mississippi basin. While three Tiffany vases cost the same as a new car, barrels of Carnival could be bought for less than the price of a headlamp.

Carnival, an American invention, was made by spraying fully formed pressed pieces with a chemical "dope", as opposed to the craft method of mixing metallic oxides into batches of raw materials. It was produced by five principal American glassworks: Fenton, Northwood, Imperial, Dugan/Diamond (picture 79), and Millersburg, with lesser contributions by Westmoreland and US Glass. Methods and popular patterns were rapidly copied across the glassmaking world, from India to Argentina, making this a complex area with nearly 2,000 patterns now recorded in almost 60 different colours.

Most Carnival glass remains relatively cheap, with modern values based on the familiar criteria of rare patterns, desirable colours, condition, etc. Orange marigold, blue, and amethyst are generally common colours, but smoke is rare. The record price for a piece of Carnival, $95,000 (£55,000), was paid for a Northwood *Peacock at the Fountain* pattern punch set in aqua-opal. However, the vast majority changes hands for under $100 (£60), and many patterns continue to be reproduced.

Steuben, a leader in fine Art Nouveau iridescent glass, was founded as a joint venture between Frederick Carder and Thomas Hawkes, of Corning's leading glass-cutting works, T.G. Hawkes. Originally intended to provide Hawkes with colourless blanks, Steuben was soon producing more daring work, including cameo, *pâte de verre*, and iridescent gold *Aurene*. Carder devised a total of around 7,000 shapes and 140 colours, and is now acclaimed a hero of American glassmaking.

Steuben was taken over in 1918 by Corning Glass, founded in 1868, whose prosperity was based on its invention and international licensing of oven-proof *Pyrex* (p.200). Demand for coloured art glass slumped during the Depression, and Carder was promoted out in 1932. His successor as chief designer, Sidney Waugh, adopted the Swedish model

▲ **80: Brilliant cutting**

Top left: Square low bowl cut in the *Radius* pattern by Straus & Sons, New York, c.1900. Lazarus Straus, a German immigrant, started his rich-cut-glass business in the basement of Macy's department store. The Straus family eventually owned Macy's and was responsible for some of the finest rich-cut-glass of the era. 28cm (11in) diam. Right: Footed ewer, made by Dorflinger & Sons of White Mills, PA, in 1901, and cut in the *Mercedes* pattern by T.B. Clark & Co. of Honesdale, PA. 29cm (11⅜in). Bottom left: Footed and handled comport bowl. Cut in the *Wamsutta* pattern by the Pairpoint Corp. of New Bedford, MA, c.1905–9. 23cm (9in).

Clockwise from top £850/$1,450; £4,400/$7,500; £1,800/$3,000

◀ ▲ ▶ **82: Depression Glass**

Left and right: Sorbet glass and carafe in the *Cubist* pattern produced by the Jeanette Glass Co., 1929–33, and the Indiana Glass Co., 1933–40. Glass: 12cm (4¾in); carafe: 26cm (10¼in). Top: 1929 catalogue illustration of the US Glass Co.'s acid-etched and gilded *Deerwood* pattern, derived from Moser's superior *Fipop*, c.1920 (p.55).

Left £5/$9, Right £20/$35

▲ **81 Steuben glassware**

Left: Modernist vase with scroll base. Signed: *Steuben SHS1983*. Originally designed in the 1950s by George Thompson, it was reissued in 1983 as part of the Steuben Historic Series (SHS). 20cm (7⅞in). Right: Frog figure with a 22-carat gold crown, one of many Steuben animals. Designed by James Houston, c.1966. Signed: *Steuben*. Background: Ship's decanter, based on an antique form, priced at $310 in Steuben's 1977 catalogue.

Left £75/$130, Right £100/$170

of sculptural objects and superior vessels in colourless and clear-tinted glass. This remains Steuben's principal focus today, often in the form of reprises of its greatest hits (picture 81).

Depression glass

Those works that survived the Crash largely did so through mass production. The necessary technologies included Owens' automatic blowing machine, with 200 operational by 1920, and the gob feeder and IS (individual section) machines, introduced from 1925, which allowed the simultaneous production of differing items within one piece of equipment. The resulting pieces are today generically named Depression glass, though this term is often used to categorize most American low-grade utility glassware made before, during, and after the Depression.

Depression glass was produced by at least 19 American works, but most notably by the Indiana, Jeannette (picture 82), Hocking (picture 83), Federal, US, MacBeth-Evans, and Hazel-Atlas companies, which produced a combined total of 92 patterns. The first, *Avocado*, was introduced in 1923, while the most enduring, Westmoreland's *English Hobnail*, spanned 1928–83. These were formed in a variety of colours and qualities, from rough, fully automatic to hand-finished, and most depended on busy patterns to disguise their poor quality.

Fenton and Blenko

Fenton Art Glass, founded at Martins Ferry, Ohio, in 1905, straddles the divide that separates craft and industrial American glass. It was a major

▲ 83: Anchor Hocking

Dating from 1880, Hocking survived the Depression, unlike many of its competitors, through the introduction of blowing machines that enabled tumblers, for instance, to be sold at "2 for a nickel (5¢)". Oven-proof *Fire King* was just one of Hocking's best selling lines. From top: Green- and yellow-stained *Kimberly* mug, 1970s, 9cm (3½in); *Good Housekeeping* magazine advertisement, 1952; opaque-white *Golden Shell* cream jug, probably 1950s, c.10.5cm (4in); and sticker for the *Peach Lustre* range, 1951–65.

£5/$9

▶ 84: Blenko

Founded in 1893, Blenko survived early disasters to become one of America's most dynamic post-war glassmakers. Drawing on myriad influences, from the Scandinavian repertoire to contemporary art, the results spanned the range of colour, shape, size, and taste. Left: *Amberina* vase, shape 6223, 1962. 31.5cm (12⅜in). Right: Publicity photograph of mould-blown spirit decanters, 1964. c.25cm (9⅞in) inc.

Vase £40/$70, Decanters £125/$210

producer of Carnival glass, but also ventured into utility and art pieces. It still produces reproductions, including so-called Mary Gregory-painted cranberry and vintage Carnival, often in its former competitors' moulds.

America's most interesting mid-ranging works, from an international viewpoint, is Blenko (picture 84). Founded in Milton, West Virginia, in 1922, it specialized in coloured window glass before it branched out into hand-made decorative and vessel glass. Unusually, design played a major role at Blenko, which employed a series of full-time designers, including Winslow Anderson (1946–53), Wayne Husted (1953–64), and Joel Philip Myers (1964–72). The result was an outpouring of distinctive wild and wacky shapes in vivid colours, which continues, still under family direction, today.

American studio glass

Myers' departure from Blenko into studio glassmaking in 1972 was indicative of a trend. Reacting against the dominance of industrially generated glass, a small core of interested artists had met at Toledo, Ohio, in 1962. Led by Harvey Littleton and Dominick Labino, the resulting workshop led directly to the foundation of the American studio-glass movement (picture 85). The key to its success was the development of miniaturized furnaces that could facilitate garage glassmaking.

Over the following years, Littleton's base at the University of Wisconsin became the incubator within which dozens of students were transformed into evangelists for home glassmaking. Thousands are now involved, from hobbyists to Dale Chihuly's 200-employee empire at Pilchuck, near Seattle; Chihuly installations (picture 86) generate millions of visitors.

▲ **85: Marvin Lipovsky**

Lipovsky, Dale Chihuly, and Fritz Dreisbach, all trained by Harvey Littleton and Dominick Labino, were the evangelists/teachers of the American studio-glass movement. Their work remains revered and they taught most of today's leading figures. Free-blown candy-stripe *Venini 7* art object, c.1974.

£2,500/$4,250

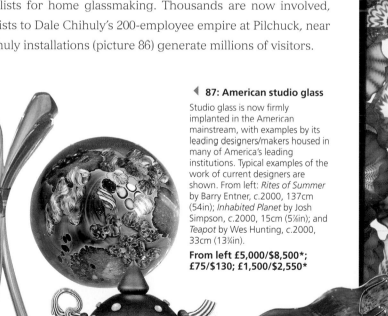

◀ **87: American studio glass**

Studio glass is now firmly implanted in the American mainstream, with examples by its leading designers/makers housed in many of America's leading institutions. Typical examples of the work of current designers are shown. From left: *Rites of Summer* by Barry Entner, c.2000, 137cm (54in); *Inhabited Planet* by Josh Simpson, c.2000, 15cm (5⅞in); and *Teapot* by Wes Hunting, c.2000, 33cm (13¾in).

From left £5,000/$8,500*; £75/$130; £1,500/$2,550*

◀ ▲ **86: Dale Chihuly**

His extraordinary creations, twinned with piratical looks and rock-star image, have made Dale Chihuly the world's most famous glassmaker. From top: unique art object (unnamed), 1968; unique *Malina Window*, 1993 , 5m (16ft); *Tangerine Macchia with Imperial Blue Lip Wrap*, 1985, 38cm (15in).

£6,000/$10,200*

◀ **88: Renaissance goblet, c.1475**
Enamelled and gilded goblet in cobalt-blue glass, made on Murano. 20.5cm (8in). Sold in 1998 for the sum below.
£144,000/$245,000

It remains to be seen which studio glass withstands the test of time (picture 87), but the happy fact remains that small-scale glassmaking is currently enjoying a dynamic renaissance in the United States.

Murano, Italy

Murano, the small Venetian lagoon island, has always occupied a unique position in the history of world glassmaking, because of its longevity, influence, colours, and quality. Its idiosyncratic position remained unique during the 20th century for different reasons. These include:

- Its output has been almost exclusively objects of no practical use.
- Only a tiny proportion of Murano glass bears indelible maker or designer marks.
- The leading makers produced anonymous "tourist trinkets" as well as branded exhibition pieces (picture 91).
- Its makers routinely copied each others' work, considering this to be a complement to the originator.
- The island remains home to scores of tiny studios that apply their work with various generic *MADE IN MURANO* stickers (picture 96).
- The presence of a maker-identifiable sticker can multiply the value of a given piece by a factor of at least 100.
- Certain leading designs have been produced for decades, while others have been and continue to be faked (picture 97).
- Some leading designers worked for several studios.
- Academic interest in Murano glass, and the literature dedicated to it, is almost exclusively focused on rare examples, and not those generally available from flea markets and junk shops.

▲ **89: Early 20th-century reproductions**
Authentic reproductions of Venetian Renaissance glassware formed the majority of the output of Murano glassmakers from c.1865 to the 1920s. Background: page from Antonio Salviati's 1867 illustrated catalogue. Foreground: Renaissance revival vase, probably by Salviati & Cie, 1890; and goblet, probably by Cappellin, c.1920. 15.5 and 13.5cm (6 and 5¼in).
Vase £150/$255, Goblet £75/$130*

◀ **90: Later Venetian Reproductions**
It can be difficult to differentiate between 1920s and later reinterpretations of classic Venetian glass. The ruby glass and cobalt bowl are probably post-war, but the jug and tumbler are probably by Salviati & Co, c.1925. From left: Ruby glass, 8cm (3in); glass and jug, latter 20.5cm (8in); cobalt-blue bowl, 6.5cm (2½in high).
Jug set £600/$1,020
Others £15–30/$25–55

Murano glass enjoys many attributes. It abounds with historic context, is generally colourful, technically demanding, and intellectually stimulating. Indeed, some of the greatest glass produced during the 20th century was made on Murano. However, "serious" Murano glass can also be a nightmare: an academic area, not one for those of limited means or those not prepared to make mistakes. It is not unusual to witness even its specialists inspecting prospective purchases with furrowed brows, fearing that they might be close to acquiring close copies or fakes.

Those happy to collect Murano glass on a superficial level can enjoy its spectrum of colours, techniques, and effects for relatively little outlay. Over the course of the 20th century, the island's glassmakers produced hundreds of thousands, if not millions, of pieces, most of them unique and of infinite variety. The vast majority of these were originally bought as pocket-money souvenirs and remain available across the world priced at similar sums (pictures 91 and 94). However, anyone wanting to acquire the finest pieces by the leading designers will need to dig deep, because these can be more expensive, weight-for-weight, than gold.

Top-end collecting in all categories is rife with the "I'm not interested in anything but the finest" syndrome. However, academics and connoisseurs of Murano glass rank as championship contenders in this respect. It is telling that when images of about 75 examples of Murano glass (picture 94), randomly collected over many years, were inspected by leading dealers in the field, their unanimous reaction was "rubbish!". This is typical of the outright snobbery that afflicts Murano glass, as, unknown to those being consulted, several of the pieces involved bore the stickers of famous makers. Specialist collectors' books invariably urge readers to base their collecting on what they like, not on potential value. This advice cannot be more strongly put than in this case.

Twentieth-century Murano glass can be divided into five distinct phases:
1900–30: The retro period, or the *Stile Liberty* A term borrowed from the London store that specialized in turn-of-the-century Arts & Crafts. During this period thin-walled ancient forms were revived and

▲ 91: Free-formed Murano animals

Animal figures have been made on Murano for almost 1,000 years. Then as now, they attracted the attentions of both the leading makers/designers and lesser figures. From left: opaque-pink elephant, designed by Ercole Barovier for Barovier Seguso Ferro, c.1935, bearing original foil sticker, one of two sold for £8,640 ($14,690) in 2003, 23cm (9in); colourless elephant with gold inclusions, probably by Ercole Barovier, c.1940, with original Barovier & Toso sticker, 11cm (4¼in); free-blown green penguin decanter, c.1950–60, with sticker for di Empoli, Florence, 25cm (9⅞in) inc.; opaque-pink cat, c.1950, applied with *MURANO GLASS* gold foil sticker, 11cm (4¼in); free-formed *Sommerso* bull, c.1960–70, 13.5cm (5¼in); crowing cockerel with colourless-over-gold body, c.1965–70, 31.5cm (12⅜in); colourless-over-turquoise flamingo on golden rock, anonymous, c.1970, 33cm (13in); and *Sommerso* duck, attributed to Alfredo Barbini, c.1960s, 14cm (5½in)

Barovier elephant £5,000/$8,500
Others £30–50/$55–85

▲ 92: Ercole Barovier 1950s & '60s

The identification of the work of individual Murano designers is fraught with difficulties because so few pieces are signed and their output was so varied. This collection shows just a small part of the work of Ercole Barovier, most from just one decade of his 50-year design career. From left: Back: Laguna *Gemmata* vase, c.1950, with blue inclusions, probably made by Ferdinando Toso, exhibited at the Venice Biennale, 1951; iridescent, lightweight *Evanescenti* vase, from a series produced over many years – this example won gold at the Milan Triennale, 1954; *Aborigeni* vase, produced in four colours – amber-yellow, purple, deep green, and lizard-green – first exhibited at the Venice Biennale, 1954; and herringbone pattern opaline *A spina* vase, first exhibited at the Venice Biennale, 1958. Front: Iridescent jade-coloured *Eugeneo* art object, 1951; and unique, iridescent bowl tinted with metalic oxides, 1959–60, 34cm (13⅜in) diam.

£600–2,000/$1,020–3,400*

▲ **93: 1960s & '70s** *Sommerso*

Known in English as colour casing. From left: vase, c.1960; table-lamp, c.1965; cut object, 1970s or '80s; and four-layer vase, probably 1970s. 8–32cm (3–12⅝in).

£35–£500/$60–850*

▲ **94: Murano "tourist glass"**

In the absence of secure designer/maker attributions, most Murano glass falls into the category of "tourist pieces". The above selection is typical of what the term is used to describe. The techniques illustrated include *Sommerso* casing; *Zibrato* patterns; gold, silver, and other metallic oxide inclusions; and paperweight-cane *Murrine*. 5.5–51.5cm (2⅛–20¼in).

£15–100/$25–170

slightly simplified, and generally formed in clear, softly tinted glass. The decoration of these pieces was often exclusively based on optically moulded ribs, diamonds, etc. The leading makers included the Barovier family (picture 92), Salviati (pictures 89 and 90), Fratelli Toso (p.26), and, from 1921, Venini and, from 1925, MVM Cappellin (picture 89).

1930 and '40s: *Stile Novecento,* **or New Century** A period of experimentation inspired by the work of Maurice Marinot (p.32). Murano glass became markedly heavier and more sculptural, and less functional. The trend was toward thick-walled vases in bold, sometimes opaque colours, with lustred finishes or with bubble or metallic-oxide inclusions. These were often applied with wings or random trails, or featured furnace-drawn nodes. The leading designers included: Ercole Barovier (for Barovier & Toso) (picture 92), Carlo Scarpa (Venini), Napoleone Martinuzzi (Venini, then Zecchin-Martinuzzi), and Flavio Poli (Seguso Vetri d'Arte).

1950s: *Forme Nuove,* **or New Form** This was the greatest, most dynamic and expressive period: one of the most dazzling decades of artistic creativity in the history of glassmaking. With a host of new designers combining imagination with superb craftsmanship, the results often left the fine art of the period looking tame in comparison. While occasionally appearing wild, the best Murano glass of the 1950s, was achieved with superb technical precision, often incorporating fine trails

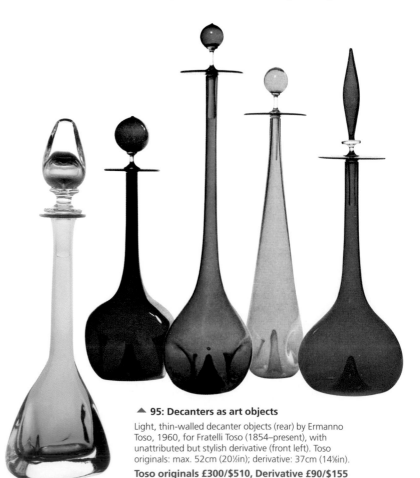

▲ **95: Decanters as art objects**

Light, thin-walled decanter objects (rear) by Ermanno Toso, 1960, for Fratelli Toso (1854–present), with unattributed but stylish derivative (front left). Toso originals: max. 52cm (20½in); derivative: 37cm (14⅝in).

Toso originals £300/$510, Derivative £90/$155

and filigree, coloured patches, deep-cut slashes, and paperweight-cane *Murrine*. The leading designers were Flavio Poli and Ercole Barovier (picture 92), Dino Martens (for Aureliano Toso), Fulio Bianconi and Paulo Venini (Venini), Alfredo Barbini, and Archimede Seguso.

1960s–80s: The calm after the storm The death of Paulo Venini in 1959 marked the end of an era in more ways than one. Venini had trained as a lawyer, but his immaculate taste and commercial acumen had propelled his glassworks onto the world stage, and drawn his compatriots with him. Calm, symmetry, and more muted colours became the order of the day. With the focus switching away from Murano, it was no coincidence that some of Venini's most distinctive designs of the period were by a Finn, Tapio Wirkkala (p.166), and an American, Thomas Stearns.

1990s–present: America returns the favour It is ironic that Murano, the spiritual home of studio glassmaking, has the American studio-glass movement to thank for its recent renaissance. After two decades or more in the artistic doldrums, Murano received the kiss-of-life through the flamboyant creations of the likes of Dale Chihuly, who had trained for a year at Venini in 1969 as a Fulbright Scholar. Repaying his debt to Murano, Chilhuly has since worked extensively with many of its maestri, most notably Lino Tagliapietra (picture 98), raising their international profile, particularly in the lucrative American market.

▲ **96: Differing Murano stickers**
From left: used exclusively by Archemede Seguso; Generic; Vistosi, also with green background.

▶ **97: Murano fakes**
Stickers can be misleading, so beware fakes. Top: free-blown green vase with opaque-green and yellow stripe, fraudulently applied with a genuine Barovier & Toso sticker as used 1971–84. 21.5cm (8½in). Below: modern vase in the style of Dino Martens for Vetreria Aureliano Toso, 1955, applied with *MADE IN MURANO* sticker. 19.5cm (7⅝in).
Left £10/$17
Right £40/$70

◀ **100: 1950s Murano silvering**
Millions of pieces of pressed and mould-blown Murano glass were embellished with fired silver decoration, usually featuring tourist scenes. These are entirely disavowed by today's purists. Decanter: 22cm (8⅝in); ashtray: 10cm (3⅞in) diam.
£10–25/$17–45

▶ **99: Non-Murano Italian glass**
From left: Free-blown *Tortoiseshell* decanter, Vetri di Empoli, Florence, 1970s, 18cm (7in) exc.; auto-blown giant decorative bottles/decanters, some examples marked *MADE IN ITALY*, probably Bormoili, Palma, 1970s, max. 58cm (22¾in); and mould-blown vase with paper sticker: *MADE IN ITALY*, possibly Bormoili, 1950s–60s. 25cm (9⅞in).
£10–40/$17–70

▶ **98: Modern Murano**
Lino Tagliapietra (1934–) is probably Murano's best-known contemporary glassmaker. Free-formed, furnace-worked, cased, and cut art object, c.1995. 60cm (23¾in).
£5,000/$8,500*

Collecting by Category

Animals

Glassmakers have attempted to capture the characteristics of animals in their work for almost as long as they have known how to create glass itself, and their variety has proved wide enough to fill a veritable Noah's Ark. Over the centuries, numerous decorators have incorporated representations of beasts in their patterns, while some glassworkers formed vessels and objects in animal shapes, whether adopting a humorous approach or remaining strictly naturalistic.

The most recurrent historical animal form has been the gin or schnapps pig, with variations produced across Europe since the Renaissance. However, the increasing scale of the glass industry, the broadening diversity of its designs, and the growth of the gift and novelty markets, most notably since the inter-war era, encouraged a huge increase in the number of bestial forms and figures. Most major glassworks in Europe and North America, from the most basic to the most exclusive, have produced ranges of animal figures over the past half-century.

▲ c.1650

Free-formed bear-shaped bottle/flask, with applied limbs, in rustic German *Waldglas*. The head serves a dual purpose as stopper and taster-tumbler. German or Bohemian. 31cm (12¼in).

£7,000/$11,900*

▼ 1928 and 1970

Cast, frosted, and polished sparrow paperweight designed by René Lalique, 1928. Engraved signature: *R Lalique, France.* 6cm (2⅜in). Pressed and frosted swan ashtray designed by Marie-Claude Lalique, c.1970. 7cm (2¾in).

Sparrow £450/$765*
Swan £45/$75

◀ 1930

Cast and polished zebra in Alexandrite glass and cut duck trinket pot. Zebra designed by Vally Wieselthier, for Curt Schlevogt, Jablonec, Czechoslovakia. 16.5cm (6½in). Duck designer unkown. 15.5cm (6in).

Zebra £400/$680
Duck £150/$255

▶ 1960

Free-formed *Pulcino* birds with copper legs and *Murrine* eyes. From a series of five birds designed by Alessandro Pianon, for Guglielmo Vistosi, Murano. The orange version is the most common. Max. 30cm (11⅞in).

£1,500–2,000/ $2,550–3,400*

◀ c.1960s and '70s

Long-tailed birds by Vicke Lindstrand (right) and Ronald Stennett-Willson (left). Lindstrand, 1960s, engraved: *Lf1,* 17.5cm (6⅞in). Stennett-Willson, (RSW5013) 1970s, *WEDGWOOD* sticker, 15.5cm (6in).

Both £65*

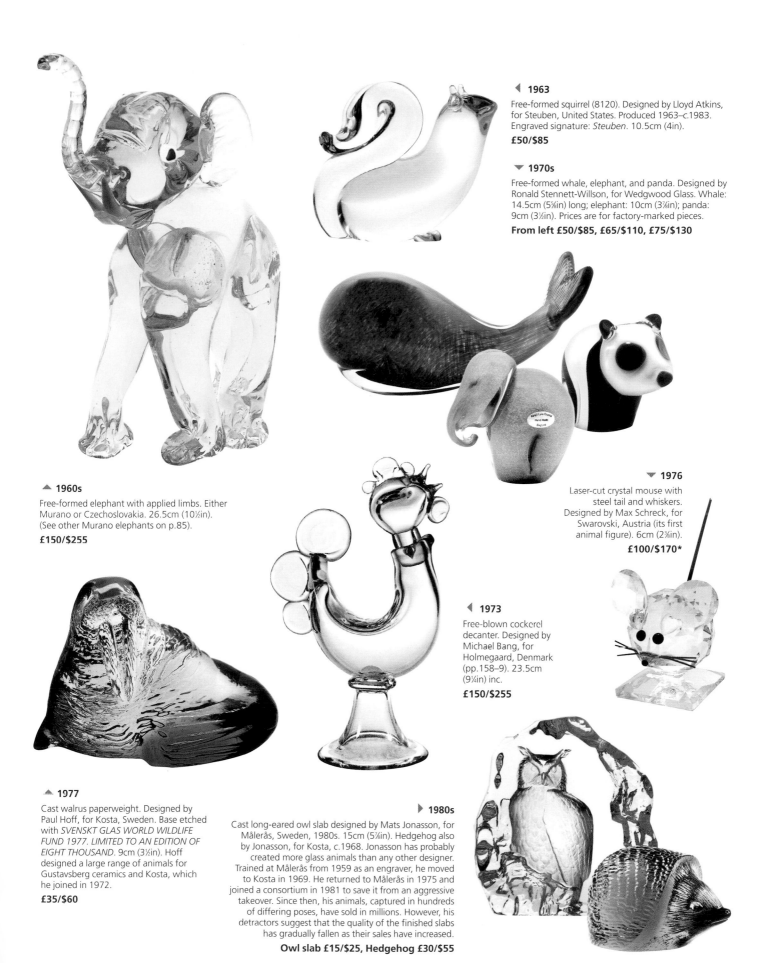

▼ 1963

Free-formed squirrel (8120). Designed by Lloyd Atkins, for Steuben, United States. Produced 1963–c.1983. Engraved signature: *Steuben*. 10.5cm (4in).

£50/$85

▼ 1970s

Free-formed whale, elephant, and panda. Designed by Ronald Stennett-Willson, for Wedgwood Glass. Whale: 14.5cm (5⅝in) long; elephant: 10cm (3⅞in); panda: 9cm (3½in). Prices are for factory-marked pieces.

From left £50/$85, £65/$110, £75/$130

▲ 1960s

Free-formed elephant with applied limbs. Either Murano or Czechoslovakia. 26.5cm (10½in). (See other Murano elephants on p.85).

£150/$255

▼ 1976

Laser-cut crystal mouse with steel tail and whiskers. Designed by Max Schreck, for Swarovski, Austria (its first animal figure). 6cm (2⅜in).

£100/$170*

◄ 1973

Free-blown cockerel decanter. Designed by Michael Bang, for Holmegaard, Denmark (pp.158–9). 23.5cm (9¼in) inc.

£150/$255

▲ 1977

Cast walrus paperweight. Designed by Paul Hoff, for Kosta, Sweden. Base etched with *SVENSKT GLAS WORLD WILDLIFE FUND 1977. LIMITED TO AN EDITION OF EIGHT THOUSAND.* 9cm (3½in). Hoff designed a large range of animals for Gustavsberg ceramics and Kosta, which he joined in 1972.

£35/$60

▶ 1980s

Cast long-eared owl slab designed by Mats Jonasson, for Målerås, Sweden, 1980s. 15cm (5⅞in). Hedgehog also by Jonasson, for Kosta, c.1968. Jonasson has probably created more glass animals than any other designer. Trained at Målerås from 1959 as an engraver, he moved to Kosta in 1969. He returned to Målerås in 1975 and joined a consortium in 1981 to save it from an aggressive takeover. Since then, his animals, captured in hundreds of differing poses, have sold in millions. However, his detractors suggest that the quality of the finished slabs has gradually fallen as their sales have increased.

Owl slab £15/$25, Hedgehog £30/$55

Suncatchers

These decorations were produced at several Scandinavian glassworks during the 1970s. The often colourful glass discs, impressed with a variety of differing motifs, were hung against windows to "catch the sun". They were formed by pouring a small quantity of molten glass onto an iron slab, flattening and rounding its edges, then pressing into it a mould impressed with the design.

The largest versions were designed by Per Lütken in1975 (p.156). Perhaps the most distinctive are Michael Bang's *Noah's Ark* series, designed as production items in 1969 and not, as suggested elsewhere, as a commission from the zoo at Odense, the town where he worked at that time. They were produced between 1970 and 1976 and sold in large numbers. The series comprises Noah himself and pairs of elephants and giraffes. Each was made in green and various shades of blue, red/amber, and coral, with diameters ranging between 5 and 20cm (2 and 8in). The smaller versions were probably made as hippie jewellery, intended to be hung around the neck on leather thongs. The largest series of suncatchers was a colourless group designed by Kerttu Nurminen for the Finnish Nuutajärvi works from 1977, several of which featured Christmas motifs.

Fishing-net floats are another form of "hanging glass" produced by several 20th-century European glassworks. Dating from shortly after the invention of glass-blowing *c*.60AD, they were used for suspending fishing nets in the sea, or tied on long ropes to identify the location of lobster and crab pots. They were often formed in brightly coloured glass to make them easier to locate. Their practical function was gradually usurped from the 1930s by the advent of more robust substitutes in metal and plastic, but they continued in production for decorative purposes at several glassworks, including Holmegaard (pp.138–161), Davidson (pp.108–15), and Nazeing (pp.180–3). New versions are now being produced at Indian and Chinese glassworks. Old examples tend to be in coarse glass and contained in net chord rather than string.

▲ ▼ **1969**
Pressed-glass *Noah's Ark* suncatchers and paperweights. Designed by Michael Bang in 1969 and produced 1970–6. 5–20cm (2–7⅞in) diam. From Holmegaard's 1970 catalogue.
Small £12/$20, Large £30/$55*

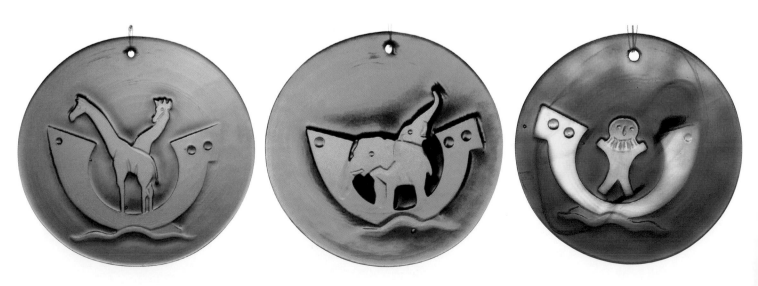

▲ **1966**

Hanging ball. Possibly designed by Michael Bang. Holmegaard produced a series of hanging balls from 1966 to 1970 in *Rubin* transparent, yellow opal, white opal, *Coral* opal, *Ocean blue*/opal, and *Edelgreen*/opal. 7.5–25.5cm (2⅞–10in) diam.

£50/$85

▲ *c.* **1968**

Hope Anchor symbol suncatcher in amber. Designed by Michael Bang. The symbol is derived from the ancient expression "Hope is the anchor of the soul." 9.5cm (2⅜in) diam.

£20/$35

▲ **1974**

Clover leaf suncatcher. Designed by Michael Bang. 13.5cm (5¼in) diam.

£20/$35

▶ **1975**

Owl-shaped suncatcher. Designer and maker unknown. 18cm (7in).

£25/$45

▲ *c.* **1965**

Turquoise *Naked Man* suncatcher designed by Erik Höglund for Boda, Sweden. Engraved: *11866/b*. 24cm (9½in).

£50/$85

▲ **1969**

Sunspot suncatcher designed by Geoffrey Baxter for Whitefriars, 1969. 18cm (7in) diam.

£80/$135

◀ *c.* **1970s**

Fishing-net ball. 15cm (5⅞in).

£15/$25

▶ **1975**

Colourless suncatcher impressed with a star. Designed by Christer Sjogren, for Lindshammar. 17cm (6¾in) diam.

£20/$35

LASIKORISTE/GLASSDEKOR/GLASSDECORATION/GLASDEKORATION/				
Design Kerttu Nurminen 1977	**DÉCOR DE FENÊTRE/** 窓の飾り物			NEW

619001	65 mm 2½ in 1/12	enkeli	angel	ange	エンゼル
		ängel	engel		
619004	65 mm 2½ in 1/12	kide	snowflake	flocon	雪片
		kristall	schneekristall		
619007	65 mm 2½ in 1/12	lintu	bird	oiseau	鳥
		fågel	vogel		
619008	65 mm 2½ in 1/12	omena	apple	pomme	りんご
		apple	apfel		
619011	65 mm 2½ in 1/12	sydän	heart	coeur	ハート
		hjärta	herz		
619090	65 mm 2½ in 1/12	1990 PRO NATURA			牛飾り物

▲ **1977**

Bell colourless suncatcher. Designed by Kerttu Nurminen. 6.5cm (2½in) diam. Background: Illustration from Iittala/Nuutajärvi's 1990 catalogue showing full range.

£12/$20

Beer glasses

Beer has been brewed for longer than bread has been baked, with known recipes dating back 7,000 years. The Pharaohs consumed it from gold goblets, and glasses designed for beer were produced during the Renaissance. Their quality ranged from the sublime, featuring luxurious decoration, to the ordinary.

The most recurrent problem with pub and tavern glasses was that their sizes were often imprecise and publicans regularly appeared in courts, charged with supplying short measures. The advent of glass-pressing and improved moulding technology from the mid-19th century overcame this problem. Sizes were regularized and each glass applied with legally enforceable marks stating their capacity.

Twentieth-century beer glasses, often bearing the names of brands and breweries, are a fast-growing area of collecting. A recent Google search for "beer glass" registered 11 million hits, many of them traceable to collectors and dealers. Central European examples, hand-enamelled in bright colours, rank among the most attractive, but even plain, undecorated ones are attracting interest for their differing methods of manufacture and capacity-authenticating marks.

▲ **1619**
Richly enamelled *Reichsadlerumpen*, incorporating the date *1619* in its decoration. Beer glasses such as this were expensive and used as symbols to express a host's wealth and status as they were passed around the table, each guest drinking in turn. 30.5cm (12in).
£8,000/$13,600

◀ **1880**
Victorian pressed beer glass, the foot impressed with *IMPERIAL ½ PINT*. Publicans were notorious for providing their customers with short measures, so glasses such as this were intended to provide the appropriate reassurance. 15cm (5⅞in).
£35/$60

▶ **1900–1918**
German beer tankard printed with *BENKELLER BRAUEREI, DEUTSCH-SUDWEST-AFRIKA WINDHUK* and its logo. Base impressed with the crown logo of the Radeberg glassworks, near Dresden, southern Germany. 20.5cm (8in). The company's 1928 catalogue illustrates this tankard, although German South-West Africa ceased to exist after 1918.
£45/$75

▲ **1910–36**
British pint beer glasses, all marked with the *GR* cipher for George V, who reigned 1910–36. From left: Dip-moulded, marked *GR323*, 13.5cm (5¼in); pressed-glass, marked *GR542*, 15.5cm (6in); mould-blown, marked *GR323*, 15cm (5⅞in). 323 was the number of the Gateshead Weights & Measures Office; 542 was Newham, London.
£25/$45, £20/$35, £20/$35

▶ **1928**
Pewter-lidded pressed-glass *Stein* tankard hand-enamelled with *GEYNER BRAU, MÜNCHEN* and its logo. Engraved with *0.5l* and the date *1912*. 18.5cm (7¼in) inc. Background: Page from the Radeberg glassworks' 1928 catalogue illustrating the same glass without the lid.
£45/$75

▶ **1920–30s**
Amber and yellow British pressed-glass half-pint and pint beer tankards. Left: *Beer Can No. 2*. Made by Bagley of Pontefract (pp.96–101). 11cm (4¼in). Right: Possibly by Davidson of Gateshead (pp.108–15). 13cm (5in).
Left £15/$25
Right £20/$35

1930–50s

Czech hand-enamelled beer glasses bearing the German names *MUNSTER BIER* and *WEIHENSTEPHANER CHAMPAGNER WEIZENBIER*, and the Czech *PILSNER URQUELL*, and their logos. 24, 26.5, and 18cm (9½, 10½, and 7in). German law demanded that every bottle and drinking glass produced in Germany should bear an engraved scratch-line and the numerical value of its contents before leaving the glassworks. The Urquell glass has a similar acid-etched mark – *HALF LITRE TO THIS LINE GR239 LCC* – which was applied at Southwark under the auspices of the London County Council.

£50/$85

1953

Pressed-glass tankards commemorating the coronation of Elizabeth II, 1953. Left: Dimpled half-pint printed with a crown and *Elizabeth R 1953*, the base impressed with *ENGLAND*. 9cm (3½in). Right: Flared-rim half-pint with *EIIR* moulded into one side, the queen's profile encircled by the wording *ELIZABETH II, CROWNED JUNE 1953* on the other. 11cm (4¼in).

£20/$35

1950s–80s

Selection of pressed and automatically blown British half-pint and pint tankards bearing the names of lagers and bitters, some of which no longer exist. 20.5cm (8in) max.

£2–10/$3–17

1970s–90s

Selection of European lager glasses. A market exists even for such glasses without significant age, though prices are low. Radeberger Bier: 20.5cm (8in).

£1/$2

c.1990

Optic-moulded half-pint tankard transfer-printed with the former logo of *TIGER BEER*, owned by the Singapore-based Asia Pacific Breweries, itself owned by Heineken. Like the beer, the glass was probably made in the Far East. 10cm (3⅞in).

£3/$5

Identification by Factory

Bagley 1871–1975

Bagley's Crystal Glass Company was probably Britain's most successful inter-war manufacturer of cheap and cheerful pressed fancy glass. Its soft-tinted ranges of vases, trinket sets, and jelly moulds sold to the working classes of Britain and its Empire in quantities of which fine-quality glassmakers could only dream.

Based near Pontefract, Yorkshire, at the centre of the bottlemaking area, Bagley's first noteworthy domestic range was *Queen's Choice* (*c*.1922), a shameless copy of the American *Chippendale*, 1907 (pp.112–13). Its *Honeycomb* pattern (1931) was similarly derived from the Jeanette Glass Company's *Cubist* range of 1929 (p.81).

Managed by cousins Percy and Stanley Bagley, glassmaker and businessman respectively, the company survived the trend toward closure and mergers through the progressive adoption of new technology. Under their supervision, the workforce increased from 200 in 1906 to over 800 in 1935.

Bagley produced large quantities of colourless domestic wares, including fridge boxes, but is best remembered for its soft-coloured blue, pink, green, amber, and blue *Crystaltynt* decorative ranges, dating from the early 1930s. The company maximized the use of its expensive moulds by manipulating the shape of some of its pieces, such as *Equinox* (1938), with tools after the moulding process to create two different shapes.

Bagley's most stylish designs were commissioned from Royal College lecturer Alexander Hardie Williamson (pp. 126–31). The full extent of his involvement remains uncharted, though it is probably safe to link Bagley's best 1930s ranges to his drawing board. Most *Crystaltynt* pieces remain common and cheap today. However, a small number of designs, including the *Koala Bear* vase (1936) (Bagley's most desirable design by far) and some table-lamps, are rare and sought-after.

The post-war ranges *Carnival* (1946), *Osprey* (1953), and black *Jetique* (1957) sold well, but Bagley slowly faded. It was taken over in 1962 and 1968, and then again in 1994. It is now owned by Stölze Oberglas AG of Austria, which employs around 200 workers producing perfume bottles for customers including Christian Dior, L'Oreal, Revlon, and Yves St. Laurent.

▲ **1933**

Pressed three-piece *Wyndham* flower set (1333) designed by Alexander Hardie Williamson. Produced 1933–75. 18cm (7in) inc. plinth. The *Wyndham* design series, vase, clock, and trinket set was registered in December 1934 (Rd No. 790482). Optional black plinths and flower-arranging inserts were made for most Bagley vases.
£25/$45

Lamp 3003

Centrepiece 3003 with block on plinth

Trinket Set. 3008 4 piece

"CRYSTALTYNT"
IS MANUFACTURED IN FOUR COLOURS
GREEN, BLUE, AMBER,
OR
ROSE PINK

BLOOM RING 6" & 9"

THE CRYSTAL GLASS CO.
KNOTTINGLEY YORKSHIRE ENGLAND

▲ **1934**

British magazine advertisement promoting Bagley's coloured fancy glass, in green, blue, amber, and rose. These colours were not augmented until the introduction of black *Jetique* in 1957. The items illustrated include the 3003 lamp, the 3003 centrepiece vase/bowl, and the 3008 trinket set. Probably all designed by Hardie Williamson.
Lamp £175/$300, Vase £30/$55, Ring trough £3/$5

▲ **1953**

Pressed *Electrolux* fridge box. Produced 1953–75, plain or embossed with *Electrolux* name. 16cm (6¼in) square. The design was derived from Wilhelm Wagenfeld's similar boxes for Vereinigte Launsitzer, Germany, from 1938 (produced until 1968). Lindshammar, Sweden, produced similar boxes for Electrolux from 1954. The Rosice glassworks, Czechoslovakia, produced unmarked boxes from 1958.

Square (illustrated) £15/$25
Rectangular £20/$35

◀ **1934**

Bagley magazine advertisement for pressed rabbit jelly moulds. Produced 1934–early 1950s in quarter-, half-, and full pint sizes (the smallest are the rarest). Bagley produced many differing moulds, of which the rabbits became one of their best selling products, although they never appeared in the company's catalogues.

Large £20, Medium £25/$45, Small £25/$45

▲ **1953**

Pressed *Osprey* tumbler and honey pot (3153). Produced *c.*1953–75. Tumbler: 13.5cm (5¼in); honey pot: 11.5cm (4½in).

Tumbler £15/$25, Honey pot £25/$45

KEY DATES

1871 Bagley, Wild & Co., bottlemakers, founded at Knottingley, Yorkshire.

1890 Name changed to Bagley & Co.

1899 Company expands rapidly under cousins Dr Stanley and Percy Bagley. Buys patent for Arnell's semi-automatic bottlemaking machine, typical of early adoption of advanced technology.

1912 Bagley establishes table-glass subsidiary, the Crystal Glass Co., to make pressed copies of fashionable cut designs, but remains principally a bottlemaker throughout its history.

c.1922 New pattern based on the American *Chippendale* introduced.

1924 Queen Mary buys selection of Chippendale copy at Wembley Exhibition, renamed *Queen's Choice*.

1933 First coloured pressed-glass, including Art Deco *Wyndham*,

Grantham, and 3002 patterns, designed by Alexander Hardie Williamson (pp.126–31).

1937 Factory visited by King George VI and Queen Elizabeth.

1939–45 Production redirected towards military needs.

1946 Colour-tinted opaque range, *Crystopal*, launched.

1957 Black *Jetique* range launched.

1962 Ownership passes to former Bagley apprentices, brothers John and Tom Jackson, after deaths of Stanley and Percy Bagley.

1968 Bottlemaking giant Rockware assumes control of Bagley/Jackson Brothers.

1976 Fancy-glass production ceases due to shortage of skilled labour.

2005 Bagley, part of Austrian-owned Stolzle Flaconnage, continues to produce high-quality bottles for cosmetics industry.

1928

Pressed and frosted *Pendant* fruit bowl (724). Design registered in 1928 (Rd. No. 742290). 22cm (8⅝in) diam.

£5/$9

BAGLEY OR NOT BAGLEY?

The full extent of Bagley's output remains unknown because numerous pieces with a distinctly "Bagley-look" and formed within its limited colour range do not appear in known catalogues or advertisements. Its well-known rabbit jelly moulds, for instance, were never mentioned in Bagley catalogues, although they were advertised in 1934. These pieces would appear to have been made by Bagley, though further research will be required before direct links can be proven.

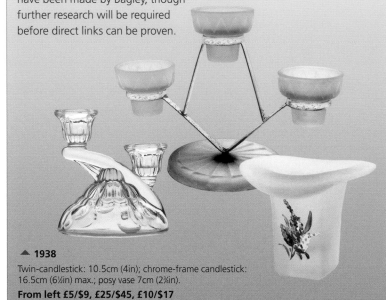

1938

Twin-candlestick: 10.5cm (4in); chrome-frame candlestick: 16.5cm (6½in) max.; posy vase 7cm (2¾in).

From left £5/$9, £25/$45, £10/$17

1931

Pressed *Honeycomb* sugar bowl and honey box. Copy of *Cubist* pattern produced by American Heisey and Jeanette glass companies (p.81). Sugar bowl: 7cm (2¾in); honey box: 6cm (23/8in).

Sugar £7/$12
Honey box £20/$35

1932

Pressed *Salisbury* vase and frosted fruit boat (2832). Produced 1932–75. Vase (sold with or without a black plinth): 17.5cm (6⅞in); fruit boat: 26.5cm (10½in) diam.

£15/$25

1933

Pressed three-piece *Spinette* diamond posy vase. Produced 1933–75. 13cm (5in) inc. plinth. Early attempts at creating this pink used arsenic, which was both expensive and hazardous. However, its use was later abandoned after the discovery that immersing a large potato into the molten glass achieved the same effect.

3-piece £30/$55

1934

Pressed *Grantham* clock and vases (all 334). Designed by Alexander Hardie Williamson. Produced 1934–75. This clock is one of two *Grantham* clock designs. The range also included a wall-hanging vase (334). Clock: 16.5cm (6½in); vases: 16cm (6¼in) (top left), 10cm (3⅞in) (bottom), 20.5cm (8in) (right).

Vases (each) £18–40/$30–70*
Clock (working) £50/$85

1936

Pressed and frosted *Tulip* lamp (3025). Probably designed by Alexander Hardie Williamson. Produced 1936–early 50s. One of several Bagley lamp designs. 24cm (9½in).

£70/$120

1936

Pressed *Koala Bear* vase. Produced for a limited time and reputedly restricted to the Australian market. Retailed with square black plinth. A metal-mounted *Kookaburra* wall lamp, probably also intended for Australia, was illustrated in the company's 1936 catalogue. 20cm (7⅞in).

£400/$680

1937

1936

Pressed bloom troughs in different shapes. Produced 1936–75, in various sizes. Other shapes included horseshoes, diamonds, hearts, and arcs. An EIIR set commemorated Queen Elizabeth's coronation in 1953. Bagley workers disliked making these as it was difficult to pour the molten glass into the moulds.

£2/$3

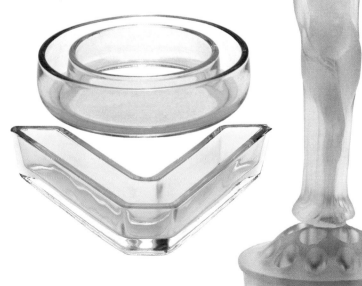

1936

Pressed *Andromeda* figurine. Produced 1936–75. *Andromeda* figures were fitted into various Bagley vases and flower blocks. The company also produced a pelican figurine. Similar figures were produced by several glassworks, though only Bagley's versions have chained or roped ankles. 20cm (7⅞in).

£15/$25

1937

Pressed *Split Diamond* water jug (3030). Produced 1937–early 1950s. Design registered in July 1937 (Rd. No. 821905). The pattern was restricted to this jug and matching tumblers. 15.5cm (6in).

£5/$9

▲ 1937

Magazine advertisement for pressed *Leaf* pattern (3055). Produced 1937–75. The design was reputedly based on an acanthus plant in an employee's garden. Dessert bowl: 14cm (5½in) diam.

£3/$5

▼ 1938

Pressed and frosted *Bedford* powder pot, part of a dressing-table trinket set. Produced 1938–c.55 13.5cm (5¼in).

£15/$25

▲ 1938

Pressed *Equinox vase* and bowl (3061). Produced 1938–75. These pieces were made in the same mould. Initially formed as a vertically-sided vase, the upper section was either paddled together with wooden tools to form the left-hand example, or opened to create the right-hand one.The closed form was also produced as a lamp (3061C) until 1975. Left: 11.5 (4½in) high. Right: 14cm diam (5½in).

Left £15/$25, Right £5/$9

▼ 1937

Pressed *Suite 59* water jug. Produced 1937–75. 18cm (7in). Tumblers in four different sizes completed the suite.

£5/$9

▲ 1938

Pressed *Fish Scale* fruit bowl on chrome plinth (3067). Produced 1938–53. The *Fish-Scale* pattern extended through a large number of differing vessels, some with chrome fittings. 21.5cm (8½in).

£15/$25

▲ 1938

Pressed *Sunburst* jugs/vases. Produced 1938–early 1950s. The "jugs" have either turned-down (left) or horizontal pourers, while the "vases" have none (right). 18 and 24.5cm (7 and 9⅝in).

Left £40/$70, Right £70/$120

METAL-MOUNTED BAGLEY

Bagley glassware was fitted into metal mounts by at least two British metalmakers: James Clarke & Sons of Stoke-on-Trent, and J. Zimmerman & Co. of Birmingham. Clark advertised chrome-plated frames containing Bagley's *Shell Ice* dish in 1950. The association between Bagley and Zimmerman resulted in dozens of items that combined Bagley dishes and bowls with Zimmerman frames during the 1950s and '60s. A Zimmerman trade advertisement from 1959 illustrated several Bagley pieces in leafy frames, and stated that Zimco produced "500 lines in Chrome Tableware…".

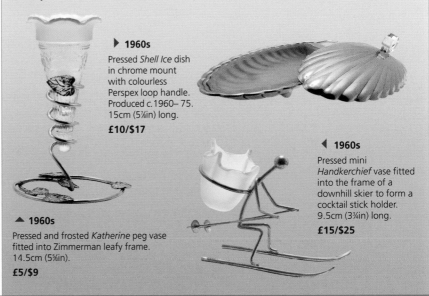

▲ **1939**

Pressed *Fish Plate* (3123). Produced 1939–75. 23cm (9in) square.

£20/$35

▶ **1960s**

Pressed *Shell Ice* dish in chrome mount with colourless Perspex loop handle. Produced c.1960–75. 15cm (5⅞in) long.

£10/$17

◀ **1960s**

Pressed mini *Handkerchief* vase fitted into the frame of a downhill skier to form a cocktail stick holder. 9.5cm (3¾in) long.

£15/$25

▲ **1960s**

Pressed and frosted *Katherine* peg vase fitted into Zimmerman leafy frame. 14.5cm (5⅝in).

£5/$9

▼ **1946**

Magazine advertisement from 1946 for pressed *Carnival* pattern (3141). Produced 1946–75. Applied to about 20 different shapes. Design registered November 1946 (849118). 2,400 pieces of *Carnival* could be produced in a single shift. Cream jug: 9.5cm (3¾in). Cheese dish 21.5cm (8½in) long.

Jug £5/$9, Dish £15/$25

▲ **1957**

Advertisement from 1961 announcing new shapes to the pressed black *Jetique* range. Produced 1957–75. Many items in the range were applied with white vitreous enamel polka dots, others with transfer-printed enamelled motifs including bouquets and Highland dancers. From left: *Handkerchief* vase: 9.5cm (3¾in); *Ocean* vase (3206): 11cm (4¼in).

£5–20/$9–35*

▼ **1975**

Pressed *Wild Oak* Handkerchief vase. Probably designed and produced in 1975, but when Bagley ceased making fancy glass in 1975, the moulds for *Wild Oak* were transferred to Rockware who produced it for a short period. 15cm (5⅞in). The centre of the base is impressed with a large White Rose, the symbol of Yorkshire. The design combined Bianconi's *Handkerchief* vases for Venini, (from the mid-1940s, p.107), with frost-textured pieces by Wirkkala and Sarpaneva for Iittala, from the early 1960s (pp.162–77).

£10/$17

Chance / Fiesta Glass 1824–2000

Chance Brothers, based at a huge 16.6-hectare (41-acre) site near Birmingham since 1824, was a family-run glassworks whose products ranged from laboratory and lighting glass to radar screens and ashtrays. It installed lighthouse lenses in 80 countries, including 75 around the USA and 45 in China; and 22,000 tons of Chance Brothers' glass were used to clad the Crystal Palace of the Great Exhibition, the most innovative building of the 19th century.

Chance's foray into domestic glass began in 1934, when it commissioned Royal College lecturer Robert Goodden (1909–2002) to design the pressed *Spiderweb* range, based on the ribbing of lighthouse lenses, and a massive seller in 1934–9/1945–53. *Aqualux*, an experiment in forming domestic vessels from glazing glass, was halted by the outbreak of war in 1939, but resuscitated in the early 1950s as *Fiesta*.

Goodden returned with further designs from 1949 to 1952, including *Waverley, Britannia, Lotus, Gossamer,* and *Cato*. However, production was focused from 1953 on heat-slumped *Fiesta,* after pressing was abandoned when exports fell because of rising protectionist tariffs.

A succession of further designs stemmed from Royal College of Art contacts from c.1955 to the early 1970s. The *Swirl* pattern and the *Giraffe* carafe (both 1955) have been tentatively linked to Goodden. These were followed in 1958 by *Night Sky,* by Margaret Casson, wife of RCA lecturer Hugh, then *Calypto* and *Anenome* by RCA student-turned-tutor Mike Harris (1959 and '62). A further series, including *Honeysuckle, Ocean Spray, Gold Spray,* and *Filigree* (1970) were commissioned from the Queensberry Hunt partnership, headed by RCA tutor David Queensbury, and executed by his former student, Sue Heaven.

Chance did not make hollow-ware, so it outsourced the tumblers, goblets, jugs, and carafes for its *Fiesta* ranges to makers including Nazeing (p.180) and Dema, Chesterfield. Its jugs were imported from Portugal, though the maker of the mould-blown *Giraffe* carafe remains unclear.

Pilkington, owners of Chance since 1945, eventually sold Fiesta to its management in 1981. The resulting company, Fiesta Glass, produced slumped *Special Occasion* items and best selling patterns, including *Swirl* and *Anenome,* until c.2000. Heat-slumping was resuscitated in 2002 by Anthony and Richard Joseph, sons of a former Fiesta Glass chairman.

◀ 1950s

The distinctive Chance logo, based on the signature of Sir Hugh Chance, company chairman. It was applied to all its products, and was impressed into some of its pressed table-glass.

◀ c.1958–70

The logo was dropped in c.1958 and replaced with a gold foil sticker.

◀ 1970–81

◀ 1981–2000

The sticker of Fiesta Glass Ltd.

CHANCE PRESSED-GLASS

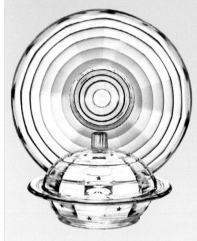

◀ 1934

Pressed-glass *Spiderweb* bowl and jam pot. Designed by Robert Goodden and produced 1934–9 and 1948–53. The *Spiderweb* pattern was clearly inspired by Chance's role as a maker of lighthouse lenses. Goodden had trained as an architect, but turned to industrial design in the 1930s, when he worked extensively with Chance. In 1948 he was appointed professor of Silversmithing and Glass at the Royal College of Art, where he remained until 1974. Bowl: 21cm (8¼in) diam.; jam pot: 15cm (5⅞in) diam.

£5–30/$9–55*

◀ 1949

Pressed-glass *Waverley* fruit bowl. Probably designed by Robert Goodden and produced 1949–53. 24cm (9½in) diam.

Pink £20/$35
Colourless/green £10/$17

◀ 1950

Pressed-glass *Britannia* dish, the recesses in the pattern highlighted in white. Probably designed by Robert Goodden and produced 1950–53. Chance publicity material stated in 1951 that "variety is provided within each by the addition of ceramic colour, sprayed on or hand applied, and by gold edging or banding". 24cm (9½in) diam.

£15/$25

The cover of the first issue of the in-house magazine, *Chance Comments*, March 1948. Also a stamp issued by Chance in 1951 to commemorate the centenary of its Lighthouse Works. The cover of the magazine features Jack Batten checking an optic on the lens of Pulau Angsa Lighthouse in the Malacca Straits.

▶ 1955

The *Giraffe* carafe, probably designed by Robert Goodden, was among the most distinctive glass shapes of the post-war era. Its blank was bought in because Chance did not produce hollow-ware. It was discontinued in 1981 when Pilkington liquidated Chance, closed the Spon Lane works, and sold its tableware division to its management. 30cm (11⅞in).

£30/$55*

▶ 1951

Graphic designed in 1951 to promote Chance's lighting glass division at the time of the Festival of Britain.

KEY DATES

1824 Robert Lucas Chance buys the British Crown Glass Co. at Smethwick, near Birmingham.

1836 Robert's bother William joins the company; name changed to Chance Brothers. Specializes in window, stained, and optical glass, including lighthouse lenses.

1851 Chance Brothers supplies all glazing glass, 300,000 sheets, for the Crystal Palace building of the Great Exhibition. 1,200 employees.

1929 Launches *Orlak*, an oven-proof range of borosilicate glass to rival Pyrex. Its shapes, based on octagons, designed by Harold Stabler of Poole Pottery. Sold to Pyrex in 1933.

1934 Robert Goodden designs pressed-glass tableware pattern, *Spiderweb*, exhibited at British Art in Industry exhibition at Royal Academy in 1935.

1939 Launch of *Aqualux*, range of dishes formed from slumped textured glazing glass. Range comprises: *Hammered*, *Flemish*, *Stippolyte*, and *Maxine* textures.

1939–45 Wartime production of technical glass.

1945 Chance Brothers bought by glazing glass giant Pilkington. Installs fully-automatic pressing machines at new subsidiary, W.E. Chance.

*c.***1947** Pressed *Lotus* range, designed by Robert Goodden.

1948 *Spiderweb* resumes production: formed in bowls, vases, sundae dishes, glasses, and jug and tumbler sets.

1949 Pressed *Waverley*, followed by *Britannia*, 1950.

1951 New pressed ranges, *Lancer* and *Gossamer*, and Fiesta, formed from shaped colourless glazing glass. Fiesta launched with *Lace* and *Greco* patterns.

1952 Pressed *Cato* and Fiesta *Willow Pattern* launched.

1953 Slump in export sales causes closure of pressed-glass plant.

1955 Most extensive Fiesta pattern, *Swirl*, launched, probably designed by Robert Goodden. Produced into mid-1990s.

1970 Textured *Carnival* and *Tinted* glass added to Fiesta ranges.

1958 Chance's *Hankie* vases first advertised in September.

1965 Pilkington sells lighthouse division to Stones of Deptford.

1970 Textured glass added to *Hankie* range.

1981 Fiesta Glass, result of management buy-out, founded to continue production of Feista range.

1980s Fiesta Glass adds *Special Occasion* items, such as golden, silver, and ruby wedding, 100th birthday, etc., items to Fiesta ranges.

2002 Production of slumped table-glass, sold under Joseph Joseph trademark, transferred to Midland Industrial Glass, Birmingham.

Fiesta

1951–present

With its bold forms and patterns, the numerous *Fiesta* designs sold in millions and became virtually ubiquitous in post-war British homes. Chance's most successful venture into table-glass, *Fiesta* was a development of the *Aqualux* range, launched in 1939, but abandoned only months later at the outbreak of war. With the exception of drinking hollow-ware, the various *Fiesta* shapes were formed from sheets of flat glass shaped by slumping them over moulds in a furnace.

Cheap, easy to clean, and well designed, *Fiesta* was launched at the Ideal Home Exhibition in 1951, and gradually grew into a huge variety of screen- and transfer-printed wares. The first design was the doily-like *Lace* pattern, which was available in black, white, *Moss*, *Russet*, *Daffodil*, and *Delphinium*.

Many early *Fiesta* designs originated from the Royal College of Art. Robert Goodden, the creator of several of Chance's pressed ranges introduced between 1934 and 1950, probably contributed the most successful *Fiesta* shape and pattern: the *Giraffe* carafe and the *Swirl* pattern, 1955. These were followed in 1958 by *Night Sky*, by Margaret Casson, the wife of one Goodden's colleague's at the RCA, and *Calypto* and *Anemone*, 1959 and '62, by Michael Harris (pp.132–7), an RCA student.

During the late 1960s/early '70s, a series of further designs was derived from Queensberry Hunt, the consultancy established in 1966 by David Queensberry, head of the ceramics department at the Royal College. Queensberry did not undertake any Chance commissions personally, and the designer of the *Psychedelic* and Op-Art *Escher Hankie* vase patterns, *c.*1970, remains uncertain. However, Queensberry's employee, Sue Heaven, contributed several patterns, including the blue linear *Honeysuckle* and *Filigree* for the *Fiesta* range around 1971.

Although Pilkington closed Chance Brothers in 1981, a management buyout team relaunched Fiesta Glass immediately. Familiar designs, such as *Swirl* and *Anemone*, continued in production as late as the 1990s (albeit adapted for screen-printing as the original method of application, on a Deffa machine, was abandoned as too complex in 1981). Fiesta Glass' focus increasingly switched toward *Special Occasion* items, printed with slogans commemorating occasions as diverse as 80th birthdays and Holy First Communions.

▲ **1951 and '57**
Publicity photograph of gold-on-ruby *Greco* (left) and *Roset* bowls (both 1951), and cased and cut ruby ashtray (1957). These designs anticipated the *Spirograph* drawing toy, invented in 1962 y British engineer Denys Fisher during resarch into bomb detonators. The pattern on the ashtray is intaglio cut. Ashtray: 12.5cm (4⅞in) long.
Bowls £15/$25, Ashtray £45/$75

1951

JOHNSON MATTHEY TRANSFERS

The post-war period witnessed a huge rise in the use of transfers on glass. This was because they were far cheaper than the traditional types of glass decoration: cutting, engraving, and enamelling. The trend was encouraged by the invention of photolithographic printing, which encouraged a wide variety of colourful, detailed, naturalistic, and humorous motifs.

Johnson Matthey, best known as a refiner of precious metals, was Britain's largest producer of transfers, most of which were produced for the ceramics industry.

◀ **1952**
Johnson Matthey trade advertisement for its transfers, from *Pottery Gazette*. The left-hand margin illustrates the method of application.
Glasses £5/$9

1952

Auto-blown pint tumbler screen-printed with *Willow Pattern*. Chance bought in all the hollow-ware from other glassworks for the *Fiesta* ranges: the tumblers from Dema Glass, Chesterfield; the goblets from Nazeing (pp.183–6). 15.5cm (6in).

£10/$17

1959

Calypto goblet. Pattern designed by Michael Harris (pp.132–7). Harris accepted this commssion while a glass design student at the Royal College of Art, where he later taught the subject. He later designed *Anemone*, the best selling pattern in the *Fiesta* range (p.133). 13.5cm (5¼in).

£10/$17

▼ 1970

Carnival coloured slumped glass. The *Carnival* series was formed in Pilkington rolled plate-glass. The short-lived range comprised: colourless, textured *Glacier* and *Cotswold*, *Hammered* (front left, 27.5cm /10⅞in long), *Small and Large Flemish* (front right, 37cm/14⅝in long), and plain *Grey Dawn* (background), imported from Belgium. The range was launched alongside the similar *Tinted* range of *Hankie* vases (p.107).

£15–25/$25–45

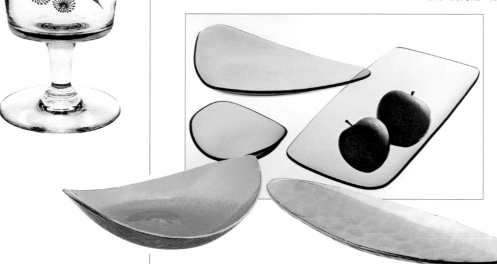

▼ 1955

A 1961 advertisement showing the *Swirl* pattern, probably designed by Robert Goodden. Items include the *Mini Bar*, comprising two differing sets of six glasses, price £4 5/- (£4.25), and the *Water Set*, of six tumblers, a *Giraffe* carafe, and a tray, priced at £2 7/6 (£2.35). The three-piece nibbles dishes, 18/9 (90p), were applied with a Design Centre approval seal. The gilt-metal frames were bought in from Birmingham metalmakers but were soon abandoned after demand outstipped an unreliable supply. The *Swirl* range, produced until the mid 1990s, extended through dozens of pieces. Carafe 31cm (12¼in).

Framed tumbler set below left £35/$60

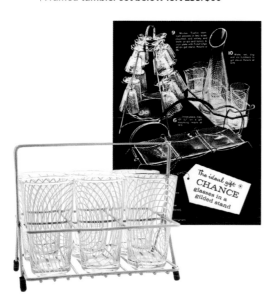

▲ 1958

Publicity photograph of *Night Sky* dish, tumblers, and *Giraffe* carafe. *Night Sky* was designed by Lady Margaret Casson, based on an astronomical chart, but it failed commercially and production soon ceased.

Entire set £90/$155

1970

▲ c.1970

Chance Brothers, and its successor, Fiesta Glass Ltd, were not the only British producers of heat-slumped table-glass. This dish, screen-printed with a *Spirograph*-type pattern, was made by one of its competitors, possibly Webb & Co., of north London. Designer unknown. 32cm (12⅝in) long.

£25/$45

▲ ▶ 1970

Honeysuckle (above) and *Filigree* (right) patterns. Both designed by Sue Heaven for Queensberry Hunt. Heaven also designed *Ocean* and *Gold Spray* at the same time. Both 25cm (9⅞in) diam.

£15/$25

Gala Greetings

▲ 1981–2000

Foreground: Slumped-glass silver appliqué 25th wedding-anniversary plate from the *Special Occasion* series. Designed by Robin Busfield, for Fiesta Glass' US distributor, Lefton & Co., in 1990. Background: Pages from Fiesta Glass' *Special Occasion* catalogue, c.1985, featuring a vast range of *Special Occasion* items. These ranged from special birthday paperweights for men and women to *Celebrity* fluted plates for milestone wedding anniversaries. By the 1980s, these items numbered over 300 and sold in their millions. As Fiesta director Tony Cartwright admitted: "Many of the designs were 20 years past their sell-by date, but they still sold so we continued to make them!"

£5/$9

▼ 1971

Chance employee screen-printing the *Canterbury* pattern (left) onto a dish. 21cm (8¼in) long. Screen-printing was introduced to replace the lithographic machine that had applied Chance's fine linear patterns, *Swirl*, *Calypto*, and *Filigree*. The patterns had to be simplified for the screen-printing process.

Dish £25/$45

▲ 1978

The transfers for *Immari* and the similar *Grantleigh* were supplied by their maker/designers, Johnson Matthey. However, *Immari* never entered commercial production and *Grantleigh* was soon relegated to the company's reject shop because of the physical difficulties arising from such large transfers.

£10/$17

▼ 2002

Bent-glass *Olive* dish and *Spectacles* tray. Both 30cm (11⅞in) long. Manufactured by Joseph Joseph. The Chance/Fiesta method of forming glassware from sheet glass was revived in 2002 by Joseph Joseph, led by Antony and Richard Joseph, twin sons of Fiesta's former managing director Michael Joseph. The resulting products continue to be decorated with transfers and screen-prints and slumped on Fiesta's old machines in Birmingham. The designs, created by Antony Joseph, Bo Lundberg, and the 3 Fish in a Tree consultancy, received an Excellence in Housewares Award in 2004.

£10/$17

HANKIE VASES

The original and ingenious *Handkerchief* vase was designed by Fulvio Bianconi and Paulo Venini for Venini, Murano, around 1948. Some were collaborations between both while others are credited to one or the other. They were exhibited in London in 1953 and featured in *Pottery Gazette* in 1955.

Numerous glassworks across Europe formed derivatives, including Holmegaard (p.157) and Bagley, which produced pressed versions, some in black *Jetique* (pp.101), from 1957. They were followed a year later by Chance's variant. Formed in glazing glass in the manner of most of the *Fiesta* range, Chance produced *Hankies* in three sizes: 17, 12.5, and 10cm (6¾, 4⅞, and 3⅝in), with the two larger ones hand bent, the smallest being moulded.

Chance's earliest *Hankies* were formed in ruby or blue-over-colourless glass off-cuts, soon followed by versions screen-printed in the manner of the *Fiesta* ranges. The patterns included *Cordon*, *Bandel*, *Polkadot*, *Blue*, *Psychedelic*, and the last, *Gingham*, introduced in 1977. A further series, *Tinted*, was formed from 1970 in textured amethyst, blue, and amber-tinted Chance rolled plate-glass and also in *Grey Dawn*, which was imported from Belgium.

◀ **1948**
Free-formed and grey-over-white cased *Handkerchief* vase. Designed by Paulo Venini, for Venini. Etched *VENINI MURANO ITALIA*. 27cm (10⅝in) high.
£400/$680

▼ **1958**
Chance Brothers slumped-glass *Hankie* vases. These early versions, in red-over-white and ruby-over-colourless, were formed from off-cuts from Chance's industrial glass. The series included blue-over-colourless intaglio-cut and white-over-colourless *Cut Pearl*.
**Left £200/$340
Right £100/$170**

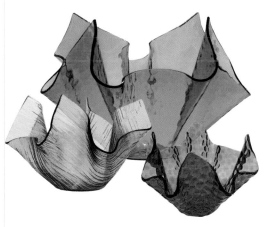

◀ **1970**
Gold, blue, and amber *Tinted* series *Hankie* vases. These were formed in off-cuts of rolled and textured plate glass. From left: *Cotswold* (gold), *Flemish* (blue), and *Hammered* (amber). Medium-sized versions are the rarest. 10, 13cm, and 17.5 (3⅞, 5, and 6⅞in) high.
**Left & centre £50/$85
Right £25/$45**

▶ **1958–90s**
The most common Chance *Hankie* vase patterns (shape No. 29). From left: *Polkadot* (introduced c.1970), *Cordon* (1958), and *Bandel* (c.1962). All were screen-printed and these small versions, called *Posy Bowls*, were produced into the 1990s. All 10cm (3⅞in) high.
£25/$45

▲ **1972**
Small *Escher* (left) and *Psychedelic* (right) pattern Chance *Hankie* vases with the original artwork for *Psychedelic* in the background. Designs attributed to Sue Heaven for Queensberry Hunt. These patterns failed commercially and were soon discontinued. 10cm (3⅞in) high.
***Escher* £50/$85, *Psychedelic* £40/$70**

George Davidson & Co. 1867–1992

George Davidson & Co. was one of Britain's largest producers of cheap fancy glass. Founded at the Teams Glass Works, Newcastle, in 1867, it specialized in pressed-glass until its closure in 1987.

Davidson's first products of note were the *Hobnail* suite, 1885, and the *Pearline* range of small baskets, salts, etc., from 1889, whose blue, *Primrose*, and *Moonshine* bodies were decorated with faux cutting and opaque-white rims. They were produced for several decades, copied at the time by the neighbouring Greener glassworks, and have recently been faked by Taiwanese glassworks.

Davidson stepped up a gear from 1891 when Tom Davidson (1860–1937), the founder's son, assumed control. He introduced a new design every year between 1889 and 1914, each being named after its year of introduction, with the exception of the 643 and 283 suites. The *Flower Dome*, perhaps the most innovative of all, was designed by Davidson himself. Introduced in 1910, these multi-holed blocks, known to some as "frogs", gave flower arrangements a greater stability than previously possible, and they sold in millions.

Davidson's most distinctive product was the random-trailed *Cloud* range, introduced from 1923, starting with purple (pp.110–11). The American-designed *Chippendale* pattern (pp.112–13), produced under licence from 1930 or '31, and bought outright from 1933, was probably Davidson's best selling range. Only three *Chippendale* shapes were produced in *Cloud*: the *1445* and *1446* bowls and a cress drainer. The success of *Chippendale* encouraged Davidson to produce the Czech-designed *Jacobean* ranges for Clayton Meyers, which had previously imported it, from *c*.1931 (pp.114–15).

Davidson introduced some stylish coloured vases during the 1930s, though their designer remains anonymous. Only one formal designer worked for Davidson throughout its entire history: W.J.G. Fullerton (1938–47). Few specific pieces have been definitively linked to him as yet, apart from the derivative *Ripple* series and *Fan Vase*.

Davidson struggled in the post-war era and was taken over in 1966 by Abrahams, a metal-plating company. However, in the absence of successful new designs, both *Chippendale* and *Jacobean* remained in production as late as the early 1970s. After a terminal decline, Davidson finally closed in 1987.

◄ Gold foil sticker
As applied to certain post-war Davidson glassware.

▲ ► 1891
Primrose-tinted *Pearline* salt. Produced 1891–1914. 3.5cm (1⅜in). And pressed blue tri-form basket (242), produced 1891–1914. One of five similar baskets (240–44), produced with and without an opaque-white upper rim. 8.5cm (3¼in).
Top £40/$70
Right £30/$55

▲ 1910
Flower Dome Block designed by Tom Davidson. Base embossed *MADE IN ENGLAND PATENT 47830/19120*. Instabilities created by their manufacture means that perfect *Flower Domes* are rare. 10cm (3⅞in).
£5/$9

◀ **1912**

Purple *Cloud* celery vase (283). A colourless version was produced 1912–42. During the 1920s, *Cloud* was produced in only amber, blue, red, and purple. 18cm (7in).

£30/$55

GEO. DAVIDSON & Co.
TEAMS GLASS WORKS,
GATESHEAD-ON-TYNE.

Manufacturers of the world renowned "DAVIDSON" Glassware, have pleasure in announcing that they have purchased the Moulds, Registered Trade Mark and Sole Manufacturing rights of the well-known "CHIPPENDALE" Glassware. This range of exquisite models is now being offered at reduced prices, and samples can be seen at the London Showrooms, 3, Charterhouse Street, Holborn Circus, E.C.1. Also, for the convenience of our numerous friends in the Provincial and Country Towns, samples of the "Chippendale" range will be carried by our representatives during the coming Autumn tours.

As all discriminating buyers realize, no stock will be complete without the elegant and charming "CHIPPENDALE" range, the beautiful quality of which is assured by it being a "DAVIDSON" production—which it has been for the last few years.

CHIPPENDALE
REG. TRADE MARK

▲ **1933–50**

Foil sticker applied to *Jacobean* glassware Produced in England by Davidson.

▶ **1933**

Davidson *Chippendale* advertisement, illustrating: low foot bowl round (T78); claret goblet (T1028); jug (pint to gallon sizes), (T420–23); vase (T1225–30); and (foreground) punch/fruit bowl, not illustrated in 1917 American catalogue.

Glass £5/$9, Fruit bowl £40/$70

KEY DATES

1867 George Davidson & Co. founded at Gateshead, near Newcastle-upon-Tyne.

1888 *Pearline* range introduced. The company launched one new product per year from this date until 1914, with each one generally named after the year of introduction, the only exceptions to the rule being the 643 and 283 suites.

1891 Tom Davidson (1860–1937) assumes control after the death of his father, George (1822–91).

1910 Tom Davidson patents *Flower Dome Block*.

1923 First *Cloud* glass colour introduced (purple), followed by blue, amber, red, orange, and green.

1929 First production of *Chippendale*, made for Charles Pratt's National Glass Co., London.

1932 *Jacobean* and *Georgian*, Czech pressed-glass patterns, enter production under licence from import agents Clayton Mayers.

1933 Company buys exclusive world rights and moulds to entire *Chippendale* range.

1937–47 Davidson employs its first and only designer, W.J.G. Fullerton.

1939–50 Production switched to basic utility and military glass.

1940–c.65 *Chippendale*-style patent *Toughened Tumblers* produced for Clayton Mayers, forming 14 per cent of Davidson's entire production.

1951 *Chippendale* patents renewed.

1954 Introduction of two new colours: black and *Lovat* (blue).

1957 New *Cloud* colour: *Briar* (amethyst/green).

1959 Davidson bought by J.M.E. Howarth and M. Pollock-Hill, the owner of Nazeing Glass (pp.180–3).

1966 Company taken over by Abrahams – chrome fittings manufacturer.

1966 Launch of colourless lead-crystal ranges.

1967 *Victorian* cut range launched, involving modern shapes with retro decoration.

1971 Solid-colour *Lunar Crystal* launched, bearing similarity to Whitefriars/Geoffrey Baxter's cased *Bark* designs.

1987 Davidson closes after losses of £160,000 in previous year.

1992 Company liquidated.

▶ **1912**

Parfait vase. Designer unknown. Produced 1912–42. This example, in matt green, was also produced in amber, purple, blue, green, and orange *Cloud*. 14cm (5½in).

£10/$17

▲ **1910**

Flower set with grid support (10/1910). Produced 1910–c.1960. The grid support insert was also fitted to the *Chippendale* 1547/10 flower set. 8.5cm (3¼in).

£15/$25

▶ **1928**

Flower bowl (697). Produced 1928–35 and 1960s. The pattern is a pastiche of *nipt diamonds*, a form of decoration as applied to Anglo-Venetian glassware, c.1670–85. It was also produced in amber, blue, and purple *Cloud* (679 and 679L) in 1928–35. 14.5cm (5⅝in).

£45/$75

▼ **1933**

Jade pressed-glass, applied to many existing shapes but no new ones bewteen February 1933 and April 1934. From left: Salt, possibly not Davidson, 3cm (1⅛in); candlestick, Davidson, 5.5cm (2⅛in); flower dome, 4.5cm (1¾in); bowl, 6cm (2⅜in). Jade was expensive to produce, costing 50 per cent more than equivalent pieces in plain colours, and was produced for just 14 months, in shiny and matt finishes.

£10–20/$17–35

1910

DAVIDSON CLOUD GLASS

Random-trailed *Cloud* was a form of coloured pressed-glassware introduced by George Davidson & Co., Gateshead, in 1923. The *Cloud* effect was achieved by adding molten trails of dark glass to lighter-coloured gathers just before the object was shaped in a manual glass press. The result was a range of strongly coloured vessels each filled with uniquely shaped ragged "clouds".

The rarest *Cloud* colours were those produced for the shortest time, namely red and orange. The range extended through all forms of fancy glass, including salad servers, ashtrays, table-lamps, boxes, and cake stands. Many of these were formed in existing moulds, some dating from as early as 1907. Only three shapes from the *Chippendale* range, two bowls and a cress-drainer, were formed in *Cloud*, though several other shapes are unique to the effect. Most *Cloud* vases and bowls were retailed with flower domes and black or matching plinths.

The *Cloud* colours were as follows: purple, 1923–34; blue, 1925–34; amber/tortoiseshell, 1928–57; *Ora* (red), 1929–32; orange, 1933–5; green, 1934–41; and *Briar*, 1957–61.

Several other companies made forms of *Cloud*, including James A. Jobling and Sowerby (UK); Walther & Söhne and Brockwitzer Glasfabrik AG (Germany); and S. Reich & Co. (Czechoslovakia).

(Dates refer to approximately the earliest use of the mould to shape them.)

◀ **1907–c.1960s**

Blue *Cloud* three-piece flower set (1907TD). Design registered by Davidson, 486298, 9/1906. *Cloud* colours available were amber, blue, green, orange, purple, and *Briar*. 13cm (5in) diam.

£35/$60

▶ **1932–40**

Green *Cloud* bowl (248F). Produced in amber, blue, green, orange, and purple. 12.5cm (4⅞in) diam. (25.5cm/10in for 699F.)

£125/$210

◀ **1925–40**

Orange *Cloud* bowl and stand (699). Produced in amber, blue, green, orange, and purple. Available at 18cm (7in) (S/696), 21.5cm (8½in) (696), and 25.5cm (10in) (699) diam.

£400/$680

▶ **1934**

Rose-tinted candlestick (from trinket set 340). Produced 1934–mid-1950s. Never produced in *Cloud*. 6cm (2⅜in).

£15/$25 a pair

▶ **1939**

Ripple pattern vase (741). Designed by W.J.G Fullerton; registered on 14/2/1939. The base embossed *G.Brit Rd: 833455 / Australia 19221*. Also made in amber, green and colourless. 18cm (7in). Also available at 13, 23, 28cm (5, 9, 11in).

£30/$55

▶ **1937–50s**

Black *Grecian* bowl (518/oval version: 519CF). The design for the original version of this bowl, the 314 round tomato dish, was patented in 1937 (Rd. No. 817751), though this black variant dates from 1959. Decorated in unfired, non-durable, household oil paints. 25.5cm (10in) diam.

£30/$55

▼ **1938**

Chevron vases (295). Designed by W.J.G. Fulleron. Registered on 12 March 1938. 16.5cm (6½in) and 21cm (8¼in).

£2/$3

▲ **1940**

Crystolac toughened tumbler. Produced 1940–c.1965 in their millions. Individual examples can be dated from the number of dots on the base: none for 1940, one for 1941, etc. This example, with three dots, was made in 1943.10cm (3⅞in).

£3/$5

▼ **1971**

Lunar Crystal posy bowl. Introduced as a cheap equivalent to Whitefriars' textured ranges. This model is virtually identical to a version produced by Davidson's competitor and neighbour, Sowerby of Gateshead. 17.5cm (6⅞in) diam.

£5/$9

Chippendale 1907–c.1970

Chippendale was probably the most distinctive of the thousands of pressed-glass patterns produced during the 20th century, and remains among the most avidly collected on both sides of the Atlantic. Originally designed in the United States in 1907, it was produced in England into the early 1970s and inspired numerous direct copies and derivative versions in both the USA and across Europe.

Chippendale was designed by William Jacobs of the Ohio Flint Glass Co. in 1907. Its name paid nominal homage to Thomas Chippendale (1717–79), though its Neo-classical lines owed more to the Scottish architect Robert Adam (1728–92) than to the English cabinet-maker.

Initially comprising 82 different vessels, the *Chippendale* range gradually grew to over 400 items. The rights to produce it and all its moulds changed hands four times in 22 years: three times within the United States, before finally passing to George Davidson & Co. of Gateshead, Britain, where it was exclusively manufactured from 1929. Davidson added to the range and exported it widely to colonial markets, though it failed to sell in Australia.

The vast majority of American *Chippendale* was produced in colourless glass, though some examples are known in a Vaseline yellow, whereas Davidson produced small quantities of it in amber and emerald and three items in *Cloud*. American pieces are marked with the impressed logo *Chippendale Krys-Tol* while British ones were sold with factory paper labels.

▲ c.1930s
Paper (left) and foil (right) *Chippendale* stickers from around the 1930s.

AMERICAN CHIPPENDALE

All these pieces were illustrated in the 1917 catalogue of the Jefferson Glass Company, Follansbee, West Virginia. Most were also produced in Britain by George Davidson & Co from 1930. The descriptions in italics are those used in the catalogue.

◄ 1917
Chrome-capped salt and pepper (T750). The 1917 catalogue illustrated versions with differently shaped aluminium caps. These examples are probably British, c.1930-40. 9cm (3½in).
£25/$45 a pair

▶ from 1917
Carnation Vase (T1253). The Krys-Tol range extended to 15 such vases (numbered 1260–83). This form is known generically as a *swung vase*: they are pressed with vertical sides, but were stretched on reheating and swung backward and forward. The rim was created by further reheating and manual tooling. 24.5cm (9⅝in).
£25/$45

◄ from 1917
Winged candlestick (T317). This particular design was registered by Benjamin Jacobs at the U.S. Patent Office on 18 June, 1907. 19cm (7½in). T314 and T319 also made, at 11.5cm (4½in) and 23cm (9in).
£40–80/$70–135 pair*

▶ from 1917
Oval sugar and cover (T953). 15.5cm (6in).
With cover £25 /$45

BRITISH CHIPPENDALE

Davidson produced *Chippendale* for the British and colonial markets under licence from 1930/31 and bought the exclusive world rights to its manufacture in 1933. Some pieces reputedly remained in production as late as c.1970. Most Davidson *Chippendale* is indiscernible from American-made pieces, except that none bears the *Krys-Tol* logo.

A fine academic line divides the designs of some pieces made by Davidson before it acquired the rights to the authentic *Chippendale* range. The candlesticks, bowl, and sherbet dishes illustrated here may not be genuine *Chippendale* pieces, but are extremely close approximations of them plagiarized and produced by Davidson before 1930.

▶ 1917

Nappy bowl in satin-finished green (T118). This shape was illustrated and described as a *Nappy* (a rimless, open dish) in the 1917 American catalogue. The satin finish on the exterior was achieved by dipping it in a hydrofluoric/sulphuric-acid solution. 24cm (9½in) diam.

£10/$17

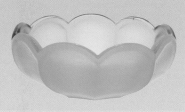

▼ 1922–36

Squat candlestick (Davidson 283). This candlestick does not appear in the 1917 American catalogue but is a shortened version of the T328 "Tall Candlestick". Regarded as a Davidson derivative and not a formal *Chippendale* shape. From top: Rose pink, c.1930; amethyst *Cloud* (produced 1923–34); jade (1931–4). Orange *Cloud* version was also produced (1933–5). 6cm (2⅜in).

£5–75/$9–130*

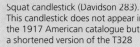

▲ 1930s

Footed Sherbert bowls, one with matching underplate. This was among the most popular of Davidson's *Chippendale* pieces, though colourless examples vastly outnumber tinted ones. Davidson also produced it in blue *Cloud* (471/2), with an underplate (279). 9cm (3½in).

£3/$5, with underplate £6/$10

CHIPPENDALE COPIES

Most successful pressed-glass patterns were copied by rival glassworks, but *Chippendale* inspired more than perhaps any other, in both the United States and Europe. Close approximations of it were produced in the USA by, among others, the Heisey, Duncan & Miller, Westmoreland, Cambridge, Indiana, and U.S. Glass companies, and in Europe by Riihimaki (Finland) and Walther & Söhne (Germany).

However, the version of *Chippendale* made by Bagley's Crystal Glass Co., of Knottingly, Yorkshire (pp.96–101), from c.1921, ranks among the most flagrant cases of glass-pattern plagiarism. Originally known as pattern 1122, it was renamed *Queen's Choice* after Queen Mary bought several pieces. Some *Queen's Choice* shows subtle design differences from its role model. Its celery or trophy vase, for instance, had a flat, horizontal rim where the *Chippendale* version was scalloped. However, in many cases, any differences between the original and the pretender are indiscernible. Bagley also produced copies of the Jeanette Glass Company's *Cubist* pattern under the trade name *Honeycomb*, and Whitefriars' *Glacier*, which it called *Wild Oak*.

▲ 1929

Chippendale "trophy vase", two copies, and a Bagley advertisement. Clockwise from top: Authentic *Chippendale Tall Celery* (T60), 19.5cm (7⅝in); unknown maker and date, possibly Jobling, 19.5cm (7⅝in); Bagley *Queen's Choice* version, 18.5cm (7¼in), as advertised to its left.

£15–20/$25–35*

Jacobean 1922–72

The *Jacobean* range of mostly colourless, pressed glassware, produced from 1923 to *c.*1980, ranks alongside *Chippendale* as the most common 20th-century glass pattern, though as yet it is not so avidly collected. It was designed between 1922 and 1930 by Rudolf Schrötter for Josef Inwald AG, an industrial glassmaker based at Rudolfova Hut, near Teplice, Czechoslovakia, which had over 1,000 employees by 1938.

Originally conceived as the *Lord* range, it was marketed as *Milord* in France, *Lirio* in Argentina, and *Jacobean* by its British import agents, Clayton Mayers, and their American counterparts, F. Pavel & Co. It proved an immediate success and within two years had been extended to 150 pieces. It was reported in Britain to have "spread all over the country like wild fire". By the mid-1930s, 275 *Jacobean* shapes were in production, with some examples formed in amber, rose pink, blue, green, and iridescent Carnival in *Marigold*.

Clayton Mayers promoted *Jacobean* with aggressive and pioneering marketing strategies. These included in-store display units, glass-for-cigarette-coupon promotions, prolific trade and public advertising campaigns, and an annual *Jacobean* Hostess who, in 1931, was the well-known actress Madeleine Carol. In that year, the company produced an advertising film, *Address Parade*, in which she demonstrated *Jacobean*'s beauty and utility. Twenty years later Clayton Mayers was first to advertise glassware on television.

A financial crisis in 1931 forced the British government to impose a 50 per cent tariff on all imported glassware. Though reduced to 20 per cent the following year, Clayton Mayers responded by persuading Inwald to switch the production of *Jacobean* to Davidson, which was already producing its principal rival, *Chippendale*. Besides colourless flint, Davidson produced certain *Jacobean* items in amber, emerald, rose, and blue.

Jacobean was produced by Sklo Union, Czechoslovakia until 1972, but Davidson's association with the pattern probably ceased in the early 1950s after Clayton Mayers acquired its own automatic glass production facilities. British production of *Jacobean* was switched during the mid-1960s to the United Glass plant at St Helens after container and domestic glass distributor Johnson & Jorgensen bought out Clayton Mayers. The final addition to the range was a beer tankard designed by Alexander Hardie Williamson (pp.126–31) in 1972.

▶ **1920s**
Foil sticker applied to *Jacobean* glassware sold in English-speaking markets, late 1920s.

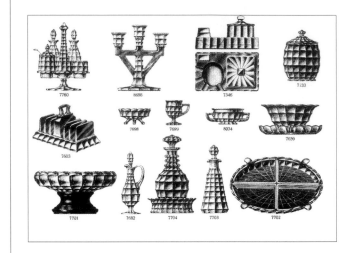

▲ **1920s**
Illustration of the *Lord* range from an Inwald catalogue.
£5–40/$9–70*

1920

▼ **Late 1920s**
Jacobean footed vinaigrette, decanter, and cruet bottle. 21cm (8¼in) inc., 33cm (13in) inc., and 22cm (8⅝in) inc.
From left £30/$55, £25/$45, £25/$45

▲ **1930s–'50**

Foil Jacobean stickers. Top: As applied to Czech-made examples pre-1933. Below: As applied to pieces made in England by Davidson, *c.*1933–50.

▲ **1930s**

Jacobean amber water jug and tankards, probably by Davidson. Tankards: 10cm (3⅞in), jug: 16cm (6¼in).

From left £5/$9, £20/$35, £10/$17

▶ **1930s**

Large, rose-tinted *Jacobean* fruit-bowl. Produced by Inwald. 16.8cm (6⅝in).

£25/$45

▼ **1950s**

Clayton Mayers' advertisement for *Jacobean* glassware, 1951, and a 1950s jug transfer-decorated with punch fruits. The text stretches credulity in suggesting that the range was "fashioned on the graceful designs of the Jacobean period" (1603–25).

Advert items £5–10/$9–17, Jug £15/$25

▼ **1930**

Page of patterns from British *Jacobean* catalogue.

Ashtray £5/$9, Lamp £300/$510

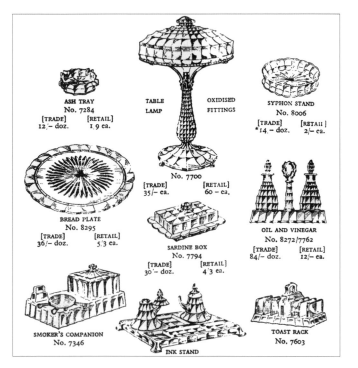

Kaj Franck 1911–89

Unassuming, methodical, and humanistic, Kaj Franck ranks among the greats of post-war design. The reason that his name has yet to be illuminated alongside the likes of Alvar Aalto and the Eames, for instance, is that the impact of his work has been so subtle. As he himself declared: "I want to make utensils that are so self-evident that they pass unnoticed." In terms of his enduring reputation, he succeeded in this aim only too well.

A glance at Franck's work illustrated on the following pages may seem, in many cases, to be unremarkable: our lives are surrounded by objects of similar appearance, many of them available from the likes of Ikea for small change. However, the design lineage of many of them is directly traceable to Franck, before whom few, or none, of them existed in their modern form.

Franck was a rounded designer/teacher. After graduating in furniture design from the Helskinki Institute of Applied Art in 1932, he worked as a window dresser and interior designer. He designed fabrics from 1938 to 1945, then worked as a designer/modeller for Arabia porcelain until 1961. He also taught design at the Institute of Applied Art in 1945–60, was its artistic director from 1960 to 1968, then its artistic professor from 1973 to 1978.

Franck's greatest love was glass, however, which he designed for Iittala between 1946 and 1950), and Nuutajärvi, where he served as artistic director from 1951 to 1976, alongside Saara Hopea until 1959, then with Oiva Toikka.

Throughout his career in designing utility ware, Franck sought to strip out everything but the essentials to form and function. He urged his students to draw inspiration from the basic objects of peasant and primitive cultures.

Franck abhorred waste, and attempted to create objects whose appeal would endure for decades rather than months. He also wanted his work to sell on its own merits, rather than on the strength of fashionable labels and designer names. Indeed, he preferred his name to be absent from his work when it was retailed, believing it to be an impediment to objective appreciation.

Franck was widely exhibited and was showered with awards. However, his greatest legacy is, without doubt, that the utilitarian glass used today was inspired by the designs of Kaj Franck more than any other.

▲ **1953**
Kaj Franck in his studio at Arabia porcelain.

▲ **1962**
Franck's signature, *K Franck Nuutajärvi Notsjö-62*, as applied to a KF106 vase with *Gauze* decoration.

▶ **1793–1993**
Nuutajärvi stickers. From top: Framed logo, 1793–1952; Fish-shaped sticker, designed by Kaj Franck, used 1952–c.1972; *ARABIA FINLAND* logo, c.1972–7, some examples also marked *FINN CRYSTAL*; blue fish logo, 1977–c.1993. Since c.1993 all Nuutajärvi production has been applied with Iittala's *i* stickers (p.173).

▼ 1958
Free-blown *Usva* (*Haze*) vases (KF106). Both designed in 1958, Amber with engraved signature dated *1958* and amethyst, *1960*. Both engraved with signatures. Amber: 11cm (4¼in); amethyst: 20cm (7⅞in).
Left £120/$205
Right £200/$340

▲ 1951
Free-formed and polished *Kajakki* (*Kayak*) art object. Engraved with "K Franck N-N51". 37cm (14⅝) diam.
£450/$765

▲ 1972
Mould-blown *Pokaali* (*Goblet*) (KF539). Produced 1972–7 in various colours. Signed *Kaj Franck Nuutajärvi Notsjö*. 16cm (6¼in) and 21cm (8¼in).
£350/$595

◄ 1966
Free-formed clear and opal *Rengaslautanen* (*Ring Dish*). Engraved *Kaj Franck Nuutajärvi Notsjö-1966*. Most Franck signatures only state the last two digits of the date. However, the full date on this example suggests that it may have been exhibited in the joint Franck/Oiva Toikka exhibition held in Helsinki in 1966. 41.5cm (16⅜in) diam.
£800/$1,360

KEY DATES

1793 Nuutajärvi Nötsjö founded under aristocratic patronage in central-southern Finland.

1932 Franck graduates as furniture designer. Military service until 1933, then furnishing-shop window dresser and interior designer.

1938 Fabric designer, Hyvinkaa wool weavers.

1939–45 Operates coastal gun battery in Finland's war against Russia.

1945 Joins Arabia Porcelain.

1946 First glass designs for Iittala after winning 2nd and 3rd prizes in design competition.

1949 Awarded grant to study glassmaking at Vetri di Napoli, Italy.

1950 Wärsilä industrial conglomerate buys Nuutajärvi Glass; Frank appointed artistic director, 1951.

1951 Franck visits Venice to hire Murano glassmakers for Nuutajärvi. Awarded Gold Medal at the Milan Triennale.

1954–7 Major participant in *Design in Scandinavia* exhibition (US/Canada).

1955 Winner of Lunning Prize.

1956 Asla Grant funds sabbatical year. Undertakes foundation course at Rhode Island School of Design, visits Massachusetts Institute of Technology, Boston, and University College Los Angeles, then tours Japan.

1957 Wins Grand Prix at the Milan Triennale.

1959 Oiva Toikka appointed Franck's assistant.

1960 Artistic Director, Institute of Applied Art, Helsinki.

1967 Devaluation of Finnish mark boosts glass exports.

1968 Remodels *Fasetti*, *Kartio*, and *Seagram* glasses for automatic production. First original design for machine production: *Prisma* (*Prism*).

1978 Designs classic 9-piece *Teema* collection for Arabia.

1979 Retrospective of Franck pressed designs at Artek, Milan.

1984 Remodels some of his 1940s utility-glass designs for Iittala in stronger colours.

1987–present More classic Franck designs remodelled and reissued.

1992 Design Forum Finland establishes the Kaj Franck Prize, awarded annually to a designer working in his spirit.

2006 Nuutajärvi continues as production centre for Oiva Toikka's glass birds and site of Franck museum.

▶ **1954 and 1958**

Mould-blown carafe (1725) containing pressed stackable tumblers (5027). Carafe designed in 1954 and produced 1954–65. 90cl (32fl oz). Tumblers designed in 1958 and produced 1958–75. Max. 35cl (12fl oz).

Full set £120/$205

▼ **1954**

Mould-blown vase (KF237). Produced 1954–56. 20–23cm (7⅞–9in).

£225/$380

▲ **1951**

Free-blown *Saippuakulpa* (*Soap Bubble*) art objects (KF113). The green version was Franck's first art object in coloured glass. Produced 1951–63. Engraved *K Franck, Nuutajärvi Notsö-54*. 18 and 23cm (7 and 9in).

Left £140/$240, Right £225/$380

1951

▲ **1952**

Mould-blow *Purnukka* (*Box*) tumblers (KF212). Produced 1952–6 and 1959, some bi-coloured. 12 and 20cm (4¾ and 7⅞in).

From left £40/$70, £60/$100, £60/$100

▶ **1953**

Free-blown *Harso* (*Gauze*) vase (KF108). Produced 1953–8. Unsigned. 15.5cm (6in).

£275/$470

Mould-blown bowls. Engraved *K Franck, Nuutajärvi Notsjö-58*. Max. 21cm (8¼in) diam.
£10/$17

▲ 1954
Pressed plates (5269). Produced 1954–68. 13.5 and 19cm (5¼ and 7½in) square.
£10/$17

1954

▼ 1954
Mould-blown vases (1405). Produced 1954–7 in various colours. The mould for the largest version was also used to produce a carafe/cocktail mixer (1610, p.120). 15, 20, and 23cm (5⅞, 7⅞, and 9in).
Signed £50–125/$85–210

▼ 1954
Mould-blown, cased, and cut *Prisma* vase (KF215). Produced 1954–68. Base engraved *K Franck, Nuutajärvi Notsjö-60*. 13, 16, 21, and 23cm (5, 6¼, 8¼, and 9in).
£250–450/$425–765*

▲ c.1955

Experimental mould-blown vase.
12.5cm (4⅞in).

£700/$1,190*

◀ ▲ 1954–6

Mould-blown *Kartio* series. Round-bottom carafe (1612), produced
1955–68, 1l (34fl oz), (some early versions have wicker coiled round the
neck); tumbler (left and above) (2744), 8–30cl (2¾–10fl oz), produced
1956–67 and 1993–present; and *Hourglass* carafe/cocktail mixer (1610),
80cl (27fl oz), produced 1954–66 and 1993–present. This group is a 2004
re-issue, modified by Oiva Toikka, Franck's former assistant.

**Original round-bottom carafe £125/$210,
Hourglass mixer £80/$135, Tumblers £8/$14**

1954

◀ 1955

Mould-blown vases.
Produced in 1955
in several colours.
20.5cm (8in).

**Left £90/$155
Right £65/$110**

▲ 1955 and 1957

Mould-blown *Kremlin Kellot* and
Kukkopullo (*Kremlin Bells* and *Cockerel*)
decanters (KF500 and 502). Designed in
1955 and 1957 respectively. Both types
produced 1957–68 in several forms,
combinations, sizes, and colours.

**From left £100/$170; £400/$680;
£850/$1,445; £600/$1,020**

▼ **1956**
Pressed candlestick (6405).
Produced 1956–present.
5cm (2in).

£15/$25

▲ **1956**
Mould-blown vases (KF241). Produced
1956–8 in yellow, lilac, violet, green, brown,
and blue. Engraved *K Franck, Nuutajärvi
Notsjö-58*. 9 and 12cm (3½ and 4¾in).

£200/$340*

▼ **1956**
Pressed-glass salts (6606).
Produced 1956–70s in
various colours.
5cm (2in) diam.

£15/$25

▲ **1956**
Pressed bowl (5377). Produced
1956–9, in various colours.
21cm (8¼in) diam.

£25/$45

▲ **1956**
Mould-blown *Lilli* tumbers
(1719). Produced 1956–67.
Max. 40cl (13½fl oz).

£45/$75 set

▲ **1956**
Mould-blown *Hourglass* vases (KF245).
Produced 1956–69 in yellow, lilac, violet,
green, brown, and blue. 17cm (6¾in).
£90/$155*

▶ **c.1958**
Filigree glass bottle, manually trailed
into a mould. Part of a series of art-
glass pieces. 8cm (3in).
£400–750/$680–1,275*

1956

▼ **1956**
Mould-blown tumblers/vases (3400).
Produced 1956–61 in several colours.
14.5–26.5cm (5⅝–10½in).
£80–120/$135–205*

▲ **1960**
Mould-blown and cased vases (KF260). Produced
1960–66 in lilac, violet, and green.
11, 22, and 14cm (4¼, 8⅜, and 5½in).
£125–225/$210–380*

◀ 1963
Mould-blown, cased, and polished vase (KF1422). Produced 1963–8 in various colours. Engraved *Nuutajärvi Notsjö*. 17.5cm (6⅞in).
£50–90/$85–155*

◀ 1963
Mould-blown *Rustica* tumbler (1771) and tankard (1833). Produced 1963–72 in amber, grey, green, and colourless. Tumbler: 12cm (4¾in); tankard: 11.5cm (4½in).
£25/$45

1960s FRANCK ART GLASS

Franck designed a significant amount of often technically demanding art glass. Most were signed, relatively expensive, and produced for short periods. Today, these inevitably tend to be more sought-after than standard production pieces.

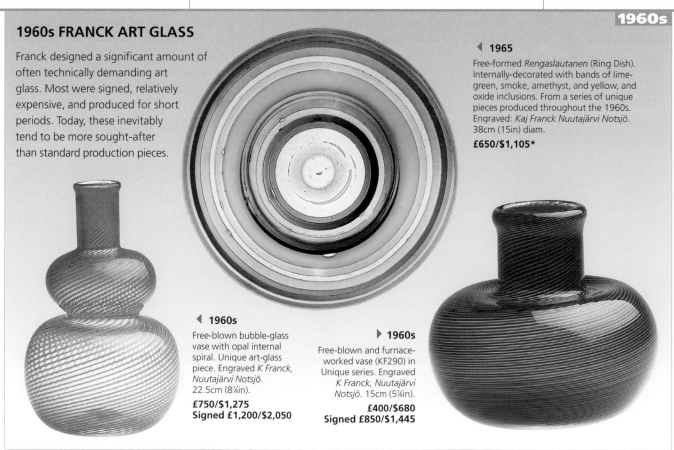

◀ 1965
Free-formed *Rengaslautanen* (Ring Dish). Internally-decorated with bands of lime-green, smoke, amethyst, and yellow, and oxide inclusions. From a series of unique pieces produced throughout the 1960s. Engraved: *Kaj Franck Nuutajärvi Notsjö*. 38cm (15in) diam.
£650/$1,105*

◀ 1960s
Free-blown bubble-glass vase with opal internal spiral. Unique art-glass piece. Engraved *K Franck, Nuutajärvi Notsjö*. 22.5cm (8⅞in).
£750/$1,275
Signed £1,200/$2,050

▶ 1960s
Free-blown and furnace-worked vase (KF290) in Unique series. Engraved *K Franck, Nuutajärvi Notsjö*. 15cm (5⅞in).
£400/$680
Signed £850/$1,445

▲ 1967
Experimental mould-blown goblets in various colour combinations. 15.5cm (6in).
£200/$340*

Free-blown and worked *Sargasso* art-glass series. Right: Designed in 1968. 27cm (10⅝in). Below: Designed in mid-1970s. 19.5cm (7⅝in). Both engraved *Kaj Franck Nuutajärvi Notsjö*

Left £80/$135
Right £60/$100

1966

◀ 1966
Mould-blown *Ryppynyppy* (*Wrinkle-Pimple*) tumblers (1772). Produced 1966–8. 10, 20 and 30cl (3½, 7, and 10fl oz).
£5/$9

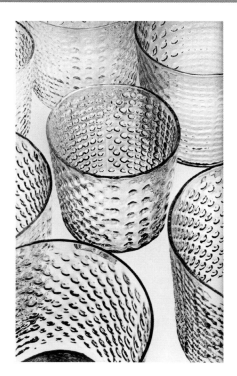

▼ 1968
Mould-blown goblets (KF486). Produced 1968–71 in numerous colour combinations. 17.5–19.5cm (6⅞–7⅝in).
£125–200/$210–340*

▲ 1970

Mould-blown colour-ring technique bowl in art-glass series. Engraved *Kaj Franck Nuutajärvi Notsjö*. 20.5cm (8in) diam.

£125/$210

▶ 1975

Mould-blown Filigree goblets (KF486). Produced 1975–7, in numerous colour combinations. Various heights. Filigree was initially revived at Nuutäjarvi in 1943 as part of its 150th anniversary celebrations. Unlike the Venetian method, the canes were inserted into moulds rather than free-formed. Franck used the method periodically between 1963 and the early 1980s.

£175/$300*

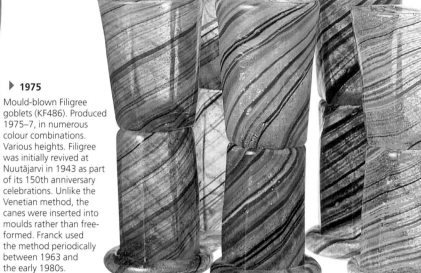

▼ 1970s

Mould-blown (left) and free-formed (right) red oxide art series. 11.5cm (4½in) and 14cm (5½in). Both engraved *Kaj Franck Nuutajärvi Notsjö*.

Left £60/$100
Right £80/$135

▼ 1981

Mould-blown Filigree bottle. Limited edition of 1,000 numbered pieces produced 1981–4 in various sizes and colour combinations. All engraved *Kaj Franck Nuutajärvi Notsjö*, and date coded – 1981: *932-019-91*; 1982: *093-082-91*; 1983: *032-083-91*; 1984: *932-084-91*.

£200–400/$340–680*

A. Hardie Williamson 1907–94

▲ 1948
Auto-blown saucer champagne/Babycham glass (P621). The saucer, or *coupe*, one of the oldest forms of drinking-glass, was remodelled by Williamson for automatic production. It is best known for having been chosen by Showerings Brewery as the glass for its pear-based Babycham drink, launched nationally in Britain in 1953. 11cm (4¼in). Background: entry from Ravenhead's 1958 catalogue.
£5/$9

Alexander Hardie Williamson was Britain's most prolific 20th-century glass designer. While his name is largely unknown, his work is instantly recognizable across the world. His most successful designs, including the *Nonik* (1948), *Paris* (1952), and *Siesta* (1973) drinking-glass ranges, remain ubiquitous to virtually every British pub, hotel, and home. However, they formed just a fraction of the 1,634 glass designs he executed between 1933 and 1974.

Williamson first designed glassware in 1933 while studying textiles at London's Royal College of Art, where he taught until 1955. The results, several colourful Art Deco vases and bowls by Bagley (p.128), are uncharacteristic, since most of his work was produced in colourless glass.

He explained his design ethos in 1951: "Traditionally, pressed glassware has been a means for producing cheap imitations of heavy, hand-cut glass tableware…. From my commencement, I have endeavoured to design a series of articles which would depart from this. The essential shape of the article is all-important and, ideally, any further enlivening of the shape should be by means of a decoration which will give light and life to the metal. At the same time, the handling of the article is also important, its weight, finish, ease of cleaning, etc. If these factors are carefully considered … it will in nearly every case lead to the production of an article pleasant to handle and look at."

Williamson glasses were exported to over 100 countries, most under the trade names of Sherdley and Ravenhead.

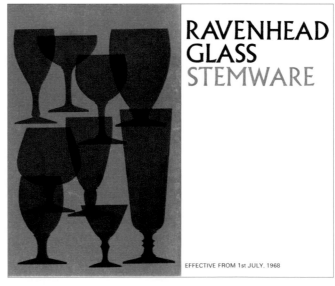

▲ 1968
Ravenhead's 1968 catalogue cover showing Williamson silhouette montage of some of his best-selling designs.

▲ **1940s**
Hardie Williamson trained as a textile designer and taught the subject at the Royal College of Art. These scraps of painted paper, seen in montage here, were probably designed in the 1940s and are from his private collection.

▲ **1956**
Hardie Williamson's most distinctive designs were probably his huge range of screen-printed tumblers, produced from 1956. The four basic shapes were applied with hundreds of different patterns, some appearing in differing colours.
£8/$14

KEY DATES

1907 Born in Hull.

1915 Family moves to Edinburgh after German Zeppelin airships bomb Hull.

1925–9 Studies lithography and commercial design, Harrogate School of Arts & Crafts.

1929–32 Scholarship student, Design School, Royal College of Art, London.

1933–55 Member of Royal College of Art teaching staff.

1933–39 Freelance designer making commissions for Bagley, pressed-glass makers (pp.96–101), and Royal Worcester porcelain.

1939 Marries Sue Plowright, fellow student at RCA.

1939–45 Royal College evacuated to Lake District; Williamson runs fabric design course.

1944–68 Freelance design consultant to Johnsen & Jorgenson, marketing agent and distributor for United Glass. Designs most of United Glass' domestic ranges.

1940s–70s Designs covers and endpapers for all 92 books in Dent Hutton's series *Children's Illustrated Classics*.

1951–55 Head of Printed Design, Royal College of Art.

1956 First two-coloured screen-printed tumblers produced at United Glass' Sherdley plant, St Helens, Lancashire.

1964 United Glass closes Sherdley; production switches to nearby Ravenhead.

1968–74 Employed directly by United Glass.

1974 Retires, spends time painting, taking photographs, and gardening at Hedfield, West Sussex.

1987 United Glass/Ravenhead sold to American bottlemaker, Libbey.

1994 Dies at Worthing, aged 87. The contents of his studio acquired by Broadfield House Glass Museum, Stourbridge.

1996 Retrospective exhibition at Broadfield House.

2000 Ravenhead sold to Durobor, owned by Belgian regional government of Wallonne/Walloon Brabant.

2001 Ravenhead closes after 150 years; 300 staff made redundant.

HARDIE WILLIAMSON AND BAGLEY

Williamson's first glass designs were for Bagley, the pressed-glass maker near Pontefract, Yorkshire (pp.96–101), in 1933/4. However, the full extent of his contribution remains unclear. A few pieces can be definitively linked to his hand, including the *Marine* bowl and the *Wyndham* vases. Several others, such as the *Bamboo* vases, are also thought to be Williamson designs. Furthermore, Bagley registered some of his designs at the Patent Office, including several pairs of Art Deco bookends, though they may never have entered production as no examples are known.

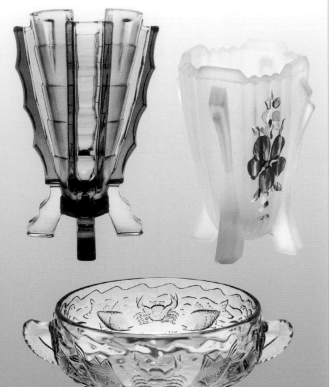

▶ **1933–4**

Anti-clockwise from top left: Pressed *Bamboo* pattern vase and clock (3007), designed in 1933, produced 1934–75, clock 12.5cm (4⅛in), vase 22cm (8⅝in); pressed *Marine* bowl (3000), designed in 1934, produced 1934–mid-'50s, design registered December 1934 (Rd. No.798843). 31cm (12¼in) diam; and *Bedford* vase (3057) designed in 1934, produced 1935–75. 9.5 and 20.5cm (3¾ and 8in).

Clock, working £50/$85, *Bamboo* vase £40/$70, Small *Bedford* £15/$25, Large *Bedford* £40/$70, Bowl £35/$60

1933

UNRECORDED WORK 1933–9

Williamson undertook a series of commissions between 1933 and 1939, when the Royal College of Art was evacuated from London to the Lake District. It is known that he designed glassware for Bagley and porcelain for Royal Worcester, but his other work from this time currently remains unrecorded. It is known that he was working for United Glass in 1944, but their pressed *Nordic* range, *c.*1936, and *Ripple* jug and tumbler set, 1938, have also been tentatively linked to his drawing board.

▲ **1947**
Pressed *Regency* fruit bowl. Publicity photograph, *c.*1950. Made in two sizes: centrepiece and individual servings.
Set £25/$45

▶ **1938**
Pressed *Ripple* jug (P370; tumbler: P417), possibly designed by Williamson. *Ripple* was inspired by Aino Aalto's *Bölgeblick* range of horizontally banded pressed-glass for Iittala of 1932 (p.21 and 163). 15.5cm (6in).
£20/$35

▲ 1947

Pressed *Doric* fruit set. Large bowl (P478): 20cm (7⅞in) diam.; plate (P584): 14cm (5½in); and small bowl (P487): 12.5cm (4⅞in). Publicity photograph, c.1950.

Set £25/$45

THE WESTLAKE MACHINE

In 1948 United Glass installed a revolutionary new machine, the Westlake, made by the giant American bottlemaker Owens-Illinois. Westlakes were capable of producing huge numbers of glasses fully automatically. Williamson's *New Worthington*, *Paris*, and *Waterloo* designs were among the first to be produced this way.

1948, 1952, 1958

From left: Auto-blown *New Worthington* beer glass (P643), *Paris* goblet (P660), and *Waterloo* goblet (P694). The *Paris* and *Waterloo* ranges comprised six sizes: 2.5–12 fl. oz (73–355ml). From Ravenhead's 1958 catalogue.

£2/$3

▼ 1948

Auto-blown *Nonik* beer glass (P708). The *Nonik* and the dimpled tankard were the most common British beer glasses of the 20th century. From Sherdley's 1958 catalogue. Half and full pint sizes available.

£2/$3

▲ 1958

Auto-blown *Bamboo* tumbler (P711). From Sherdley's 1958 catalogue. 10.5cm (4in).

£1/$2

1973

▼ 1973

Auto-blown *Siesta* tumbler with original packaging. The "icy" texture was copied from similar effects developed by Tapio Wirkkala (pp.166–71) and Timo Sarpaneva (pp.172–7), but *Siesta* was much cheaper and sold in far greater numbers than equivalents by Iittala. 12cm (4¾in).

£1/$2, Boxed set £20/$35

SLIM JIMS

Slim Jims is the generic name given to a series of auto-blown tumblers designed by Alexander Hardie Williamson for Sherdley from 1956, then Ravenhead from 1964. They were modelled on the similar *Swanky Swig* tumblers produced by several American glassworks from around 1933 to 1970, many sold containing Kraft mustard and mayonnaise.

The earliest two-colour designs were applied to an existing shape, the *Conical*, later renamed the *Cooler*. Other shapes, all designed by Williamson, were added during the 1960s, including vertical-sided *Slim Jims*, contoured *Chunkies*, and barrel-like *Chubbies* and *Gaytime*. Three-colour schemes were introduced c.1960.

The range proved a huge commercial success over 20 years and was applied with hundreds of patterns and colour variations. Certain examples include the word *ENGLAND* in the design, others do not. Production of Ravenhead types ceased in the late 1970s.

Hardie Williamson created his tumbler designs by painting each colour onto separate sheets of transparent film. The sheets were then taped together, with the foremost colour on the uppermost sheet, followed by the second and third colours in descending order. Once in the correct sequence, Williamson then bladed the laminated sheets into the required shape to fit around a blank tumbler.

▲ **Conical/Cooler**
The most common shape, later renamed the *Cooler*. 12cm (4¾).
£5/$9

▲ **Slim Jim**
14cm (5½in).
£7/$12

▲ **1965**
United Glass/Johnsen & Jorgenen catalogue launching a new range of Williamson-designed *Slim Jims*, *Chunkies*, and *Conicals*. *Slim Jims* cost 9/11d (50p/85c) for six, *Chunkies* were 8/11d (45p/77c), and *Conicals* 6/3d (31p/53c).

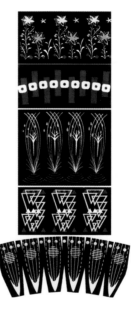

▲ **1965**
Series of Hardie Williamson original design films, shown here against black grounds for clarity. The bottom pattern has been bladed to allow it to be wrapped around the body of a tumbler. From Hardie Williamson's private collection.

▲ **1965**
Original design trial for the *Queen of Diamonds* from Williamson's *Royalty* series of *Slim Jims*. From Hardie Williamson's private collection.

▲ **Chunkie**
11cm (4¼in).
£7/$12

▲ **Chubbie**
Intended as an "easy-grip" party glass. 11cm (4¼in).
£7/$12

▲ **Toddie**
10cm (3⅞in).
Most £5/$9
This example £10/$17

▲ **Gaytime**
The rarest shape, with a thick base and gilded rim. 15cm (5⅞in).
£10/$17

NON-WILLIAMSON PRINTED GLASSWARE

Collector demand is beginning to focus on Hardie Williamson in general, and his printed tumblers in particular. However, Ravenhead was not the only glassworks to produce screen-printed glassware. In Britain, Dema Glass, Chesterfield, made a series of similar tumblers from the late 1960s, and London-based importers/distributors Clayton Mayers (pp.115) advertised its *Colourcraft* range widely in the 1970s. Screen-printed glassware was also produced in France, by J.G. Durand.

▲ **1970s**
Set of 1970s screen-printed Dema tumblers in original packaging. c.15cm (6in).
Set £20/$35

▲ **1950s & '70s**
Group of 1950s and '70s printed tumblers and salt and pepper shakers. All marked *France* except the left-hand tumbler (*Foreign*).
Salt and pepper £5–20/$9–35
Tumblers £3–10/$5–17*

Michael Harris 1933–94

MDINA GLASS

▲ **1968**

Mdina logo. Designed by Michael Harris, based on St Thomas's Tower, which was originally intended to be the site of the Mdina glassworks.

1973–5 Paper sticker. "England" included on early versions.

1974–82 The flame logo. Also white-on-black and applied as a seal on the base of most pieces made in 1974.

1982–89 Also gold-on-black.

1989–present Variations include gold-on-black and black-on-clear and 30th anniversary, 2003.

Harris' signature Dated 1979. The inclusion of the date is rare.

Mike Harris, entirely untrained in practical glassmaking, quit his post as a Royal College of Art lecturer in 1968 to become Britain's first studio-glass artist. During nine years at the RCA, Harris became frustrated with its lack of hot facilities. Matters came to a head after meeting leading American studio glassmakers Dominic Labino and Sam Herman, whose hands-on creative drive was previously unknown in Britain.

Within months, Harris had quit the RCA, assembled 10 tons of equipment and moved to the Mediterranean island of Malta, where he established his first studio with a partner, Eric Dobson. Instituting a policy retained throughout his career, Harris recruited only those apprentices who were entirely without glassmaking experience. Learning as he worked, his creations were expressed in hot Mediterranean colour combinations – a tendency he retained when he returned to England in 1972 to found Isle of Wight Studio Glass.

Since his death in 1994, Harris's legacy has been maintained by his wife Liz, and elder son Tim, at the Isle of Wight, and his second son, Jonathan, at his specialist cameo and *Graal* (p.199) studio at Ironbridge, Shropshire. Although Harris began working with virtually no practical experience, the three glassworks established during his career, two Maltese and one British, continue to flourish, with scores of his former apprentices now spread across the globe.

◀ **1959**

Printed and auto-blown *Calypto* tumbler. Produced 1959–mid-90s as part of the *Fiesta* range (pp.102–7). 11.5cm (4½in).

£5/$9

▶ **1960**

Harris with the internal dividing wall, constructed from foil-backed textured glazing-glass, that he designed for the P&O cruise ship *Canberra*.

◀ 1962

Transfer-printed and heat-slumped *Anemone* dish with metal mount. Produced in 1962–mid-1990s. *Anemone* was the first all-colour design in the *Fiesta* range. 21cm (8¼in) diam.

£5/$9

▲ 1963–4

Unique mould-blown *Bark* vase. Designed and mould made by Harris during visits to Rogaška Slatina, a Yugoslavian glassworks. Similar to later Whitefriars' *Bark* vases, the idea probably derived from Timo Sarpaneva's *Finlandia* series for littala, 1964 (p.174).

◀ 1962

Unique engraved goblets commissioned by the Royal College of Surgeons to commemorate the opening of their new headquarters in 1962. Engraved by Harris. Applied to a goblet from Whitefriars' *Embassy* service, designed by James Hogan, c.1942.

▶ 1964

The *Sunday Times* Fashion Award, 1964. Unique piece, designed and engraved by Harris.

▼ 1964

Mould-blown dish commissioned by the Royal Society of Arts to commemorate the 400th anniversary of the birth of William Shakespeare. Designed and engraved by Harris. Engraving applied to Whitefriars bowl (8972), designed by Barnaby Powell, c.1930. 28.5cm (11¼in) diam.

KEY DATES

1933 Born at Belper, Derbyshire, England.

1950–51 Interest in glass stimulated during foundation year at Stourbridge Art College.

1955–6 Military service.

1956 Marries textile designer Elizabeth Silvester (1933–).

1956–60 Student of glass design at Royal College of Art, London.

1959 Early design commissions include screen-printed *Calypto* range, based on eucalyptus leaves, for Chance Brothers (p.105).

1961–7 Works with Ronald Stennett-Willson to establish hot-glass facility at Royal College of Art.

1962 Designs *Anemone* range for Chance for £50 fee.

1963–8 Tutor in Industrial Glass at Royal College of Art.

1963/64 Supervises new production methods at Yugoslavian works, Rogaška Slatina, where he designs and produces his first *Bark* vases.

1967 Works with American studio glassmakers, Dominic Labino and Sam Herman.

1968 Quits RCA, replaced by Sam Herman. Founds Mdina Glass Ltd on Malta with partner Eric Dobson.

1969 After several setbacks, Mdina enters production at Ta'Qali airfield, Malta.

1970–71 Early commissions from London store Heal's and Rosenthal.

1971 Harris recruits experienced Whitefrairs glassmaker Vincente Boffo, followed by his son Ettore.

1972 Thirty workers employed at Mdina, but Harris family leaves Malta. Sale of his shares to Eric Dobson completed in 1973.

1973 Production starts at new site near St Lawrence, Isle of Wight.

1979 Design Council Award for *Azurene* range.

1984–8 Isle of Wight employs 34; 85 per cent of production exported.

1985 Eric Dobson sells Mdina to Joe Said, the Harris' first Maltese apprentice.

1989 Michael and Elizabeth Harris found new works on Gozo, Malta. Prototypes made by Michael and Tim Harris at Isle of Wight. Gozo works sold to the Brooks family in 1995.

1994 Elizabeth, Tim, and Jonathan continue Isle of Wight Studio Glass after death of Michael Harris.

1998 Jonathan Harris leaves to join Richard Golding's Okra Studio. Founds his own studio in 2000, Ironbridge, Shropshire.

2005 Production continues at Isle of Wight, with 15 employees.

▼ 1968

Mould-blown *Bark* bottle-vases and vase. Mdina's *Bark* range was directly descended from the colourless trial pieces Harris had made during visits to Yugoslavia in 1963 and '64. Formed by the traditional "half-post" method, used by German, Scandinavian (picture 35, p.21), then later Americans, for forming flasks. 33, 21, 30, and 23cm (13, 8¼, 11⅞, and 9in).

Bottles £85–175/$145–300
Vase £75/$130

▲ 1969

Cast-glass sculpture blocks. After casting these blocks, Harris glued series of them together to form two-dimensional sculptures mounted in steel frames. 6.5cm (2½in) square (the first production 15cm (5⅞in) square).

£40/$70

▼ 1970

Mould-blown *Attenuated Bottles*. Originally designed by Harris, they continued in production at Mdina into the 1980s. The tortoiseshell examples are post-Harris. Max. 42cm (16½in).

£120–150/$205–255*

1968

▲ 1968

Free-formed paperweights in Harris' distinctive colourways. Paperweights were among Mdina's first products, being small and cheap; they were aimed at Malta's tourist trade. They have been produced continuously since 1968 at Mdina, and by the Harris family at Isle of Wight Studio Glass since 1973. 6.5 and 4.5cm (2½ and 1¾in) diam.

£25/$45

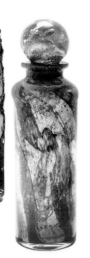

▼ 1968

Mould-blown and trailed decanters and rare bottle-vase. The pronounced shoulder of the decanters made decorative use of the swollen "overblow" resulting from blowing them into an open-topped dip-mould. The trails were applied manually to the body, then flattened on a stone "marver".

Decanters £50/$85
Vase £350/$595

▲ 1970

Free-formed *Side-Stripe Lollipop*, *Fish*, and *Cut Ice* vases/art objects. The most distinctive and longest-enduring of Harris' designs, variants of which are still produced at Mdina and by Tim Harris at Isle of Wight. These shapes have erroneously become known among collectors as "axe" vases, a term derided by Harris himself. The planes on the front section of the *Cut Ice* version (right) were cut and polished by Gulemeyr, Malta's leading glass merchant as Harris lacked the required facilities. 18, 26, and 23cm (7, 10¼, and 9in).

Left (post-Harris) £50/$85
Centre £250/$425, Right £200/$340

▶ 1970

Free-formed *Chalice*, produced 1970–2. The trailing applied to the large knops on the stems was among the earliest duties of Vincente "Poppa" Boffo, recently recruited from Whitefriars. *Chalices* were produced at Mdina for many years, but only those with gently curving lower bowls are attributable to the Harris period. 21cm (8¼in).

Unsigned £125/$210, Signed £300/$510

▼ 1971

Large, internally decorated *Crizzle Stone* art object. Base engraved *Michael Harris, Mdina Glass, Malta*. 18.5cm (7¼in). Harris applied his name to relatively little of his output, believing, firstly, that it had been created not by him personally but rather by his entire staff, and, secondly, "that our best work will be executed tomorrow".

£1,100/$1,870

▲ 1970

Internally trailed and free-formed vase. 16.5cm (6½in).

£150/$255

POST-HARRIS MDINA

Mike Harris sold Mdina to his business partner, Eric Dobson, and left Malta in 1972. The large number of surviving Harris designs illustrated in a late 1970s brochure were credited to Dobson. In 1985, Dobson sold Mdina to Joseph Said, one of Harris' original Maltese apprentices, who remains its managing director. However, Harris' design imprint has faded from Mdina's current output and his name is omitted from the current official history.

Harris' resistance to signing Mdina's output was scrapped on his departure, with the introduction of the distinctive looping engraved *Mdina* signature.

Said's brother, Paul, left to found Mtarfa Glass in 1980. Another Maltese glassworks, Phoenician, established by Leonard Mulligan, operated for many years near to Harris' original site at Ta'Qali. Gozo Glass, founded by the Harris family on Gozo in 1989, continues today in the hands of the Brooks family.

▲ 1972

The Dremel-engraved Mdina signature was applied only after Harris' departure.

▲ 1980s

Free-formed seahorse paperweights. Adopted after Mdina was commissioned to produce a glass chess set. 12–15cm (4¾–5⅞in).

£10/$17

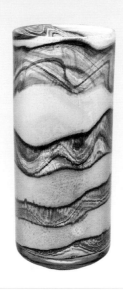

◀ 1970s

Mould-blown *Earth* or *Earthtones* cylinder vase. Signed *Mdina*. 20cm (7⅞in).

£40/$70

▶ 1980s

Mould-blown vase with applied aquamarine trails. Unsigned. 16cm (6¼in).

£30/$55

1972

ALUM BAY GLASS

Not all "Isle of Wight glass" is Isle of Wight Studio Glass. Island Glass was founded by Michael and Lynn Rayner in a garage at Totland on the Isle of Wight in 1972, just before the Harris family arrived on the island. Ten years later, the Rayners moved their studio and shop to the Needles Pleasure Park, a major tourist attraction at nearby Alum Bay, and renamed it Alum Bay Glass.

The glassworks was acquired in 1997 by its landlord, the Needles Pleasure Park Company, which replaced its gold foil label, used since 1983, with a new logo.

Alum Bay Glass is now managed by Colin Green, who joined as an apprentice in 1987 and who has designed all its ranges since 1997. Virtually the entire output of its five fulltime glassmakers is sold to tourists through its shop.

1973

▲ **1972–present**
Alum Bay stickers. Left: Gold foil with red writing, 1972–97. Right: Buff-and-black logo, 1997–present.

◄ **1998**
Free-blown and colour-splashed *Snowdrop* vase. Designed by Colin Green. 18cm (7in).
£10/$17

▼ **1973**
Free-blown and furnace-worked *Aurene* range. Produced 1973–80, in blue/gold. Max. vase: 40cm (15¾in); bowl: 17cm (6¾in) diam.
From left £40/$70, £250/$425, £250/$425, £180/$305, £90/$155

▼ **1973**
Free-blown *Pink Strap Swirl* vase. Produced in 1973, also in blue and turquoise. 8.5cm (3¼in). Continuing his resistance to signatures, Harris marked his Isle of Wight production during 1973 only with an idiosyncratic seal, created by pressing the rounded head of a coach bolt into a small blob of glass applied to the base (see inset picture). The Isle of Wight flame logo was incorporated into this seal in late-1973 and used through 1974, after which stickers were used.
£90/$155

▲ **1973**
Free-blown *Tortoiseshell* range. Produced 1973–80. Harris developed *Tortoiseshell* at Mdina. However, the striations on Isle of Wight versions are applied horizontally rather than vertically. Base sealed with the Isle of Wight flame logo seal. 16, 14.5, and 11cm (6¼, 5⅝, and 4¼in).
From left £70/$120, £90/$155, £45/$75

▼ **1975**
Free-blown and furnace-worked *Seaward* range. Produced in 1975. 13, 8, and 25cm (5, 3, and 9⅞in). A successor to *Tortoiseshell*. Both colourways originally conceived and produced by Harris on Malta in the early 1970s.
£80–150/$135–255

▲ 1978

Free-formed and cased *Lollipop* vase/art object. Harris made his first *Lollipop* vases at Mdina around 1970 and continued to produce them until c.1980. 17cm (6¾in).

£65/$110

▼ 1979

Free-blown and gold- and silver-leafed *Azurene* range. Produced 1979–87 in black, pink, green, and blue. Black still in production. *Azurene*, the result of collaboration between Harris and RCA graduate William Walker, was the first ever range of glassware with gold and silver leaf applied to its surface. Its success transformed the fortunes of the Isle of Wight studio, winning a Design Council Award and by 1984, new orders joined a two-year waiting list. 7, 18.5, 7, 20, and 23cm (2¾, 7¼, 2¾, 7⅞, and 9in).

£40–90/$70–155

▲ 1983

Free-blown *Dog Rose* colourway from *Meadow Garden* range, its surface decorated with coloured canes and chips. One of eight colours in range. Designed by Elizabeth Harris and produced 1983–8. *Meadow Garden* was intended to depict wild flowers, created by contrasting coloured chips and canes against the background colour. The similar *Flower Garden* (1989–2004, also by Elizabeth Harris) used shards and canes on colourless glass. 22 and 15cm (8⅜ and 5⅞in).

£50–80/$85–135

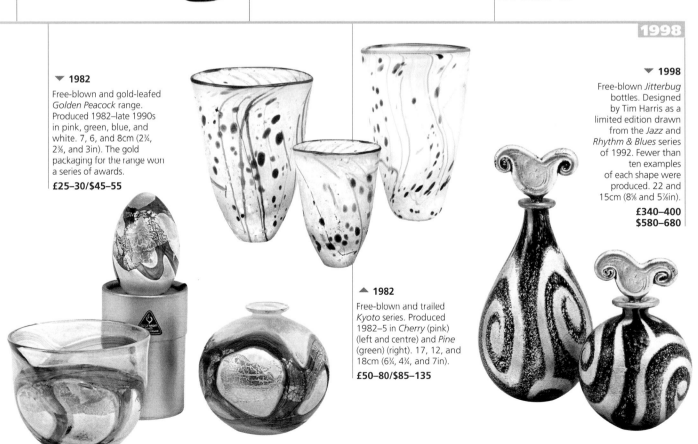

▼ 1982

Free-blown and gold-leafed *Golden Peacock* range. Produced 1982–late 1990s in pink, green, blue, and white. 7, 6, and 8cm (2¾, 2⅜, and 3in). The gold packaging for the range won a series of awards.

£25–30/$45–55

▲ 1982

Free-blown and trailed *Kyoto* series. Produced 1982–5 in *Cherry* (pink) (left and centre) and *Pine* (green) (right). 17, 12, and 18cm (6¾, 4¾, and 7in).

£50–80/$85–135

▼ 1998

Free-blown *Jitterbug* bottles. Designed by Tim Harris as a limited edition drawn from the *Jazz* and *Rhythm & Blues* series of 1992. Fewer than ten examples of each shape were produced. 22 and 15cm (8⅜ and 5⅞in).

£340–400 $580–680

Holmegaard

Holmegaard's contrasting contributions to European glass-making during the 19th and 20th centuries could hardly stand in greater contrast. Like all Scandinavian makers, its early products were derivative and inconsequential. However, its fortunes were transformed between 1930 and 1980 when the designs of three individuals catapulted Danish glassware onto the international scene.

Jacob E. Bang, Per Lütken, and Bang's son Michael worked for Holmegaard and its sister company Kastrup for a total of 122 years from 1927 to 2000. Lütken remained at the works for an extraordinary 56 years, designing everything from exhibition pieces, through multi-element services, to catalogues and brochures.

Holmegaard, established as a bottleworks in 1825 under aristocratic ownership, began producing table-glass within its first decade. Various production methods and decorating techniques were adopted gradually over its first century following technical and aesthetic developments pioneered elsewhere.

As late as 1938, 11 years after Jacob Bang's recruitment, the company's catalogue was still dominated by pieces derivative of anonymous late 19th-century Bohemian, German, English, and French factories. Its ranges spanned plain, cut, and engraved mould-blown and pressed utilitarian wares, but was led by Bang's soft-tinted 54-piece *Viol* and 100-piece *Primula* services.

Lütken was recruited from art school in 1942 to fill the void created by Bang's temporary departure into ceramics. Some of his earliest designs were applied to Bang shapes, but his rapid ascent of the learning curve was manifested in hundreds, then thousands, of designs that ranged between subtle and audacious.

Following in his father's footsteps, Michael Bang gained experience in ceramics and glass before joining Holmegaard's Odense plant in 1968. With failing health forcing his early retirement in 2000, his career is perhaps best remembered for his bold and vivid colour-cased *Palette* utilitarian and lighting ranges.

Other designers contributed to Holmegaard's success, but the significant and widespread influence of Danish glass in the post-war period is almost entirely attributable to the combined output of the Bang-Lütken-Bang triumvirate.

◀ **1860**
Cobalt-blue preserve jar of a type known in England since the 1760s, made at Holmegaard about a century later. 28.5cm (11¼in).

£400/$680

▲ **1865**
Group of three-part mould-blown vessels of a type produced in Britain, Ireland, and the United States from c.1810, but made at Holmegaard during the 1860s. Milk jug: 14cm (5½in).

£45–85/$75–145*

▲ **1900**

Venetian Revival goblets with rope stems and applied petals, made at Holmegaard around 1900. 25cm (9⅞in) max.

£60/$100

▶ **1920–22**

Acid-cameo vase in the Daum manner. Probably designed by Axel Enoch Boman for Holmegaard. 32cm (12⅝in).

£250/$425*

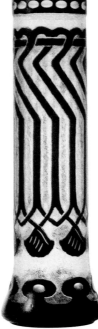

▲ **1934**

Mould-blown and trailed vase (2658). Designed by Jacob E. Bang as part of an extensive range of avant-garde, experimental, and exhibition pieces he developed during the 1930s. 23cm (9in).

£350/$595*

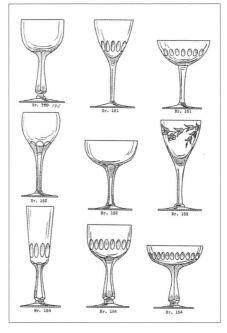

▲ **1938**

A page of typically old-fashioned drinking-glasses from Holmegaard's 1938 catalogue.

Glasses £10/$17

▶ **1927–present**

Kastrup and Holmegaard stickers.

| **Kastrup** 1927–40 | **Kastrup** 1940–56 | **Kastrup** 1956–65 | **Holmegaard** 1925–35 | **Holmegaard** 1936–66 | **Holmegaard** 1966–79 | **Holmegaard** 1980–present |

KEY DATES

1825 Founded at Fensmark, 100km (62 miles) south-west of Copenhagen, by Countess Henriette Danneskiold-Samsøe, directed by Norwegian glassmaker Christian Wendt. Early production exclusively bottles, but tableware introduced during 1830s. Cutting from 1835, enamelling from 1847.

1847 Second glasshouse founded at Kastrup. Bottle production augmented by table-glass from 1867 and pressed glass from 1875.

1873 Kastrup sold to finance Holmegaard expansion.

1905 Holmegaard hires first outside designer, ceramicist Svend Hammershøi (1873–1948).

1920s Kastrup leader of conglomerate that includes Hellerup bottleworks, and Odense lighting and pressed-glass.

1920–2 Holmegaard produces cameo glass by Axel Enoch Boman.

1926–41 Jacob E. Bang (1899–1965) chief designer at Holmegaard.

1935 Holmegaard becomes public limited company after descendants of founding Danneskiold-Samsøe family sell their shares.

1942–98 Per Lütken (1916–98) resident designer at Holmegaard.

1957–65 Jacob E. Bang chief designer at Kastrup.

1957–71 Christer Holmgren (1933–) designs for Holmegaard, sometimes in collaboration with his wife, Christel.

1962 Otto Brauer, glassblower at Odense, designs iconic *Gulvæse* (*Floor Vase*), based on Lütken's 1958 design.

1965 Holmegaard amalgamates with Kastrup, Hellerup, and Odense to form Kastrup & Holmegaard Glasværk, based at Fensmark.

1968 Michael Bang (1944–), son of Jacob, appointed designer at Odense. Production at Kastrup ceases.

1979 Hellerup closed.

1985 Holmegaard bought by Royal Copenhagen (owners of Venini, Venice, and Orrefors/Kosta/Boda, Sweden).

1990 Odense closed.

1998 Death of Per Lütken.

2002 Michael Bang retires due to ill health.

Jacob E. Bang 1899–65

Holmegaard 1927–41, Kastrup 1957–65

Jacob E. Bang is universally acknowledged as the father of 20th-century Danish glass design. He was not the first artist to work for Holmegaard, but the consistency and diversity of his work during his 16 years at the company in the prewar period introduced a unique identity to Danish glass.

Bang was educated at the Royal Danish Academy of Fine Arts, then trained as an architect before joining Holmegaard in 1927; he remained as its artistic director from 1928 to 1941. His early work, typified by the pastel-tinted *Primula* service, drew on both the past and contemporary work by the likes of Gate and Hald at Orrefors (pp.186–9) and Elis Burgh (1881–1954) at Kosta. As he gained in confidence, his designs flowered during the 1930s, as seen in a wide range of individual and often avant-garde styles.

He left Holmegaard in 1941 to design ceramics for Nymolle (1936–) and took on occasional architectural work. He returned to glass full-time in 1957 when appointed chief designer for Kastrup, where he remained until his death in 1965, the same year that the company amalgamated with Holmegaard. His later work included a distinctive series of widely influential smoke-grey and yellow vessels, some with optic-moulded banding that recalled his earlier work.

PRIMULA

Primula was a 100-piece range of table-glass designed by Jacob E. Bang for Holmegaard from 1930. It was produced in several soft-tint colours, including smoke-brown and mauve. Most of the items from the *Primula* range incorporate a double knop, as featured on the lid of the cheese bell and the base of the candlestick below.

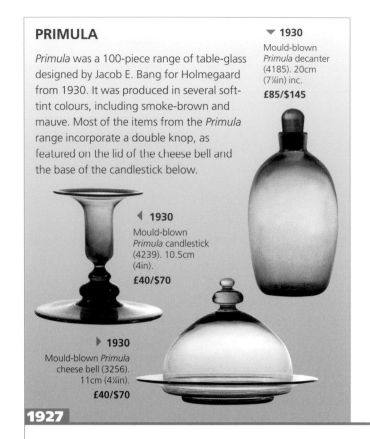

▼ **1930**
Mould-blown *Primula* decanter (4185). 20cm (7⅞in) inc.
£85/$145

◀ **1930**
Mould-blown *Primula* candlestick (4239). 10.5cm (4in).
£40/$70

▶ **1930**
Mould-blown *Primula* cheese bell (3256). 11cm (4¼in).
£40/$70

1927

▲ **1927**
Mould-blown and enamelled *Snapsemand og Snapsekone* (*Man and Wife*) (2209). Man: 26.5cm (10½in).
£150/$255

▲ 1930
Mould-blown smoke-topaz liqueur
decanter (4089). Produced 1930–36.
Matching glasses also available (4428).
18.5cm (7¼in).
£200/$340

▼ 1934
Optic-moulded violet bowl.
20cm (7⅞in) diam.
£200/$340

▲ c.1936 and '62
Optic-moulded, solid-colour vases designed from
c.1936. Left: From the *Capri* series (13939)
designed for Kastrup in 1962. 36cm (14⅛in). Right:
Designed for Holmegaard in 1936, and produced
1936–70. 21cm (8¼in). These pieces are often
mistaken in England for similar designs by
Geoffrey Baxter for Whitefriars.
Left £150/$255, right £90/$155

▼ 1928
Mould-blown smoke-topaz vase (3428).
Produced 1928–36. 29cm (11½in).
£250/$425

1937

EXHIBITION PIECES

These decanters and a jug are from a series of avant-
garde mould-blown exhibition pieces by Bang.

▶ 1934
Jug with applied
trails. 16cm (6¼in).
£150/$255

◀ 1934
Decanter (2677).
15cm (5⅞in) inc.
£250/$425

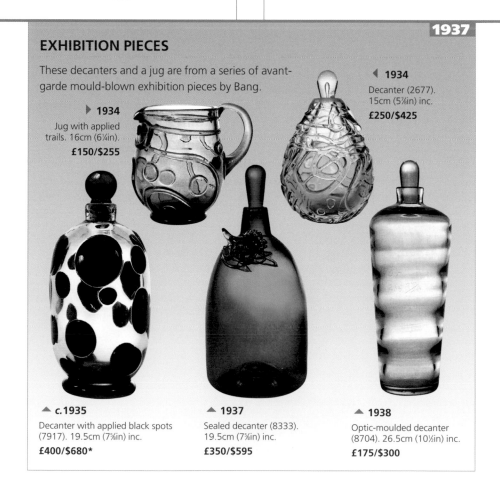

▲ c.1935
Decanter with applied black spots
(7917). 19.5cm (7⅝in) inc.
£400/$680*

▲ 1937
Sealed decanter (8333).
19.5cm (7⅝in) inc.
£350/$595

▲ 1938
Optic-moulded decanter
(8704). 26.5cm (10½in) inc.
£175/$300

APPLIED FIGURES

These are from a series of designs by Bang with applied figures from the 1937 Holmegaard exhibition, *Den Permanente, 10 Years of Danish Glass*. The exhibition marked Bang's first decade at Holmegaard.

◀ **1937**
Free-blown, furnace-worked, sealed prunts, and sealed amber carafe. 27.5cm (10⅞in).
£1,000/$1,700*

◀ **1937**
Free-blown blue-lidded punch bowl. 45.5cm (18in).
£1,000/$1,700*

▲ **1937**
Free-blown and sealed blue punch bowl. 28.5cm (11¼in).
£1,500/$2,550*

1937

▼ **1937**
Optic-moulded *Anenome* dessert dish (644). 13cm (5in) high.
£65/$110

▲ **1937**
Mould-blown and sealed schnapps decanter and glass. Decanter: c.20cm (7⅞in). Glass: c.5cm (2in).
Decanter £75/$130
Glass £20/$35

1937

Pressed-glass and enamelled jug from *Broskø* range. Produced 1938–67. It is a close copy of Aino Alto's version for littala/Karhula of 1932 (p.21 for pattern drawing, and p.163). 15.5cm (6in).

£35/$60

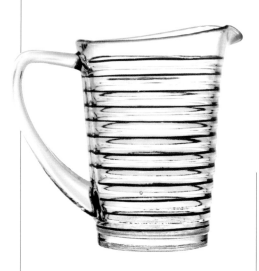

1938

Mould-blown and enamelled spirit decanter. Enamelled in blue, yellow, and red with the jolly toast: *Never too much, Never too little, Never too rarely, Never too often!* 22.5cm (8⅞in).

£150/$255

1954

Mould-blown, cased, and furnace-shaped bubbled ashtray (504). Designed for Kastrup. 8cm (3in) diam.

£20/$35

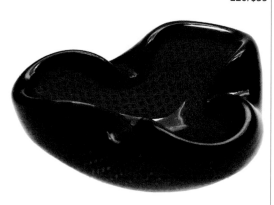

1937

Optic-moulded aqua ice bucket with wicker handle (8715). Designed for Holmegaard in 1937 and produced in 1937 and 1954–75.

£50/$85, With drainer and tongs £100/$170

1941

Mould-blown piggy bank with applied features. Reissued in 1956 to raise money for Hungarian refugees after the uprising against the Russian occupation. Max. 21cm (8¼in).

Left £500/$850, Right £100/$170

▲ **1957**
Optic-moulded, solid-colour vase in *Odelgrön* (*Edel Green*) (16163). Designed for Kastrup and produced c.1957–65. 20.5cm (8in).

£45/$75

▶ **1957**
Optic-moulded, solid-colour decanter and vase. Designed for Kastrup and produced: c.1957–65. 14.5 and 36.5cm inc (5⅝ and 14⅜in).

Decanter £100/$170
Vase £50/$85

▼ **1960**
Mould-blown, teak-stoppered, turquoise *Green Line* and opaque-white decanters with wicker neck grip. Designed for Kastrup and produced 1960–5. 34.5cm (13⅜in) and 33.5cm (13¼in) inc.

£250/$425

▼ **1957/8**
Mould-blown, solid-colour vase. Designed for Kastrup and produced c.1957/58–65. 16cm (6¼in).

£65/$110

▲ **1958**
Mould-blown, solid-colour vase. Designed for Kastrup in 1958 and produced c.1959–65. 15cm (5⅞in).

£50/$85

1961–2

Mould-blown solid-colour *Capri* series vases and carafe (right, 240846). Designed for Kastrup 1961–2 and produced 1962–5. Carafe: 25cm (9⅞in).

**Vases from left £110/$190, £150/$255, £75/$130
Carafe £80/$135**

1964

Mould-blown, trailed, and sealed solid-colour *Antique Green* bottle-vase. Designed for Kastrup in 1964 and produced 1965–70. The seal, in the form of a girl's face, was derived from similar versions designed by Erik Hoglund, for Boda, Sweden. 23cm (9in).

£150/$255

1965

1960

Mould-blown and colour-cased tube vase (390070). Designed for Kastrup. 26cm (10¼in).

£80/$135

1965

Mould-blown *Hurricane Lamps* (591750). Designed for Kastrup and produced 1965–78. From Holmegaard's 1970 catalogue.

£75/$130

1964

Mould-blown and sealed solid-colour *Antique Green* range. Designed for Kastrup in 1964 and produced 1965–9. Each piece sealed with the monogram *JB*. From Holmegaard's 1969 catalogue. Tallest vase: 23cm (9in).

From left £60/$100, £45/$75, £50/$85

Per Lütken 1942–98

Holmegaard 1942–77

While many of the themes common to Per Lütken's work were derived from contemporary sources of inspiration, its subtlety made him one of the most influential glass designers of his generation.

Trained in technical drawing and painting at the Copenhagen School of Arts and Crafts, Lütken joined Holmegaard in 1942, and remained as its artistic director until his death in 1998. When he was asked to propose a title for a book about his work to be published in 1986 to celebrate his 70th birthday, unsuprisingly Lütken chose his favourite maxim: *Glass is Life*.

Over the course of an astonishing 56-year career, Lütken designed not only every conceivable form of table-glass, incorporating techniques such as pressing, casting, blowing, and free-forming, but also most of Holmegaard's promotional material. He produced pieces for every official exhibition of Danish handicraft for three decades, many of which were adapted for commercial production. Lütken pieces are commonly applied with the engraved signature *Holmegaard* followed by the production date framing his own *PL* monogram (e.g. *19PL59*).

So what made Lütken so great? Perhaps the answer is best explained by Ronald Stennett-Willson (pp.224–33): "Glassware always comprises two lines, the inner and the outer, and it's the combination of the two that makes a piece interesting. Per Lütken understood that better than any other 20th-century glass designer."

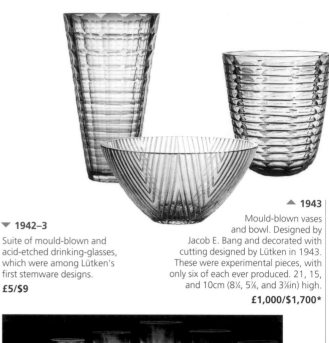

▼ **1942–3**
Suite of mould-blown and acid-etched drinking-glasses, which were among Lütken's first stemware designs.
£5/$9

▲ **1943**
Mould-blown vases and bowl. Designed by Jacob E. Bang and decorated with cutting designed by Lütken in 1943. These were experimental pieces, with only six of each ever produced. 21, 15, and 10cm (8¼, 5⅞, and 3⅞in) high.
£1,000/$1,700*

1942

▼ **1947**
Mould-blown and glue-blasted ice bucket (13243). A unique exhibition piece. 13cm (5in).

The numbers stated in captions for Per Lütken designs fall into two categories: four-digit, which are Lutken's own numbers taken from his hand-drawn pattern books, and longer seven- or eight-digit Holmegaard production numbers, which would have been used for internal factory purposes and ordering.

Mould-blown and trailed bowl/vase, from the *Caravellen* series. Designed in 1950 for an exhibition. 14cm (5½in) diam.

£450/$765*

▶ **1952**

Mould-blown and swung *Bone* vases – experimental pieces that never entered commercial production. However, derivatives of this design were made, most notably in Sweden. 15.5cm (6in) and 18cm (7in).

£70/$120

▲ **1952**

Mould-blown *Beak* and *Heart* vases in aqua (15734, 14405, 14403, 15732). *Beaks* produced 1952–76, *Hearts* produced 1955–76, all in various sizes in aqua and smoke. From Holmegaard's 1971 catalogue.

From left £70/$120, £40/$70, £60/$100, £40/$70

1953

◀ **from 1951**

Mould-blown and swung *Næbvase* (*Duckling* or *Beak Vases*). Designed from 1951 and produced in numerous sizes, colours, and forms 1952–76. Max. 30.5cm (12in).

From left £90/$155, £40/$70, £130/$220, £120/$205

▼ **1953**

Catalogue entry for mould-blown and furnace-worked *Tivoli* cocktail service (17823 and 14938). Produced 1953–80, in colourless and smoke. From Holmegaard's 1963 catalogue.

Martini mixer £75/$130, Glasses £5–10/$9–17 each

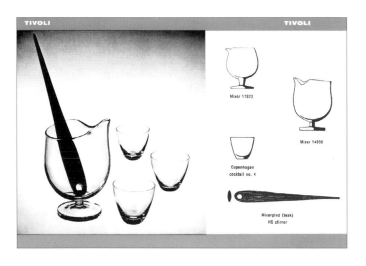

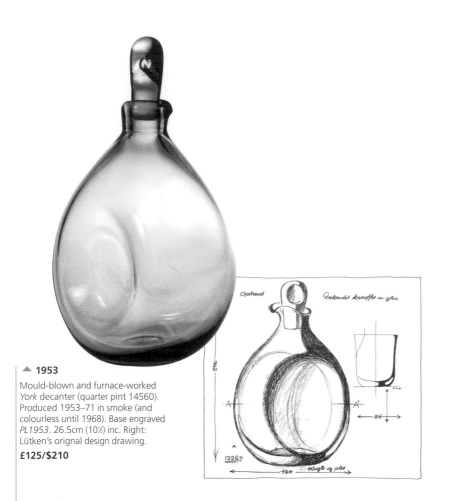

▲ 1953

Mould-blown and furnace-worked *York* decanter (quarter pint 14560). Produced 1953–71 in smoke (and colourless until 1968). Base engraved *PL1953*. 26.5cm (10½) inc. Right: Lütken's orignal design drawing.

£125/$210

▲ 1955

Mould-blown *Hellas* vase in smoke (15388). Produced 1955–77 in aqua and smoke. 15.5cm (6in).

£60/$100

1953

▲ 1953

Free-formed bowl in *Titan* yellow (14591). Designed in 1953 and produced as a limited series from 1953. Base engraved *Holmegaard 1955*. It is a copy of a similar bowl designed by Hugo Gehlin in 1942, for Gullaskruf, Sweden. 29.5cm (11⅝in) diam.

£75/$130

▼ 1955 and '56

Holmegaard advertisement in *Pottery Gazette* for mould-blown *Aristocrat* decanter (16588) and *Scanada* glasses. Glasses (also known as *Canada*) produced 1955–90; decanter produced 1956–74, in colourless and smoke. Decanter: 37.5cm (14¾in) inc.

Decanter £100/$170, Glasses £8–15/$14–25

△ 1955
Cased, mould-blown ashtray
(15912–18). Base engraved *15918*.
6cm (2⅜in) diam.
£100/$170

▶ ▼ 1956
Mould-blown *Unamak* vase
(3411026–28) and ashtray (3410001).
Both designed in 1956; vase produced
1957–76 and ashtray 1956–67, both
in aqua and smoke. Ashtray engraved
19PL59, 6cm (2⅜in) high; vase
engraved *19PL62*, 18.5cm (7¼in).
Left £30/$55, right £65/$110

△ 1956
Mould-blown hurricane lamp (181735),
produced 1956–70. From Holmegaard's
1970 catalogue.
£60/$100

▼ 1956
Mould-blown *Winston* service (16192). Produced
1956–73 in colourless, *Odelgrön (Edel green)*, and
smoke. From left: wine glass, teak-stoppered decanter,
tumbler, and jug. From Holmegaard's 1970 catalogue.
**Decanter £150/$255, Glasses £10–15/$17–25,
Jug £35/$60**

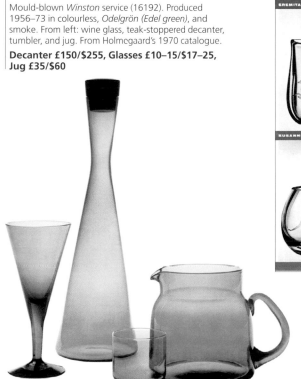

△ 1957
Catalogue entry (1963) for mould-blown
and engraved *Eremitage* (15473–74),
Louise (341281), and *Susanne* vases
(15387). Produced 1957–76. Some
examples of the deer vase (top left) are
engraved *AB*, the monogram of Jacob's
brother Arne Bang (1901–83), who
designed the motifs.
£100/$170*

◀ **1958**

Mould-blown vase (1286). This vase served as the role model for Holmegaard's iconic *Gulvæse* (*Floor vase*), 1962, credited to Otto Brauer (p.161). 14cm (5½in).

£60/$100

▶ **1958**

Mould-blown *Labrador* vase (1624). Designed in 1958 and exhibited in New York in the same year. Base engraved *19PL58*. 39.5cm (15⅝in).

£200/$340*

▲ **1959**

Lütken's distinctive *PL* monogram framed by the date *1959*. Holmegaard ceased the application of date-related signatures in 1961.

1958

◀ **1960**

Mould-blown *Greenland* series. From left: tumbler (17657), vase (17706), broad-based "carafe" vase (17720), and cylinder vase (17652–6). Designed in 1960 and produced 1961–4. Carafe-shaped vase: 20cm (7⅞in). Extreme right vase: 32.5cm (12¾in). Advertisement by Bowman & Son, Holmegaard's UK agent.

From left £30/$55, £110/$190, £125/$210, £90/$155

▼ **1960**

Publicilty photograph of rolled and shaped *Fried Egg* ashtray. Produced 1960–70 in smoke (170522, 170514, and 170506) and *Safire* (290528, 290510, and 290502).

£30/$55

GREENLAND BY HOLMEGAARDS OF DENMARK

EDWARD BOWMAN & SON LTD.

GAMAGE BUILDING HOLBORN LONDON E.C.1   HOLBORN 6540

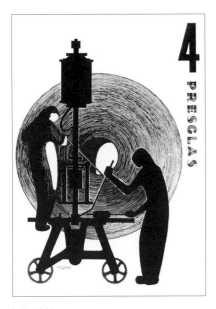

▲ **1960**

Lütken etching of manual glass-pressing. From Holmegaard's 1960 catalogue.

▼ **1960**

Mould-blown *Roskilde* jug (101436, colourless; 161430, smoke). Produced 1960–72. 30cm (11⅞in).

£80/$135

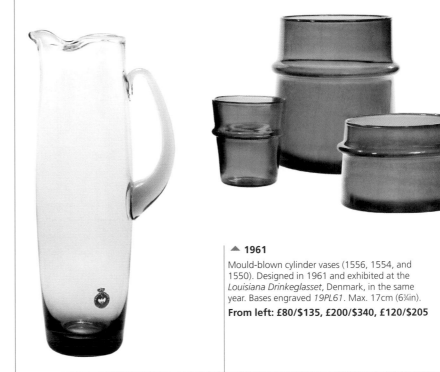

▲ **1961**

Mould-blown cylinder vases (1556, 1554, and 1550). Designed in 1961 and exhibited at the *Louisiana Drinkeglasset*, Denmark, in the same year. Bases engraved *19PL61*. Max. 17cm (6¾in).

From left: £80/$135, £200/$340, £120/$205

▲ **1961**

Mould-blown and trailed *Krukker* vase (1517). Designed in 1961 and exhibited in New York in 1962. Base engraved *HOLMEGAARD PL 20-44 1962*. 10cm (3⅞in) high.

£250/$425

▼ **1962**

Mould-blown cylinder vases (17826–8). Produced 1962–4, in solid *Rubin* and cobalt blue. Max. 27.5cm (10⅞in).

From left £120/$205, £45/$75, £70/$120

▲ 1963

Mould-blown *Majgrøn* (*May-Green*) range. From left: carafe (460105), vase (46022), vase (460121), and carafe (460097). Produced 1963–70. From Holmegaard's 1969 catalogue.

From left £45/$75, £45/$75, £25/$45, £45/$75

1963

▼ 1965

Dip-moulded and trailed carafe (2007). 32cm (12⅝in). Unique exhibition piece.

▲ 1966

Mould-blown and pressed hurricane lamps (261719 and 261727). Designed in 1966 and produced 1967–70. From Holmegaard's 1970 catalogue.

Left £80/$135, Right £60/$100

▲ 1963

Pressed *Skjold* box. Produced 1963–71. 10cm (3⅞in).

£45/$75

▼ 1965

Cast-glass ashtray from the *Riflet* range. Pieces of this type are commonly associated with Pukeberg, Sweden, who specialized in cast glass. 10cm (3⅞in) wide.

£20/$35

1966

Mould-blown *Moonstone* range. From left: bowl (280412), vase (280032), candlestick (280628), and vase (280057). Produced 1967–70. From Holmegaard's 1970 catalogue.

From left £30/$55, £45/$75, £50/$85 a pair, £35/$60

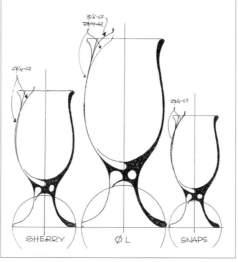

1966

Mould-blown *Pearl* goblets. Produced 1966–72. Original design drawing dated: 3/5/66.

£10–15/$17–25

1969

Clay-moulded *Lava* vase/art object. Base engraved *2258*. 22.5cm (8⅞in). Unique exhibition piece.

1968

Mould-blown and cased *Carnaby* range. From left: 600080, 390245, 390098), 390310, and 561308. Designed in 1968 and produced 1969–76. From Holmegaard's 1970 catalogue. Max. 26.5cm (10½in).

From left £165/$280, £110/$190, £250/$425, £80/$135, £60/$100

1967

Mould-blown *Havanna* range in smoke-brown. Carafe and vases (vases: 27291 and 2676). Designed in 1967 and produced 1968–9 (also in lavender blue). 12–35cm (4¾–13¾in). From Holmegaard's 1968 catalogue.

From left £70/$120, £50/$85, £35/$60

▼ 1969

Clay-moulded *Lava* range (611517, 610055, 610402, 610048, and 610014). Designed in 1969 and produced 1970–7. From Holmegaard's 1970 catalogue.

£150–300/$255–510*

▲ 1970

Free-blown *Blue Lava* series vases. From left: 610089, 610105; front: 610618. Produced 1970–7. From Holmegaard's 1970 catalogue.

From left £200/$340, £50/$85, £300/$510

1969

▲ 1969

Mould-blown *Tivoli* service (669804, etc). Produced 1969–90. Holmegaard advertisement, 1971. Decanter: 22.5cm (8⅞in). Not to be confused with Lütken's *Tivoli* cocktail suite, 1953 (p.147)

Decanter £50/$85, Glasses £10/$17

▼ 1970

Free-formed opaque *Perlemer* vase (2389), goblet (34145910), and bottle (2419). Max. 16cm (6¼in).

£75–150/$130–255*

▲ 1970

Mould-blown bubble-glass vase (2149). 16.5cm (6½in). Unique exhibition piece.

▲ **1970**
Free-blown and furnace-worked *Maskekrukker* (*Mask vase*) (2301–07). Designed in 1970 and produced in 1971. Lütken developed this series for an exhibition at the Kunstindustrimuseet, Copenhagen, in October 1971. 23–37cm (9–14⅜in). Unique exhibition piece.

▼ **1970**
Mould-blown olive-green *Vintergaek* (*Snowdrop*) decanter. 23.5cm (9¼in) inc.
£150/$255

▲ **1973**
Clay-moulded decanter (2759). Designed in 1973 and exhibited in Stockholm the same year. 31cm (12¼in) inc. Unique exhibition piece.

▼ **1970**
Opaque colour-splashed vase (2397) in *Unica* (limited edition) series. Base engraved *19PL70 HOLMEGAARD 2397*. 20cm (7⅞in).
£250/$425*

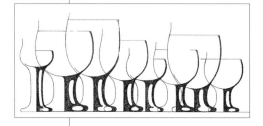

▲ **1971**
Mould-blown *Inn Glass* service designed in 1971 and produced 1972–99. 9.5–15.5cm (3¾–6in). (Matching decanter: 23cm/9in inc.) Lütken drawing of one of his most successful designs.
£5–10/$9–17

▲ **1974**
Mould-blown opaque *Cascade* vase (3135). Designed in 1974 and produced 1975–9. Base engraved *19PL75*. 11cm (4¼in).
£35/$60

The Holmegaard name is occasionally spelt "Holmegaards", as if a plural. This is because the glassworks was originally built on a farm owned by the Holmegaard family, and thus was Holmegaard's farm. However, the possessive apostrophe used in English does not occur in the Danish language .

1975

Clay-moulded vase/art object (2811). Designed in 1975 and exhibited in New York the same year. 22cm (8⅝in). Unique exhibition piece.

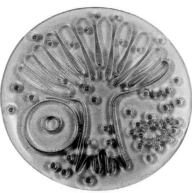

▶ **1975**

The Four Seasons cast reliefs. Limited series of 2,500 sets to commemorate 150 years of Holmegaards Glasværk, 1825–1975. All 38cm (15in) diam.

£150–225/$255–380

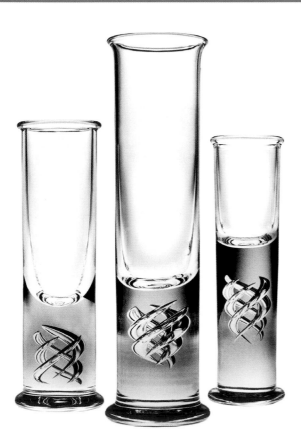

◀ **1980**

Mould-blown *Labrador* candlestick. Design derived from 1958 exhibition range. 25cm (9⅞in).

£150/$255

◀ **1979**

Mould-blown and furnace-worked *High Life* glasses. Produced 1979–2002. Originally sold in pairs.15, 16.5, and 21.5cm (5⅞, 6½, and 8½in).

From left £22/$40, £30/$55, £15/$25

◀ **1982**

Free-formed, cased, opaque colour-splashed exhibition port glass (3309, wine glass 3308). Designed by Lütken to commemorate his 40th anniversary at Holmegaard (1942–82). Port glass: 19cm (7½in), wine glass 16cm (6¼in).

£250/$425*

▶ 1982

Furnace-worked, colour-splashed *Africa's Rose* bowls (3157–8). Designed for *Living Arts* exhibition in Bryanston, South Africa, 1982. Inspired by South Africa's national flower, the protea. 37cm (14⅝in) diam.

£110/$190*

▼ 1985

Free-blown and furnace-worked *Folded Bowl* (3405–7). Designed for exhibition in Nykøbing, 1985, but entered commercial production as the *Laguna* bowl, 1985–2000. 30–55cm (11⅞–21⅝in). (For similar *Handkerchief* vases see p.107.)

£150/$255*

▲ 1986

Mould-blown service (3434–36). One of Lütken's last designs, designed for his retirement exhibition. Jug: 27cm (10⅝in). Unique exhibition pieces.

▲ 1984

Free-blown and colour-splashed *Cascade* bowl (3379–86). Designed for Australian exhibition, 1984. 12–20.5cm (4¾–8in).

£150/$255

▼ 1985

Pin-blown *Boblevæse* (*Bubble Vase*) art object (3432–3). Designed for exhibition in Nykøbing, 1985. Blown by piercing a gob of hot glass with a damp stick, the humidity on the stick vapourized and expanded the glass. The foot was then shaped and the piece finished in the usual manner. 25cm (9⅞) and 30cm (11⅞in).

£150/$255

1986

GLASS IS LIFE

▲ 1986

Lütken at his retirement exhibition in 1986, and the cover of the retrospective book of his 45-year career, published the same year.

Michael Bang 1944–

Holmegaard 1968–2002

Michael Bang became entranced by the vital and spontaneous processes of glassmaking while visiting Holmegaard as a child with his father, Jacob (pp.140–5), and began to design vessels at the age of 13. His early commitment to glass was tested by two spells working with ceramics, at Royal Copenhagen (1962–4), and with Bjørn Wimblat (1964–6). He then worked at Ekenås Glasbruk, Sweden (1966–8), before being appointed permanent designer at Holmegaard's Odense plant. He moved to its principal factory at Fensmark in 1974.

"There is something alchemic about making glass," he said. "The most important factor is teamwork. Working with the craftsmen is akin to conducting the soloists in an orchestra: you have to cooperate because it is almost impossible to succeed alone. I strive for taut forms, as simple as possible. I want to give people more than function, I want to give them an experience."

Michael Bang's career ground to a premature halt around 2000 due to the progressive advance of Alzheimer's disease. He never achieved the longevity or design diversity of his father or Per Lütken, but his colourful ranges of *Palette* kitchen and lighting glass remain among the most distinctive of Scandinavia's 20th-century glass forms.

▼ **1969**
Mould-blown, colour-cased *Napoli* series. Produced 1969–71. From Holmegaard's 1971 catalogue.
From left £30/$55, £65/$110, £45/$75, £30/$55

1969

▲ **1970**
Mould-blown *Palet* (*Palette*) range, including salt and pepper pots, spice jars, herring dishes, and oil and vinegar bottles. Produced 1970–5. From Holmegaard's 1971 catalogue. For prices, see right.

▶ **1970**

Mould-blown and opaque colour-cased table lamps. Designed in 1970 and produced from 1971 (*Parasol*, 1971–8; *Astronaut*, 1971–5; *Parasol*, 1971–8; *Victoria* 1971–5). From Holmegaard's 1971 catalogue.

From left £80/$135, £80/$135, £200/$340, £65/$110

▲ **1981–3**

Mould-blown and furnace-worked *Cluck-Cluck* decanter. Based on a traditional form made for over 1,000 years, and produced at Holmegaard since the mid-19th century. Michael Bang produced a wide range of variants, including one with a crown-shaped stopper and another leaning as if drunk. This example is an exhibition piece. 26cm (10¼in).

Production examples £40/$70*

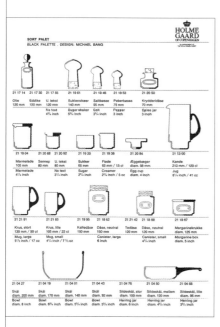

▲ **1970**

Catalogue entry for *Sort Palet* (*Black Palette*) range of colour-cased kitchen glassware. Produced 1970–5. Despite its name, the *Black Palette* range was made in opaque-white and cased in blue, yellow, orange, green, and amber. From Holmegaard's 1971 catalogue.

Salts £50/$85 pair, Storage jars £35/$60, Herring dishes £45/$75

▽ **1971**

Mould-blown *Hulvæse* (*Hole vase*). Designed for Odense and produced 1973–8. This example 18cm (7in), but made in several sizes.

£40/$70*

▲ **1981**

Auto-blown flask. Shape designed by Michael Bang in 1981; decoration for this example designed by Harald Wiberg in 1991. This flask is among Holmegaard's most common shapes, having been produced annually from 1981 to 1992 as a collectors' series. Before 1991 they were applied with different Christmas designs by Jette Frølich. 16.5cm (6½in).

£5–10/$9–17

Other Designers

Jacob Bang, Per Lütken, and Michael Bang were Holmegaard's most significant designers, but several others also made contributions. They include Siegfried Wagner, Ole Winther, Nanna and Jørgen Ditzel, Hjørdis Olsson, Charlotte Rude, Bent Severin, Christer and Christel Holmgren, and Otto Brauer.

Bent Severin's range of *Princess* glasses, 1957, were among Holmegaard's best-sellers, particularly in the United States, and demand for second-hand examples has soared since production finally ceased. Christer Holmgren, Lütken's assistant from 1957 to 1971, contributed many designs, some jointly with his wife, Christel.

Austrian-born Christel and Swedish Christer both studied design before meeting in Denmark during the 1960s. Settling in Naestved, a short drive from Holmegaard, they established a consultancy, C & C Holmgren, in 1971, designing a broad range of graphics, toys, and household items, from cast-iron candlesticks to plastic spatulas. Christer's *Neck Glass* for Holmegaard was truly a product of its age: a large, footless goblet supplied with a leather thong. The thong, referred to as a "third hand", was used to suspend the glass around users' necks, allowing them to "smoke, eat, shake hands – or even hold another drink".

The credit for Holmegaard's most recognizable design is also assigned outside the Bang-Lütken triumvirate. The individual credited with variously sized and coloured *Gulvæse* (*Floor Vase*), Otto Brauer, was not a draughtsman but a glass-blower at the company's Odense works. Introduced in 1962, its shape, resembling a giant Bordeaux wine bottle with a wide lip, was formally devised in 1962, but was clearly inspired by Lütken's bottle-vases (1958) (p.150) and the jug from Jacob Bang's *Capri* series (1961) (p.145).

Over their production span (1962–80) *Gulvæse* variations included giants measuring 35.5cm (14in) tall, and bright red, blue, and orange colour-cased versions. The largest most colourful versions have become increasingly sought after, but collectors should be aware of reproductions of the smaller sizes in solid-colours, made for Ralph Lauren.

◀ **1957**

Mould-blown *Princess* series glasses. Designed by Bent Severin, for Kastrup, in 1957 and produced 1958–84. The best-selling range of glasses that Holmegaard ever produced. 10, 16.5, and 10.5cm (3⅞, 6½, and 4in).

£5–15/$9–25

1955

▼ ▶ **1955 and 1962**

Mould-blown *Viking* carafes. Designed by Ole Winther, for Torben Anton, a Danish wine company. Blue and green produced 1955 and 1962–70 respectively. The blue is sealed with a Viking mask and the green with a *CE* cipher for Cherry Elsinore, a Danish cherry wine. Auto-blown versions are known bearing the logo of British wine merchants Stowells of Chelsea. c.22cm (8⅝in).

£25/$45*

1962

Mould-blown *Gulvæse* (*Floor Vases*). Designed by Otto Brauer, for Odense. Produced 1962–80. Cased examples are the most sought after. Max. 35.5cm (14in).

From left £25/$45, £350/$595, £400/$680, £40/$70, £60/$100

1971

Mould-blown and blue-trailed *Blå Time* decanter. Designed by Christel and Christer Holmgren. 20.5cm (8in) inc.

£70/$120

1970

Mould-blown *Hivert* (*Down the Hatch*) schnapps decanter. Designed by Hjørdis Olsson and Charlotte Rude, for Odense. Originally supplied with metal-mounted cork stopper. 15cm (5⅞in).

Without stopper £40/$70
With stopper £80/$135

1971

1958

Mould-blown *Largo* (*Silver Birch*) service (1379–99). Designed by Christer Holmgren and produced 1958–75. Holmegaard promotional artwork, 1961, wrongly crediting Per Lütken as the designer.

£5–15/$9–25*

1971

Carneval series. Designed by Christel Holmgren and produced 1971–3.

Small punch glass £15/$25
Punch bowl with ladle £250/$425

1959

Mould-blown and furnace-worked *Natblå* vase (32338). Designed by Nanna and Jørgen Ditzel, for Odense. 25cm (9⅞in).

£150–250/$255–425*

CARNEVAL
DESIGN: CHRISTEL HOLMGREN - EXNER

HOLMEGAARD OF COPENHAGEN

Iittala 1881–present

Although hardly a household name, Iittala is widely regarded by design connoisseurs as the most important glassmaker of the post-war period. Its history can be divided into two strands: the economic, which has seen its ownership change hands several times, and the artistic, which has been dominated by Tapio Wirkkala (1915–85) and Timo Sarpaneva (1925–2005): two towering figures of industrial design.

Iittala entirely lacked a glassmaking identity until 1932–6, when a series of competitions elicited the iconic Modernist designs of the husband-and-wife architectural team Aino and Alvar Aalto. Although their association with the works was short-lived, Aino's *Bölgeblick* range of horizontally banded pressed-glass (1932) and Alvar's asymmetrical *Savoy* vase (1935) placed Iittala on the international stage.

Despite the Aaltos' contributions, Iittala's international repute rests solidly on the original, subtle, and influential work of Wirkkala and Sarpaneva, who, between them, contributed designs for almost 90 years. After Wirkkala's death in 1985, and Sarpaneva's withdrawal during the 1990s, the artistic mantle shifted to various designers, most notably Valto Kokko (1963–93), Jorma Vennola (1975–86), and Harri Koskinen (1995–).

The problem with the burgeoning talents of Wirkkala and Sarpavena was that Iittala was probably too small for the both of them and this led to a rivalry of John Lennon and Paul McCartney proportions. Wirkkala, the "Lennon" to Sarpaneva's "McCartney", won three Grand Prix at the 1951 Milan Triennale, and his accelerating international reputation as a "genius" left Sarpaneva increasingly alienated and embittered. Yet while Wirkkala arguably possessed the greater talent, Sarpaneva won a Grand Prix in 1954 and made important contributions to Iittala's success. In the final analysis, the competitive tensions between the two brought out the creative best in both and, in the process, helped to define the vocabulary of modern design.

The fact that Iittala produced some of its bestselling designs over several decades dents their "collectability". For instance, while an original 1930s Aalto *Savoy* vase would be worth thousands of pounds, a modern version would struggle to match its current design shop price. Conversely, short-run pieces, such as Sarpaneva's *Finlandia*, are far safer bets.

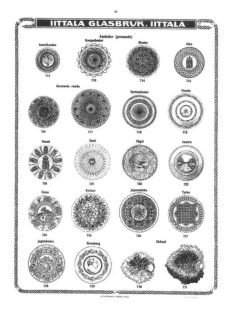

◀ **1913**
Page of pressed-glass plates from Iittala's illustrated catalogue. The patterns illustrated are evocative of similar examples produced by American and other European glassmakers from the 1840s.
£5–10/$9–17

▲ **1920**
The Karhula logo from the front cover of the company's illustrated catalogue.

▲ **1930**
Bohemian-style cut and engraved Art Deco decanters or perfume bottles made at Karhula/Iittala during the 1930s. The necks are ground for silver mounts. Contemporary photo.
£150/$255

◀ 1947
Finnish advertisement illustrating Tapio Wirrkala's recent *Kantarelli* (*Chanterelle*) vase/art object and glass building bricks. This image encapsulates Iittala's dilemma: whether to promote itself as a maker of fine or industrial glass.

▼ 1949
Finnish advertisement for Karhula/Iittala storage jars.

▲ 1936
Architect Alvar Aalto's pressure-blown *Aalto* vases have proved to be Iittala's most iconic design. Originally named *Eskimo Woman's Leather Trousers*, the *Aalto* became known as the *Savoy* vase before gaining its current name in 1975. From Iittala's 2005 catalogue.
Large price variations according to age:
£35–3,500/$60–5,950*

◀ 1932
A 1948 advertisement for Aino Aalto's Modernist *Bölgeblick* pressed-glass tumblers, which remain among Iittala's bestsellers.
£5/$9

◀ 1946
Mould-blown and enamelled shot-glass. Base enamelled *Iittala-46*. Karhula/ Iittala glass was often enamelled during the 1930s and '40s. 7.5cm (2⅞in).
£70/$120

KEY DATES

1881 Iittala founded near Hämeenlinna, Finland, 105km (65 miles) north of Helsinki. Produces domestic glassware.

1891 Karhula founded at Karhula, on the Baltic coast, 135km (85 miles) east of Helsinki. Produces bottles.

1915 Karhula bought by engineering conglomerate Ahlström.

1917 Iittala bought by Ahlström.

1917 Civil war follows Finland's independence after 600 years. Republic of Finland founded in 1919.

1925–33 Eric Ehrstrom artistic director of Karhula/Iittala.

1930s Series of design competitions attracts designs by Aino and Alvar Aalto, Göran Hongell, Arttu Brummer, and Gunnel Nyman.

1933 Karhula/Iittala wins Grand Prix for glass at Milan Triennale.

1933–57 Göran Hongell artistic director.

1936 Alvar Aalto's *Eskimo Woman's Leather Trousers* vase wins design competition at the 1937 Paris exhibition and enters commercial production.

1945 Ahlström divides production: Karhula to make bottles; Iittala to make pressed and blown table-glass.

1946 Another competition discovers Tapio Wirkkala and Kaj Franck; both join Iittala's design staff.

1950 Timo Sarpaneva joins Wirkkala as resident designer at Iittala; Franck leaves to join Nuutajärvi, owned by Finnish shipbuilding conglomerate Wärtsilä.

1956 Iittala "i" logo, originally designed to accompany Sarpaneva's *i-line* collection, adopted as company logo.

1985 Death of Tapio Wirkkala.

1985 Ahlström buys Riihimäki glassworks, which it closes in 1990.

1987 Ahlström merges Iittala with Nuutajärvi. Ahlström owns 80 per cent of new glassworks, Wärtsilä 20 per cent.

1990 Finnish Hackman Group buys Iittala-Nuutajärvi.

1995 Ahlström sells Karhula to American bottlemaker Owens-Illinois.

2004 Iittala regains independence through management buyout after Hackman sold to the ALI Group.

The Iffland Portfolio

▲ Göran Hongell
Mould-blown colourless vase (*6212*). Exhibited in Paris in *1937*.
£100/$170*

▲ Kaj Franck
Mould-blown spirit flask, with engraving by Teodor *Käppi*, Iittala's finest engraver. *75cl* (26½fl oz).
£80/$135

▲ Tapio Wirkkala
Free-formed vase with wild animals, including a moose and a bear, engraving attributed to Teodor Käppi. The surface was apparently sand-blasted or acid-etched, then selectively polished. 33.5cm (14in).
£1,000/$1,700

▲ Rikhard Jungell
Mould-blown cut and engraved bowl (*5027*) with engraving by Teodor Käppi (*K3165*). 28.5cm (11¼in) diam.
£250/$425

▲ Tapio Wirkkala
Cased and free-formed, opaque-white, shell-shaped ashtray (3317–5014). Designed in 1947 and exhibited at the Milan Triennale in 1951. Produced commercially until 1963. 12 and 15cm (4¾ and 5⅞in) diam.
Early example £600/$1,020, later £150/$255

In 1947, in an attempt to confirm its status as a leading producer of "designer glass", Iittala hired the German-born Finnish photographer Heinrich Iffland (1897–1943) to shoot a series of exhibition pieces by its leading designers. The line-up comprised the head of the design team, Göran Hongell (1902–73), Kaj Franck (1911–89), Rikhard Jungell (1900–73), Gunnel Nyman (1909–48), and Tapio Wirkkala, who had just joined the company.

Some of the images in the resulting folio of black and white prints were used for occasional advertising purposes. However, most were then forgotten and remained stored in Iittala's archive. They were finally redis-covered in 2004 during research for this book and are published here for the first time in over 50 years. In most cases, the whereabouts of the pieces illustrated are unknown, and information, such as their sizes, production techniques, and design numbers, is restricted to occasional pencil-written notes on the reverse of some of the prints. These jottings are incorporated into the appropriate captions above and opposite, in italics for clarity.

▲ **Gunnel Nyman**
Mould-blown cut bowl for Karhula (*6209*) with engraving by Teodor Käppi (*K3162*). Exhibited in Paris in 1937.
£1,200/$2,050

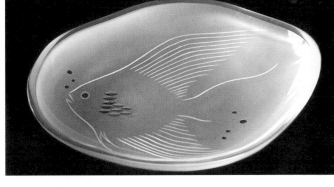

▲ **Gunnel Nyman**
Mould-blown polished fish dish for Karhula (*6211*) with engraving by Teodor Käppi (*K3164*). Exhibited in Paris in 1937.
£2,500/$4,250*

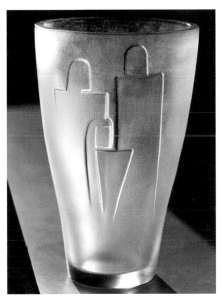

▲ **Gunnel Nyman**
Mould-blown vase for Karhula (*6310*) of extraordinary Modernist design, the surface matted by sand-blasting or acid-etching.
£800/$1,360

▲ **Gunnel Nyman**
Mould-blown and cut *Rye Field* vase for Karhula (*6311*), cutting by Rikhard Jungell (*S/2125*). Exhibited in Paris in 1937. 11cm (4¼in).
£600/$1,020

▲ **Gunnel Nyman**
Mould-blown and polished vase for Karhula. Mention of *Käppi* in notes suggests the presence of engraved decoration, though none is apparent. 27.5cm (10⅞in).
£800/$1,360

Gunnel Nyman was one of the brightest lights in mid-20th-century glass. Trained at Helsinki's Institute of Applied Art, she initially worked in furniture, then later in textiles, wallpaper, ceramics, and silver. However, she remains best known as Finland's leading glass designer of the 1940s.

Nyman freelanced for all of Finland's fine glassworks: Riihimäki (1932–47), Karhula (1935–7), then Iittala (1946–47), and Nuutajärvi (1946–8). The designs illustrated here provide a snapshot of the range of her work: spanning plain, engraved, moulded, and cut glass. However, bubble inclusions, one of her most distinctive decorative forms, are absent from the examples shown here.

The success of her designs prepared the path for the series of outstanding Finnish women designers, including Helena Tynell and Nanny Still (pp.208–19), that rose to international prominence after Nyman's premature death in 1948.

The notes and design numbers written on the reverse of the prints suggest that all these pieces were produced for the World Exhibition in Paris, 1937.

Tapio Wirkkala 1915–85

Iittala 1946–85

▼ **1946**
Mould-blown shot-glass. Designed
in 1946 and produced c.1947–50.
Karhula/Iittala glassware was
enamelled at Karhula pre-1939, but
the enamelling department moved to
Iittala in 1945. 6cm (2⅜in).
£60/$100

▲ **1947**
Finnish newspaper advertisement, 1948,
showing mould-blown and engraved
Varsanjalka (*Foal's Foot*) vase (3215), to
celebrate the acquisition of an example by the
Museum of Modern Art, New York. Produced
1947–59. 12–26cm (4¾–10¼in).
£100–350/$170–595*

1946

Tapio Wirkkala was one of the giants and distinctive characters of post-war design. A Renaissance man, he worked in wood, plastics, metal, ceramics, and architecture, and created postage stamps, hand tools, and jewellery, though he remained, above all, a glassman.

A big, bearded, pipe-smoking bear of a man with fat, stubby fingers and a twinkle in his eye, Wirkkala spent half the year at his home in Lapland, in Finland's most northerly tip. Surrounded by its alternately verdant and ice-blasted expanses, he immersed himself in its traditions, its people, its wildlife, its silence, and its textures. The natural patterns created by temperatures of down to -50°C (-58°F) and searing winds were features common to many of his glass designs.

Trained in decorative carving, Wirkkala personified the hands-on, get-dirty approach to his craft. When relaxing, he went fishing or shaped scraps of wood with his pocket-knife; when working, he would carve his own moulds or rub shoulders with the blowers at the furnace mouth.

He enjoyed his considerable fame and acted as a sometime ambassador for his country. However, once snug in his log cabin in a far-flung forest, not even a presidential invitation could shift him. In design terms, Wirkkala's powers of observation, combined with a clear sense of line and function, elevated his work into a league of its own.

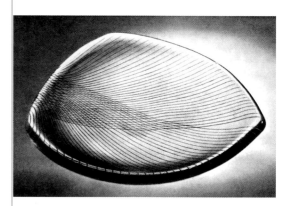

▲ **1946**
Mould-blown, furnace-worked, and engraved
Leaf Dish (3213). Designed in 1946 and
produced 1947–9. From Heinrich Iffland's series
of photographs (pp.164–5), as used for a Finnish
newspaper advertisement, 1948.
£4,000/$6,800*

▼ 1946 and 1947

Iittala publicity photograph, c.1951, showing free-formed, mould-blown, and engraved *Kantarelli* (*Chanterelle*) vases (3200, 3800, and 3280), which won the Grand Prix at the Milan Triennale, 1951. Left: Free-formed and engraved; designed in 1946 and produced 1947–57. 20cm (8in). Centre and right: Mould-blown and engraved; designed in 1947 and produced 1948–57 and from 1981. 10 and 21cm (3⅞ and 8¼in).

1946 original (50 made) £30,000/$51,000*
1947 original (50 made) £20,000/$34,000*
1948–57 production £2,000/$3,400*

MILAN TRIENNALE, 1954

These pieces formed Wirkkala's entry at the 1954 Milan Triennale and the images are contemporary Iittala photographs. The bubbles were created by piercing the glass with a wet stick while still ductile, then sealing it. The bubble was formed by steam, created by the extreme heat. Holmegaard designer Per Lütken and Dartington's Frank Thrower adopted similar techniques during the 1950s and '70s (P157).

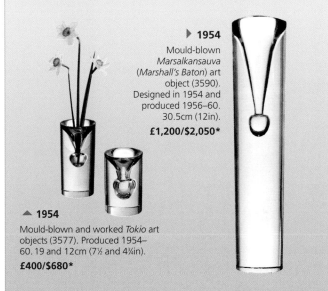

▶ 1954

Mould-blown *Marsalkansauva* (*Marshall's Baton*) art object (3590). Designed in 1954 and produced 1956–60. 30.5cm (12in).

£1,200/$2,050*

▲ 1954

Mould-blown and worked *Tokio* art objects (3577). Produced 1954–60. 19 and 12cm (7½ and 4¾in).

£400/$680*

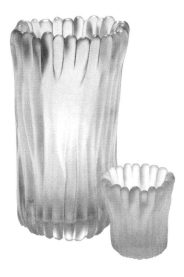

▲ 1950

Mould-blown and acid-matted *Jäkälä* (*Lichen*) vases (3515), exhibited at the Milan Triennale, 1951. Produced 1950–64. 21 and 9cm (8¼ and 3½in).

Left £800/$1,360, Right £200/$340

▲ 1953

Finnish magazine advertisement for mould-blown and engraved *Tatti* (*Boletus*) vases (3366 and 3552). Produced 1953–9. 7.5–18cm (2⅞–7in).

Small £100/$170, Largest £1,000/$1,700

▼ 1953

Mould-blown, furnace-worked, and engraved art objects (3341–3). Designed in 1953 and produced in the early 1950s. 12–23cm (4¾–9in) diam. Internal Iittala drawing.

£50–1,000/$85–1,700*

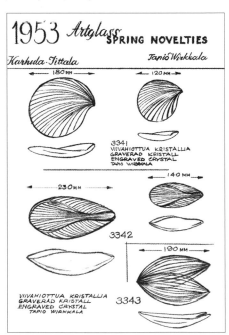

▲ **1958**
Mould-blown and sand-blasted colour-cased vase/art object (3578). Designed in 1958 and produced 1959–66 in blue, lilac, and grey. 22cm (8⅝in).
£80–120/$135–205

▼ **1959**
Mould-blown, sand-blasted, and colour-cased vase/art object (3305). Produced 1959–66. 14 and 20cm (5½ and 7⅞in). From Iittala's 1962 catalogue.
£120–300/$205–510*

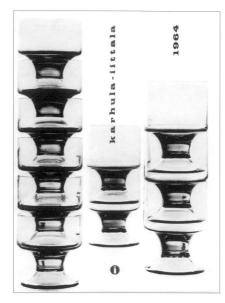

▲ **1963**
Stacks of mould-blown *Forest* glasses (2102). Produced 1963–72. 5–25cl (2–8¾fl oz). Front cover of Iittala's 1964 catalogue.
£15/$25

▼ **1959**
Iittala publicity photograph of mould-blown bottles (2507–08). Produced 1959–66 (tall version) and until 1968 (short version). 75 and 125cl (25 and 45fl oz).
£40–50/$70–85*

▲ **1960**
Mould-blown, sand-blasted, and colour-cased vase/art object (3306). Produced 1960–65. 18cm (7in).
£120–300/$205–510*

WIRKKALA AT VENINI AND ROSENTHAL

Wirkkala's name was propelled onto the international design scene through his displays at the Milan Triennales in 1951 and '54. So it was inevitable that he became a target for companies wishing to revitalize their image and ranges. The first to recruit his services was Philip Rosenthal. Wirkkala's association with Rosenthal AG resulted in hundreds of drawings submitted 1956–79, mostly for ceramics. Wirkkala's occasional contributions to Venini 1965–79 were marked by an abandonment of textured colourless glassware in favour of hotter and uncharacteristically flamboyant designs.

▼ **1965**
Rosenthal publicity photograph of the mould-blown and cut *Polaris* service (2520). Designed in 1965 and produced by Rosenthal Porzellan AG from 1966 for an unknown period.
£5/$9

▼ **1966**
Free-blown and furnace-worked *incalmo Bolle* bottles. Produced by Venini 1966–present. 19, 21, 41.5, 34.5, 25cm (7½, 8¼, 16½, 13½, and 10in).
£300–900/$510–1,530*

▲ **1966**
Free-blown and furnace-worked *Coreano* vase. Produced by Venini 1966–present. 35cm (13¾in).
£500–1,200/$850–2,050*

▼ **1966**
Mould-blown *Mesi* (*Honey*) tumbler (2013) and vases (2774). Produced 1966–85/71 respectively. Tumbler: 14cm (5½in); vases: 16.5 and 18cm (6½ and 7in). Factory technical drawing by Sirkka-Liisa Löflund.
£20/$35

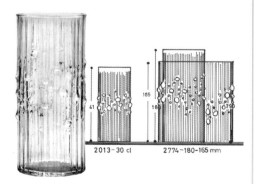

2013–30 cl   2774–180-165 mm

ULTIMA THULE

This distinctive series remains Wirkkala's best-known and most commercially successful design, elements of which are still in production. It first appeared in 1968, and the following year was selected as the in-flight glass service on Finnair. Wirkkala carved its original graphite moulds, but these were soon replaced by metal ones.

▲ **1968**
Ultima Thule bowl (2332), jug (2432), and tumbler (2052). Produced 1968 (jug 1970)–present. 6.5, 19.5, and 10cm (2½, 7⅝, and 3⅞in).
£10–40/$17–70*

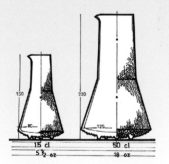

▲ **1970**
Carafes from *Ultima Thule* service (2532). Produced 1970–88. 15 and 22cm (5⅞ and 8⅝in). Factory technical drawing by Sirkka-Liisa Löflund.
£30–60/$55–100*

▲ **1968**
Bowls and dishes from *Ultima Thule* series (2332). Produced 1968–present. 11.5–37cm (4½–14⅝in) diam. Factory technical drawing by Sirkka-Liisa Löflund.
£10–100/$17–170*

▼ **1969**

Page of Wirkkala vases being produced at Iittala in 1969 but originally designed in 1955–69. Factory drawings by Sirkka-Liisa Löflund.

£45–200/$75–340*

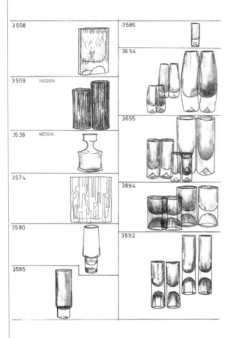

3508	3586
	3654
3509 NEOSIN	
	3655
3538 NEOSIN	
3574	3894
3580	3892
3585	

1969

▶ **1969**

Mould-blown *Hopla* tumbler (2017). Designed in 1969 and produced 1970–80. 12cm (4¾in). Factory technical drawing by Sirkka-Liisa Löflund.

£10/$17

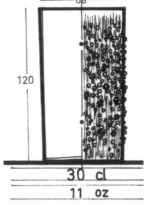

68

120

30 cl

11 oz

▼ **1969**

Mould-blown *Aslak* tumblers (2025). Designed in 1969 and produced 1970–88. 6.5, 7.5, 9, 10, and 13.5cm (2½, 2⅞, 3½, 3⅞, and 5¼in). Factory technical drawing by Sirkka-Liisa Löflund.

£5–10/$9–17

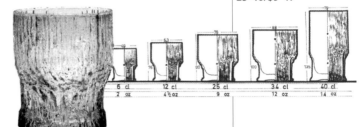

6 cl / 2 oz, 12 cl / 4½ oz, 25 cl / 9 oz, 34 cl / 12 oz, 40 cl / 14 oz

FINLANDIA VODKA

Owned by the Finnish state alcohol monopoly Alko, Finlandia vodka was launched internationally as a premium brand in 1970. With an eye on the American market, Wirkkala was commissioned to design a bottle that would suggest an impression of ice, the Arctic, and the wilderness.

The resulting award-winning *Finlandia* bottle, produced 1970–90, was created by Wirkkala, working alongside Iittala engineer Tapio Jääskeläinen. Wirkkala also designed the *Finlandia* tumbler, pairs of which were supplied with the bottle in gift sets. The bottle was made at Karhula, the tumblers at Iittala. A total of two million tumblers were produced. This series should not be confused with Sarpaneva's series of the same name (p174).

▲ **1969**

Mould-blown *Finlandia* vodka tumbler (0179). Designed in 1969 and produced 1970–73. Supplied as a free gift with bottles of Finlandia vodka. 6cm (2⅜in).

£5/$9

FIND FINLAND

SPIRIT OF WHITE REINDEER
cools you
warms you
Fresh, fiery, refreshing.

Cheers! Kippis!

FINLANDIA
80 PROOF · 100% GRAIN NEUTRAL SPIRITS 4/5 QUART
Vodka of Finland
Imported in This Bottle

FINLANDIA VODKA BY ALKO. Australian Agents: Finnish Sauna Co. of Aust. Pty. Ltd. 64 Penshurst Street, Willoughby 2068

▲ **1969**

Iittala advertisement for the *Finlandia* vodka bottle. Designed in 1969 and produced 1970–1990. Probably Wirkkala's best-selling design. 1l (34fl oz).

£2/$3

▼ **1971**

Mould-blown *Finlandia* carafe (0143). 27.5cm (10⅞in).

£60/$100

▼ 1974

Cast plaque/paperweight showing aerial view of the Karhula glassworks. Produced in 1974 to celebrate its centenary, 1874–1974. 11cm (4¼in) diam.

£40/$70

▲ 1978

Centrifuge-cast *Stellaria* candle-holder (2656). Produced 1978–present. 7cm (2¾in).

£10/$17

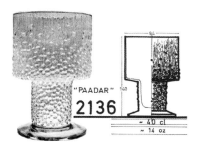

▲ 1970

Auto-blown *Paadar* goblet (2136). Produced 1970–3. The goblet took its name from Lake Paadar, beside which Wirkkala's cabin was situated. Factory technical drawing by Sirkka-Liisa Löflund. 14cm (5½in).

£10–20/$17–35

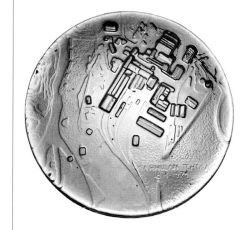

▼ 1972 and 74

Iittala publicity photograph of *Niva* (*Rushing Stream*) service (2731). Glasses produced 1972–92; decanter designed 1974 and produced 1975–86. Max. glass: 22cm (8⅝in).

Decanter £35/$60, Glasses £5–10/$9–17

Solaris från iittala.
Design Tapio Wirkkala

Solaris-tallrikarna finns i 4 storlekar och dessertskål.
Tål maskindisk. Färdigt presentförpackade.

▲ 1975

Swedish magazine advertisement for centrifuge-cast *Solaris* dish (2200). Produced 1975–95. The idea for *Solaris* was developed from the *Pilkkoavato* (*Hole in Ice*) artwork designed and made for Finland's President Urho Kekkonen in honour of his 70th birthday. Max. 30cm (11⅞in) diam.

£20–70/$35–120*

1982

▼ 1982

Mould-blown *Tapio* decanter (2501). Designed in 1982 to accompany the *Tapio* glasses service that had been exhibited at the Milan Triennale, 1954, and produced since 1956. Produced 1983–present. 25cm (9⅞in) inc.

£25/$45

Timo Sarpaneva 1926–2005

Iittala 1948–2005

As a child, Timo Sarpaneva pumped bellows while his grandfather beat iron in his village forge. "Everything was made by hand", he later recalled. "There was a place and special value for everything."

Timo Sarpaneva was a great designer in several media and received the most prestigious international awards. He won the Grand Prix at the 1954 Milan Triennale, and the Lunning Prize two years later. His work was avidly acquired by the world's leading museums and collectors. His *Orkidea* sculpture (1953) was chosen as the "most beautiful object of the year" in the United States, and his *Lancetti* art object (1952) is arguably superior. His ingenious, cast *Festivo* candlestick (1967) has remained a bestseller for 40 years. Yet this acclaim could not defend him from the insecurities he felt when being compared to larger-than-life Wirkkala.

After studying graphic design at Helsinki's School of Appplied Art, 1941–8, Sarpaneva rejected an unpaid job at Riihimäki and was about to join Holmegaard (pp.138–61) when Karhula-Iittala offered him a superior position. "The glassworks became my second home. The heat, smoke and sparks, how familiar all of it was!" he said. "Glass released me from the conventional and the three-dimensional ... and took me on a journey to a fourth dimension. Its external colours are only a small part of the whole. Inside it one can hide a whole landscape of the mind".

▼ **1952**
Mould-blown and polished *Lansetti II* (*Lancet*) art objects (3842). Produced 1952–7. *Lansetti* vases won the Grand Prix for glass at the Milan Triennale, 1954. Max. 26cm (10¼in).
Left £3,000/$5,100
Right £6,000/$10,200

1952

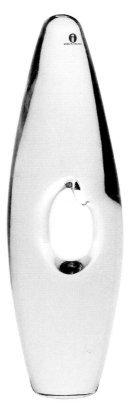

▶ **1953**
Free-formed, stick-blown, and polished *Orkidea* (*Orchid*) art object (3568). Designed in 1952, revised in 1985, and produced 1953–73 and 1985–present. This example produced *c.*1990. The series won the Grand Prix at the Milan Triennale, 1954, and was given Most Beautiful Object of the Year Award by *House Beautiful* magazine (USA) in the same year. 27cm (10⅝in).
Standard examples £150–450/$255–765* (double for early examples)

I-LINE

The *i-line* series (1956), Sarpaneva's first range of mould-blown glass, was intended to bridge the void between art glass and household/utility glass. It was marketed at a sophisticated international clientele and sold only in design shops and leading department stores. The range was produced in three colours of Sarpaneva's own making: lilac, blue, and broken green, together with an existing grey and colourless. Its distinctive "i" symbol was later adopted as Iitala's logo.

▲ **1956**
The Iittala "i" trademark logo, designed in 1956. Originally intended exclusively for the *i-line* series, but used for other products since the 1960s.

▲ **1956–7**
Mould-blown *i-402* decanter and *i-104* tumblers. Decanter produced 1957–62, tumblers 1956–67 and 2002. Decanter: 31.5cm (12⅜in). Tumblers; see below.
Decanter £60/$100, Glasses £10/$17

▼ **1956**
Mould-blown *Bird Bottles*, *i-400* (left) and *i-401* (right). Designed in 1956. i-400 produced 1957–66, i-401 1957–68. 19 and 17cm (7½ and 6¾in).
£120/$205

▶ **1957**
Mould-blown *i-403* carafe (32687–8). Produced 1957–64. Engraved *TIMO SARPANEVA IITTALA*. 25.5cm (10in).
£80/$135

▲ **1956**
Mould-blown *i-104* tumblers. Designed in 1956 and produced 1956–67 and 2004. Sarpaneva developed the lilac, blue, and broken green colours specifically for the *i-line* range. 5, 6, 6.5, and 8cm (2, 2⅜, 2½, 3in).
£10/$17

▼ **1957**
Steam-blown and flared colour-cased dish, unnamed (32476). Base engraved *TIMO SARPAVENA*. 35cm (13¾in).
£400/$680

▲ **1959**
Mould-blown and flared *Pinottava Pullo* (*Stackable Bottles*) (2509). Designed in 1959 and produced 1960–4. 11–16cm (4¼–6¼in).
£125–150/$210–255*

▲ 1961
Mould-blown carafe/vase (2518).
Produced 1961–c.1966.
24.5cm (9⅝in).

£100/$170

▲ ▼ 1964
Mould-blown, metal-mounted *Tsaikka* cups and saucers (2007–9). The glass was designed in 1957 and produced 1957–77, but the metal mounts were not designed until 1964 (produced 1964–77). 8cm (3in). Line drawing from Iittala's 1990 catalogue.

£10/$17

▲ 1964
Iittala advertisement for mould-blown *Pisaranrengus* (*Expanded Rings*) jug (2425) and tumblers (2005). Tumblers produced 1964–70, jug 1965–77. Tumblers: 8cm (3in); jug: 15cm (5⅞in). The series was made in the opal-white glass produced by Iittala's lampshade department.

Jug £75/$130, Tumblers £20/$35

FINLANDIA

The *Finlandia* series, one of Sarpaneva's most successful designs, came about by accident. He wanted to see the effect created by attacking ductile glass with a wood saw. So, a rough wooden mould was made and molten glass poured in. The sawing failed, but the effect impressed on the surface of the glass by the burnt wooden mould was impressive. All early *Finlandia* pieces were blown into wooden moulds that gradually disintegrated with use, but later commercial versions used metal moulds.

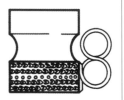

▲ 1964
Examples from the *Finlandia* series, blown in wooden moulds (3350–56). Produced 1964–71. 9.5–35cm (3¾–13¾in). Internal factory technical drawing by Sirkka-Liisa Löflund.

£100–200/$170–340*

▶ 1964
Wood-mould-blown smoke-grey *Finlandia* bowl/vase (3357). Produced 1964–70. Engraved *TIMO SARPANEVA 3579*. 5cm (3¾in).

£100–200/$170–340*

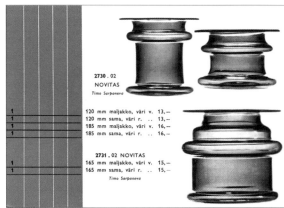

▲ 1965
Mould-blown *Novitas* vases (2730–33). Produced 1965–9. 12–18.5cm (4¾–7¼in). From Iittala's 1966 catalogue.

£25/$45

▼ 1967

Range of graphite-moulded *Festivo* candlesticks (2665). Produced 1967–present. The range was originally launched to celebrate the 50th anniversary of Finnish independence, but went on to become one of the company's most successful designs. 8–31.5cm (3–12⅜in). The largest example made is reputedly about one metre (40 inches) tall. From Iittala's 1977 catalogue.

£15–150/$25–255*

▼ 1967

Double-walled, mould-blown, and cased Heal's bowl/art object. Designed in 1967 and produced in 1968. Base engraved *TIMO SARPAVENA*. Heal's, the prestigious London furnishing store, was an important Iittala retailer. This piece was among a range of *Unica* objects designed for a Sarpaneva exhibition held at Heal's premises in 1969. 23cm (9in).

£100/$170

▲ 1967

Graphite mould-blown *Crocus* vase (2742). Produced 1967–81 (this example from before 1970.) Base engraved *TS*. *Crocus* and *Crassus* vases (see below) were designed simultaneously and formed by the same method. As with the *Finlandia* series, early examples of both were blown into graphite moulds, but metal moulds were used for later versions. 15cm (5⅞in).

£40/$70

▼ 1967

Pressure-blown *Satula* art objects/vases (3380). Produced 1967–71. 23 and 30cm (9 and 11⅞in). Internal technical drawing by Sirkka-Liisa Löflund.

£20 50/$35 85*

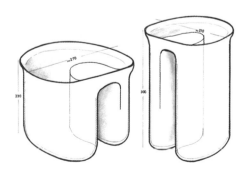

▲ 1968

Graphite-moulded *Festivo* goblet (2140). Produced 1968–84. The success of *Festivo* candlesticks, launched the previous year (see above), encouraged the design of this *en-suite* goblet. 19.5cm (7⅝in).

£10/$17

▲ 1967

Graphite-moulded *Crassus* vase (2743). Produced 1967–81. Base engraved *TS*. 15 and 22cm (5⅞ and 8⅝in).

£70/$120

▶ **1968**
Cover of German design magazine *Die Schaulade*, August 1970, showing mould-blown *Senaattori* (*Senator*) wine goblet (2104). Right: champagne flute from the same series. Both produced 1968–81. Goblet: 17.5cm (6⅞in); flute: 17cm (6¾ in).

£10/$17

iittala innovates

Kekkerit—Finnish for "party"—is iittala's newest glass. Shaped like a snowball, Kekkerit is a robust, happy goblet. In five sizes, from dainty liqueurs to hearty chalices. Next time you shop for a present, look for Kekkerit's elegant gift package with the poem on it. And when buying glass, always look for this mark:

i

iittala USA ltd.
225 Fifth Ave.
New York, N.Y. 10010
(212) 689-7430

in Canada:
R.G. How Limited
411 Des Recollets St.
Montreal, Quebec

◀ **1970**
American advertisement for machine-blown *Kekkerit* (*Party*) goblet (2105). Designed in 1970 and produced 1972–86. The *Kekkerit* series was the first to be blown in Iittala's Gemini machines. 7 and 9cm (2¾ and 3½in).

£5–10/$9–17

▲ **1977**
Graphite-moulded *Ritari* (*Knight*) goblet (2139). Designed in 1977 and produced 1979–81. 6–36cl/2–13fl oz. Cover illustration of Iittala's 1979 catalogue.

£15/$25

▲ **1981**
Hand-cast *Arkipelago* candlesticks (2647). Produced 1981–present. The hand-formed *Arkipelago* range comprised several different shapes and was intended as a collectors' series. It included drinking glasses and sculptures measuring up to 61cm (24in) in height.
£10–35/$17–60

▼ **1992**
Mould-blown and sand-blasted *Marcel* vase (33002). Produced 1992–8. The *Marcel* range, which included three series of drinking-glasses, was designed specifically for Mäntyniemi, the new official residence of the President of Finland. 18.5cm (7¼in).
£30–300/$55–510*

▼ **1984**
Free-blown, multicolour-cased, and cut *Claritas Anubis* art object (3631). Produced in 1984. From the handmade and finished *Claritas* series designed for the presentation and VIP market. 23.5cm (9¼in).
£300–1,000/$510–1,700*

SARPANEVA AT VENINI

1992

Sarpaneva designed several pieces for Venini, the leading Murano glassmaker, in 1989. His contributions to Iittala had been reducing for years, largely due to the company's decision around 1970 to produce virtually all its output on automatic machines. These reduced the importance of the designer/craftsman relationship at the centre of Sarpaneva's creative ethos. Venini's production, by contrast, was still handmade and finished.

▲ **1989**
Mould-blown and furnace-worked *Kukinto* vases. Produced 1989–present. Clearly influenced by Fulvio Bianconi's *Handkerchief* vases for Venini (c.1946) (p.47), but more so by Inkeri Toikka's *Poimu* vase for Nuutavjarvi, mid-1970s. 26 and 47cm (10¼ and 18½in).
Let £200/$340, Right £400/$680

▲ **1989**
Mould-blown and furnace-worked *Aava* and *Vire* decanters/art objects. Produced 1989–present. 38 and 27.5cm (15 and 10⅞in).
Left £300–500/$510–850*
Right £500/$850

Liskeard 1970–present

Liskeard is a micro-glassworks, situated in the small Cornish town from which it takes its name. It was founded in 1970 by John Randle, formerly Professor of Thermal Dynamics at Sheffield University.

John Randle had always been fascinated by glass and wished to spend his retirement gainfully occupied. After scouring far-flung areas of Britain for cheap premises, he finally found and bought Pavlova Mill and Broken Hill House, a former corn and wool store with associations with the Australian wool industry, in Lisekard. Randle staffed his venture with several glass-blowers and a cutter, some of whom arrived via Whitefriars and King's Lynn, which had been recently taken over by Wedgwood (pp.230–33).

Liskeard worked in a soda-lime glass containing a small amount of lead, melted in a half-ton tank furnace. It made at least two complete, Swedish-style services, *Lyner* and *Tamar*, named after local rivers, and several tankards. The services each comprised several forms of wine glass and a tumbler, some decorated by former Whitefriars' cutter, Bill Horwood.

Liskeard also made a particularly distinctive but confusing vase. Named the *Knobbly*, it bore an uncanny resemblance to the shape, colour, and size of the *Knobberly* produced at Whitefriars 1964–72. The Whitefriars version had been designed by William Wilson and Harry Dyer in 1963, while Liskeard's was the brainchild of its employee/director Jim Dyer, Harry's son or brother. Liskeard versions can be distinguished by a series of decorative nodes, created by pressing steel tubes into the hot glass metal, and by having their bases sealed with the work's distinctive *LG* logo.

The works was bought in 1979 by Tim Bristow, a former apprentice of Mike Harris on the Isle of Wight (pp.132–7). Working under the name of Liskeard Studio Glass, Bristow produced free-blown colour-streaked vases, birds, paperweights, and hand-pressed ashtrays with a Harris-esque flavour. Liskeard changed hands again in 1983, when the site was bought by Liam Carey, who had worked there as a schoolboy and as an apprentice from 1976. Carey had demonstrated precocious skills after joining Liskeard and was soon making paperweights, drinking-glasses, and decorative vases. He continues at the same premises today, trading under the name Merlin Glass.

◀ **1970–9**
The Liskeard Glass *LG* logo was applied like a wax seal onto the bases of numerous Liskeard vessels and objects.

KNOBBLY VASES

◀ **c.1972**
Liskeard *Knobbly* vases. Designed by Jim Dyer. The turquoise model is known as *V1*, the amethyst version as *B1* – these are both sealed with the Liskeard *LG* logo. Max. 18.5cm (7¼in).
£30–40/$55–70*

◀ ▼ **1963**
Whitefriars *Knobberly* vases. Designed by William Wilson and Harry Dyer. From left: *Ruby* lamp base (9612); *Streaky Meadow* green vase (9608), and *Kingfisher* blue vase (9610). Produced 1963–80 at the latest, in the Whitefriars colour range in plain and streaky. 24, 12.5, 16.5cm (9½, 4⅞, 6½in)
£45–80/$75–135*

1970s

Pencil-drawn and mimeographed page of goblets G1, G2, G4, and G5 from Liskeard's only known catalogue of the Randle era. All were 17cm (6¾in) high except G4, which was 18cm (7in).

£5/$9

c.1970

Mould-blown *Lyner* service. Designed by John Randle. 12.5–16.5cm (4⅞–6½in).

£5/$9

c.1970

From left: mould-blown *Lyner* and *Tamar* candlesticks. Designed by John Randle. *Lyner*: 25cm (9⅞in); *Tamar*: 21.5cm (8½in).

**Plain £30/$55
Cut £40/$70**

c.1972 and '77

Mould-blown and hand-formed tankards. Designed by Duncan Randle. Other versions of the left-hand tankard were sealed with a Celtic Cross. 13.5 and 18.5cm (5¼ and 7¼in).

Plain £10/$17, Sealed £15/$25

c.1970

Free-formed swan, with Liskeard Glass sticker. It is similar to the swan produced by Whitefriars from c.1960 – further evidence of the stylistic link between the two glassworks. These birds were formed by Jim Dyer and Duncan Randle at a rate of around 200 per day. 21.5cm (8½in).

£20/$35

1979–83

Free-blown and colour-splashed vases (*G1–G3*). From a folio of four similar pages from Tim Bristow's Liskeard Studio Glass catalogue.

£20–45/$35–75*

1980

Spun-glass bowl. Designed and made by Liam Carey. The ductile glass was placed on a wheel and "thrown" like a piece of clay 23cm (9in) diam.

£45/$75

Nazeing 1928–present

Every nation with a significant glass industry needs a works like Nazeing Glass. Tiny Nazeing's survival as a small, family-owned unit in this era of mega-corporations owes everything to flexibility. It has been sustained through periods of famine largely through the success of its factory shop – the world's first at a glassworks – and by undertaking unglamorous commissions.

The company has occupied its present site at Nazeing, Essex, since 1928. It survived a catastrophic flood in 1947 only by selling a 50 per cent stake to an investor. The most collected items from Nazeing's history are its mottled and swirling pastel-coloured art-glass ranges produced during the 1930s and '50s. Originally retailed through fashionable London stores, they are often mistaken today for the products of better-known works.

Since the late 1950s, when public taste switched toward cooler, Scandinavian styles, Nazeing has found its bread and butter elsewhere: hand-pressed advertising ashtrays, produced at the rate of three million annually during the 1970s and '80s, and stemware for NATO and international airlines, including Concorde.

Nazeing has produced an astonishing variety of industrial, pharmaceutical, lighting, glazing, architectural, promotional, catering, and domestic glassware, as well as bomb-proof windows for prisons. These commissions have been mould-blown, pressed, or centrifugally cast, and sometimes decorated with cutting, gilding, acid-etching, or transfers.

Nazeing developed a vitrified glass for the nuclear industry and continues to press-mould railway signal lenses. It has undertaken commissions for hundreds of clients, including Nestlé, Dartington, and Wedgwood.

Not all of Nazeing's output has been unglamorous and unrecognized. Its award-winning *Paris Pullman* service, by Ronnie Stennett-Willson (p.224) and the updated *Executive Suite*, designed by Roger Phillippo, were used for decades by British Transport hotels. As its owner, Stephen Pollock Hill, recalls, "We called ourselves 'the biggest producers of handmade stemware in the Commonwealth'. However, we gradually lost the business to companies like JG Durand (p.73), which could make millions of glasses a week on automatic machines, so moved into more profitable areas of special designs and short runs."

▲ 1930s–'50s   ▲ 1960s   ▲ 1980s

▲ 1950s   ▲ 1960s   ▲ 1980s

◀▼ **1952 and 1975-85**

At its peak, Nazeing pressed 3,000,000 promotional ashtrays annually. They were made by 16 men working in four teams 5½ days per week. They proved so profitable that Roy Lakin, director of Whitefriars Glass, joked that Nazeing was no longer a glassworks but a money-making machine. The most common examples bear the names of Guinness, Rothmans, and brewers Bass Charrington, Double Diamond, Harp, Skol, and John Smiths. They were wholesaled by Reginald Corfield Ltd, 1975–83, then Wade/PDM, a subsidiary of Wade Potteries. Some examples are marked: *REGICOR* and/or *NAZEING MADE IN ENGLAND*. The Guinness ashtray (below) was among the first pressed pieces produced by Nazeing. The works produced millions of ashtrays, and hundreds of thousands for Guinness, but only early examples bear the wording: *PRODUCED IN GT BRITAIN FOR ARTHUR GUINNESS & SONS BY NAZEING GLASS WORKS LTD, BROXBOURNE, HERTS.* 23cm (9in) diam. The gold was replaced by ochre in the 1970s after a 500 per cent rise in the price of gold.
Illustrated in advert £5/$9 Guinness £40/$70

Small

Medium

Large

◀ **c.1955**

Pressed pint tankard transfer-printed with a huntsman and hounds. Nazeing pressed and blew numerous forms of beer glasses, including versions transferred with slogans and trade names. Decorated by Mayhill Glass, co-owned by Nazeing shareholders Malcolm Pollock-Hill and Robin Meyer. 15cm (5⅞in).

£5/$9

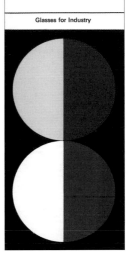

▼ 1970

Cover of Nazeing's 1970 industrial glass catalogue. Its illustrated contents include lenses and domestic, directional, marine, pavement, and deck lighting.

NAZEING

Glasses for Industry

▶ **c.1960**

Left: *Player's No.6* pub carafe. Nazeing *Water Bottles* in smoke and amber, introduced during the 1950s, were later applied with the *Player's No.6* cigarette logo in gold and became a familiar sight in British pubs throughout the 1960s. Right: Ice-effect versions were later produced for Carling and Bass Charrington beers. Both 19.5cm (7⅞in).

£10/$17

▲ **1968**

Nazeing produced mould-blown drinking-glasses for hundreds of customers. This example, the same shape as supplied for Chance Brothers' *Fiesta* range (p.105), was commissioned by Roger Pilkington to commemorate his year as Master of the Glass Sellers' Company. The decoration, designed by David Knight, was based on an engraving of Old London Bridge in the Museum of London. 13cm (5in).

£30/$55

KEY DATES

1928 Kempton family, owners of Vauxhall Glass, London, buys 15-acre farm, The Goats at Nazeing, about 32km (20 miles) north of London, to relocate its works.

1935 Malcolm Pollock-Hill buys works.

c.1935 New range of 40-shape bubbly/random coloured art glass; retailers include Heal's, the leading furnishing store.

1939–45 Wartime production: black *Vitrite* glass and technical light bulbs and tubes.

1947 Nazeing works hit by major flood. 70 employees, full and part-time.

1948 Robin Meyer buys 50-per-cent stake in company to save Nazeing from closure.

1949 Mayhill Glass, owned by Robin Meyer and Pollock-Hill, established at nearby Hoddesdon to decorate Nazeing glass.

1952 Glass-pressing introduced.

1952 *Paris Pullman* and *Tower* suites, designed by Ronnie Stennett-Willson (pp.224–33). *Paris* goblets advertised until at least 1985.

1953–4 Opaque-white shapes transferred with Norman Thelwell's gymkhana cartoons.

1960s Output includes ashtrays, naval lanterns, signal and lamp lenses, skylight panels, antique-style glazing bullseyes, and plain and retro crystal services.

1963–2003 RCA-trained Roger Phillippo consultant designer to Nazeing.

1970s–'80s Nazeing produces 40,000 mould-blown glasses monthly; employs 180.

1972 Nazeing buys order book and moulds of Sowerby, recently closed. Nazing produced ex-Sowerby vases in ruby, amber, and blue until 1980.

1973 Factory shop opens, selling pub glasses and seconds, turns over £64,000 in first year.

1984/85 Factory shop sales peak at £350,000, 20 per cent of company turnover.

1991 Nazeing's top clients include: Thorn Lighting, Wade (ashtrays), Thorpe Lighting, Air New Zealand (stemware), Whitbread (ashtrays), BNFL (raw glass for encasing nuclear waste), Westinghouse (railway signal lenses), and Standex (restaurant candle holders).

2002 Lead crystal abandoned in favour of barium-based crystal.

2005 Nazeing's 35 employees produce glazing blocks for Prison Service, lenses and lighting glass, mould-blown table-glass, etc.

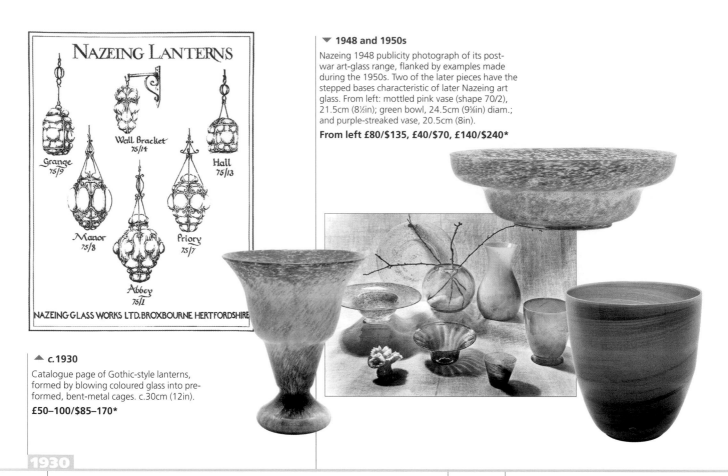

NAZEING LANTERNS

Grange 75/9

Wall Bracket 75/14

Hall 75/13

Manor 75/8

Priory 75/7

Abbey 75/1

NAZEING GLASS WORKS LTD. BROXBOURNE HERTFORDSHIRE

▲ **c.1930**

Catalogue page of Gothic-style lanterns, formed by blowing coloured glass into pre-formed, bent-metal cages. c.30cm (12in).

£50–100/$85–170*

1930

▼ **1948 and 1950s**

Nazeing 1948 publicity photograph of its post-war art-glass range, flanked by examples made during the 1950s. Two of the later pieces have the stepped bases characteristic of later Nazeing art glass. From left: mottled pink vase (shape 70/2), 21.5cm (8½in); green bowl, 24.5cm (9⅝in) diam.; and purple-streaked vase, 20.5cm (8in).

From left £80/$135, £40/$70, £140/$240*

▲ **1936–8**

Bubbly, streaked, and mottled art glass. From left: Blue vase, 16cm (6¼in); pink lamp (shape 16), 17.5cm (6⅞in); green basket vase, 13.5cm (5¼in) diam.; and green vases, max. 22cm (8⅝in). The background image illustrates pieces introduced in 1936 and '38. While all these pieces are invariably attributed to Nazeing, doubts remain in some quarters over whether the blue vase was made by the company.

From left £40/$70, £40/$70, £20/$35, £50/$85, £120/$205, £120/$205*

▼ **c.1948**

Publicity photograph of one of Nazeing's few pressed-glass ranges, *Barleycorn*. It probably entered production in the late 1940s, but appears to have been short-lived. Nazeing produced another range, *Fantasia*, mostly in green, during the 1950s.

£5–10/$9–17

▼ **1952**

Mould-blown and drawn-stem *Paris Pullman* goblets. Designed by Ronald Stennett-Willson (pp.224–33) and produced at Nazeing 1952–86. Its purchasers included British Transport hotels and Air New Zealand, which used it for its first-class in-flight service. Nazeing used this advertisement unaltered, apart from its phone number, during *Pullman*'s entire production span. 300ml (½ pint) goblet: 13.5cm (5¼in).

£10/$17

THE PARIS PULLMAN SUITE

The rim of a wine glass is of importance to those who appreciate fine glass. At Nazeing four separate hand processes are applied to the edge of a glass before we feel it is good enough for your lips.

The Paris Pullman Glass was designed to give a new look to the traditional Paris pattern. It has been approved by the Council of Industrial Design and is in demand throughout the world.

NAZEING GLASS WORKS LTD.

BROXBOURNE HERTFORDSHIRE TEL HODDESDON 63078

Nazeing's *Bristol Blue* range. Nazeing was commissioned to produce the series by Bristol City Museum after the original was discontinued by its previous maker, Thomas Webb & Sons, in 1984. Its shapes were variously inspired: the *New Worthington* goblet, centre, was originally designed by Alexander Hardie Williamson in 1948 (pp.216–31), while the knopped goblet, centre extreme right, was modelled on an antique example, *c.*1820.

£5–30/$9–55*

▲ **1970**

Promotional photograph of pressed breakfast bowl impressed with recesses for grapefruit pips and the words: *TINKER, TAILOR, SOLDIER, SAILOR, RICH MAN, POOR MAN, BEGGARMAN, THIEF.* The bowls were made for a collect-tokens offer for Nestlé Evaporated Milk. Over 300,000 sky-blue versions were produced 1971–2, though Nestlé had expected orders of 500,000 and considered the promotion a failure. About 2,000 black versions were produced in the late 1980s.

£10/$17

1985

▲ ▶ **1972**

Nazeing bought the orders, stock, and moulds of Sowerby, Britain's leading Victorian pressed glassmaker, after its closure in 1972. Nazeing continues to press lenses formed in old Sowerby moulds for railways in Britain, Pakistan, Australia, India, New Zealand, and Egypt. It also produced variously shaped ex-Sowerby dishes for Boots the Chemist throughout the 1970s. Bowl: 16.5cm (6½in) diam.

£5/9

Tarquin
Two Hand Cut Hiball Glasses
Wedgwood® Crystal

▲ **1983**

Mould-blown *Rufus* and *Tarquin* tumblers (FJT30). Designed by Frank Thrower, for Wedgwood Glass, but produced at Nazeing. Nazeing sub-contracted for glassworks that lacked sufficient capacity or technology. It made these tumblers, in colourless and midnight smoke, and in plain or optic-moulded *Ripple*. The cutting of the *Tarquin* versions was applied at Wedgwood's plant at King's Lynn (pp.230–3). *Rufus:* 8cm (3in).

Singles £5/$9, Boxed set £20/$35

Orrefors 1898–present

Orrefors, founded in the tiny village of the same name in Sweden's Småland region in 1898, was the 20th century's most influential glassworks. Dozens of other makers enjoyed periods of critical and commercial success, but none came close to rivalling Orrefors' sustained commercial and artistic success. Some managed to attract two or even three significant designers, but Orrefors has employed a constant stream of notable artists since Simon Gate joined the company in 1916.

Gate and his colleague, Edward Hald, were the linchpins of Orrefors' meteoric rise from obscurity. Gate remained at Orrefors until his death in 1945, and Hald for 61 years until 1978, many of them spent as its managing director. Within a generation, they had been joined by Nils Landberg, Sven Palmqvist, Vicke Lindstrand, John Selbing, and Edvin Öhrström. Between them, this illustrious group of seven individuals dedicated a total of 257 years to the company, and this strong foundation is the principal reason for the continuity that remains the overriding characteristic of Orrefors glass.

Initially, Orrefors was entirely overshadowed by the older, larger, and more prestigious Kosta. Its transformation began in 1915 when its estate was bought by Gothenburg paper magnate Johann Ekman, originally with the sole intention of harvesting its forests for his mills. By great fortune, Eckman's representative at Orrefors, Albert Ahlin, quickly developed a passion for glassmaking and recruited several of Kosta's leading craftsmen to set the story in motion.

Orrefors' success was founded on the principle of high quality at reasonable price, using genuine materials, to produce simple, organic, ergonomic, and fashionable forms. As another leading Swedish glass designer, Tyra Lundgren, observed: "Orrefors has become the pride of the nation – and justifiably so – to such an extent that its products may truly be described as 'art'. Indeed, even the socially inclined speak of its art glass rather than its luxury glass. Orrefors is unique in that it is able to make art out of glass: odd glass, thin, thick, coloured, complicated and expensive glass, and glass without purpose. There can hardly be anyone who does not take pleasure in the beauty of its multitudinous designs. It is Orrefors that made Swedes interested in glass."

ORREFORS' SIGNATURE CODES

Orrefors was one of the few 20th-century glassworks to apply engraved signatures to most of its output. This practice lapsed for standard production items during the 1970s; also, pieces made by its sister company, Sandvick, were never signed, and marks are often absent from individual glasses. However, the remainder was generally applied with the scripted name *orrefors* followed by a code, comprising a series of letters and numbers that identify the designer and design date of a piece.

While the codes for art pieces are complex, those for production pieces followed a formula employed for two generations: *orrefors* + designer letter + method of decoration + design number. With the information provided in the system below, it is possible, for instance, to deduce that an item signed *LA1457* was designed by Vicke Lindstrand, has cut decoration, and was awarded the production number 1457. More complex digits generally mean that the item in question did not form part of Orrefors' standard production.

LEADING DESIGNER CODES

Orrefors' designer codes were changed in 1970. Those predating that date appear before the slashes below:

Olle Alberius	1971–93	A
Gunnar Cyrén	1959–70, 1976–	B
Simon Gate	1916–45	G/SG
Edward Hald	1917–78	H/EH
Lars Helsten	1972–	T/LH
Jan Johansson	1969–	J/JJ
Nils Landberg	1927–72	N/NL
Vicke Lindstrand	1928–40	L/VL
Ingeborg Lundin	1947–71	D/IL
Edvin Öhrström	1936–57	F/EÖ
Sven Palmqvist	1928–71	P/SP

Principal decoration codes:

A: Cut glass	D: Lighting glass
E: Matt finish	F: Cut overlay
I: Enamelled glass	P: Pressed-glass
U: Blown, furnace-worked glass	

◀ **1920–98**

Orrefors not only signed a majority of its production but also applied it with stickers until 1998.

Sticker 1: 1920–40, foil sticker, light blue-gold (1920–50 foil sticker, red-gold and gold for seconds).

Stickers 2 and 3: 1960–98, cellophane sticker, burgundy and black.

Sticker 4: 1980–98, cellophane sticker, green, for seconds.

▼ **1933**

Photo montage of pressed-glass kitchenware from French magazine article about Orrefors. The fridge boxes (left) were modelled on Wagenfeld's designs for Schott. Several other Swedish, American, German, and Polish glassworks produced similar storage jugs (right). Polish glassworks still produce them today for Ikea.
£5–15/$9–25

◀ **1954**

John Selbing is an unsung hero of Orrefors' history. He recorded tens of thousands of items in his role as the company photographer and designed several iconic pieces, including these *Globe Over Cone* art objects. 48cm (18¾in).
£1,000/$1,700

▲ **1918**

Swedish magazine advertisement for Simon Gate and Edward Hald's "Modern" *Venise* designs for Orrefors.

▶ **1969**

Gunnar Cyrén had trained in silversmithing before joining Orrefors (1959–70), but his drawing skills, honed as a magazine illustrator, emerge most strongly through his work in glass. These he expressed through engraving and, in this case, the enamelling applied to this *Cykelturen* (*Cycling*) bowl.
£800/$1,360

KEY DATES

1898 Orrefors Glasbruk founded at Orrefors in Småland province, southern Sweden.

1913 Gothenburg paper magnate Johan Ekman buys Orrefors' estate for its wood. Albert Ahlin, appointed manager of glassworks, recruits Kosta glassmakers Oscar Landås and Knut Bergqvist.

1915/16 Graphic artist Simon Gate joins design staff, recommended by architect John Åkerlund.

1916 *Graal*, a new, complex technique for decorating glass internally, developed by Knut Bergqvist. Exhibited for the first time at Stockholm department store, NK (Nordiska Kompaniet).

1917 Orrefors takes over Sandvik glassworks at Hovmantorp to produce low-cost domestic glass.

1918 Young painter Edward Hald joins Orrefors' design staff. Managing director 1933–4.

1922 Orrefors establishes an engraving school, directed by Bohemian Arthur Diessner.

1925 Paris Expo Grand Prix awarded to Gate, Hald, and three blowers; 36 Grand Prix awarded to Swedish participants, out of 15,000 medals awarded.

1927 Orrefors glass prominent at Swedish design exhibition at Museum of Modern Art, NY, then Detroit and Chicago.

1929 Orrefors employs 36 full-time engravers.

1930 Stockholm Exhibition marks aesthetic turning point as engraved decoration gives way to bold forms often colourless and with simple, undulating, mould-blown decoration.

1930–57 Sculptor Edvin Öhrström engaged as designer two months per year.

1933 Suicide of Swedish's leading industrialist, Ivar Kreugar, after Wall Street Crash hits Swedish economy.

1932–73 John Selbing, Orrefors photographer, occasional designer.

1937 New air-trap technique, *Ariel*, developed by Vicke Lindstrand and others.

1937 Paris Exposition marks Gate's finale as glass designer.

1948 50th-anniversary exhibition at NK store, Stockholm.

1956 Orrefors major player in influential touring exhibition Design In Scandinavia.

1958 Hald's official retirement.

1959–70 Gunnar Cyrén (1931–) member of Orrefors design team.

1983 Retrospective Hald exhibition, National Museum, Stockholm.

1997 Orrefors Kosta Boda bought by Royal Scandinavian Group.

2005 Orrefors Kosta Boda bought by Swedish conglomerate New Wave Group for around £2.5 million. 67 job losses.

Simon Gate 1883–1945

Orrefors 1916–45

Simon Gate was the fiery soul in Orrefors' early rise from obscurity to international acclaim, while Edward Hald provided its rationale. Gate and Hald collaborated regularly, indeed, they shared the same desk until 1924, and each designed decoration to be applied to each others' shapes.

A plump farm boy, Gate's open, sensual, and intuitive approach blossomed during his art-college training. Yet for all his spontaneity, he remained a conservative who found inspiration in Renaissance Venice, Bohemian engraving, Baroque symmetry, and English Regency-period (c.1800–25) glass cutting. His repertoire spanned the gulf between inexpensive drinking suites for Orrefors' Sandvik subsidiary and grand fittings for the transatlantic liner, the *Stockholm*. Both Gate and Hald were awarded gold medals at the Paris Exposition in 1925, albeit along with 15,000 other medal winners.

Gate's son, Bengt, recalled that his father was "never so even-tempered or in such great good humour as when he was designing. He was always an extremely hard worker: he would get up at 5am and could happily go on until two or three in the morning." Sadly, Gate's personal life disintegrated towards the end of the 1930s: his wife left him, he turned to drink, and died a debtor.

▼ **1916**
Mould-blown and cut *Triton* vases. 24 and 31cm (9½ and 12¼in).
£1,250–2,500/$2,200–4,250*

1916

▶ **1918**
Mould-blown service (G521). Designed for Sandvik. Retailed by Heal's, London, under the name *Astrid* until 1966. Decanters (G521/11 and 12): 38.5 and 32cm (15⅛ and 12⅝in) inc.
Decanters £110/$190
Glasses £10/$17

1923

Mould-blown decanter (G623). Designed for Sandvik. Certain designs for Sandvik were produced for many years. This piece is illustrated in several design books. 26cm (10¼in) inc.

£250/$425

▼ 1925

Mould-blown, furnace-worked, and engraved *Paris Pokalen* (*Paris Cup*). Blown by Knut and Gustav Bergqvist; engraved by Gustaf Abels and Elis Rydh. Exhibited at the 1925 Paris Exposition. Though a museum piece, similar examples can be had for the price below. 74.5cm (29⅜in).

£10,000/$17,000*

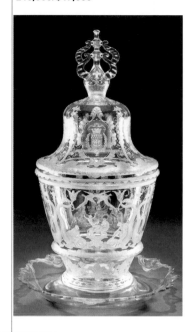

▼ 1941

Publicity photograph of mould-blown and engraved *Javanese Dancers* vase (2572). Standard production piece. 21cm (8¼in).

£450/$765*

▲ 1935

Mould-blown, cut, and engraved smoked vase (G1448). Base engraved *Gate 1448 A3/14/9/ 1937*. 20cm (7⅞in).

£180/$305

▲ 1923/4

Optic-moulded *Slottsglas* (*Palace Goblet*). Designed with Knut Bergqvist. Produced in smoke, turquoise, and amethyst. Exhibited in Gothenburg in 1923. 26cm (10¼in).

£5,000/$8,500

▼ 1932–4

Mould-blown decanters and toothpick holder/ cocktail glass. Left decanter engraved *of GU107/13* (1932); cut decanter engraved *of GA406/37* (1933); glass engraved *of GA285/18* (1934). Part of a large range of influential black-footed and -stoppered Gate designs. 20.5, 19.5, and 7cm (8, 7⅝, and 2¾in).

Left to right £160/$270, £180/$305, £60/$100

▲ 1937

Mould-blown 24-element drinks service (G1239). Max., water jug: 21cm (8¼in). From Orrefors' 1938 catalogue.

Decanter £125/$210

Edward Hald 1883–1980

Orrefors 1917–78

Edward Hald was a cool, sophisticated artist from a middle-class background who became the public face of Orrefors for over 50 years. Amiable but aloof, he had studied economics at Liepzig, architecture in Dresden, and trained under Matisse before turning to glass in 1918. It was a choice frowned upon by his contemporaries. "They treated us with disdain," he later recalled. "They regarded our medium as a sort of minor art suitable for those of inferior talent. Seldom did they apply any form of intellectual or social approach to our work."

Adopting a far more radical, Modernist approach than Gate, Hald's designs tended towards open, lighter, and dynamic themes, often with wit or a sting in the tail. Where Gate played an important role in the development of *Graal* (p.198), Hald's greatest contribution to Orrefors was as its managing director between 1933 and 1944.

After surviving the economic fallout following the Wall Street Crash, Swedish industries were crippled 1939–45 when the Baltic was mined by the Allies to impede Nazi shipping. Employing steely determination, Hald slashed his staff (including Vicke Lindstrand) and sourced the materials that were essential to ensure Orrefors' survival. Post-war, Hald's design role diminished as he became an international ambassador for the work of Orrefors' new designers, including Landberg, Palmqvist, and Lundin.

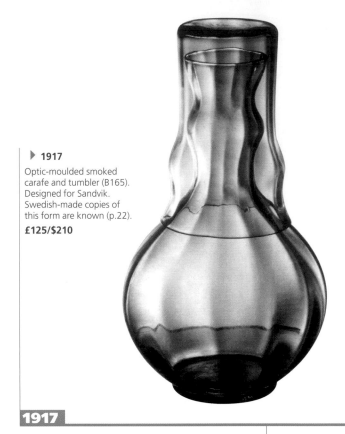

▶ **1917**
Optic-moulded smoked carafe and tumbler (B165). Designed for Sandvik. Swedish-made copies of this form are known (p.22).
£125/$210

1917

◀ **1918**
Mould-blown and engraved *Wild Strawberries* service (H88). The shapes are very similar to those of Gate's *Astrid* service designed in the same year (p.186).
Decanter £225/$380
Glasses £20/35

1920

Mould-blown and engraved bowl/vase *Bollspelande Fickor* (*Girls Playing Ball*). One of Hald's best-known designs, directly inspired by his former teacher Henri Matisse. 23.5cm (9¼in).

£3,500/$5,950*

1933

Optic-moulded bowl. Engraved *orrefors HU103/1*. 23.5cm (9¼in) diam.

£75/$130

1921

Mould-blown and engraved *Fyrverkeriskålen* (*Fireworks*) bowl. Typical of Hald's use of the entire surface to create a single 3D image. Produced into the 1970s in blue and colourless glass. 21cm (8¼in).

£2,000-5,000*

1945

Mould-blown schnapps decanter, engraved with a portrait of Winston Churchill (production number HU2953). An example of this decanter was presented to Churchill in 1945 by Sir Victor Mallet, Britain's wartime ambassador to Sweden. c.20cm (7⅞in).

£100/$170

1945

1920–25

Montage of Hald decanter design blueprints. All these pieces were produced during the 1920s. People-shaped decanters were a traditional feature of Scandinavian glassmaking (pp.75, 78, and 140).

£200/$340*

1932

Mould-blown *Grace* bowl. Produced almost continuously 1932–2003. 11 and 20cm (4¼in and 7⅞in) diam.

£20/$35

1933

Mould-blown and polished spirit decanters. Right engraved *orrefors H/21796/1*. 22.5cm (8⅞in) inc. One of Hald's most enduring shapes, the decanter was applied with differing engraved decoration designed by several Orrefors designers over many years. Cheap, Italian-made copies with nylon-pegged stoppers are common. The engraved scene (left) is taken from the biblical story *Susannah and The Elders*.

Engraved £200–800/$340–1,360*
Plain £80/$135

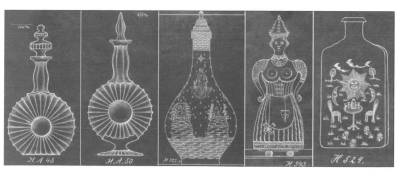

Nils Landberg 1907–91

Orrefors 1927–72

▲ 1940
Mould-blown cocktail shaker. Base engraved *orrefors NUL2575/31*. 23cm (9in) inc.
£85/$145

1940

▼ 1945
Mould-blown and engraved guitar decanter and shot glass (N3005). From the cover of Orrefors' 1950 catalogue.
From left £225/$380, £10/$17

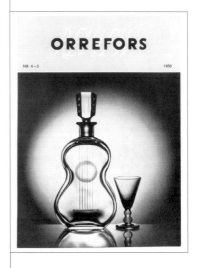

Nils Landberg, who remained at Orrefors for 45 years, is probably its most underrated designer. He joined in 1927, aged 20, straight from Gothenburg School of Arts and Crafts. After serving an apprenticeship in Orrefors' engraving school, he decorated some Gate and Hald designs, worked on Hald's magnificent *Celestial Globe* (1930) and other items in standard production.

He was promoted to Orrefors' design team in 1936, contributing engraved pieces for standard production while continuing to work on large public engraving commissions. His role remained subordinate until the early 1950s, when he played a pivotal role in switching Orrefors' style from its monumentalist past to its lighter, subtler future.

Landberg contributed numerous engraved designs, most notably a loose, organic bottle-vase in 1953. Yet the defining characteristics of his work were simple, bold, light shapes reliant on form more than technique. His *Gabriel* candlesticks of 1956 are still in production, and the deceptively simple *Dusk* series (also 1956) inspired a legion of copyists. He made more designs for Sandvik than any of his contemporaries.

His finest design was probably the *Tulpan* (*Tulip*) goblets (1954), which were drawn from a single gather of glass and won the Gold Medal at the Milan Triennale, 1957. Masterblower Henry Karlsson recalled them as "the most difficult, most exciting and most enjoyable glass I ever made...".

◄ 1953
Free-blown and engraved bottle-vase. The design is a souvenir of Landberg's training at Orrefors' engraving school. The pattern was adopted for commercial use on service N3420 in 1954. 30cm (11⅞in).
£800/$1,360

▲ 1954

Free-formed and cased *Tulpanglas* (*Tulip glass*). Engraved *Orrefors Expo N310-57*. 48.5cm (19⅛in). Also publicity photograph of *Tulpan* series, Landberg's most acclaimed design. Some customers wanted versions over a metre tall." The *Tulpan* series won the Gold Medal at the Milan Triennale, 1957.

£500–1,200/$850–2,050*

▼ 1957

Mould-blown *Illusion* wine glass. From the *Illusion* service of similarly tall-stemmed, smokey-green glasses designed for Sandvik. Unsigned. 19cm (7½in).

£5/$9

▲ 1957

Publicity photograph of mould-blown *Pedestal* vases. Unsigned. Although advertised 1957–8, these vases do not appear in Orrefors' catalogues, so were probably made by Sandvik. Blue example: 36cm (14⅛in).

£30/$55

▼ c.1965

Free-blown vase with opaque-blue and white banding. Engraved *orrefors N4123-230*. 17cm (6¾in).

£150/$255

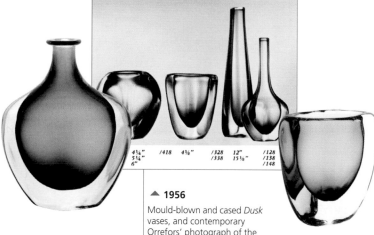

◄ 1956

Free-formed and drawn *Gabriel* candlestick. One of Landberg's most influential designs and still produced today (p.51). Also produced in smoke. Made in three sizes: 19, 23, and 27cm (7½, 9, 10⅝in).

£50/$85

▲ 1956

Mould-blown and cased *Dusk* vases, and contemporary Orrefors' photograph of the series. The coloured example engraved *NU3538/2*. Geoffrey Baxter's *Scandinavian* vase series for Whitefriars (9650-04) in 1965–9 was directly copied from these designs. 16cm (6¼in).

£110–200/$170–340

Sven Palmqvist 1906–84

Orrefors 1927–72

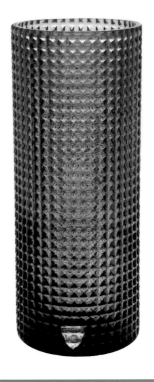

◀ **1950**
Mould-blown *LT* cylinder vase. The textured finish probably derived from Palmqvist's experiments with *Kraka* netting. This example is from the collection of Alexander Hardie Williamson (p.126). 18cm (7in).
£50/$85

Sven Palmqvist is equally respected for his pioneering glass-forming and decorating techniques as he is for his designs. So, perhaps it is no surprise that his career began as an apprentice at the furnace mouth rather than at art school. He joined the Hjertsö glassworks in 1921, where he spent five years as a glass- and mould-maker, before joining the Orrefors engraving school.

Following a similar path to his contemporary, Nils Landberg, he joined Orrefors' payroll when appointed as Simon Gate's assistant in 1928, then became a member of its design team in 1936. Palmqvist rectified his lack of formal training by spending extended periods in the 1930s at art schools, twice in Stockholm, then as an occasional sculpture student at the Académie Ranson in Paris, 1936–9.

Like Landberg, Palmqvist made his greatest contributions after 1940. *Ravenna* and *Kraka*, new forms of internal decoration, were developed simultaneously during the 1940s, and his invention of centrifuge casting, which was originally conceived in 1934, was finally perfected and exhibited in 1954. While *Ravenna* and *Kraka* remain unique to Palmqvist, the centrifuge, a revolutionary method of spinning rather than blowing glass, has since become a standard production method around the world.

1941

KRAKA

▲ **1944–88**
Like *Graal* (p.185, 198–9), *Kraka* was built up through layers of coloured glass, though the effect involved a fine mesh rather than an engraved or blasted central core. The area of glass around the net was sandblasted, then the resulting blank cased within a layer of colourless glass. Early examples are usually in one colour or have large brown nets (*Brynja/Fisherman's Crochet*), with three-colour examples (blue and yellow, etc) generally later. Left: 1964 example, engraved *ORREFORS Kraka 349 Sven Palmqvist*. 20.5cm (8in). Main photo from Orrefors catalogue 1975.
£350–1,500/$595–2,550*

◄ **1954**

Free-blown and swung opaline *Selina* vase. Engraved *orrefors PU3090/5*. 46cm (17⅞in). This is a rare example of Orrefors' opal glass. The *Selina* series was developed from 1948 in association with W.E.S. Turner, the British glass technologist. Palmqvist felt that its opalescence resembled the colour of moonbeams.

£50–250
$85–425*

CENTRIFUGE CASTING

Palmqvist observed as early as 1934 how cream rose when rotated in a butter churn and wondered if glass would behave similarly. His first experiments, based on a hand-cranked machine, had limited success. Despite resistance from Orrefors' blowers, who feared for their jobs, Palmquvist persevered and was granted a patent covering the process. A buyer for the NK department store was impressed by the idea and placed an order sufficient to justify commercial trials. The *Fuga* range went on sale in 1954 and won the Grand Prix at the Milan Trienalle in '57. The technique is widely used today, still under Palmqvist's patent, especially in Sweden.

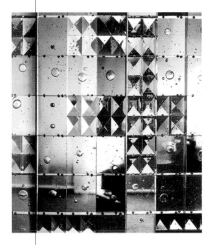

▶ **1954**

Centrifuge-cast *Fuga* bowl. Produced 1954–83. Right: *Fuga ORREFORS* moulded onto its base, as with all *Fuga* pieces. 12.5cm (4⅞in) diam.

£50/$85

▼ **1960s**

Wall of cut and polished glass *Fugal Blocks*. Glass blocks remained the subject of Palmqvist's interest for over 20 years from the beginning of the 1960s. Ranging between 12.5 and 25cm (4⅞–9⅞in), they were sold individually or incorporated into architectural projects, such as the entrance to the Television Building, Stockholm, 1970, from which this example is taken.

£150–400/$255–680*

RAVENNA

▲ **1948**

Palmqvist said that *Ravenna*, his most important contribution to art glass, was intended to resemble "coloured air". It involved casing glass plates, masking and sandblasting them, then filling the cavities with coloured glass powder. The resulting blanks were then reheated and blown into a mould. The results were unveiled at Stockholm's NK department store in 1951.

£300–900/$510–1,530*

▼ **1959**

Mould-blown *Rhapsody* (PS1850) service (retailed as the *S* service in UK), which typically extended to 30 different vessels. Decanter: 26cm (10¼in) inc.

Decanter £85/$145

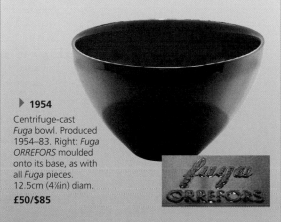

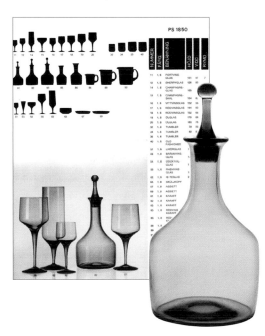

1960s

▲ **1960**

Free-blown and cut vase. Engraved *PA36342*. This cut-fern design was applied to five differing vessels: PA3634/1–5. 11cm (4¼in).

£50–250/$85–425*

Vicke Lindstrand 1904–83

Orrefors 1928–40, Kosta 1951–74

Victor "Vicke" Lindstrand, a 24-year-old commercial artist, was recruited by Orrefors in 1928 to lighten the workloads of Gate and Hald as they prepared for the 1930 Stockholm Exhibition. His radical, loose designs did more than any others to invigorate Orrefors in the 1930s, when he was among the leading Modernists in Scandinavian design.

Raised in a home filled with music, he abandoned the lute and the piano after realizing that he would never achieve virtuoso status, turning instead to the pencil. He adapted to glass with apparent but surprising ease, applying sinuous, figurative decoration, inspired by his background in graphics, to strikingly bold forms. By the mid-1930s, acclaim and demand for his artistic creations rivalled if not eclipsed those of Gate and Hald.

Lindstrand's contribution went beyond design into technique, with major roles in the development of *Ariel* (from 1937; p.198–9) and *Mykene* (1936). Yet he will probably be best remembered for his extraordinary series of marine vases, including the *Pearl Divers* (1931–5), which created a unique marriage of glass and sculpture.

Wartime shortages of materials and customers forced Lindstrand's departure from Orrefors in 1940. He designed ceramics for Upsala-Ekeby and Karlskrona until 1951, when he was reunited with glass at Kosta, where he remained for 23 years.

▼ **1930**

Mould-blown and enamelled *Cirkus* (*Circus*) vase. Black enamelling was developed in late 17th-century Bohemia and was known as *Schwarzlot* (*black lead*) (p.52). The *Cirkus* vase, unveiled at Lindstrand's first exhibition in Stockholm, 1930, clearly demonstrated his background in graphic art. 29cm (11½in).

£4,000/$6,800*

1930

◀ **1930–31**

Optic-moulded and engraved *Pearl Divers* vase with black foot. From a pre-war series decorated with similar deeply engraved underwater scenes, many now in museums. The heroic treatment of the male form is evocative of images from Soviet/Nazi propaganda. The *Shark Killers*, from 1936, remains the most sought-after of the series. 35cm (13¾in).

£3,000–10,000
$5,100–17,000*

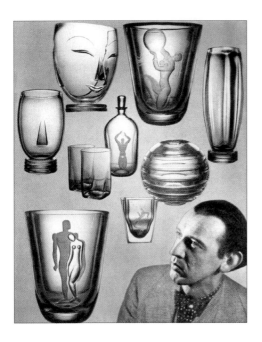

▲ 1936

Lindstrand's portrait and selection of his new designs from Orrefors' 1936 catalogue. Lindstrand's bold modern approach, derived from contemporary art, gave Orrefors' output a new dimension.

£200–2,000/$340–3,400*

▼ 1936

Mould-blown, acid-etched, and cut *1457* service. From Orrefors' 1936 catalogue.

£10–250/$17–425

▲ 1937

Mould-blown, cut, and selectively polished *Torso* vase. The graphic image was created entirely with contrasting matt and polished cut surfaces. 20cm (7⅞in).

£1,200–2,500/$2,050–4,250*

▼ 1936

Free-blown *Mykene No.4* vase. Lindstrand's *Mykene* was a variation of the *Graal* technique. It involved the selective addition of carborundum powder to a small bubble of blown glass, which was then overcased in a second layer. The powder gasified when the glass was reheated and manipulated, creating an image composed of millions of bubbles. 22cm (8⅝in).

£2,500/$4,250*

▲ 1936

Mould-blown and glue-blasted *LU154* service. After cooling, each piece was blasted with chips of dried glue under compressed air to leave an impression similar to wind-blasted ice. The asymmetrical shapes are remarkably similar to Alvar Aalto's vases of identical date (p.163). Decanter: 25cm (9⅞in); glass: 7.5cm (2⅞in).

£50–100/$85–170

▲ 1939

Mould-blown *Persika* decanter. Engraved *LU155*. This monolithic piece, in contrast to his graphic pieces, was among Lindstrand's last designs for Orrefors. 24.8cm (9⅞in).

£110/$190

Ingeborg Lundin 1921–92

Orrefors 1947–71

Before the Second World War, some Swedish glassworks had employed women designers, including Tyra Lundgren (Kosta, 1935), Gerda Strömberg (Strömberg, from 1933), and Monica Bratt (Reijmyre 1937–58). However, Ingeborg Lundin, who spent 25 years at Orrefors, distinguished herself both by being its first female designer and by the contrasting character of her creations.

Lundin joined Orrefors in 1947 after completing her training as an art teacher, and held her first exhibition just a year later, showing a range of engraved asymmetrical opaline vases. Her break from Orrefors' traditional formality must have reverberated throughout the works. As the Kosta designer/sculptor Erik Höglund (pp.42 and 78) recalled after her death: "Seriousness and humour were both present in the sensuous figures...a refreshing contrast to the works of Öhrstrom, Palmqvist and Landberg".

During the 1950s, her *Timglas* (*Hourglass*) glasses and *Äpplet* art objects brought her international attention, the latter attracting the epithet of "the world's best-known piece of '50s glass". She also produced a series of lesser-known drinks services for Sandvik at this time.

After Edvin Öhrström's departure from Orrefors in 1957, Lundin adopted his mantle and became freer and more overtly artistic. While her engraved designs proved commercially unsuccessful, she is best remembered for her series of subtle *Ariel* bowls and vases (p.199), for which she has been described as "the airy spirit of Swedish glass".

▶ **1952**
Mould-blown cocktail shaker/decanter. Engraved *orrefors DU3310*. This decanter was first illustrated in the 1952/53 *Studio Yearbook*, accompanied by a set of matching glasses. 21cm (8¼in) inc.
£80/$135

1952

1953 ▼
Free-blown *Timglas* (*Hourglass*) glasses, which provided the centrepiece of Orrefors' display at the H55 exhibition at Helsingborg, 1955. 25–45cm (9⅞–17¾in).
£1,500/$2,550

1955

Free-blown and cased *Äpplet* (*Apple*) art object. Launched at the Milan Triennale in 1957. Examples of this iconic piece are held by numerous museums, including the V&A, London. 44cm (17⅜in).

£2,000–2,500/$3,400–4,250*

1960

Publicity photograph of mould-blown and cut carafe, decanter, and jugs from the *3806* service, which comprised goblets of seven sizes, four differing tumblers, bowls, etc.

Decanter £100/$170, Jugs £40/$70

1968

Mould-blown vase with grey/green/blue inclusions. This rustic design was an echo of Erik Höglund's earlier work for Boda. 38.5cm (15⅛in).

£150/$255

1960

Mould-blown and cut *3658* vases. Left: Vase engraved *orrefors D3658-321*. 16cm (6¼in). Right: Larger version from Orrefors' 1969 catalogue. The range comprised 10 different shapes.

Small £100/$170, Large: £400/$680

1964

Mould-blown and cased opaque-orange vase. Other vases in this series were in clear tinted glass. 22cm (8⅝in).

£150/$255*

1960s

Mould-blown opaque-blue and white and colourless bowl. Engraved *orrefors D4136-420*. 18cm (7in).

£80/$135

1961

Mould-blown and cut *Carina* wine glass. Produced 1961–present. The shape and cutting were modelled on English facet-stem wine glasses, c.1770. 17cm (6¾in).

£5/$9

GRAAL AND ARIEL

The history of Orrefors is distinguished not only by its designers but also by the development of a series of revolutionary fabricating and decorating techniques. The best known of these, *Graal* and *Ariel*, were created by Orrefors designers working alongside master glassmakers at the furnace mouth. Unlike most forms of glass decoration, both rely on effects created within the finished piece as opposed to surface treatments.

Graal was developed from 1916 and *Ariel* in 1937, but variations of both are still produced at Orrefors. Indeed, most new recruits to its design staff appear compelled to experiment with at least one of them as a rite of passage. Their striking visual effects, and the technical challenges involved in their creation, have also attracted the attentions of innumerable studio glassmakers in Sweden and beyond.

Graal, a development of overlaying or casing, starts with a small blank that is gradually coated with several layers of coloured glass. The resulting multilayered piece is then etched, cut, or engraved with the desired motifs, then reheated to around 450°C (842°F), fixed to a blowing iron, coated with an outer layer of clear glass, and finally blown and shaped.

Graal, dating from 1916, was developed by Orrefors' master blower Knut Bergqvist and designer Simon Gate, and first exhibited in 1917. The technique has been adopted by many of Orrefors' leading designers, including Edvin Öhrström in the 1930s and '40s, Edward Hald in the 1950s (pp.188–9), Ingeborg Lundin in the 1960s (pp.196–7), Eva Englund, and Martti Rytkönen since the 1990s. The technique has been adopted by numerous other designers.

Ariel was first created in 1937 by Vicke Lindstand, Gustav Berqvist, and Edvin Öhrström, a young sculptor recently recruited to Orrefors' design staff. *Ariel* differs from *Graal* in that it contains air pockets, as well as differing colours, under the colourless outer casing. These are achieved by sandblasting the multicoloured blank to create series of cavities. *Ariel* is most closely associated with Öhrström, who spent 20 years developing its possibilities before leaving Orrefors in 1957. His vase *Ariel No.125* achieved the highest price ever paid for a piece of glass in Sweden when it sold for almost 1 million krone (about £100,000/ $170,000) in 1988. In contrast to this exceptional price for an exceptional piece, fine examples by leading designers and makers start around £750 ($1,275).

▶ c.1917 *Graal*

Graal Valkyries vase. Designed by Simon Gate for Orrefors. In 1917, the Swedish art critic Gregor Paulsson predicted that Gate's designs "will prove something of an époque in the history of Swedish glass manufacture". 31cm (12¼in).

£35,000–50,000/$60,000–85,000*

◀ Engraved blank

Graal blank, its multicoloured layers engraved to create the desired pattern. This would later be reheated, blown to shape, and generally overcased in colourless glass. Made by Tim Harris for Isle of Wight Studio Glass 2000. 9cm (3½in).

◀ 1937 *Graal*

Graal Chameleon vase, very few produced. Designed by Edvin Öhrström. After joining Orrefors in 1936 to relieve pressure on Gate, Öhrström produced hundreds of *Graal* and *Ariel* vases, decorated with figurative and abstract motifs over his 21 years at the works.

£40–50,000/$70–85,000*

▶ 1937 *Graal*

Fiskegraal (Fish Graal) vase. Designed by Edward Hald. Base signed *orrefors HU421P*. Unlike most *Graal* and *Ariel* pieces, *Fiskegraal* entered mainstream production and thousands were produced 1937–88 (this one 1960). 11cm (4¼in).

This example £600/$1,020
Others £400–800/$680–1,360*

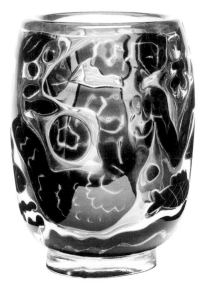

◀ **1937 *Ariel***

Ariel vase. Designed by Edvin Öhrströrn for Orrefors. Öhrström tended to number rather than name his *Graal* and *Ariel* vases. 16.5cm (6½in). Sold for the sum below in 2003.

£4,500/$7,650

 1967 *Graal*

Unnamed *Graal* vase. Designed by Ingeborg Lundin. Engraved *Orrefors. Graal. Nr 314-67. Ingeborg Lundin*. Lundin joined an exclusive group of female glass designers when recruited by Orrefors in 1947. Best known for her 1957 sculptural *Äpplet* (*Apple*) (p.197), she brought a light, sensual contrast to the Orrefors look through services and studio work alike. 19cm (7½in) diam.

£1,000/£1,700*

▶ **1990 *Graal***

Graal Embrace vase. Designed by Eva Englund, for Orrefors. Englund, who joined Orrefors from Pukeberg in 1974, generally created figurative motifs for her many *Graal* vases, which she continued to produce after leaving to establish her own studio in 1990. 25–30cm (9⅞–11⅞in).

£5,000/$8,500*

▶ **1969 *Ariel***

Ariel Face vase. Designed by Ingeborg Lundin, for Orrefors, and produced 1969–88. Lundin adopted *Ariel* after Öhrström's departure in 1957. Most of her pieces feature geometric patterns against coloured backgrounds. c.17cm (6½in).

£1,500/$2,550

◀ **2000 *Litograal***

Untitled *Litograal* vase. Designed by Per Sunderberg for Orrefors. Sunderberg joined Orrefors in 1994, when he was already an established studio glassmaker. With his *Litograal* technique, the design is sandblasted onto a thin layer of porcelain enamel, which gives the glass the impression of having been printed. 17cm (6¾in).

£500–800/$850–1,360

◀ **1970s *Ariel***

Ariel vase. Designed by Ronald Stennett-Willson (pp.224–33), for Wedgwood Glass. 16.5cm (6½in). Signed *RSW*. Stennett-Willson spent years importing Orrefors glass into Britain.

£800/$1,360

Pyrex 1915–present

Corning Glass of New York State introduced its Pyrex range of ovenproof glassware in 1915. Its development was a fortuitous by-product of demand by American railroad companies for frost-proof signal lamp lenses. Boron-based borosilicate glass, from which Pyrex is formed, was probably invented by the British amateur scientist Michael Faraday (1791–1867) and later developed by the German glass technologist Otto Schott (1851–1935). However, it was only after the wife of a Corning scientist successfully baked a cake in one of the company's new car battery casings, made of the same material, that its domestic potential was realized.

British and colonial rights to the Pyrex brand were acquired in 1921 by James A. Jobling of Sunderland, where it continues in production today. The latitude granted by Corning to Jobling resulted in a twin-track approach, with American designs produced alongside British ones. So, for instance, Pyrex jelly moulds, hot-drinks mixers, and pie-crust aerators or "birds" are relatively common in the British and Commonwealth markets but unknown in the USA. Similarly, numerous popular American designs were never adopted by Jobling.

Some Jobling Pyrex pieces were developed in-house, such as the chicken roaster, 1936, whose shape was determined by employees working empirically on a large stuffed chicken brought to the works, whereas the *Streamline* series, from 1931, was designed by the respected Harold Stabler, best known for his designs for Poole Pottery. In 1951, the company recruited a trained designer, John Cochrane, who worked in association with the Design Research Unit and the Stuart advertising agency.

Pyrex inspired competitors both in the United States and abroad, but is still produced across the world, and remains a leading brand name of the 20th century. With its basic and evolving lines continuously restyled, Pyrex may be regarded as the glassware that most clearly reflects the evolving aesthetics of its age.

◄ 1935
Advertisement in British *Good Housekeeping* magazine, proclaiming that complete Pyrex dinner services were "What hostesses have been waiting for!" It goes on to suggest: "What a thrill to see your table gleaming with this radiant glassware – and what a pleasant surprise when you discover how inexpensively a whole set works out." Earlier advertising strategies had played on the luxury of Pyrex.

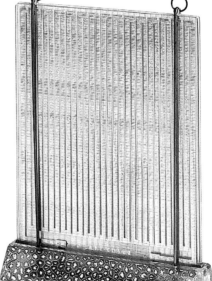

◄ 1937
Pyrex electric radiator. Designed by René-Andre Coulon, and produced by St Gobain/Société Pyrex. The metal heater filaments were contained within Pyrex glass panels on a moulded glass base enclosing an electric lamp. 61cm (24in).
£450/$765

◄ 1921–50s
Three differing logos were applied to British-made Pyrex. The first, with the *JP* (Jobling Pyrex) monogram and *PYREX MADE IN ENGLAND* within a circle, was used 1921–mid-30s. This was followed by *JAJ* (James A. Jobling) above a crown and *MADE IN ENGLAND*. The simplified *PYREX* logo, designed by Milner Gray of the Design Research Unit, was introduced in 1953. The disappearance of the *JP/JAJ* monogram reflected the end of the Jobling era after the family sold its interest to Pilkington in 1949. The cartoon KING PYREX figure was created by TIM and used for promotional purposes during the 1950s.

▶ **1942**

American *Silver Streak* electric iron by Sanders Inc. Produced c.1942–5 in Pyrex glass, chromed steel, and plastic. When restrictions on the use of metal for domestic use were introduced after the United States joined the Second World War, Sanders formed the iron's upper body in Pyrex. This rare survivor sold for £1,200 ($2,050) in London in 2000. However, a red version was sold by the same auctioneer in 2004 for only £230 ($390)! 23cm (9in).

◀ **1960s**

The heat- and frost-resistant properties of borosilicate glass were first recognized by Otto Schott in the late 19th century. The company he founded, Schott at Mainz, Germany, still produces technical glass today. This advertisement for Schott's iconic glass teapot and ovenware appeared in the 1960s.

Tea set £250/€425*

▲ **1961**

British Pyrex advertisement in *Ideal Home* magazine repeating a time-honoured scenario: the husband has invited his boss for dinner, but alas, his poor wife! "Her cooking was wonderful [Clear Pyrex!]: but oh dear!...her table! There was no dash, she thought, no sparkle, nothing different—modern, gay! [Enter husband wildly, on scooter, bearing selection of Pyrex Opal products. Curtain, music....]"

KEY DATES

1915 The first Pyrex ovenproof glassware produced by the American Corning Glass Works, Corning, NY. The name "Pryex" was drawn from *Pyr*, Greek for "fire", and *Rex*, Latin for "king".

1921 Ernest Jobling Purser, manager of Greener & Co. (founded 1858), Wear Flint Glass Works, Sunderland, granted Pyrex manufacturing rights for Britain and the Empire excluding Canada.

1922 Corning introduces 100th transparent ovenware Pyrex shape.

1922 Jobling Purser renames Greener as James A. Jobling Ltd.

1922 Corning & Saint Gobain form joint venture, Le Société Pyrex, to manufacture Pyrex in France for France, Belgium, Holland, Spain, and Italy. Similar licences were granted for Germany and Japan in 1927 and 1930 respectively.

1927 Jobling/Pyrex sales: £80,000; its payroll reaches 1,000.

1927 Jobling builds 60-ton tank furnace and introduces fully automatic presses for Pyrex production. The factory also expands to accommodate new finishing plant, packing, and warehousing.

1939 Sprayed *Colourware* (jade green, powder blue, and canary yellow) introduced by Jobling, then ceases due to outbreak of war.

1939 End of cut and engraved ranges and distinctive knobbed casserole handle, all dating from early 1920s.

1939 Introduction of *Green Line* range, distinguished by fine olive-tinted concentric lines.

1946–58 Ninety-four per cent rise in British Pyrex sales.

1949 Ernest Jobling Purser retires, selling Jobling to glazing-glass giant Pilkington.

1954 Pilkington sells its remaining 40 per cent stake in Jobling to Corning, USA.

***c*.1955** Red added to sprayed *Colourware* range.

1957 Opaque-white Pyrex *Opalware* introduced; Jobling ceases production of all domestic "fancy" glassware.

1961 Introduction of opaque-white bodied *Pyrosil*, decorated with blue cornflower silhouettes. A glass-ceramic, it had been developed by Corning/Pyrex to protect the nose cones of NASA space rockets.

1974 Total of 4,750 employed in the production of Pyrex worldwide, of which 3,500 worked at three locations in Sunderland.

1975 Jobling renamed Corning Ltd.

1994 Corning sells Pyrex brand and plants to US Parker Pens-to-building tools conglomerate Newell-Rubbermaid. Production maintained in Sunderland at old Greener glassworks.

METAL-MOUNTED PYREX

Pyrex was initially marketed as a luxury product in both the USA and Britain and priced accordingly. In 1927, a Jobling advertisement typically suggested that, "Amid the sparkle of silver and glass, PYREX dishes add the same note of beauty."

This approach was underlined by the cutting and intaglio engraving applied to otherwise standard casseroles between 1918 and the mid-1930s, which added 75 and 50 per cent to their prices respectively. This initial cachet also encouraged Pyrex and others on both sides of the Atlantic to mount pieces within metal frames. In an era when domestic help had become increasingly expensive, the hostess could now transfer a casserole from the oven into the frame and then onto the dining table while maintaining the appropriate decorum.

The earliest Pyrex mounts were in silver-plate, followed in the 1930s by stainless steel (or Staybrite, as it was known), aluminium, and chrome versions. The distinctive "knob handle", which had been adorned all casserole dishes since the early 1920s, was dropped in 1939.

1920s

▲ **1920s**

Pyrex casserole in silver-plated mount. Glass embossed with *JP* monogram and *MADE IN ENGLAND*. Metal unmarked. 34cm (13⅜in) diam.

£50/$85

▲ **1930s**

Pyrex casserole in chrome-plated liner stamped to create a "hand-beaten" look and marked *PEWTER [BR]*. 24.5cm (9⅝in) diam.

£25/$45

PYREX CLONES

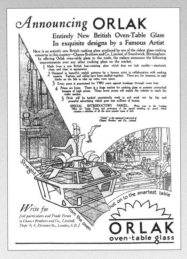

▲ **1929**

Trade advertisement announcing launch of Chance Brothers' *Orlak* range in 1929. *Orlak* was the first Pyrex clone. It was designed by Harold Stabler (1873–1945), industrial designer and art director of Poole Pottery. Stabler's services were retained by Jobling when it bought and promptly closed Orlak five years later.

▼ **1940s**

Thomas Webb and George Davidson (pp.108–15) made limited attempts at capturing a share of the ovenproof glass markets. Webb advertised *Duroven* briefly in the late 1940s, and *Silbo* appeared in Davidson's 1940 catalogue, but examples are rare.

▲ **1962**

Phoenix heat-resistant glass casserole. Embossed with the *Phoenix* logo, *MADE IN ENGLAND*, and design registration number *872873*, dating it to 1962, just four years before the company went into liquidation. Also *Phoenix* ovenware paper sticker, *c.*1935. It was named *Phoenix* because it rose from the ashes of Orlak, whose plant at Smethwick was just 16km (10 miles) from the Phoenix works at Bilston. Phoenix proved a constant irritant to Jobling, most especially as it produced a clearer, brighter glass than Pyrex. It was based on a pure sand mined at Loch Aline on the Isle of Mull. 10cm (3⅞in).

£15/$25

◀ **1921–c.58**

The (British) sauce or gravy-boat was a Jobling design unknown in the United States. Its shape, only slightly modified over its 50-year lifespan, appeared in numerous colour variations. The early "closed" handle was abandoned because it proved difficult to force molten glass into its loop. A design modification during the 1930s resulted in the new "tab" handle, which was moulded horizontally, then reheated and manipulated by hand into the desired shape. With the problem resolved through improved moulding technology, the closed handle had returned by 1960. From top: Colourless, with moulded *JP* logo mark for 1921; jade-green *Colourware* version, introduced in 1939; powder-blue *Colourware* in new shape, c.1950; yellow Phoenix copy of Jobling/Pyrex design, c.1955, marked *PHOENIX/MADE IN ENGLAND*; Pyrex red *Colourware* (red proved problematic and was not produced until c.1954); and bordeaux *Opalware* (p.204) with screen-printed *Hawthorn* pattern, c.1958. Saucer. 21cm (8¼in) wide.

£8/$14

FLAMEWARE

Flameware, a form of Pyrex that could be used directly on gas and electric hobs, was produced 1936–79. The first items in the range included teapots, coffee makers, and saucepans. These were tinted light blue and had green trade markings until 1946 to distinguish them from other forms. A large range of coffee percolators joined the range from the late 1950s. *Flameware*, an alumino-borosilicate glass, was superseded from 1979 by amber/brown-tinted *Vision*, a robust glass-ceramic rather than pure glass, made at Corning's plant at Bagneaux, near Paris.

◀ **1936**

Flameware teapot. American design, produced 1936–70s. Stainless-steel band stamped *PYREX 6336*. 22cm (8⅝in) diam.

£25/$45

▶ **1936**

Flameware saucepan. American design, produced 1936–70s. Embossed *PXM1 USA*. Made in three sizes and with optional egg-poaching inserts. 31cm (12¼in) diam.

£25/$45

▼ **1930**

Pyrex jelly mould. One of the earliest British Pyrex designs. Embossed *JAJ* logo and *MADE IN ENGLAND*. 8cm (3in).

£5/$9

 1934

Willow pattern transfer-printed meat plate. British design. Embossed *PYREX BRAND 313*. 35cm (13¾in) diam. The *Willow* service, comprising not only casseroles but plates and side-dishes, marked a departure for Jobling/Pyrex by providing customers with entire dining services. Advertisements of the period declared that these were just "what hostesses have been waiting for!" (p.200).

£20/$35

Ye "Olde Hall" Quality Staybrite Tableware
Registered Trade Mark.

YE OLDE HALL CASSEROLE STANDS.
Provisional Patent.

PLAIN MODELS.

		Round.		Oval.		Square.
Reference No.	...	S373.	S374.	S375.	S376.	S377.	S378.	S379.
For Pyrex Dish No...		A267.	A268.	A269.	A293.	A297.	A294.	A800.
Capacity, Pints	...	1½	2¼	3¼	1½	2¼	3	2¼
Price Complete	...	23/-	27/6	32/6	23/-	27/6	32/6	33/3
Stand only	...	17/6	21/-	25/-	17/6	21/-	25/-	25/-

PIERCED MODELS.

		Round.		Oval.		Square.
Reference No.	...	S464.	S465.	S466.	S467.	S468.	S469.	S470.
For Pyrex Dish No...		A267.	A268.	A269.	A293.	A297.	A294.	A800.
Capacity, Pints	...	1½	2¼	3¼	1½	2¼	3	2¼
Price Complete	...	27/-	31/6	36/6	27/-	31/6	36/6	37/3
Stand only	...	21/6	25/-	29/-	21/6	25/-	29/-	29/-

Any other design to order.

▲ **1935**

Pyrex casseroles in stainless-steel mounts from Old Hall catalogue. Prices ranged from 17/6 (75p/$1 30c) and 37/3d (£1.75/$3).

£25/$45

OPALWARE PYREX

Opaque-white *Opalware* Pyrex, introduced in 1957, dramatically widened the decorator's horizons because it offered a neutral background similar to porcelain and its surface provided a firm anchor for enamel decorating pigments. This was partly because it was formed in a fluoride-opal soda glass rather than borosilicate. It was made resistant to extreme temperatures by tempering, which required reheating otherwise finished vessels and cooling them rapidly with blasts of cold air. Initial *Opalware* ranges were sprayed in the same manner as *Colourware* but by automatic machines, which replaced hand-spraying at Jobling

c.1955. *Opalware* also offered designers new possibilities for transfer- and screen-printed patterns.

Screen-printing was used on flat surfaces, though later designs were applied onto curved pieces by rotating them against screens. Transfers were preferred for multicoloured designs because of difficulties in registering the differing layers. Each enamel transfer was floated away from its backing paper in water, then placed on the vessel, with any surplus moisture being mopped away. The vessel was then placed on a conveyor belt that carried it though a furnace to fire the enamels and on into a tempering furnace for toughening. Each vessel was then inspected and packed.

▲ **1958**

Cinderella series
Mixing bowl with screen-printed *Gooseberry* pattern. American design, introduced to Britain in 1959. This popular shape was sprayed in blue, pink, and yellow, and with differing patterns. Sets, comprising four sizes, retailed in Britain for 45/- (£2.25/$3 85c) when launched.

£15/$25

◀ **1960**

Sprayed *Hostess Set* in lacquered brass frame. British design. Glass embossed *JAJ PYREX MADE IN ENGLAND*. The glass pots were also sold individually as ramekins. Set: 17.5cm (6⅞in) diam.

Set £25/$45, Ramekins £3/$5

▲ **1958**

Turquoise *Gaiety* series casserole with screen-printed *Snowflake* pattern. American design, introduced to Britain in 1959. 22cm (8⅝in) long.

£15/$25

▼ **1960**

Sprayed *Tableware* plates and "porriger". All embossed *PYREX TABLEWARE*. The porriger was designed by the Design Research Unit in 1952. The plates have gilded borders. Plates: 21.5, 25, and 16.5cm (8½, 9⅞, and 6½in) diam.; porriger 15.5cm (6in) diam.

Set of 6 plates £12/$20

▶ **1963**

Opalware casseroles with differing polychrome transfer patterns (top: *Harvest*; bottom: unknown). British designs, probably by Anthony Welsh. 26cm (10¼in) diam.

£10/$17

▲ **1965**

Border of *Opalware* meat plate with printed *Matchmaker* pattern. British design. *Matchmaker* was also transfer-printed onto some vessels according to their shape.

► 1958

Drinks mixer and rolling-pin, introduced in the same year. British design, probably by John Cochrane. The mixer was for preparing powdered bedtime drinks, and the hollow rolling-pin was corked for filling with cold water. Mixer: 24cm (9½in); rolling-pin: 36cm (14⅛in).

£15/$25

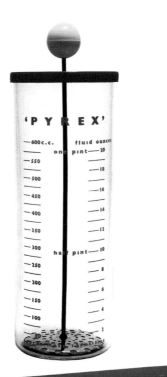

▲ 1939

Jade-green sprayed *Colourware* mixing bowl. British design, probably by John Goss. Embossed *PYREX No 301*. 9.5cm (3¾in). Jade-green, powder-blue, and canary-yellow sprayed and fired enamel pigments appeared briefly in 1939, were withdrawn 1939–45, and re-introduced in 1952. Red, previously problematic, joined the range in the mid-1950s.

£5/$9

▲ 1966

Drinkup tumbler in avocado plastic holder. (Also available in yellow, red, and blue.) British design, by Tony Welsh. Tumbler printed *PYREX MADE IN ENGLAND* with the *JAJ* logo. The handle was turned upside down in 1969. 7cm (2¾in) inc.

£3/$5

1939

1979

◄ 1970

30cl (10fl oz) Pyrex *Drinkups* and an Arcoroc copy (right). British design, possibly by Tony Welsh. 13cm (5in). Copies of the Pyrex design, in toughened soda glass, were produced by the French glassmaker Cristal d'Arques under the brand name ARCOROC.

£5/$9

▼ 1952–3

The *Jockey Cap* soup bowl from the *Easy-Grip* range. British design, by the Design Research Unit. 16cm (6¼in) diam.

£3/$5

◄ 1979

Vision saucepan. American design. Embossed *VISION CORNING FRANCE 1.5l*. 14.5cm (5⅝in) high.

£8/$14

Riihimäki 1910–90

Riihimääein Lasi Oy, (or Riihimäki Glass Works), was established at Riihimäki, 60km (40 miles) north of Helsinki in 1910 by M.A. Kolehmainen, a blower formerly employed by Karhula. Its early table-glass catalogues illustrate a wide range of derivative mould-blown domestic wares typical of most Scandinavian glassworks of the period, and it also made bottles and window glass from 1919 to 1924. During the 1930s, its domestic production broadened to include cheap pressed wares, iridescent Carnival glass, some Orrefors-esque engraved pieces, and a series of bold Art Deco vases with deep geometric Czech-style cutting.

Like Iittala, Riihimäki's output did not achieve individuality until the late 1930s. The catalysts for this change were its associations with Gunnel Nyman, Finland's first great glass designer (p.165), and Arttu Brummer (1891–1951), a teacher and later art director of Helsinki's Institute of Applied Art. As a respected interior designer, Brummer substantially bolstered Riihimäki's design legitimacy.

After the war, the works gradually assembled a team of design graduates. They included Helena Tynell (1946–76), Nanny Still (1949–76), Tamara Aladin (1959–76), Aimo Okkolin, who emerged as a designer during the mid-'50s, and Erkkitapio Siiroinen (from 1966).

Despite periodic downturns, at its peak in 1968 the plant employed 1,200 people in the production of 30,000 tons of glass products annually, making it one of Scandinavia's largest glassworks. However, its troubles began around 1970, when the oil crisis greatly increased its production costs. Then, in 1973, Finland began to dismantle its historic protectionist tariffs on imported glassware. Finding its products increasingly uncompetitive in its home market and the international market increasingly tough, Riihimäki ceased making table and decorative glass in 1976. In 1985, Ahlström, the Finnish multi-national conglomerate that already owned Karhula Iittala, bought Riihimäki, only to close it five years later.

Riihimäki's numerous ranges of distinctive, colour-cased vases were widely exported across Europe and to the United States, where their low prices generated significant sales, so they remain fairly common. Conversely, its art-objects, some of which were labour-intensive to produce, were more expensive and are now rare.

1912–37
Designed by architect Oiva Kallio.

1938–76
Also used in some cases until 1990.

1969–76
Lynx pawprint meant to indicate that glass was handmade.

1960s
Used for export only.

Late '60s/early '70s
Probably used for export only.

c.1967–76
Used for export only.

1977–90
Used for automatic production only.

◀ **1925**
Mauve-tinted *Venise* dessert dish with applied scrolled feet (3059). From a c.1925 Riihimäki catalogue. 8cm (3in) high.
£15/$25

▲ **1965–71**
The Riihimäki archive is held at the Finnish Glass Museum, based at the old Riihimäki glassworks. However, the company catalogues fail to identify the designers of certain pieces, including those in the bottom row, while other known Riihimäki pieces, including those in the top row, are not illustrated at all.
Top row £90/$155, £60/$100, £70/$120
Bottom row £40/$70*

1942

Pressed
commemorative art
object acid-etched
1939–1942. One of a
series, with similar
examples illustrated in
Riihimäki's 1941
catalogue. 8cm (3in).

£100/$170

▲ **1963**

Aimo Okkolin, who trained as a glass-cutter and engraver,
generally designed luxury and presentation pieces, which
remain rare. However, his mould-blown *Stromboli* vase (1436),
shown left and centre, designed in 1962 and made in five
sizes, probably sold more than any other. The right-hand vase
(6012), from 1982, was one of his last designs. 18, 15,
24.5cm (7, 5⅞, 9⅝in).

£20/$35, £20/$35, £30/$55

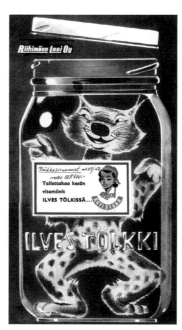
▲ **1956**

Finnish advertisement for container
glass using a cartoon representation of
the company mascot and logo, a lynx.

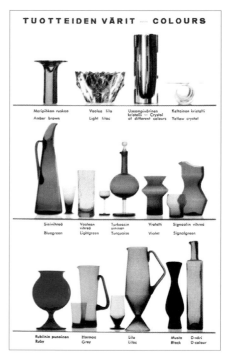

TUOTTEIDEN VÄRIT — COLOURS

▲ **1962**

Riihimäki's range of colours and shapes, as
illustrated in its catalogue. The objects were
designed by Nanny Still, Helena Tynell, and
Aimo Okkolin.

KEY DATES

1910 Riihimäen Lasi Oy founded at Riihimäki by
Kolehmainen family.

1928 Riihimäki design competition won by Henry Ericsson,
who contributes many designs.

1930 Aimo Okkolin (1917–82), son-in-law of the owner, joins
works and soon becomes apprentice glass-cutter.

1929 Range of iridized *Carnival* glass launched at Turkku
industrial fair.

1933–47 Gunnel Nyman freelances for Riihimäki.

1939–45 Production of fancy glass suspended, though series
of commemorative pieces date from this period.

1946–76 Helena Tynell (1918–) is Riihimäki designer.

1949 Teodor Käppi, Finland's leading engraver, joins Riihimäki's
Kauklahti plant from Iittala.

1949–76 Nanny Still (1926–) is part of Riihimäki design team.

1952 Kauklahti plant closes, Käppi moves to Riihimäki, where
he engraves blanks designed by Tynell and Still.

1955 Okkolin's art objects acclaimed at Helsinki Fair.

1959 Antti Kolehainen, son of managing director, develops first
of a new series of colours based on metallic oxides.

1959–76 Tamara Aladin joins Riihimäki design team.

1965 Antti Kolehainen becomes managing director after
death of his father, Ville.

1966 Design competition winner, Erkkitapio Siiroinen, joins
Riihimäki freelance design team.

1972 Riihimäki and Nuutajärvi production agreement from
beginning of 1976: Riihimäki to cease making pressed-glass in
return for Nuutajärvi stopping production of lead crystal.

1973 Oil crisis plunges Riihimäki, and others, into financial crisis.

1974 Okkolin retires due to ill health after 44 years at Riihimäki.

1976 Production of handmade glass ceases at Riihimäki. Outraged
by the news, Okkolin destroys all his design drawings. Crystal
blanks bought in from Austria, Italy, and Turkey.

1981 Finnish Glass Museum, founded 1961, moves to Riihimäki site,
where it remains today.

1985 Ahlström buys Riihimäki, but closes it permanently in 1990.

Helena Tynell 1918–

Riihimäki 1946–76

Helena Tynell's training as a sculptor at Helsinki's Institute of Applied Art resonated throughout her career as a glass designer for Riihimäki from 1946, and later both in lighting glass and in her own studio work. Asked what kind of glass she liked to design, she beamed: "Big, bold and colourful!"

Tynell began her career in 1943, drawing in the mornings for Taito, a lamp manufacturer, and sculpting ceramics at Arabia in the afternoons. Ceramics extended her feeling for form, but she was drawn to glass by the spontaneity of its manufacture. "That was the deciding factor," she explained.

Her early designs for Riihimäki were often engraved with figurative and abstract motifs, reflecting her admiration for the Orrefors aesthetic. Most of these were applied by Teodor Käppi, the leading Finnish glass engraver, who had joined Riihimäki from Iittala (pp.162–3) in 1949. Tynell temporarily left glass in 1952 after the birth of her second child to experiment with metal sculpture. However, it was a visit to Italy in 1961 that transformed her attitude toward glass, her preferred medium: "It was like a bolt of lightning," she recalled. "Glass suddenly became something three-dimensional and much richer than before."

Tynell's designs became bolder, larger, and more colourful, typified by several series of mould-blown, cast, and pressed monumental vases. After her husband's death and the cessation of fine glassmaking at Riihimäki in 1976, she joined Bega-Limburg, a German lamp manufacturer, for whom she designed lighting glass, stationery, and brochures. In 1993, she returned to Finland and to studio glassmaking.

▼ **1946**
Mould-blown and engraved *Kaulus* (*Collar*) vases. Designed in 1946 and produced c.1947–c.1958. 30 and 12cm (11⅛ and 4¾in). From Riihimäki's 1958 catalogue.
Left £145/$250, Right £60/$100

1946

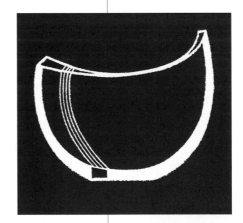

▼ **1960**
Free-formed and engraved *Lintupuu* (*Bird Wood*) dish (6649). 27.5cm (10⅞in) diam. From Riihimäki's 1960 catalogue.
£125/$210

▲ **1957**
Mould-blown dish (6635). Designed in 1957 and produced in 1958. 18cm (7in). From Riihimäki's 1958 catalogue.
£300/$510

▲ 1961

Mould-blown *Pingviini* (*Penguin*) service (1270–1, 1764). Designed in 1961 and produced 1962–5. From Riihimäki's 1962 catalogue. Decanters: 65cl and 1l (22 and 34fl oz).

Glasses £30/$55, Large decanter £160/$270, Small decanter £120/$205

▼ **1964**

Mould-blown *Tippa* decanter (1727) and *Mehulasi* tumblers (1017 and 1032). Produced 1964–6. The square version of this decanter, *Noppa* (1725), is rarer. Contemporary publicity photo. Decanter: 150cl (50fl oz); tumblers: 10 and 50cl (4 and 20fl oz).

**Decanter £135/$230
Set of 6 tumblers:
small £50/$85, large £70/$120**

◀ **1963**

Mould-blown *Katedraali* (*Cathedral*) bottle vases (1435). Designed in 1963 and produced 1964–5 in turquoise, green, lilac, violet, yellow, and amber. 30–46cm (11⅞–18in). Riihimäki publicity photograph.

**30cm £125/$210*
35cm £175/$300*
46cm £300/$510***

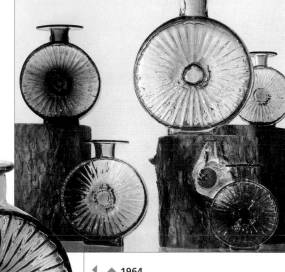

◀ ▲ **1964**

Finnish advertisement for mould-blown *Aurinko* (*Sun*) vases (1394). Produced1964–74 max. Max. 32cm (12⅜in). Left: Riihimäki made narrow-lip versions of *Aurinko*. 12.5cm (4⅞in). These were copied by an Italian glassworks, possibly Bormioli, which are difficult to distinguish from the originals though they tend to be lighter and slightly rougher.

**Wide-lip: 17cm £70/$120*, 23cm £120/$205*, 32cm £200/$340*
Narrow-lip: original £30/$55, copy £10/$17**

▼ **1966**
Mould-blown *Corona* sculptures (6607).
Produced 1966–70. 14.5–30cm (5⅝–11⅞in).
**14.5cm £200/$340, 22cm £350/$595,
30cm £550/$935**

▼ **1966**
Mould-blown
Kynttilänjalka bowl
(1941). 28cm (11in) wide.
£40/$70*

▲ **1966**
Mould-blown *Palkki* (*Girder*)
vases (1307). Produced 1966–75.
12–20cm (4¾–7⅞in).
£30–60/$55–100*

1964

▶ ▼ **1964**
Mould-blown *Pala* (*Ice
Cube*) vases (1393).
Produced 1964–76.
6–23cm (2⅜–9in).
£12–45*

▶ **1966**
Mould-blown *Pultti*
(*Bolt*) vases (1329).
Produced 1966–9.
12 and 18cm (4¾
and 7in).
**12cm £15/$25,
18cm £40/$70**

Mould-blown *Piironki* (left), *Aitan Lukko* (*Grain Barn*, centre), and *Ahkeraliisa* (*Busy Lizzy*, right) vases (1306, 1311, and 1309). *Aitan Lukko* and *Piironki* produced 1968–74. *Ahkeraliisa* produced 1968–9. All 21cm (8¼in). These designs and *Emma* (see below) formed a series called *Vanha Kartano* (*Country House*).

Most colours £90/$155*, Red £125/$210*, Signed £150/$255*

Helena Tynell
"Vanha Kartano"
"Emma"

RIIHIMÄEN LASI

◄ ▲ **1968**
Mould-blown *Emma* vase (1310).Produced 1968–74. 21cm (8¼in). Left: Finnish magazine advertisement for *Emma*, 1968.

£80–140/$135–240*

▲ **1968**
Cast *Metsä* (*Forest*) sculpture (6610). Produced in two sizes: 14cm (5½in) 1968–76 and 26cm (10¼in) 1968–72. 19cm (7½in) also produced.

£150–225/$255–380*

PIKKU MATTI (LITTLE MATT)

This series was inspired by Zacharias Topelius' children's story of *Pikku Matti* (Little Matt), who wore his grandfather's clothes to greet the regional governor because his own were too worn. Impressed by Matti's efforts, he rewarded the family for the respect they had accorded to him. As Tynell explained, "I had read the story as a child and later recalled it as a simple, true drama of a little boy's struggle to find his place in the adult world".

◀ ▼ **1969**

From left to right: Mould-blown *Pikku Matti* (*Little Matt*), *Isoäiti* (*Grandmother*), *Maaherra* (*Governor*), and *Isoisä* (*Grandfather*) decanters (1761–4). Produced 1969–70. Max. 90cl (1½ pints).

Decanters (blue)
£125–225/$210–380
Set with 6 glasses £300/$510*

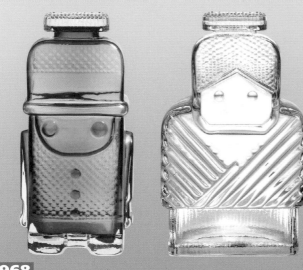

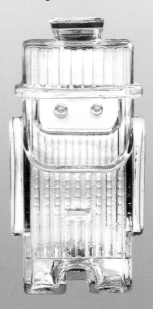

1968

▼ **1970**

Mould-blown *Viktoriana* vase (1446). Produced 1970–72. 18–24cm (7–9½in).

£80–125/$135–205*

▲ **1968**

Mould-blown tumbler (1628). Designed in 1968 and produced 1969–70, in colourless and blue. 4 and 30cl (1½ and 10fl oz). Sold with *Pikku Matti* series (above).

£12/$20

▼ **1970**

Mould-blown *Brokadi* (*Brocade*) vases (6615). Produced in two sizes: 20cm (7⅞in) 1970–3; 23cm (9in) 1970–5. From Riihimäki's 1970 catalogue.

£85–120/$145–250*

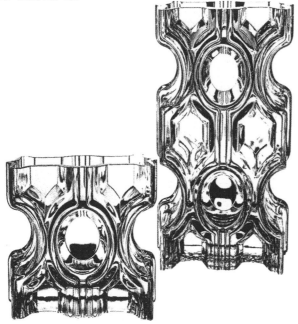

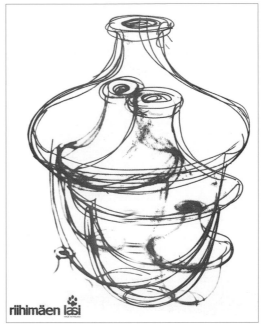

riihimäen lasi

▲ **1975**

Design sketch for mould-blown *Tammenterho* (*Acorn*) decorative bottle (1747). Produced in 1975. 17–25cm (6¾–9⅞in). Cover of Riihimäki's 1975 catalogue.

▶ **1973**

Mould-blown *Der Kreisel* ceiling lamp. Designed for Limburg Glashütte, Germany. 35cm (13¾in).

£750/$1,275

▼ **1971**

Mould-blown *Päivänkukka* vase (1409) in colourless, red, and amber. Produced 1971–6. 20–33cm (7⅞–13in). From Riihimäki's 1976 catalogue.

Red £100–200/$170–340

▲ **1971**

Mould-blown *Onnenlehti* (Four Leaf Clover) vase (1218 and 1410). Produced 1971–6. 14–28cm (5½–11in).

14cm £80/$135, 23cm £110/$190, 28cm £165/$280*

1409	PÄIVÄNKUKKA vase/vas
	Helena Tynell
height	200 mm
colours	clear, amber, ruby
packing	1 GB
transp. unit	12 pcs

Nanny Still 1926–

Riihimäki 1949–76

Nanny Still, who designed glassware for Riihimäki for 27 years, became a celebrity in Finland and one of its most vigorous ambassadors after marrying an American businessman and settling in Brussels in 1959.

Still's career began in 1949, while she was still a student at Helsinki's Institute of Applied Art, when her entries to a design competition organized by Riihimäki caught the jury's attention. Though her earliest designs never entered production, her distinctive services, including *Viiru* (1955), *Black & White* (1956), and *Rosso* (1957) sold well. However, it was the extraordinary *Harlekini* series (1958) that established Still's international reputation.

Like other leading designers, Still several explored other media. She designed wooden objects, such as salad bowls and candlesticks, as well as ceramics, jewellery, graphics, and cutlery and pans.

Still's resentment that Riihimäki was unjustly overshadowed by its neighbour, Iittala, exploded in 1958 when she found that Tapio Wirkkala had excluded her entries to the Brussels Expo, 1958, in favour of those from Iittala and its sister company, Nuutajärvi. While her work was reinstated after the ensuing row, Still remained rather an outsider, possibly because she spoke Finland's minority language, Swedish, and because she lived in Belgium.

Still returned to Riihimäki several times a year to develop new design ideas until the early 1970s, when the works ceased to produce handmade glass. She returned to glass during the 1990s with a series of sculptural studio pieces.

▶ **1950**
Mould-blown *SV* tumbler (T/339, renumbered SV6410 in 1957) and decanter. Produced 1950–60. Decanter: 21.5cm (8½in) inc. Tumbler 5.5cm (2⅛in).
Decanter £70/$120
With 6 glasses £120/$205

1950

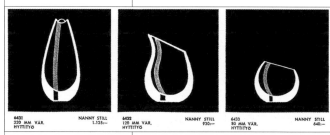

▲ **1953**
Mould-blown *Vuokko*, *Kieli*, and *Pallo* vases with filigree inclusions (6431–3). All designed in 1953, and produced 1954–60 (*Vuokko*), 1954–8 (*Kieli*), and unknown (*Pallo*). 22, 12, and 8cm (8⅝, 4¾, and 3in). From Riihimäki's 1958 catalogue.
From left £125/$210, £100/$170, £70/£120

▶ **1955**
Finnish magazine advertisement for pressed *Viiru* (*Stripe*) series (5038; 13 elements). Produced 1955–67. Jug (max.) 19cm (7½in).
£5–25/$9–45*

▲ 1955

Finnish magazine advertisement for mould-blown *Black & White* service (1124, 1172–3). Produced 1955–57 (*Violet* from 1964; *Turquoise* from 1968).

Jugs £50/$85, Glasses £8/$14

▼ **1957**

Finnish magazine advertisement for pressed *Rosso* service. Designed in 1957 and produced 1959–62. Tumbler (5044): 15 and 20cl (5 and 6½fl oz). Jug (5112). Plate (5267): 15.5cm (6in) diam. Sugar (5531). Cream jug (5532).

£10–30/$17–55*

▶ **1959**

Mould-blown *Decorative Bottles* (1734). Bases engraved *RIIHIMÄEN LASI OY NANNY STILL*. Produced 1959–68. 31.5 and 32cm (12⅜ and 12⅝in).

£150/$255

6458
300 MM VÄR.

NANNY STILL
7.200:—

▲ **1956**

Mould-blown and cased *Juhannussalko* (*Midsummer Pole*) art objects (6458). Produced 1956–60. 30cm (11⅞in).

£450/$765

▶ **1958**

Finnish magazine advertisement for mould-blown *Harlekini* service (1061 etc.; 24 elements). Designed in 1958 and produced in 1959–71. Decanter 28cm (11in) inc.

Interlocking bottles £400/$680
Decanter £225/$380

▼ 1961

Mould-blown *Ilmapallo* (*Balloon*) vases (1430–33). Produced 1961–2 in colourless, amber, and lilac, and with shorter stems. 20–33cm (7⅞–13in).

20cm £140/$240, 33cm £200/$340

▼ 1966–8

Mould-blown *Grappo* goblet and tumbler (1843, etc.,15 elements). Designed 1966–8 and produced 1967–73. Coloured versions also produced. Both 12cm (4¾in).

£10/$17

▲ 1964

Mould-blown tumbler from a cocktail service alternately known as *Siniparta* and *Blue Beard* (1036, etc.; nine elements). Designed in 1964 and produced 1965–8. 8cm (3in).

£15/$25

1961

▼ 1964

Mould-blown, half-post method *Flindari* service (1708, etc.; 16 elements). Produced 1964–8 (later examples pressed). Decanters: 22.5 and 26.5cm inc. (8⅞ and 10½in inc.); tumbler: 7cm (2¾in). *Flindari* won the International Design Award of the American Institute of Interior Designers, 1965.

Decanters £100–200/$170–340*, Glasses £10/$17, Tumblers £7/$12

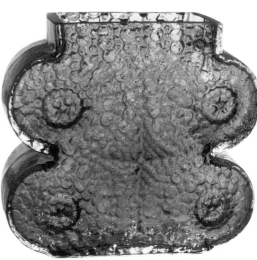

▲ 1967

Mould-blown *Nebulosa* vase (1415). Designed in 1967 and produced 1968–9 in colourless and orange cased. 18cm (7in).

£135/$230

▲ 1967

Mould-blown *Candida* candlestick (1947). Designed in 1967 and produced 1968–72 in colourless, amber, and olive. 20 and 28cm (7⅞ and 11in).

20cm £45/$75, 28cm £65/$110

▼ 1967

Mould-blown *Sulttaani* candleholder (1910) and decanter (1774). Produced 1967–9. 23 and 31cm inc. (9 and 12¼in inc.)

Candlestick £75/$130
Decanter £220/$375
Glasses £7/$12

▲ 1967

Mould-blown *Fenomena* vase (1419). Designed in 1967 and produced 1968–72 in colourless, orange, and olive. 20 and 28cm (7⅞ and 11in).

20cm £50/$85*, 28cm £75/$130*

▼ 1967

Mould-blown *Paraati* vase/candlestick (1943). Designed in 1967 and produced in 1968. 13cm (5in).

£50/$85

▲ 1967

Mould-blown *Stelleria* vase (1413). Produced 1968–9. 18cm (7in).

£135/$230

▲ 1967

Mould-blown *Pompadour* vase/candlestick (1945 and 1405). Produced 1967–73. Both 19cm (7½in).

Left £55/$95
Right £75/$130

▲ **1967**

Mould-blown *Kometti* vase (1414). Designed in 1967 and produced 1968–9. 18cm (7in).

£135/$230

▶ **1968**

Mould-blown *Pagoda* vase (1403). Produced 1968–9 in colourless and olive cased. 22 and 28cm (8⅝ and 11in).

22cm £50/$85
28cm £80/$135

▲ **1969**

Mould-blown *Apollo* candle lamp (1960). Designed in 1969 and produced 1970–6. 26.5cm (10½in). Range shown illustrated in Riihimäki's 1976 catalogue.

£50/$85

▼ **1968**

Riihimäki advertisement for semi-auto-blown *Grapponia* decanters (1742) and bowl (5565). Produced 1968–75 in colourless, yellow, blue, and green. Bowl: 9.5cm (3¾in) diam.

Bowl £15/$25, Decanter £40/$70

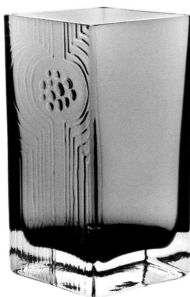

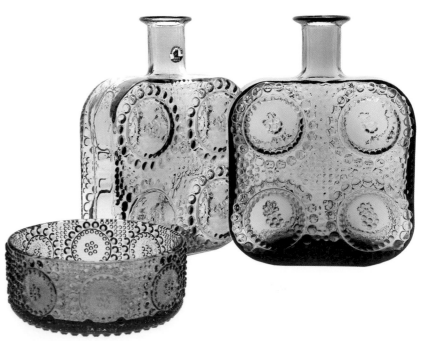

▲ **1967**

Mould-blown and cased *Lucullus* vase (1494/2). Produced 1967–8 in colourless and coloured. 20–30cm (7⅞–11⅜in). One of a series of 11 designs in the *Lucullus* series (1494/1–4).

20cm £50/$85, 25cm £85/$145, 30cm £120/$205

▲ **1970**

Mould-blown *Tiimalasi* vases (1442 and 1444). Designed in 1970 and produced 1971–6 in colourless, ruby, and olive. *Tiimalasi* appeared in four shapes (1441–4), all 18cm (7in).

£70/$120

▶ **1971–3**

Auto-blown *Lumitähti* (*Snowstar*) decanter (1704). Designed 1971–3 and produced in 1973 and 1975. Sold in sets with four tumblers. 16.5cm (6½in) inc.

£75/$130

▲ **1973**

Mould-blown *Railo* vase (1308). Designed in 1973 and produced 1974–5. 7.5–19.5cm (2⅞–7⅝in).

12cm £20/$35, 16cm £40/$70, 19cm £60/$100

▶ **1973**

Mould-blown *Bodega* bottle-vase (1303–4). Designed in 1973 and produced in 1974 in colourless, amber, and olive. 28.5cm (11¼in).

£60/$100

▼ **1973**

Mould-blown *Kyynel* decorative bottle (1717). Designed in 1973 and produced in 1974. Sold with cork-mounted metal stopper (see above). 19cm (7½in).

£55/$95

▲ **1970**

Mould-blown *Pajazzo* vases (1301). Designed in 1970 and produced 1971–4 in yellow/olive, yellow/*Rubin*, and yellow/blue. 13, 18, and 25cm (5, 7, and 9⅞in).

13cm £70/$120, 18cm £200/$340, 25cm £140/$240

▲ **1973**

Mould-blown *Ella* vase (1318). Produced 1973–5 in colourless, blue, and olive. 18cm (7in). A second *Ella* vase (1317) has a globular bowl.

£50/$85

Tamara Aladin 1932–

Riihimäki 1959–76

Tamara Aladin remains something of a mystery figure because remarkably little is known of her life and career beyond a few basic details. While entire books have been dedicated to the work of her contemporaries, Nanny Still, Helena Tynell, and Aimo Okkolin, the full extent of Aladin's own design output remains uncharted.

She studied ceramics at Helsinki's Institute of Applied Art (now the University of Art and Design) from 1951 to 1954. She then reputedly designed ceramics for Arabia, and also briefly worked as a hostess for Finnair. She joined Riihimäki's roster of freelance designers in 1959 and made regular contributions until 1976 when mould-blown production was abandoned. One of her last jobs was to redesign the Carmen candlestick (1970) for automatic production.

Aladin designed a limited number of art-glass pieces and drinks services. However, the majority of her designs were for tall cylindrical vases, each produced in the full range of the company's colours. Several dozen shapes entered serial production and they were widely exported. Her best-known pieces include *Kehrä* and *Amuletti* and the series of *Tornado* and *Hurricane* vases, some of which bear the engraved signature *RIIHIMÄEN LASI OY TAMARA ALADIN*.

Adding to the mystery, certain particularly idiosyncratic vase designs widely attributed to Aladin do not appear in known examples of Riihimäki pattern books and catalogues (p.206) – possibly because they were supplied exclusively to particular retailers, but not otherwise available.

▼ **1961**
Mould-blown unnamed glasses (1075) and decanter (1749). Designed in 1961 and produced in 1962.
Jug £200/$340
Glasses £10/$17

1961

▲ **1963**
Mould-blown *Series X* service (1754, 1756, 1763, and 1761). Produced from 1963 in colourless and lilac.
Decanters £300/$510
Glasses £25/$45

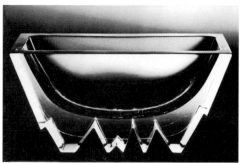

▲ **1965**

Mould-blown, cased, and cut-crystal *Viidakko* (*Tooth*) bowl (6753). Designed in 1965 and produced 1966–8. 24cm (9½in) long, (as a vase, 25 and 30cm/9⅞ and 11⅞in).

25cm vase £170/$290*
30cm vase £220/$375*

▶ **1966**

Mould-blown textured vases (1461, 62, and 65). Produced in 1966–7. 16–28cm (6¼–11in).

£15–30/$25–55*

▲ **1968**

Mould-blown *Kleopatra* jug (1502 and 1504). Produced 1968–76. 25cm (9⅞in). The *Kleopatra* series comprised 13 differing forms and sizes, each in amber and ruby (1500–1511).

£50/$85

▼ **1967**

Mould-blown vases (1472). Produced 1967–8; and included in *Export Collection*, 1976. 20cm (7⅞in).

£45–60/$75–100*

▲ **1965**

Kajo vases/art objects (6754), cased in five colours. Designed in 1965 and produced 1966–8. Max. 18cm (7in).

£300–500/$510–850*

▲ **1966**

Optic-moulded *Luna* glasses.

£5/$9

▼ **1970**
Mould-blown *Ruusu* vase (1477).
Produced 1970–76. 20cm (7⅞in).
£45/$75

▲ **1970 and 1976**
Carmen candlesticks (1964). Left: Mould-blown version, produced 1970–74. 20cm (7⅞in). Centre and right: Auto-blown versions, produced from 1976. 14cm (5½in).
Left £55/$85*, Right £12/$20

▲ **1972**
Pressed *Rengas* candlestick (5682).
Produced 1972–5. 6.5cm (2½in).
£10/$17

1968

▼ **1970**
Mould-blown *Mesimarja* candlestick (1965). Produced in 1970.
11cm (4¼in).
£20/$35

▲ **1972**
Mould-blown *Amuletti* vase (1733).
Produced 1972–4. 19.5cm (7⅜in).
The *Amuletti* series comprised three differing vases (1731–3).
£75–120/$130–205*

▲ **1968**
Mould-blown *Kehrä* vase (1496). Produced 1968–76. 20 and 25cm (7⅞ and 9⅞in).
£65/$110

▲ 1972

Mould-blown *Tornado* and *Hurricane* vases (1341 and 1348). Produced 1972–6. 16 and 21.5cm (6¼ and 8½in). The *Tornado* series comprised six differing shapes and sizes (1339–44). Some examples signed *TAMARA ALADIN RIIHIMAKAEN LASI OY*.

£65–135/$110–230

▲ 1976

Group of mould-blown vases included in Riihimäki 1976 *Export Collection*. 18–22cm (7–8⅝in)

£18–45/$30–75*

▼ 1972

Mould-blown *Tuulikki* vases (1517–20). Produced 1972–6. The *Tuulikki* series comprised four differing shapes (1517–20). 18 and 20cm (7 and 7⅞in).

£25–45/$45–75*

▲ 1976

Mould-blown *Sirkka* vase series (1526; 1528–30 shown as catalogue entries). Produced in 1976 in ruby, amber, olive, and colourless. All 20cm (7⅞in).

£25–40/$45–70*

▼ 1976

Swedish magazine advertisement for mould-blown, opaque-white, and colour-splashed *Koralli* series, comprising cylinders (1312), spheres (1313), and bowls (1285).

£40–65/$70–110*

Ronald Stennett-Willson 1915–

▲ **1958**
The cover of Ronald Stennett-Willson's 1958 book *The Beauty of Modern Glass*.
Book £75/$130*

Ronnie Stennett-Willson was probably the most dynamic figure in British post-war glass. Though untrained in business or design, he founded and operated two glassworks, ran retail and wholesale companies, compiled two influential books, served as a lecturer in glass at the Royal College of Art, and designed hundreds of production items.

Stennett-Willson was fluent in the language of contemporary glass. He wrote the text and laid out the pages for his two books, *The Beauty of Modern Glass* (1958) and *Modern Glass* (1975), both largely based on photographs from the *Decorative Art Studio Yearbooks*. He also visited most of Sweden's leading glassworks, both as a buyer and as a commissioning designer. Orrefors, Björkshults, Strömberg, Ekenås, and Johansfors manufactured his designs, and he had exclusive British rights to Kosta, Orrefors, and Pukeberg.

He combined the roles of academic, businessman, designer, and glassmaker. Acting as a sales representative, then managing director and talent scout for his wholesale and retail shops, placed him face to face not only with designers and manufacturers, but also with customers and department-store buyers. Identifying what sold, to whom, and for how much helped him to understand the market.

His close familiarity with Scandinavian glass left an indelible impression on him. He drew influences from Kaj Frank, Per Lütken, Tapio Wirkkala, Timo Sarpaneva, Jacob Bang, Simon Gate, Nils Landberg, and Riihimäki, and his best work stands comparison with such illustrious names.

▲ **1960**
Mould-blown *Canberra* vases (LSW601–03). Designed for Lemington, and produced 1960–62 in steel, amethyst, and honey. Max. 38cm (15in). The photograph was used by the Design Centre to announce its award for these vases in 1960.
From left £200/$340, £70/$120, £100/$170

Colour Range

Lemington Glass is available in the six modern exciting colours of the Harlequin sets illustrated above—Gold, Lilac, Steel, Ruby, Blue and Green; and also in Crystal. However, not every Lemington design is manufactured in the full colour scale. You will find details of the colours available for each particular design in the price list.

Lemington Glass is packed in attractive gift boxes and display packs decorated with a design based on the traditional Lemington cone.

LSW 812

Distributed by J. Wuidart & Co. Ltd. 15 Rathbone Pla

▲ **1960–62**

Lemington Glass catalogue showing two forms of Stennett-Willson-designed *Harlequin* sets in gold, lilac, steel, ruby, blue, and green. Left: 9cm (3½in), right 8.5 (3¼in).
Tumblers £10/$17, boxed set £120/$205
Shot glasses £5/$9, boxed set £60/$100

▶ **1975**

The cover of Ronald Stennett-Willson's 1975 book, *Modern Glass*.
Book £60/$100*

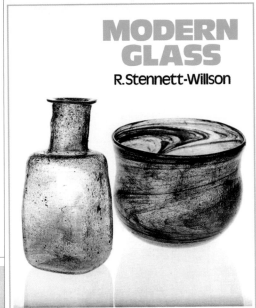

MODERN GLASS
R. Stennett-Willson

◀ **1961**

Stennett-Willson glassware is here included among the accoutrements in a chic bathroom in the early 1960s. Note the Lemington floor vase on the right, and a vase and a bowl on the window sill. Standard bathroom advertisement, from *Ideal Home*, April 1961.

KEY DATES

1915 Born, Padgate, Cheshire, England.

1935–9 Employed by Rydbeck & Norström, London, importers of Swedish glass.

1939–45 Captain, Royal Tank Regiment.

1946–51 Rejoins Rydbeck & Norström.

1951–64 Sales manager, then managing director, J. Wuidart & Co., importers of Orrefors and Kosta glass and Rörstrand ceramics.

1950s Designs glassware manufactured in Sweden by Björkshults, Ekenås, Strömberg, and Johansfors.

1958 Author and designer of *The Beauty of Modern Glass*.

1959 Designs glassware for GEC subsidiary Lemington Glass.

1960 Wins Design Centre Award for *Canberra* vases.

1961–6 Part-time tutor of Industrial Glass, Royal College of Art.

1963–6 Proprietor of *Choses*, Hampstead shop. Joint venture with Elizabeth Martins, whom he marries in 1964.

1964–6 Opens Wilmart wholesale shop.

1967 Founds King's Lynn Glass, Norfolk.

1969 Wedgwood buys King's Lynn Glass for £150,000; Stennett-Willson retained as managing director and designer.

1975 Author and designer of *Modern Glass*.

1979 Retires from King's Lynn; founds Langham Glass with King's Lynn blower Paul Miller.

1982 Wedgwood acquires 50 per cent share in Dartington Glass and merges it with King's Lynn; Frank Thrower designs new products.

1986 Wedgwood merges with Waterford Crystal.

1992 King's Lynn glassworks closes.

2004 Retrospective exhibition at King's Lynn Arts Centre.

Wuidart 1869–1980s

RSW for Wuidart 1951–64

J. Wuidart & Co. was a long-established import company (founded 1869) based in Holborn, London. By the 1940s, its primary business was being the UK agent for Orrefors and Kosta glass, and Röstrand porcelain. Little is currently known of the company's early history and it never produced catalogues. However, it did enjoy the exclusive rights to retail the *Wealdstone* range of optic-wave moulded vases produced at Powell's Whitefriars Glassworks, London, between 1930 and 1936. The series was initially designed for a rival London glass import/wholesaler, Elfverson & Co., which distributed Strömberg glass in Britain. However, Wuidart secured exclusive rights to *Wealdstone* from c.1932 and exhibited it at the *British Industrial Art* exhibition in 1933.

Wuidart's place in glass-design history is bolstered by a recent discovery in the Kosta archives. A drawing of a cocktail glass with two bands of acid-etched patterns and light diamond cutting is credited to J. Wuidart & Co., dated *20 Okt 1940* and given the pattern number *7534/W*. The design and shape is recognizable as a cocktail glass from the *Pall Mall* range of lightweight soda glass service-ware sold in Britain and across the Empire between the wars. It comprised decanters, several shapes of glasses and tumblers, dessert dishes, etc. *Pall Mall* glasses of differing qualities are known, but it would appear that at least some can now be attributed to Wuidart and Kosta.

Joining Wuidart in 1952, Stennett-Willson designed new ranges of glassware for the company each year between 1953 and 1956, which were advertised in the *Studio Yearbooks*. Despite undertaking outside design commissions, Stennett-Willson remained at Wuidart, first as sales manager, then as managing director. This required him to tour Scandinavian glass and ceramics works, meeting their designers, discussing their work, and witnessing production techniques at first-hand, all of which provided him with invaluable experience for the future. He finally left Wuidart in 1964 to form Wilmart, his wholesale glass importing business (p.229), and *Choses,* his retail shop.

Wuidart continued to distribute Waterford Crystal in the UK into the 1980s under the name Waterford-Wuidart, but disappeared after the merger that created Waterford-Wedgwood in 1986.

WEALDSTONE

Most Wuidart glassware was manufactured in Sweden, but at least one of its ranges was made by Whitefriars. Marketed under the name *Wealdstone*, it probably encompassed 91 shapes, mostly optic-moulded vases and bowls in three shades of blue, green, and amber. Reputedly designed by Barnaby Powell, it was originally commissioned by Elfverson & Co., another London-based importer of Swedish glass. However, the *Pottery Gazette* reported in 1931 that Wuidart had obtained the exclusive distribution rights, which it retained until at least 1936.

◄ **1930s**
Vases from Whitefriar's optic wave-moulded *Wealdstone* range. Designer probably Barnaby Powell, but often thought to be Barnaby Powell. The range was exclusive to Wuidart c.1932–9. Max. 25cm (9⅞in).
£80–120/$135–230*

1931

▼ **1940**
Left: Design drawing from the Kosta archives of a *Pall Mall* cocktail glass, dated October 1940, and credited to J .Wuidart & Co. Right: *Pall Mall* glass similar to the pattern drawing, but with an acid-etched rather than a cut lower band. 11.5cm (4½in).
£3/$5

WUIDART

Many of the objects imported by Wuidart originated from the existing ranges of various Swedish glassworks. For example, this candleholder, applied with Wuidart's silver and black foil retail sticker, was bought in from Gullaskruf, one of the many glassworks later absorbed into the Orrefors empire.

▼ **1950**

Green pressed candleholder. Designer unknown, for Gullaskruf, Sweden. 5cm (2in).

£20/$35

▼ **1954**

Mould-blown and pinched carafe. Manufactured by Björkshult and distributed by Wuidart & Co. Designed in 1954 and produced 1955–7. 15.5cm (6in) and 19cm (7½in). Note: This carafe was never stoppered but was retailed with seven tumblers, one of which served as a cover.

Small £25/$45, Large £45/$75

▲ **1955**

Knop-stemmed goblets manufactured by Björkshult and distributed by Wuidart & Co. Produced 1955–7. 15 and 12cm (5⅞ and 4¾in).

£15–25/$25–45

▼ **1953**

Jug, decanter, and advertisement for mould-blown *Vortex* service. Produced 1953–4. Manufactured by Stevens & Williams and distributed by Wuidart & Co. Trade advertisement in *Decorative Art Studio Yearbook*, 1953–4. Jug: c.20.5cm (8in). Decanter: c.30.5cm (12in).

Jug £45/$75, Glasses £15–25/$25–45, Decanter £250/$425

GILBEY COMMISSION

1960

Stennett-Willson received numerous commissions during his career. The largest of all, a series of glasses and a carafe to mark the centenary of Gilbey's Gin, comprised 250,000 items. This proved too large for any British manufacturer and was undertaken by the Orrefors subsidiary, Sandvik. Two glasses were fitted with metal handles to suit American drinkers' dislike of touching iced glasses.

◀ **1959**

Gilbey Commission carafe manufactured by Orrefors, Sweden. Designed by Stennett-Willson and produced 1959–61. 26cm (10¼in).

£35/$60

◀ **1959**

Paper sticker originally applied to all Gilbey Commission pieces.

▲ **1960**

Wuidart advertisement illustrating Stennett-Willson's Gilbey Commission service below Orrefors and Waterford glass and Rörstrand porcelain, which Wuidart distributed in Britain. Note the glasses with metal handles (bottom left).

Lemington Glass 1787–1995

RSW for Lemington 1960–2

Lemington Glass, founded near Newcastle in 1787, was a GEC subsidiary specializing in handmade glass, from radar screens to lighting glass. In 1959, when the production of light bulbs was switched to a new automated plant at Howarth, Yorkshire, it commissioned designs from Stennett-Willson to increase the diversity of its utility wares.

The result, a range of almost 40 vessels, drew on Stennett-Willson's familiarity with Scandinavian models. For example, his floor vase (LSW613), huge and small, echoed Jacob Bang's recent version for Holmegaard (1958), while his use of harlequin colours was probably derived from Reijmyre, Sweden. Other pieces variously offered hints of Orrefors, Stromberg, Iittala, and Riihimäki. His ingenious tumbler (LSW611), whose low centre of gravity made it virtually impossible to overturn, was itself widely copied, though its derivatives were machine-made.

As yet without a glassworks of his own, Stennett-Willson steered the manufacture of some of his freelance designs towards Lemington. The most notable of these was the service for the P&O liner *Canberra* (launched in 1960), for which he won a Design Centre Award.

Lemington, which had employed 700–800 during the 1970s, closed in 1995 with the loss of 150 jobs.

▶ **1959–60**
Mould-blown soft-tinted storage jars (LSW31 and 33). Designed by Stennett-Willson, for Lemington, 1959–60 and produced 1960–62 in steel, amethyst, and honey (not shown). Max. 20cm (7⅞in). Applied with London Design Centre seals of approval.

Short £45/$75
Tall £75/$130

`1959`

◀ **1960–2**
Lemington foil label. Text reads: *MADE IN ENGLAND LEMINGTON R STENNETT-WILLSON DESIGN*. Both blue and red backgrounds are known.

◀ **1959–60**
Mould-blown smoke-grey vases (LSW614, 620, and 619). Designed by Stennett-Willson, for Lemington, 1959–60 and produced 1960–62. Max. 30.5cm (12in). Arrangement from Stennett-Willson's retrospective exhibition, 2004.

£35/$60

▶ 1960
Three-page centre-fold of Lemington Glass's 1960 catalogue. The montage illustrates most of Stennett-Willson's designs for the company.
Giant floor vase £800/$1,360 Others £10–80/$17–135

◀ 1960
The logo for the annual Design Centre award for glassware, which Stennett-Willson won for his *Canberra* vases, commissioned for use aboard the P&O liner of the same name (p.224).

THE DESIGN CENTRE AWARDS 1960

▼ 1959
Mould-blown tumblers (LSW17). Designed by Ronald Stennett-Willson for Lemington in 1959, and produced 1960–2. 9cm (3½in).
£10/$17

STENNETT-WILLSON/ WILMART

1970

While still working at Wuidart, lecturing at the Royal College of Art, designing for Lemington, and running his Hampstead shop, *Choses*, Stennett-Willson opened another shop in London in 1964. Wilmart, also based in Hampstead, was intended as a flagship for Stennett-Willson the designer, and to wholesale his work to caterers. He also used Wilmart as an importing agent, most notably for the Swedish Pukeberg glassworks.

The Wilmart range comprised four services. These were the *Canberra*, made at Lemington, and three services made by Nazeing Glass (pp.180–3): the *Tower*, commissioned for use in the Rib Room at the Carlton Tower Hotel, opened in 1961; the *Pullman*, designed for British Rail's luxury Pullman carriages; and the *Crawford*, which was a speculative design for Wilmart, named after Crawford Street, the site of its premises.

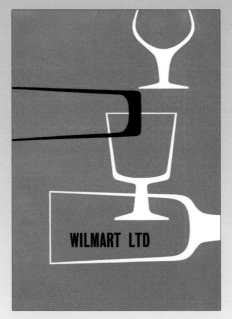

▲ 1961
The Contemporary-style design on the cover of the Wilmart Ltd catalogue, 1961, designed by Stennett-Willson, features silhouettes of *Pullman*, *Crawford*, *Canberra*, and *Tower* glasses (top to bottom).

▲ 1964
Advertisement for Wilmart's stand at the Blackpool Trade Fair. The photograph of the stand, designed by Stennett-Willson, shows his own glass beneath new ranges by Pukeberg (Sweden) and Wiesenthalhütte (Germany) and Norwegian Stavangerflint ceramics.

RSW for King's Lynn/Wedgwood 1967–79

After two decades spent teaching and writing about glass and designing, wholesaling, and retailing it, the next logical step for Stennett-Willson was to manufacture it. He chose a site at King's Lynn on the north Norfolk coast.

The furnaces, ancillary equipment, and 15 skilled glass-makers were imported from Sweden. Production started at King's Lynn Glass in 1967 with 35 employees, soon rising to 50. As Stennett-Willson had noted in *The Beauty of Modern Glass*, 1958: "A small glass factory making hand made glass with skilled workers has a flexibility which enables it to turn out an astonishing variety of articles in surprisingly large quantities." Eight years later that was just what he was doing.

His knowledge of Scandinavian glass shows in the variety of King's Lynn's output, which comprised 138 items within two years. Most were awarded names drawn from towns surrounding King's Lynn, including *Sherringham*, *Cromer*, *Sandringham*, and *Blakeney*. The *Tower* service (RSW1) and the form of the angular vase (RSW10) survived from Wilmart and Lemington, but most were new designs. They encompassed plain and cut services, mould-blown, coloured and textured pieces, paperweights, and unusual candlesticks.

▼ 1967
Candlesticks: (from left) *Sheringham*, *Brancaster*, and two variants of *Sandringham*, the latter inspired by Nils Landberg's *Gabriel* (p.191). *Sheringham* was the most sought-after, and multi-disc versions are extremely rare today.

Sherringham: 0-ring £25/$45, 9-ring £1,200/$2,050
Brancaster (short to tall) £20–60/$35–$100
Standard *Sandringham* £25–80/£45–135
Drip-pan *Sandringham* £110/$190

`1967`

KING'S LYNN/WEDGWOOD GLASS MARKS

The marks and stickers applied to King's Lynn/Wedgwood glassware changed five times in about 12 years. From top:

1967–9
King's Lynn paper sticker of the company logo above the words *LYNN ENGLAND*.

1969
WEDGWOOD ENGLAND paper sticker.

1969–c.1971
Sand-blasted stylization of Josiah Wedgwood's *Portland* vase, as applied to Wedgwood bone china c.1876–1900, above the word *WEDGWOOD*. The mark was sand-blasted rather than acid-etched for safety reasons.

c.1971–6
Portland vase logo dropped, leaving the word *WEDGWOOD* (not shown).

c.1976–8
WEDGWOOD CRYSTAL paper sticker.

c.1978–81
WEDGWOOD England paper sticker.

c.1981–82
Oval gold foil sticker with the words *Wedgwood Glass Hand Made Crystal England*.

◀ 1967
Mould-blown *Lynn* goblet. Produced 1967–9. One of Stennett-Willson's best designs, but surviving examples are rare. 12.5cm (4⅞in).
£95/$160

▼ 1967
Mould-blown and colour-cased vases. Produced 1967–9. From left: *Angular* (RSW10); *Rustic* (RSW20); and *Top Hat* (RSW21). *Angular* is commonly confused with a similar, single-colour vase by Geoffrey Baxter for Whitefriars, 1961. From left: 15.5, 19, 9cm (6, 7½, 3½in).
From left £90/$155, £90/$155, £60/$100

BRANCASTER, NORFOLK, AND BLAKENEY

In common with other glassmakers, Stennett-Willson increased his range while controlling costs by creating several items in the same moulds. For instance, the *Brancaster*, *Blakeney*, and *Norfolk* services, including two decanter shapes and 13 forms of drinking-glass, were blown in the same moulds. They also shared the same stopper as the RSW43 decanter. The only differences were that *Brancaster* was left plain while *Blakeney* and *Norfolk* were cut with differing patterns.

1967

From left: Mould-blown *Brancaster* decanter (RSW2); cut *Blakeney* goblet (RSW38/8); and cut *Norfolk* decanters (RSW37 and RSW37-ship). From left: 25.5, 15, 25.5, 23cm (10, 5¾, 10, 9in).

Glass £20/$35, Decanters £90/$155

▲ **1967 and '69**

Left: Mould-blown *Sheringham* decanter (RSW44). Produced 1967–9. Right: Dimple-based whiskey decanter (RSW60). Produced 1969–72.

Left £90/$155, Right £70/$120

▼ **1968**

Mould-blown textured vases (RSW25). Produced 1968–c.1970. Both 18cm (7in). So-called *Moon Crater* vase (left) was designed to commemorate 1967 moon landing.

£80/$135

▲ **1967**

Mould-blown and hand-jointed *Sheringham* goblet (RSW16). Produced 1967–9. As with the candlesticks (p.230), the *Sheringham* goblet was difficult to make. This was reflected in its high price of 47/6d (£2.35/$4), and it was abandoned after the Wedgwood takeover. 16cm (6¼in).

£100/$170

KING'S LYNN PAPERWEIGHTS

Wholesale and retail experience had shown Stennett-Willson the commercial viability of paperweights. The air-trap *Saturn*, the facet-cut *Galaxy* and the *Topiary* were all included in his debut range at Lynn. The air-trap *Saturn* was available in two groups of sizes, 10–13cm (4–5in) (RSW11), and 26–36cm (10¼–14⅛in), described as a "doorstop" (RSW12). Prices ranged from 26/- [£1.30] for a small RSW11 to a wallet-sapping £10 (£17) for the largest RSW12.

1967

Air-trap *Saturn* paperweight (RSW11). Produced 1967–73. 10cm (4in). A larger version (RSW12) was made as a "doorstop".

£20/$35

1967

Free-formed blue *Topiary* paperweight (RSW11). 10cm (3⅞in). Colour variations included: amethyst, yellow, topaz, cranberry, pink, opal , green-blue, pink, turquoise, and green speckle.

£25/$45

1967

Facet-cut blue *Galaxy* paperweight (RSW14). Produced 1967–73. 10cm (3⅞in). Colour variations included: amethyst, topaz, pink, yellow, pale blue, white opal, and green.

£45/$75

▼ **1968**

Mould-blown posy vase (RSW26). Produced 1968–72. 11cm (4¼in).

£30/$55

WEDGWOOD GLASS

"Wedgwood took over King's Lynn because it felt that we would add a string to its bow in the American market," recalls Stennett-Willson. "Wedgwood had distributed Waterford Crystal in the US for several years and, envying its success, saw Lynn as a potential money-spinner."

While Lynn's original investors were pleased to take a profit, Stennett-Willson, who had been his own master for nearly 20 years, was less than delighted. As he put it: "It wasn't as if I had less control under the new regime, I had no control whatsoever. However, times change and we had to change with them." He remained as managing director of Wedgwood Glass until his retirement in 1979, contributing hundreds of further designs.

In 1982, three years after Stennett-Willson's departure, Wedgwood bought a 50 per cent stake in Dartington Glass and merged its operations with King's Lynn. Frank Thrower (pp.242–7), previously Dartington's resident designer, became the artistic director of the newly expanded Wedgwood. However, Wedgwood abandoned glassmaking in 1988 after its merger with Waterford Crystal, and the King's Lynn factory was sold to Caithness Glass.

1968

Wedgwood's takeover of King's Lynn in 1969 had little visible short-term effect, as the covers of these two catalogues (King's Lynn 1968, Wedgwood 1969) show.

1968

▼ **1970**

Mould-blown *Flame* tumblers (RSW128). Produced 1970–c.1972. *Flame* was among Stennett-Willson's least favourite designs and it was produced against his wishes. Retailed in boxed pairs. 14.5cm (5⅝in).

£20/$35

▲ **1968**

Bubble-stopper decanter (RSW43). Produced 1968–74 in three colours. 31cm (12¼in) inc.

£80/$135

WEDGWOOD GLASS WITH JASPERWARE CAMEOS

Numerous items of Wedgwood glass, including goblets, bells, candlesticks, and paperweights, were issued as commemorative souvenirs from 1972 to 1982, some acid-etched, others set with ceramic cameos. The latter were designed by Stennett-Willson at the specific request of Wedgwood chairman Arthur Bryant to combine his company's traditional products with glass.

The first were goblets, produced in 1972 to commemorate the silver wedding of Queen Elizabeth and the Duke of Edinburgh. The goblets, in blue or topaz, echoed the shape of Regency-period rummers, with generous bowls applied with circular rings containing unglazed *Jasperware* profiles. The rings were cut with shallow facets and framed by v-grooved wreaths. The portraits, by the sculptor Arnold Machin (1911–99), had previously appeared on British postage stamps and coins. The blue goblets were applied with white portraits on blue backgrounds, the topaz ones with white on black.

The most popular themes included British royal milestones and historic American figures, such as George and Martha Washington and John Paul Jones. The Montreal Olympics were celebrated in 1976, 900 years of the Tower of London in 1978, the bi-centenary of Stephenson's *Rocket* in 1981, and, perhaps more bizarrely, the 50th anniversary of the circumnavigation of the globe by a Graf Zeppelin in 1979.

▲ **1968**

Mould-blown vases/candlesticks (RSW58), designed to accept fat and slim candles. Designed in 1968 and produced in 1969. 10.5cm (4in).

£45/$75

1972

Mould-blown and cut royal commemorative goblet with applied Wedgwood jasperware portrait of Prince Charles. Produced 1972–82. 13cm (5in).

£55/$95

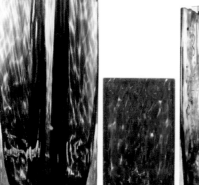

▲ **1970**

Dip-moulded and colour-splashed vases. Left: Triangular-sectioned vase made as a trial piece and never entered commercial production. Middle and right: RSW251 and 252. Produced 1970–4. 15.5 and 21.5 (6 and 8½in).

£65–80/$110–135*

▼ **1973 and 1975**

Cast and etched Christmas paperweights. Wedgwood Glass produced a different weight each year 1973–84. 1975 example: 11.5cm (4½in).

**Left £35/$60
Right £20/$35**

▼ **1975**

Free-formed and colour-cased *Lilliput Owl* (SJG5007). 11cm (4¼in). Stennett-Willson designed a menagerie of glass animals in a variety of colours during the 1970s, some of which are also illustrated on pp.88–9.

£30/$55

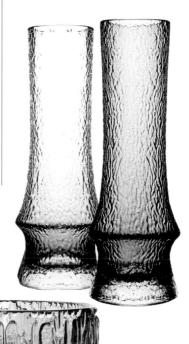

STENNETT-WILLSON STUDIO VASES

1975

"Studio" pieces were produced by many commercial glassworks during the 20th century. However, they were rarely profitable because they were generally time-consuming, technically demanding, and required the involvement of the leading glassmakers. However, they pleased their designers, boosted company prestige, and sometimes led to new production pieces. As Stennett-Willson recalled of his vases: "We regarded them as exhibition pieces. Some of them were very difficult and laborious to make, requiring as many as five different colour layers and taking a team as long as eight hours to form." The bases of some are engraved *RSW* and with the date of manufacture.

1974–6

Mould-blown and colour-cased *Ariel* studio vases. All engraved *RSW*. 11.5 and 15.5cm (4½ and 6in). These top-of-the-range vases were based on the *Ariel* technique for trapping air pockets within the contrasting colour casings developed at Orrefors (pp.198–9) from 1936 by Edvin Öhrstöm, Vicke Lindstrand, and Gustav Bergkvist.

**Front £400/$680
Rear £800/$1,360**

▶ ▼ **1975**

Mould-blown textured vases and bowl (RSW267). Produced 1975–c.1978. Bowl: 19cm (7½in) diam. Vases: 21cm (8¼in).

**Bowl £45/$75
Vases £65/$110**

Stuart 1881–present

Stuart & Sons/Stuart Crystal was Britain's most distinctive 20th-century producer of cut glass and employed two of its leading designers in that medium: Ludwig "Lu" Kny and John Luxton. During the 1930s, Stuart was also the country's most prolific maker of enamelled table-glass, and produced a series of pieces designed by fine artists for exhibition purposes. The purchase and closure of Stuart by Waterford Crystal in 1995 marked the end of Britain's 300-year heritage as the world's leading maker of cut glass.

Frederick Stuart bought the Red House Glass Works near Stourbridge, the centre of the British fine-glass industry, in 1881. The brick furnace cone at its centre remains the area's last remaining complete example and is now a museum. The works remained in the shadow of its more illustrious competitors, Stevens & Williams and Thomas Webb, until it recruited the design services of Lu Kny in 1918 (overleaf).

Kny's early designs reflected the popular taste of the period, being retro-based and unmemorable. This changed in 1927 with the arrival of Geoffrey Stuart. Encouraged by Geoffrey's artistic, dynamic approach, Kny's designs became less busy and more stylish.

Stuart remains best known as the producer of the designs of fine artists such as Erik Ravillious, Laura Knight, Paul Nash, and Graham Sutherland. The results, mostly applied with acid signatures, were used to promote "good design" at showcase exhibitions and are rare today.

John Luxton (1920–) maintained Stuart's post-war design standard. A Royal College graduate, Luxton found his urges toward Modernism stiffled by conservative management: his preference for less being often overruled by directives toward more. Nonetheless, Luxton's best work, much of it directed toward the American market, expresses strong individuality.

◀ **1887**
Mould-blown and cut decanter, set with floral *Medallion Cameo*. Designer unknown. Stuart patented *Medallion Cameos* in 1887, described in the *Pottery Gazette* as the "latest production for this season, a most delicate and entirely novel effect". 30cm (11⅞in) inc.
£800/$1,360

▼ **1907**
Mould-blown, cut, and intaglio-engraved *Beaconsfield* wine glass (17298). Designer unknown. Produced from 1907 until at least 1975, the *Beaconsfield* pattern proved one of the 20th century's most enduring glass designs. 17cm (6¾in).
£15/$25

▼ **1909**
Mould-blown and green-trailed tazza and vases. Decoration designed by A. Stainer. This form of applied decoration proved to be one of the most distinctive forms of British Art Nouveau glass.
From left £200/$340, £400/$680, £280/$475

1  **2**

3 **4**

◀ **1924–**
1: Paper sticker, 1924–c.1935.
2: Logo acid-etched onto all Stuart pieces from c.1930.
3: Oval gold and green paper sticker, c.1935–70s.
4: New logo introduced after the Waterford takeover, 1985.

▲ 1927
Stuart cut and intaglio-engraved rose bowls and vases, as available from the Glass Department at Harrods and as illustrated in the Harrods catalogue, 1928–9. Their retro appearance was supported by the fact that of the 34 services in Stuart's 1927 catalogue, 27 of them were based on pre-1918 designs.
£10–60/$17–100*

◀ 1964
Mould-blown and cut *Rhythm* decanter. Designed by John Luxton, Stuart's leading post-war designer, who remained at the works 1949–85. Later examples had differing stoppers with air-twist inclusions. 33.5cm (13¼in). Background: catalogue page of *Rhythm* glasses.
Decanter £100/$170
Glasses £5–10/$9–17

▲ 1985
Mould-blown *Gold & Ebony* vases with gold-leaf decoration. Designed by Iestyn Davies, later of the Blowzone Studio, Stourbridge. This range was made at the Scottish Strathearn glassworks at Crieff, bought in 1985 but closed in 1992. This range is commonly confused with similar pieces designed by Michael Harris (p.137). 17 and 11cm (6¾ and 4¼in).
£50–30/$85–55

KEY DATES

1881 Fredrick Stuart (1816–1900) buys Red House Glass Works, founded in 1787, near Stourbridge. Changes name to Stuart & Sons.

1887 Patent for *Medallion Cameo*.

1900 After Stuart's death, his sons run works, with Robert Stuart as chief designer.

1918–37 Lu Kny (1869–1937), son of famous engraver, chief designer. Robert Stuart designs shapes, Kny their decoration; 15,000 new designs enter pattern books.

1920 Stuart employs 413, up from 176 in 1908. Acid-polishing of cut-glass becomes standard practice.

1924 Stuart logo registered. Acid-etched onto the base of most production items from 1927.

1921–6 Twenty shapes of ringed *Stratford* service registered with Patent Office.

1927 Of 34 services in new catalogue, 27 designed pre-1918. Geoffrey Stuart encourages introduction of enamel decoration. 600 enamel designs enter pattern books.

1929 Third of new designs added to catalogue have enamel decoration.

*c.***1930** Bright green and amber colours re-introduced.

1930 Company employment reaches 665.

1931 Engraved decoration largely disappears from Stuart's repertoire.

1934 New works built; production ceases at Red House in 1936.

1934 Stuart produces designs by leading artists, including Laura Knight, Paul Nash, and Eric Ravillious, for national exhibitions.

1939–45 Wartime production. End of enamelled decoration.

1946–65 Frederick Stuart (1884–1965) managing director.

1949–85 John Luxton (1920–) chief designer.

1950 Stuart employs 400.

1952 British glassmakers allowed to sell "fancy" glass into home market for first time since 1939.

1954 First post-war catalogue to include new designs.

1980 Stuart buys Strathearn Glass, Scotland; production ceases in 1992.

1995 Stuart sold to Waterford Wedgwood Group.

2000 Site closed, but products bearing the Stuart name still being marketed by Waterford Crystal.

Ludvig "Lu" Kny 1869–1937

Stuart 1888–1937

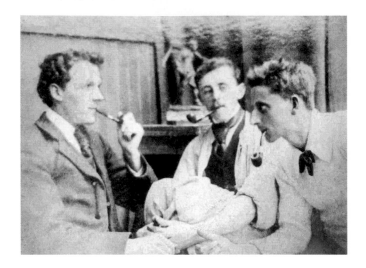

Lu Kny, (pictured above, left), was son of the great Stourbridge engraver, Frederick Kny, and worked for Stuart & Sons from 1888 to 1937. Originally employed as a freelance engraver, he became its chief designer in 1918.

During the 1920s, Kny worked closely with Robert Stuart, son of the company founder. Robert designed most of the shapes and straight-line cut designs while Kny tended towards more curved and floral patterns. Stuart glass from this period incorporating flowers, leaves, and fruit is attributable to Kny. Towards the end of the 1920s, he developed a distinctive trend toward applying fine v-grooved outlines around eye-shaped leaves.

Geoffrey Stuart helped to move Stuart's output toward more adventurous themes. Amber and green were revived as standard production colours and Kny's new designs included several ranges of drinks services. With British Art Deco cut-glass largely unfashionable today, Kny is best-remembered for his extensive ranges of colourful enamelled cocktail services, (pp.240–1).

▲ **1921**

Mould-blown *Stratford* service. Each shape was registered as it was introduced from 1921. The registration numbers were often acid-etched onto the foot of each piece, together with the Stuart logo and *Made In England*. Applied with numerous decorative forms into the 1970s. Left: Advertisement for green-tinted *Stratford* in 1930. Right: Amber *Stratford* decanter and glass, from service 25931. Decanter: 26.5cm (10½in) inc. Background: Image from Stuart's 1938–9 catalogue.

Decanter £65/$110, Glasses £2–5/$3–9

1921

▼ **1921–35**

Series of mould-blown decanters variously decorated with copper-wheel and intaglio engraving and cutting. Arranged in chronological order from Stuart pattern books published 1925–35. Stuart designers were adept at applying evolving and different decorative styles to numerous differing shapes.

£40–100/$70–170*

▲ c.1925

Mould-blown vase cut with swags and a floral border. 22cm (8⅝in).

£120/$205

▼ 1929–30

Mould-blown and cut vase. The cut swags on this vase, drawn from the Regency repertoire, c.1810–20, continued a theme that Kny had originated around 1925. 14cm (5½in).

£80/$135

▶ 1930

The *Green* and *Amber* ranges, with cutting designed by Kny for colourless pieces c.1928–30, were issued collectively in these colours in 1930.

£50–200/$85–340*

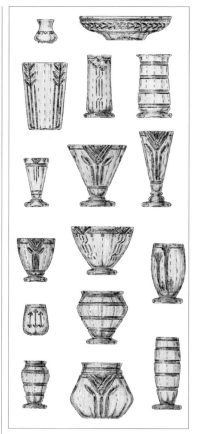

▲ 1929

Mould-blown *Waterford* pattern powder pot (26393) and vase (25894). Powder pot: 10.5cm (4in). Some examples are signed *Kny*. The theme of Kny's *Waterford* pattern was derived from the 18th-century repertoire, but not that of the Waterford glassworks (1783–1851). It originated in Bohemia c.1760 and was adopted by English cutters c.1770–85. The romantic fiction that Ireland was a major producer of Georgian glass cutting originated from Elizabeth Graydon-Stannus, an Anglo-Irish glass dealer, whose book, *Irish Glass*, 1921, rewrote the subject to her own self-interest. As with other Stuart patterns, shapes were added to the range throughout the 1930s.

Pot £45/$75, Vase £140/$240

▼ 1930

Mould-blown vases cut with Art Deco vertical lines and broadleafed floral pattern. 23 and 28cm (9 and 11in). Variations of this distinctive pattern appeared among Kny's designs throughout the 1930s, including his *Green* and *Amber* catalogue in 1930 (see above).

From left £80/$135, £250/$425

▲ 1930

Publicity photograph of mould-blown and cut *Villiers* sherry set and cocktail glass (25404). Glass: 11.5cm (4½in).

Decanter £150/$255
Glasses £10–15/$17–25

ELECTRIC LAMPS.

The Registered Name "Stuart" is marked on every piece.

▼ **1931–2**

Mould-blown *Stratford* almond dish with stylized laurel leaves and berries. Etched *Stuart England Rd 682592.* 9cm (3½in) diam.

£30/$55

▲ **1934**

Mould-blown, frosted, and cut table-lamps (28102, 27246, 27205, 27204, and 28215). Dating from 1934, but illustrated in the 1938 catalogue, these lamps combine many of Kny's most familiar signature motifs, including the *Waterford* pattern, far right. Surviving examples still fitted with their shades are extremely rare.

£300–500/$510–850*

▲ **1931**

Mould-blown and cut ship's decanter and matching cocktail glass. This retro-shaped decanter continued in production until at least 1939, appearing in that year's catalogue cut with two further patterns. Decanter: 30.5cm (12in). Glass: 17cm (6¾in).

Decanter £150/$255
Glasses £10–15/$17–25*

▼ **1931**

Mould-blown and cut cocktail glass (25404). Made in two sizes, this shape was produced in differing patterns until at least 1939. 15cm (5⅞in).

£10–15/$17–25*

▼ **1934**

Mould-blown Art Deco cocktail glasses with amber feet, one enamelled, five cut. Shapes probably designed by Geoffrey Stuart and decoration by Lu Kny. Max. 12cm (4¾in).

£25–50/$45–85*

◄ **c.1935**

Mould-blown and cut vase (27480). This precise vase was introduced in 1935. However, its cut leaf pattern was first applied c.1930, and the shape was used for several other patterns, including model 26469, dating from 1931–2. 18cm (7in).

£70/$120

c.1935
Mould-blown *Stratford*
fruit bowl with stylized,
floral, Art Deco cutting.
Acid-etched *Stuart
England Rd 681309*
(1921). 17cm (6¾in).

£70/$120

▲ **c.1935**
Mould-blown fruit bowl, cut with
a seeded and dotted border and
set on a green plinth foot. Etched
Stuart England. This atypically
bold, modernist design is absent
from all known Stuart catalogues
and advertising. It was possibly an
exhibition or experimental piece.
22.5cm (8⅞in) diam.

£250/$425

▼ **1937**
1950s advertisement for mould-blown *Ellesmere*
decanter and glass. *Ellesmere* combined two of
Kny's favourite motifs: ferns and bright-edged
leaves. Stuart's 1938–9 catalogue illustrates this
decanter shape applied with three other cut
patterns (27862, 27882, and 27886).

Decanter £150/$255, Glasses £5–15/$9–25

▼ **1935**
Mould-blown and cut *Startime* tumbler. The moulded
star pattern on the foot of the tumbler is characteristic
of several Stuart blanks. *Startime* (27542) was another
of Kny's most commercially successful designs,
enduring into the 1960s. Also, printing block
illustrating a *Startime* decanter and wine glass. The
block, pictured here in reverse, was used for
advertising. Tumbler: 10cm (3⅞in).

Decanter £80/$135, Tumbler £5–10/$9–17*

▼ **1937**
Mould-blown and cut vase (93309,
L2239). This example typifies the
best of British inter-war cut-glass.
The pattern was applied to several
other shapes, including a stemmed
vase (93809). 35.5cm (14in).

£300/$510

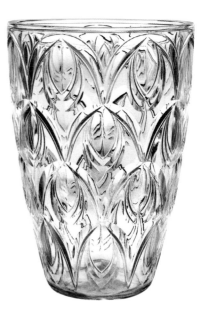

▲ **c.1935**
Mould-blown and engraved *Woodchester* cruet set
(27749) and vase (28417), decorated with ferns, one of
Kny's favourite motifs (see *Ellesmere* above). Over 30
shapes in the *Woodchester* pattern were illustrated in
Stuart's 1938–9 catalogue, most featuring the matted
discs applied to this vase. Vase: c.20cm (8in).

Vase £65/$110, Cruet set £25/$45

STUART ENAMELLING 1928–39

The extensive ranges of enamelled glassware produced by Stuart during the inter-war period remain among its most distinctive. When originally introduced, they were intended to fill a gap in the company's production between cheap, undecorated pieces and expensive cut ones. Fulfilling these hopes, brightly enamelled glassware became a cornerstone of the company's production, with over 600 designs introduced between 1928 and 1939.

The patterns, mostly comprising floral subjects, were all designed by Lu Kny until 1933, when Geoffrey Stuart began to contribute more fashionable Art Deco schemes incorporating flashes, sunrays, and zigzags. Most of the vessels used for enamelling were drawn from Stuart's existing repertoire, most commonly its mould-blown *Stratford* service, introduced from 1921. Most designs were composed using three colours, but six colour schemes are not rare.

Their appeal relied on a combination of eye-catching designs and relatively low prices. Stuart's 1938–9 catalogue illustrates six versions of the same honey pot. These cost 3/6 (18p/30c) for a plain example, and 12/3 (61p/$1) for an extensively cut one. The enamelled version cost 4/3 (21p/35c), the second-cheapest option.

The enamels, based on metallic oxides, were applied within transferred outlines with camel-hair brushes by teams of women and girls working beside large windows overlooking the Stourbridge canal. The designs took a similar amount of time to apply as cut decoration, but the women and girls who applied them were paid less than cutters, enabling their work to be retailed fairly cheaply.

 1930
Mould-blown, *Stratford*-pattern dessert dish enamelled with a fruiting plant and butterflies.
£35/$60

▶ *c.***1932**
Mould-blown sorbet dish enamelled with thistles. The foot bears the etched wording *STUART ENGLAND*, together with the number *681643*, a reference to the design registration number of this particular shape from the *Stratford* service (p.236). 9cm (3½in).
£30/$55

◀ **1930**
Free-formed amber vase with dark internal streaks and enamelled with moths and butterflies. From a short-lived range introduced in 1930. 18.5cm (7¼in).
£300/$510

 1933 and 35
Mould-blown preserve jar (without its lid), beer glass, and sugar bowl enamelled with flowers. The preserve jar (pattern 27258) was one of only three remaining enamelled designs illustrated in Stuart's 1938–9 catalogue. Beer glass: 17.5cm (6⅞in).
£30–45/$55–75

▼ **1935**

Stuart pattern page of hand-drawn and coloured designs for enamelled cocktail shakers and glasses. Dated February 1935. The shakers would have been fitted with chrome mounts after the enamels had been fired (see right).

▼ **1935**

Mould-blown cocktail shaker with chrome mount, and glass enamelled with intentionally gruesome-looking spiders. The complex webs were entirely hand-painted. Shaker c.22cm (c.9in).
Complete set £350/$595*

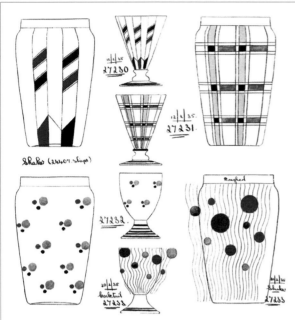

▲ **c.1935**

Cocktail glass enamelled with a huntsman. 11cm (4¼in). The colours were hand-painted within a black-outline transfer before firing.
£35/$60

STUART ENAMELLING KEY DATES

1928 First enamelled designs enter Stuart pattern book in August. Motifs include pansies, tulips, crocus, oranges, cherries, and bi-coloured chevrons. Many applied to ringed *Stratford* range, introduced in 1921. *Stratford* cocktail glass enamelled with strutting cockerel illustrated in Harrods' 1928–9 catalogue, priced 27/- (£1.35/$2 30c) per dozen.

1929 108 new enamelled patterns, 25 per cent of all new Stuart designs. Abstract designs include *Mosaic*, *Carnival*, and *Egyptian*.

1930 189 new enamelled patterns, 28 per cent of factory total; 37 designs also featured cut decoration, made for Army & Navy Stores, London.

1930 Amber vessels first applied with enamels.

1931 Increase in non-floral designs.

1933 *Persian* pattern introduced, with gold outlines containing pastiches of the decoration of *Persian* pottery in black, yellow, red, orange, brown, and green.

1933 First enamelled designs by Geoffrey Stuart, mostly jazzy, Art Deco patterns.

1933 Some patterns applied freehand without transferred outlines.

1933 First cocktail set features *Red Devil* motifs (26664).

1934 *Crowing Cockerel* cocktail set (26814), each glass decorated with between one and six chicks. Another set features fighting cocks with glasses showing a single bird in differing colours: black, red, orange, yellow, green, and blue.

1935 Cocktail sets with spiders and snakes.

1936 Lager set for Army & Navy stores features huntsman among trees, one of six differing hunting subjects.

1938 626 enamelled designs from a total of 4,000 recorded Stuart's pattern books in the decade since 1928.

1939 Just three enamelled designs illustrated in Stuart's last pre-war catalogue.

Frank Thrower 1932–87

◄ 1967–present

From top: 1967–8, original version printed on paper, later on cellophane; 1968–83, gold or red version used for first class, black for seconds; 1983–6, gold for firsts, black for seconds; and 1986–present. Dartington maintained very high quality standards, especially for the first 15 years of its production. The rejects, labelled *Seconds*, were sold in the company shop and in the annual sales at Selfridges, Heal's, Liberty, and Harrods .

Frank Thrower was the most successful British glass designer of the post-war era. Endowed with good looks, a strong ego, and irrepressible drive, he designed over 500 pieces during his 20-year association with Dartington. Since Thrower created over 95 per cent of its ranges, in many respects he is Mr Dartington.

After working in the shadow of Ronald Stennett-Willson at Wuidart (pp.226–7), Thrower went solo, making his name as a super-salesman for Portmerion Pottery, whose annual production he sold in his first few months. With time on his hands, he designed his first glassware, the *Victoria* and *Rummer* goblets, which he had made in Sweden and later became central elements of Dartington's production. In 1963 he met Peter Sutcliffe, millionaire philanthropist, and together they set up Dartington.

Leading a playboy lifestyle in London, Thrower was a man of his times. His clean, Swedish-style designs for Dartington between 1967 and 1985 captured the essence of their age and became ubiquitous in the homes of the stripped-pine generation.

As Mike Newton, Dartington's photographer for 30 years, observed: "Frank was a really good designer, perhaps not a great one, but he worked really hard to build Dartington into something special. At its peak it was as good as Orrefors and it was British, handmade, unpretentious and affordable."

1967 ►

Press-moulded *Seal* salt cellar (FT24) in *Kingfisher*, given to Dartington staff and dignitaries attending the opening of the factory in June 1967. Moulded inscription: *19D67*. 6cm (2⅜in) diam.

£25/$45

▲ 1968–9 and 1979

Mould-blown *Daisy* (FT59), designed 1968–9, and *Marguerite* (FT228), designed in 1979, vases in *Flame*, *Midnight*, blue, and colourless. *Flame* and *Midnight* were early colours but blue was not produced until the 1980s. All 14.5cm (5⅝in), though *Marguerite* was made in several sizes.

From left £45/$75, £35/$60, £35/$60, £25/$45

◀ **1967–8**

This frieze of Thrower's classic Dartington glasses was printed onto its corrugated cardboard packaging from 1971. Before then, Dartington glass had been retailed loose. Glasses designed 1967–8. From left: *Rummer* (FT104), *Victoria* (FT33; two sizes), *Inga* (FT54), *Sharon* (FT115), and *Bulldog* (FT111).

£10/$17

▶ **1967**

Thrower's designs were each awarded an "FT" production number and an often humorous marketing name. The latter were usually coined at the Holland Park office during heavy Carlsberg Special Brew drinking sessions. These decanters were named (from left): *Follow The Vin* (FT49), *Tor* (FT27), *Wanted On Voyage* (FT15), *Holding Company* (FT44), and *Show Stopper* (FT85).

£30–40/$55–$70

◀ **1967 and 1994**

Giant mould-blown *Sunflower* floor vase (FT35). Designed in 1967 and produced for three years in colourless, *Midnight*, and *Kingfisher*. However, it was revived in 1994 in cased dark blue and green. The bases of the later versions were acid-etched with a *D* and *VA No1033*. 38cm (15in).

£450/$765

KEY DATES

1932 Born Harringay, London.

1953–60 Salesman for London-based glass and ceramic wholesalers, J Wuidart & Co (pp.226–7).

1960 Sales director, Portmeirion Pottery, Wales.

1963 Meets Peter Sutcliffe of Dartington Hall charitable trust. Sutcliffe wants to found an enterprise to help halt the population drain in southwest England, whose population had halved in 50 years. Decide to establish a glassworks.

1965 Eskil Vilhelmsson hired to oversee construction of new 2,800 sq m (30,000 sq ft) glassworks. Vilhelmsson had started as a glassblower at Hovmantorps and rose to become its director. Had been works manager at Björkshult since 1956.

1966 Twenty glassworkers recruited from Swedish glassworks Orrefors, Kosta, and Boda; cutter brought in from Stourbridge.

1967 Dartington Glass opens at Torrington, Devon, with 35 employees and 5 local apprentices. Thrower sales manager and chief designer. £50,000 turnover.

1970s Some successful ranges sub-contracted to other glassworks.

1972 Wins Duke of Edinburgh Award for Design and Design Council Award for Design.

1975 Introduction of centrifuge casting for grapefruit dishes, *Hollywood*, and *Daisy* bowls.

1979 Forty per cent increase in annual turnover to £2.5 million, 200 employees, products exported to 53 countries.

1970s–80s 100,000 paying visitors annually to factory.

1982 Wedgwood buys 50-per-cent stake in Dartington (230 employees) and merges it with loss-making King's Lynn works (pp.230–3). Thrower chief designer of combined company, English Country Crystal. Thrower designs 70 new pieces for Wedgwood Crystal in 14 days.

1987 Death of Frank Thrower, months after being awarded an MBE.

1987 Waterford takes over Wedgwood, and Dartington.

1988 Dartington turnover: £7.5 million.

1989 Rockware Group buys 75-per-cent stake in Dartington: 50 per cent from Waterford, 25 per cent from the Trust. Name changed to Dartington Crystal.

1994 Dartington enters private ownership after management buyout led by long-term managing director Eric Dancer.

2000 300 employed at Dartington.

2004 Dartington taken over by Enesco Group Inc.

2005 110 employees. Britain's sole remaining major glassmaker.

THE FT1 COMMEMORATIVE TANKARD

The FT1 tankard was among the first of Thrower's 500 designs for Dartington. It was reproduced annually as a commemorative collectors' piece, each time applied with a different motif intended to celebrate its subject. In some years they were issued in limited editions of between 10–5,000, and sometimes engraved with an individual number.

They were issued as follows: **1967–8** Foundation of Dartington Glass. **1969** Dartington Hall Rose and Hart heraldic crest. **1970** *Mayflower*, 350 years since voyage. **1971** Offa, King of Mercia, introduced first penny coin, *c.*971AD. **1972** Munich Olympics (see bottom right). **1973** Edgar, first king of all England, 1,000 years since coronation. **1974** William Caxton, 500 years since first printing press. **1975** 400 years of St Paul's Cathedral. **1976** US Independence, bicentenary (see centre). **1977** ER Jubilee, 25 years. **1978** 25th anniversary of coronation. **1979** Derby bicentenary (see left). **1980** Discovery of the dodo, 300 years. **1981** FA Cup, centenary. **1982** Maritime England, *SS Dartington*. **1983** *Orient Express*, centenary. **1984** National Society for the Prevention of Cruelty to Children, centenary. **1985** JS Bach death, 300 years. **1986** *Doomsday Book*, 900 years. **1987** MCC (Marylebone Cricket Club), bicentenary. **1988** Dartington Crystal, 21 years. **1989** City of London, 800 years. **1990** Battle of Britain, 50 years. **1991** Mozart, death bicentenary. **1992** Dartington Crystal, 25 years.

1967

▶ **1969**

Mould-blown *Barbican* tankard with applied seal (FT105). This version was applied with the Prince of Wales' feathers to commemorate his investiture. A version for the *Mayflower* was produced in 1970, followed by two undated versions featuring kings, with the inscriptions: *King Eadearre* and *Anglis Regem Sicno Fatearis Evnde*.
£35–45/$60–75

▼ **1967–92**

FT1 tankards. 12.5cm (4⅞in).
£25/$45

◀ **1967–8**

Mould-blown *Face Vase* (FT52). 23.5cm (9¼in). Thrower's early designs included three *Face* vases, inspired by Erik Höglund (p.78): this and two square-sectioned versions (FT16 and 43), both 14.5cm (5¾in). From Dartington's first photographically illustrated catalogue, 1968.
£150/$255

◀ **1967**

Mould-blown FT4 decanter with applied neck ring. The FT4 was clearly inspired by Kaj Franck's *Kremlin Bells* decanter series for Nuutajärvi, Finland (p.120). However, British consumers found its off-beat shape too daring, and it was soon withdrawn as a commercial failure. 27.5cm (10⅞in) inc.
£100/$170

1968 ▶

Mould-blown *Irish Coffee* glass with applied handle (FT83). 14cm (5½in). This was Thrower's bestselling stemware design, and it was echoed in his later work for Wedgwood: the *Seamus* coffee glass (FJT20), *Genevieve* cream and sugar (FJT21), and *Alexander* water pitcher (FJT16).
£5/$9

▲ **1968**

Mould-blown vases in *Midnight* and *Kingfisher*. From top, left to right: FT58, FT60, FT62, FT65, FT66, FT84, FT88, FT98, FT101. 8–24cm (3–9½in). Most were also produced in colourless and *Flame* (red). These vases rank as one of the most bizarre series in post-war glass. While some were derivative – the FT101 is copied from Sarpaneva's *Crocus* vase for Iittala (p.175) – most were without precedent.

£15–45/$25–75

▲ **1971**

Centrifuge-cast *Grapefruit Dish* (FT148). 11.5cm (4½in) diam. Dartington adopted centrifuge casting, invented by Sven Palmqvist c.1954 (p.192–3), despite early reservations about adopting further production methods. Their production was switched to Nazeing c.1973 (pp.180–3).

£15/$25

◄ **1969**

Mould-blown *Nipple* vase (FT95). Produced in colourless, *Midnight*, *Kingfisher*, and *Flame*. The decoration on this self-proclaimed "X-Certificate" vase was based on the physiology of the human nipple. 14.5cm (5⅝in). (FT108 version, 11cm/4¼in.)

£25/$45*

▼ **1971**

Pressed *Avocado Dish* (FT137), sold in boxes of pairs, with original box. Dartington's first pressed-glass product. Early examples made at Dartington have polished rims while later ones, with unpolished rims, were sub-contracted. 6cm (2⅜in). Thrower's mould-blown triangular-sectioned *Avocado Dressing Servers* (FT146), 6cm (2⅜in), were soon discontinued.

Single £2/$3, Boxed set £20/$35

▲ **1969**

Mould-blown *Polar* water jug (FT109). 20cm (7⅞in). The ice-textured *Polar* collection, inspired by Wirkkala (pp.166–71) and Sarpaneva (pp.172–77), included matching tumblers, a fruit set (FT109/2–3), and a square-section vase (FT101).

£30/$55

▲ **1971**

Mould-blown *Dimple* vase/candleholder (FT143). This example engraved in diamond-point by Kim Thrower with the interior of a Gothic church and the inscription *Plaistow, 6th June 1936*. 17cm (6¾in). Developed from a shorter version designed in 1967 (FT10): 8, 12.5, and 15cm (3, 4⅞, and 5⅞in).

£25/$45

▲ 1971

Mould-blown *Kitchen Collection*. The pieces of the cork-stoppered *Kitchen Collection* were Dartington's first boxed products, all previous pieces having been sold loose. Most were new designs, though the *VIN* carafe (FT49) dates from 1967. The new items were (from left): Oil and vinegar bottles (FT113), 12.5cm (4⅞in); salt and pepper (FT114), 9cm (3½in); bottles, plain or blasted with *THE MIXTURE* or *SALAD DRESSING* (FT145), 77cl (27 fl oz); *PASTA* jar (FT121), 33.5cm (13¼in); jam pot (FT123), 11.5cm (4½in); *Bung Ho!* storage jars (FT112), 12.5 and 13.5cm (4⅞ and 5¼in); sugar shaker (FT122), 14.5cm (5⅝in); egg cups (FT136), 5.5cm (2⅛in). Not illustrated: taller salt and pepper (FT135), 8cm (3in). The *PASTA* jar proved difficult to make and was sub-contracted to Magnor Glassverk, Norway. Contemporary photograph by Mike Newton.

Most £5–20/$9–35, PASTA jar £35/$60

1971

▼ 1978–9

Optic-moulded *Diablo*, *Etruscan*, *Roman*, and *Flare* vases (FT283, 286, 285, and 284). 23, 18, 26, and 27.5cm (9, 7, 10¼, and 10⅞in). Thrower's first attempt at the ancient technique of optic-moulding was commercially successful; the technique is liked by glassmakers because its effects can disguise poor glass and blowing errors. It was soon adopted for further designs, most notably for English Country Crystal, formed after Dartington's takeover by Wedgwood in 1982.

£25/$45

1979

1977 ▼

Centrifuge-cast *Daisy* range (FT186/5, 186/4, and 186/6). Made in colourless and *Midnight*. The *Daisy* range proved extremely successful and was gradually expanded to include a fruit bowl and dishes (FT206), 32 and 17cm (12⅝ and 6⅝in) diam.; bread platter (FT214), 19cm (7½in) diam.; and cheese platter (FT215), 26.5cm (10½in) diam. From Dartington's 1985 catalogue.

£15/$25

▲ 1978–9

Mould-blown *Volterra* (FT222), *Candy* (FT 224), and *Inkwell* (FT 223) floor vases. 26, 29.5, and 26.5cm (10¼, 11⅝, 10½in). The *Candy* vase box (centre) was designed by Thrower's son Kim. Thrower derived the form for *Candy* from Holmegaard's *Gulvase* (p.161). Dartington possessed neither the production capacity nor the necessary colour ranges for this series so they were sub-contracted, reputedly to Wood Brothers of Worsbrough, near Barnsley, Yorkshire.

£85–110/$145–145*

WEDGWOOD TAKEOVER/ ENGLISH COUNTRY CRYSTAL, 1982

Ronnald Stennett-Willson's retirement in 1979 (p.232) left Wedgwood Crystal without direction and making losses. So, when Wedgwood chairman Sir Arthur Bryan met Frank Thrower in 1982, he quickly posed the question: "Can you do anything for us?"

The answer was English Country Crystal, a joint-venture established within months, with Wedgwood buying 50 per cent of Dartington for cash, shares, and property valued at £1.6m. The new company was controlled by Eric Dancer and Jan Mollmark, Dartington chairman and managing director, and with design and sales under Thrower. Dartington kept its name and ranges while King's Lynn produced cut stemware and new Thrower designs, most produced in colourless and *Midnight*, plain or optic. Most of his designs for Wedgwood were made in various sizes.

Thrower threw himself into the project with typical gusto, producing around 70 new designs for Wedgwood within two weeks. However, tensions grew between Thrower and Dancer as the former became increasingly exhausted by his workload and the latter resentful of Thrower's huge income, derived from his director's salary and sales-based design royalties.

▲ **1982**
From left: Mould-blown *Portia* glass (FJT29), 21cm (8¼in); optic-moulded *Orson* vase (FJT5), 15.5cm (6in); mould-blown *Horatio* decanter (FJT13), 22cm (8⅝in); optic *Rufus* tumbler (made at Nazeing) (FJT30), 8cm (3in); mould-blown *Grace* bud vase (FJT2), 28cm (11in); and mould-blown *Diana* candlestick (W30), 20cm (7⅞in), based on Stennett-Willson's *Sandringham* (RSW23), 1967 (p.230).
Tumbler £5/$9, Decanter £75/$130, Rest £20/35

◀ **1982 & 1986**
Wedgwood stickers. 1982: Red for firsts, black for seconds. 1986: The Devon Collection was directed at the American market but was also sold elsewhere. Many pieces were modified versions of Stennett-Willson designs, and all were given WUS numbers.

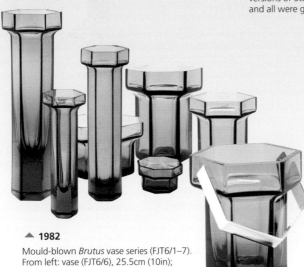

▲ **1982**
Mould-blown *Brutus* vase series (FJT6/1–7). From left: vase (FJT6/6), 25.5cm (10in); vase (FJT6/1), 16cm (6¼in); fruit bowl (FJT6/6), 19cm (7½in) diam.; (FJT6/2), 21cm (8¼in); vase (FJT6/8), 11cm (4¼in); cocktail dish (FJT6/6), 5cm (2in); vase (FJT6.7), 13.5cm (5¼in); and ice bucket (FJT6/7), 13.5cm (5¼in).
£25–65/$45–110*

▶ **1982**
Mould-blown *Marcel* decanter (FJT15) with *Arthur* candlesticks (W29), descended from Stennett-Willson's *Brancaster*, (RSW15), 1976. The *Marcel* and similar *Gaston* decanter (FJT14) were also fitted with ball stoppers. Decanter: 35.5cm (14in); candlesticks: 26.5, 13, and 19cm (10½, 5, and 7½in).
Decanter £65/$110 Candlesticks £25–35/$45–60*

Where to See & Buy

Where to buy

The last five years have seen a major transformation in the way that collectors acquire new pieces. Time was when serious contenders had to tour shops, fairs, and auction houses in the hope of spotting potential additions to their holdings. That hit and miss approach has been superseded, at least in part, by the advent of Google and eBay. The internet has become a major factor in the increasingly international nature of modern collecting. The ability to bolster a collection while sitting at home, examining objects available in Wiesbaden or Minneapolis, is having predictable results. Today, collectors can not only locate rarities with an ease that would have been inconceivable a decade ago, but are also able to sell their surpluses online to finance their new acquisitions. Collections have always evolved through trading, but now the internet is turning many active participants into part-time dealers.

Of course, the net is not for everyone. Its processes can be laborious and frustrating. The sheer volume of pieces available can be intimidating; sizes can be deceptive; photographs are often unduly flattering and descriptions inaccurate; post and packing add to headline prices, and the risks of breakage and dishonesty inevitable. Many simply enjoy browsing through shops and markets until they find something they like.

Unfortunately, rising property values and taxes, in addition to the internet, have caused the closure of hundreds if not thousands of antique and junk shops in both Europe and the United States. Yet, while traditional antique shops are closing, there has been a marked rise in the number specializing in the type of retro-glass, and other functional and decorative objects, featured on these pages. However, as this book will reach many different countries, it lacks the space to recommend individual shops across the globe.

Our own shop/exhibition complex *Glass Etc*, is situated in the historic town of Rye on Britain's Sussex Coast, where readers will be most welcome. Comprising a 100-square-metre shop, an adjacent exhibition room and outbuildings, it stocks a broad range of glassware, including a large quantity of the types of glass illustrated here. Lectures devoted to the subjects of current exhibitions are held regularly throughout the year.

Glass fairs

Glass fairs tend to come and go the world-over. It is hazardous to suggest specific locations as local knowledge is required. However, two biannual British fairs have endured for many years, with dealers offering a wide variety of antique, 20th-century, and contemporary glass (see below).

Glass clubs

Most nations have clubs dedicated to furthering the appreciation and understanding of glass. In Britain, these include the Glass Circle, the Glass Association, and the Friends of Broadfield House Glass Museum. Their members' perception of glass ranges from passing interest to hard-core, and from the general to the specific. The United States is home to the National American Glass Club, the American Cut Glass Association, and numerous more specialist organizations, while the International Association for the History of Glass serves a wider membership.

Most clubs impose fairly cheap membership fees, publish newsletters, and organize trips. In recent years, British club members have visited the Czech Republic, Venice, and the United States, while the Americans have visited Britain and other European glassmaking centres. Details about all of these, including membership forms, can be found on the web.

Where to visit

The world's finest glass museums are the Corning Museum of Glass (CMG) and the privately-owned Glasmuseum Passau . The CMG specializes in glass of all nations and periods, from Roman to contemporary, whereas Passau is exclusively dedicated to Bohemian/Czech glass, 1750–1950. The CMG is inconveniently situated in Corning, a small town in New York State, a three hour drive from New York City. Passau is a small German town on the Rhine at the junction of the Austrian and Czech borders. Both have collections of more than 30,000 pieces. Other museums include Britain's Broadfield House Glass Museum, the Smålands Glass Museum of Växjö, Sweden, and the Finnish Glass Museum at Riihimäki. All are situated at the geographic centre of each country's historic glass industries and emphasize local production.

The problem for most museums is a lack of both funding and space, which leaves their staff overworked and more pieces in storerooms than on public display. The Corning Museum of Glass has taken a lead by emptying its stores into a series of "study galleries", where all its holdings are exhibited, albeit in cramped conditions. Others have followed this path, such as the Österreichisches Museum fuer Angewandte Kunst (MAK) in Vienna, where large quantities of glass can be viewed in its basement. The magnificent Glass Gallery at the Victoria & Albert Museum, London, displays most of its extensive collection, from the 16th century to the present, with most prominence and space given to 20th-century pieces.

Fairs

The Cambridge Glass Fair
Chilford Hall Vineyard
Linton, Cambridgeshire
CB1 6LE, UK
www.cambridgeglassfair.com

The National Glass Collectors Fair
The Heritage Motor Centre
Gaydon, Warwickshire
CV35 0BJ, UK
Tel: +44 (0)1260 271975
www.glassfairs.co.uk

Museums

Austria
MAK
Stubenring 5, A-1010 Vienna
Tel: +43 1 711 36 0
www.mak.at

Britain
Broadfield House Glass Museum
Compton Drive, Kingswinford
West Midlands, DY6 9NS
Tel: +44 (0)1384 812745
www.dudley.gov.uk/glassmuseum
(Stourbridge glass, c.1700–2000)

Victoria & Albert Museum
Cromwell Road, London SW7 2RL
+44 (0)20 7942 2000
www.vam.ac.uk

Czech Republic
Jablonec Museum of
   Glass & Jewellery
U Muzea 398/4
466 01 Jablonec nad Nisou
Tel: +420 483 369 011
www.msb-jablonec.cz
*(Glassware and paste jewels
and beads)*

Museum of Glass at Novy Bor
Namesti Miru 105, Novy Bor, 47301
Tel: +420 424 222 196
link via www.bohemian-glassworks.
(Czech and German glass)

Denmark
Glasmuseet Ebeltoft
Strandvejen 8
8400 Ebeltoft
Tel: +45 8634 1799
www. www.glasmuseet.dk
(Contemporary glass)

Finland

The Finnish Glass Museum
Tehtaankatu 23, FI-11910 Riihimäki
Tel: + 358 (0)20 758 4108
www.riihimaki.fi/lasimus

Germany

Glasmuseum Passau
Am Rathausplatz, D - 94032 Passau
Tel: +49 (0)851 35071
www.glasmuseum.de
(Bohemian/Czech glass, 1750–1950)

Holland

Glasmuseum Schiedam
Tijdelijk onderkomen
Boterstraat 81, 3111 NB Schiedam
Tel: +6 11017511, www.glasmuseum.nl
(Emphasis on post-war glass)

Italy

Museo del Vetro di Murano
Fondamenta Giustinian 8
30121 Murano, Italy
Tel/Fax: +39 041 739586
www.museiciviciveneziani.it
(Murano glass of all periods)

Sweden

Smålands Museum
Järnvägsgatan 2, Box 102
S-35104 Växjö
Tel: +46 470 70 42 00
www.smalandsmuseum.se
(Mostly Swedish glass)

United States

Corning Museum of Glass
One Museum Way, Corning, NY
14830-2253, Tel: +1 800 732 6845
www.cmog.org
(All eras)

Museum of Glass
1801 East Dock Street
Tacoma, WA 98402-3217
Tel: +1 253 284 4719
www.museumofglass.org
(Contemporary glass)

Others

For a more complete list of the
world's glass museums visit:
www.glassart.org/museums.html

Glossary

Acid-badge Signature or logo applied with acid.

Acid-etching Decoration achieved with hydrofluoric and/or sulphuric acids.

Acid-cameo Vessel of two or more coloured layers, selectively corroded by acids to reveal a pattern or design in shallow relief.

Air-trap Decorative inclusion of air pockets within the glass. Not to be confused with *Ariel*.

Ariel Specific method of decorating glass with internal structured air pockets. Developed at Orrefors (pp.198–9).

Auto-blown Blown automatically by a machine.

Aventurine Decorative effect intended to simulate aventurine quartz, created by including metallic particles in the batch of raw materials. Mostly used on Murano.

Bohème Shortened form of *façon de Bohème*, meaning in the Bohemian style.

Cameo Decorative effect similar to acid-cameo, but created by manual carving rather than by the application of acids.

Blank Generally, fully-formed and cooled but undecorated piece.

Borosilicate glass Heat-resistant glass, such as Pyrex, composed of boron, sand (silica), aluminium oxide, and sodium or potassium.

Carnival glass Glassware iridized by spraying its surface with a chemical "dope", pioneered in the United States from *c*.1900.

Cased Formed with two or more layers of contrasting colours. Always handmade.

Cast To create/created by pouring the glass into a mould.

Centrifuge-casting Method of forming glassware by spinning it at high speed against a mould. Invented by Sven Palmqvist at Orrefors (p.193).

Contemporary Decorative style popular in post-war Britain.

Cutting Decorative effect created by grinding patterns into the surface of glass with stone, or later, carbarundum wheels.

Dip-mould Open-topped mould, often shaped like a flower-pot, into which glass is blown, then withdrawn without needing to open the mould.

Free-blown Blown without the aid of a mould.

Furnace-worked Decorated while still hot and maleable, a process generally requiring repeated furnace reheatings. Known in the United States as the "off-hand" technique.

Engraving Application of motifs, patterns, or signatures by pressing glassware against small abrasive-coated copper wheels.

Gob A small gather of ductile glass taken from a furnace.

Graal Specific term for a rare form of internal glass decoration developed at Orrefors (pp.198–9).

Half-post method American name for a traditional German and Scandinavian method of blowing flasks. It required the first gather of blown glass to be coated in a second layer of glass up to the level of the lower neck to provide strength.

Hand-pressed Formed by being squeezed against a mould by the force of a manually operated lever.

Intaglio Decorative effect midway between cutting and engraving. The glass is applied against small abrasive wheels to create generally broad, curved cuts.

Mark Term interchangeable with "signature".

Marver A stone or metal slab against which ductile glass is flattened or shaped.

Modernist Decorative style of the inter-war period, distinguished in glass by bold sculptural forms.

Mould-blown Formed by a blower's breath forcing ductile glass against a mould.

Murrine or **Murrhine** Italian name for the small decorative canes commonly found in paperweights.

Optic-moulded Decorative patterns formed within the glass by a mould. Most common forms include swags, zigzags, and diamonds.

Pâte de verre French term for glass formed by mixing crushed glass with a binding agent. The resulting clay-like substance is manually forced against a mould, then vitrified in a furnace.

Pressed Same as "hand-pressed" but generally implies the use of mechanical force.

Prunt Applied decorative feature, normally a small blob of glass often moulded with a pattern in relief.

Sand-blasting Frosted effect or signature achieved by firing sand at the surface of glass under compressed air.

Satin-surfaced Frosted effect achieved by dipping fully-formed objects in acid.

Signature Mark applied to a finished piece of glass, usually its base. Used variously to identify the country of origin, maker, designer and/or date.

Single-colour Formed in a single colour, as opposed to casing, which involves the use of contrasting colours.

Slumped Formed by placing sheets of flat glass over a mould and allowing it to slump into shape when heated in a furnace.

Sommerso Italian term for "cased".

Swung vase A vase initially formed in a mould, then removed and swung backward and forward while still malleable to stretch it vertically.

Texture-moulding Similar to optic-moulding but used to create textures rather than patterns.

Transfer-printed Applied with acrylic transfers, known in the United States as "decals".

Venise Shortened version of *façon de Venise* – in the manner of Venetian glass, or Venetian-style.

Bibliography

As mentioned elsewhere, rising interest in 20th-century glass has been mirrored by a surge in the number of books devoted to the subject. This trend should be welcomed by academics and collectors who might reasonably expect them to answer the basic questions concerning the pieces they illustrate: what is it, who designed and made it, and when? With these being such obvious requirements, why do so many fail to deliver?

The answer is that it is often far more difficult than one might imagine to pinpoint reliable information. With few authors prepared to undertake the research required to ensure a worthy end-product, mediocre books on glass outnumber solid ones. Further, many collector/writers, encouraged by the falling cost of printing, have opted to self-publish. While the financial returns may appear superficially greater, the quality of the resulting books can be dubious, with many better at provoking further questions than providing answers. Poor images, incoherent or gushing text, and a lack of context, hard facts, and even indexes, are too often the hallmarks of self-published books. As this is the case, the following list focuses on the best and ignores the rest.

Select bibliography and recommended reading

Aav, Marianne *et al.* (eds) *Timo Sarpaneva* (DesignMuseo, 2002)
(120 pages. Good text, comprehensive exhibition catalogue.)

Aav, Marianne (ed) *Tapio Wirkkala: Eye, Hand & Thought*
(Museum of Art & Design, Helsinki, 2002)
(400 pages. Excellent text and good exhibition catalogue.)

Benson, Nigel *Glass of the '50s & '60s* (Miller's, 2002)
(64 pages. Good, affordable beginners' guide.)

Curtis, Jean-Louis *Baccarat* (Thames & Hudson, 1992)
(Good text and images, corporate-sponsored.)

DeBoni, Franco *Venini Glass* (Allemandi, 1996)
(260 pages. Preface by Dan Klein, 175 colour images, and 62 pages of design blueprints, 1921–35.)

Dodsworth, Roger (ed) *British Glass Between the Wars* (Dudley, 1987)
(116 pages. Well illustrated and written exhibition catalogue.)

Evans, Stuart, (*et al.*) *Pyrex, 60 Years of Design*
(Tyne & Wear Museums, 1983)
(94 pages. Exhibition catalogue. Good text. Black-and-white images.)

Hayhurst, Jeanette *Glass of the '20s & '30s* (Miller's, 1999)
(64 pages. Good, affordable beginners' guide.)

Henrikson, Alf (*et al.*) *1742–1992, Kosta 250* (Kosta, 1992)
(250 pages. Good corporate-sponsored study.)

Jackson, Lesley (ed) *Whitefriars Glass* (Richard Dennis, 1996)
(160 pages. Outstanding single-factory study.)

Jackson, Lesley *20th Century Factory Glass* (Mitchell-Beazley, 2000).
(256 pages. Comprehensive, strong on text, weak on images.)

Koivisto, Kaisa (ed) *Nanny Still – Ice Maiden* (Finnish Glass Museum, 2003)
(120 pages. Exhibition catalogue. Reasonable text, most designs illustrated in miniature.)

Koivisto, Kaisa (ed) *Helena Tynell, Design 1943–93*
(Finnish Glass Museum, 1993)
(120 pages. Exhibition catalogue. Good text, most designs illustrated in miniature.)

Koivisto, Kaisa (ed, *et al.*) *Kaj Franck, Theme & Variations*
(Hackman, undated)
(Comprehensive exhibition catalogue. Most designs illustrated in miniature.)

Loomis, Jean Chapman *Krystol! Krystol!* (Loomis, 2001)
(160 pages. Reproduces entire 1915 US *Chippendale* catalogue.)

Lütken, Per *Glass Is Life* (Nordisk Forlag Arnold Busck, 1986)
(120 pages. Image-orientated exhibition catalogue. Contains drawings of most Lütken designs.)

McConnell, Andy *The Decanter, An Illustrated History of Glass from 1650*
(Antique Collectors' Club, 2004)
(550 pages. 2,500 examples illustrated.)

Mergl, Jan, and Pánková, Lenka *Moser, 1857–1957* (Moser, 1997)
(352 pages. Excellent text and images. Not comprehensive.)

Mergl, Jan, and Pánková, Lenka (*et al.*, eds)
Das Böhmische Glas 1700–1950 (Passauer Glasmuseum, undated)
(900 pages in seven volumes. German text, but wealth of excellent images. Volume VI: *Jugendstil in Böhmen*; Volume VI: *Art Deco & Moderne*.)

Opie, Jennifer *Ceramics & Glass in the 20th Century* (V&A, 1989)
(184 pages. Exhibition catalogue. Black-and-white images.)

Polak, Ada *Modern Glass* (Faber, 1962)
(160 pages. Interesting "period piece". Black-and-white images.)

Ricke, Helmut, and Thor, Lars *Swedish Glass Factories, 1915–1960*
(Prestel, 1987)
(432 pages of original catalogue pages reproduced.)

Ricke, Helmut; Thor, Lars; and Gronert, Ulrich
Glas in Schweden, 1915–60 (Prestel, 1986)
(310 pages. Exhibition catalogue. German text. Black-and-white images.)

Vigier, Lorenzo, and Pina, Leslie
Smoke & Ice, Scandinavian Glass 1930–2000 (Schiffer, 2002)
(224 pages. Strong on images but weak text, no dimensions, and vague date attributions.)

Wickman, Kerstin (ed) *Orrefors, A Century of Swedish Glassmaking*
(Byggforlaget, 1998)
(256 pages. Good, comprehensive, corporate-sponsored work.)

Informative Websites

www.cloudglass.com Comprehensive, well-ordered site dedicated to *Cloud* glass generally and the output of George Davidson & Co. (pp.108–15) in particular.

www.pressglas-korrespondenz.de Devoted to pressed glass of all nations and eras. Started in 1998, it now reproduces 800 catalogues and associated articles. However, German-based and difficult to navigate.

Index

Acknowledgments

The guide prices suggested in this book are largely based on a survey conducted at Cambridge Glass Fair, England, in February 2006. The collectors and dealers involved were: Nigel Benson (20thcentury-glass.com), Elaine Evans and Tim Boalch, Stuart Davie, Michele Guzy (nopinkcarpet.com), Stephen Hazell-Smith, Geoff Lawson, Scott T. Paterson (retro-gallery.com), Danny Walker, and Ron Wheeler (artiusglass.co.uk). Further specialist information was obtained from: Warren and Teddie Biden (brilliantglass.com), Graham Cooley, Jeff Purtell (steubenpurtell.com), Erik Wagena and Danielle Kuipers (glas-design.nl), and Richard Wallis (richardwallisantiks.com).

As mentioned in the introduction, books of this scope are never the work of an individual working in isolation. The most important tribute of all is due to my wife, Helen, who has suffered, sometimes silently, during the two years of long days of research, photography, and writing that were required for this book. She accompanied me on our voyage to Scandinavia and located and scanned many of the catalogue pages and archive images contained here. It has also involved a degree of expense and domestic disorder that would have been impossible without her acquiescence.

I would also like to thank Anna Sanderson for commissioning this book, and for her advice and support. The diligence and good humour of my general editor, the unflappable Catherine Emslie, have proved invaluable, and thanks to Colin Goody for his layout designs.

The input of a large number of kind and patent individuals has greatly helped in my quest. They include: Peter Abraham, Mike Adelson, Nigel Alder, Nick and Kelly Allen, Frank Andrews, Simon Andrews, Emily Asquith, Gail Bardhan, Marina Barovier, Stuart Bean, Nigel Benson, Warren and Teddie Biden, Aldo Bova/Galeria Rosella Junck, Paul Bishop and Christina Glover, Bill Brookes, Bob Burke, Tony Cartwright, Keely Cameron, Elizabeth and Liam Carey, Suzanne Carlson, John Clark, Willie and Sally Clegg and Harvey Ferry, Mary Cross, Sean Dale, Stuart Davie, John Delafaille, Richard Diwell, Peter Elliot, Elaine Evans and Tim Boalch, Carol Findlay, Ann French, Delia Garrett, Sam Gibson, Siegmar Geiselberger, Christine Gollidge, Hilary Green, Janice Green, Adamm Gritlefeld, Emer Gunter, Michelle Guzy, Eva-Marie Hagström, Jon Hall, Richard Halliday, Hazel Hammond, Liz and Tim Harris, Robin Hawkins, Chris Hawkins, Stephen Hazell-Smith, John Henderson, Jill Hickmott, Otto Holtkamp, John Henderson, Norman Howell, Lene and

Carsten Rist Larsen, Geoff Lawson, Bill Lee, Robert Leech, Ron Lukian, John Luxton, Petr Jech, Michael Jeffrey, Michael Joseph, Christine Keilty, Gordon Kessler, Simon and Tracy Kahn, Liz McAvoy, Anne McConnell, Karie Moodie and John Smith at Broadfield House Glass Museum, Victoria Morrall, Robert Muuci, Mike Newton, Mie Levy Nielsen, Sarah O'Brien, David Queensberry, Derek and Betty Parsons, Roger Phillippo, Stephen Pollock-Hill, Jeff Pertell, Kim and Richard Press, Eric Reynolds, Richard Van Riel, Joseph and Nevise Said, Jim Sinclair, John P Smith, Linda and Stuart Smithson, Ronnie Stennett-Willson, Chris and Val Stewart, Rhonda Summerbell, Alan Taylor, Brett Taylor, Kim and Inga Thrower, Borek Tichy, Geoff Timberlake, Glen and Steve Thistlewood (carnival-glass.net), Nick Toldi, Valerie Townsend, Ian Turner, Maggie Tyrrell, Barbara and Chris Yates, Richard and Kiss Wallis, Maurice Willey, Ron Wheeler, and Rod Woolley. Apologies are offered to all those whose names have slipped through the net.

Finally, great efforts have been expended in attempting to make the information contained here as accurate as possible. Nevertheless, it will doubtless contain certain mistakes. I would happy to receive communications advising me of information that supplements or contradicts the text or captions contained in any of the sections. These should be addressed to andy@decanterman.com.

Picture credits

With the exception of those listed below (in alphabetical order by first name), all the pictures used in this book have been reproduced with kind permission by Andy McConnell, who has also photographed most of them, shooting on location in in Britain, Finland, Sweden, and Denmark.

l = left, r = right, b = bottom, t = top, c = centre

Alan Taylor (uklighthouse.info) 103tl; Anchor Hocking Glass 82tr; Ann Marie Sutherland 80b; Anne McConnell 182br; Musée de Baccarat (baccarat.fr) 72t; Barbara Beadman 103c; Bob Burke 79bl; Boda Archive (kostaboda.se) 74b; Brenda Rodd 128bl; Brett Taylor 237br, 238tl, 238bl; Broadfield House Glass Museum 13bcl, 41t, 41bc, 63b, 64t, 67bl, 69bl, 99cr, 126tl, 126br, 127l, 127r, 129t, 129bl, 129bc, 130b, 193tl, 235tl&bc, 236, 237tr, 237cr, 238tr, 239tr, 241l; Bukowski, Helsinki (bukowski.fi)175tc; Cambridge Glass Fair (cambridgeglassfair.com) 107tcr, 107bc; Christie's (christies.com) 92tr, 200bl, 201tl; Circa Glass (circaglass.co.uk) 231tr, 233bcr, 243l; cloudglass.com 108t, 112bl; Dale Chihuly 47br, 83br; Danny Walker 1, 81bcr, 84bcl; Dartington Crystal (dartington.co.uk) 242tl, 246t, 246bl; Debbie & Gary Phillips 215tr; Derek & Betty Parsons 181tr; Dorotheum, Vienna (dorotheum.com) 27t, 29tr, 31b, 55tl, 88c; Finnish Glass Museum 162t&c; Galleria Marina Barovier, Venice (barovier.it), Venice 35b, 85br, 86br, 87br; Galleria Rosella Junck, Venice (rossellajunck.it) 26; Geoff Timberlake 183tr; glas-design.nl 78t, 79cr, 79r, 91cl, 211tr, 211br, 212, 213bl, 213br, 216br, 217tr, 217bl&bc, 218c, 219tl, 219bl; Glasgalerie Michael Kovacek, Vienna (kovacek.at) 13bcr, 29bl, 52, 53, 54bl, 88tr, 88bl; Graham Cooley 33br, 37t, 45br, 51cl, 66t, 82bl, 89r, 105cr, 105br, 106tl, 106bl, 107tl, 130t, 131t, 134tl, 134tr, 135bl, 136bl, 148tr, 178cr, 182bl, 199br, 224tl&br, 225c&c, 227tr, 227bl, 227br, 228r, 229t, 229cl, 229b, 230tl & tcl, 230tr, 230cr, 231tl&tr, 231b, 232tl, 232br, 233tl&tc, 233b, 235tr, 243r, 244t, 244bc, 246br, 247; Graham Cooley & Glaspiration 245tl; Hazel Hammond 81br; Holmegaard Glasværk, Denmark (holmegaard.com) 14t, 21b, 35t, 38b, 44t, 75bc, 89c, 138-140, 141tl, 141b, 142, 143tl&tc, 143b, 144tl, 144tcr&tr, 145, 146, 147t, 147br, 148tl&tc, 148bl, 149tl, 149b, 150b, 151tl, 151tr, 151b, 152-153, 154, 155t, 155bc&br, 156tl, 156b, 157tc&tr, 157b, 158, 159t, 159bl&bc, 160, 161tl, 161bc&br; House of Brilliant Glass, Portland, Oregon (brilliantglass.com)15t, 62b, 81t; Iittala Archives 36c, 39tr, 39c, 50t, 161tl, 162b, 164-165, 166l, 166tr, 166br, 167t, 167bc&br, 168t, 168bl, 169tc, 169b, 170tl&tr, 170cr, 170bc&br, 171bc, 172t, 173tl, 173b, 174tr, 174br, 175tl, 175bl, 176tl, 176b, 177bl; Isle of Wight Studio Glass (isleofwightstudioglass.co.uk) 9r, 198tl; Isle of Wight Studio Glass/Harris Family 132-133, 134tc, 134bc, 134br, 135 tl, 135tc, 136tr, 136c, 136br, 137tl, 137tc, 137b, 179bl; Janice Green 150, 177tr, 191bcr; John Bailey 72bl, 86bl; John Clark 46bl, 135tr; John Luxton 41br, 45bl; John P Smith 27b; Kim & Richard Press 107tr; Kosta Archive (kostaboda.se)16br, 42b, 75tl, 76tl, 76bl, 79 tl, 89br, 226bl; Lalique SA (cristallalique.fr) 49t; Liam & Elizabeth Carey (merlinglass.co.uk) 178c, 179tl&tr, 179cl, 179cr, 179br; Liz McAvoy 116cl, 117tl; Lobmeyr (lobmeyr.at) 55bl; Mallet Antiques (mallettantiques.com) 234tr; Mark West (markwest-glass.com) 63c, 71cl, 88cr; Maurice Willey 80b; Michael Joseph 105tr, 106tr, 106cr, 106br, 107bcr; Michelle Guzy (nopinkcarpet.com) 219br, 221br, 222tl&tc; Mike & Debbie Moir 32r; Mike Taylor 60r; Moser Archive (moser-glass.com) 54br; Multi-faceted Glass 45t, 167bl, 172b, 174bl, 175br; Nazeing Glass Works/Stephen Pollock-Hill 69bc, 180t&c, 181b, 182tl&cl, 183tl, 183cl, 183cr; Nick Allen 72bc; Nick Toldi 17tr, 65br, 237cl, 240bl; Nigel Wiggin 203br; Nuutajärvi Archive, Finland (iittala.com) 118t, 118bl, 119, 120t, 120bl, 120br, 121tcr, 121tr, 121bc, 121br, 122, 123tl, 123tr, 123b, 124-125; Ornela (ornela.cz) 31c, 58br; Orrefors Archive (photographers: John Selbing/Per Larsson/Winells Ateljé)(orrefors.com) 16t, 22br, 34bc, 34br, 38t, 48b, 51r, 75c, 77tl, 184-185, 186t, 187tcl, 187bl, 187br, 188, 189tl, 189tcl&tcr, 189bcl, 189bl, 190tl, 190tr, 190b, 191tcl, 191tcr, 191bc, 191bl, 192tl, 192br, 193tr, 193bl&bcr, 194, 195t, 195cl, 195bcr, 196tl, 196br, 197t, 197bc&bcr, 197bl,198tr&bl, 199c, 199bl; Paul Tucker 44br, 211bc; Peter Abrahams 240tr; Petr Jech 56br; Siegmar Geiselberger (pressglas-korrespondenz.de) 114t; Richard Wallis Antiks (richardwallisantiks.co.uk) 156tr, 157tl; Riedel (riedel.com) 56bl; Lynda and Michael Adelson (seekersgallery.com) 51l, 83bl; Simon & Tracey Kahn/Refraction 191br, 197br; Sotheby's (sothebys.com)10, 12t, 13t, 14c, 17b, 28tr, 30, 32c, 37b, 47bl, 58bl, 70tl, 70cl, 70bc, 70br, 74t, 80t, 84tl, 85l, 86t, 117tr, 117br, 191tl, 199tl; Stephen Hazell-Smith 187tcr&tr, 198br; Stephen Pollock-Hill 245tr; Steuben Glass 81c (steuben.com); Stuart Davie 168br, 173tc, 174tl; Willie Clegg & Harvey Ferry (thecountryseat.com) 28tl, 46t, 69br, 226t; Barovier & Toso Museum & Archive (barovier.com) 85br, 86br; Treadway Gallery (treadwaygallery.com) 28bl, 29cl, 80t; Valerie Townshend 99clc; Venini, Venice (venini.com) 22c, 46br, 76br, 169tl, 169tr, 177br; Victoria & Albert Museum, London, Ceramics & Glass Department Library 84cl; Waltraud Neuwirth 54t; Waterford-Wedgwood plc (waterford.com)/Broadfield House Glass Museum 234cr&br, 237c, 237bc, 238br, 239br, 240br, 241c&r; Woolley & Wallis, Salisbury (woolleyandwallis.co.uk) 31t